THE COSMOLOGICAL ARGUMENT FROM PLATO TO LEIBNIZ

LIBRARY OF PHILOSOPHY AND RELIGION

General Editor: John Hick, H. G. Wood
Professor of Theology, University of Birmingham

This new series of books will explore contemporary religious understandings of man and the universe. The books will be contributions to various aspects of the continuing dialogues between religion and philosophy, between scepticism and faith, and between the different religions and ideologies. The authors will represent a correspondingly wide range of viewpoints. Some of the books in the series will be written for the general educated public and others for a more specialised philosophical or theological readership.

Already published

William H. Austin	THE RELEVANCE OF NATURAL SCIENCE TO THEOLOGY
Paul Badham	CHRISTIAN BELIEFS ABOUT LIFE AFTER DEATH
Patrick Burke	THE FRAGILE UNIVERSE
William Lane Craig	THE *KALĀM* COSMOLOGICAL ARGUMENT
	THE COSMOLOGICAL ARGUMENT FROM PLATO TO LEIBNIZ
Lynn A. de Silva	THE PROBLEM OF THE SELF IN BUDDHISM AND CHRISTIANITY
Padmasiri de Silva	AN INTRODUCTION TO BUDDHIST PSYCHOLOGY
Ramchandra Gandhi	THE AVAILABILITY OF RELIGIOUS IDEAS
J. C. A. Gaskin	HUME'S PHILOSOPHY OF RELIGION
H. A. Hodges	GOD BEYOND KNOWLEDGE
Hywel D. Lewis	PERSONS AND LIFE AFTER DEATH
Hugo A. Meynell	AN INTRODUCTION TO THE PHILOSOPHY OF BERNARD LONERGAN
F. C. T. Moore	THE PSYCHOLOGICAL BASIS OF MORALITY
Dennis Nineham	THE USE AND ABUSE OF THE BIBLE
Bernard M. G. Reardon	HEGEL'S PHILOSOPHY OF RELIGION
John J. Shepherd	EXPERIENCE, INFERENCE AND GOD
Patrick Sherry	RELIGION, TRUTH AND LANGUAGE-GAMES
Robert Young	FREEDOM, RESPONSIBILITY AND GOD

Further titles in preparation

THE COSMOLOGICAL ARGUMENT FROM PLATO TO LEIBNIZ

William Lane Craig

First published 1980 by
THE MACMILLAN PRESS LTD
London and Basingstoke
Associated companies in Delhi
Dublin Hong Kong Johannesburg Lagos
Melbourne New York Singapore Tokyo

Printed and bound in Great Britain by
Redwood Burn Limited
Trowbridge & Esher

British Library Cataloguing in Publication Data

Craig, William Lane
The cosmological argument from Plato to Leibniz – (Library of philosophy and religion).
1. God – Proof, Cosmological
I. Title II. Series
211 BT102

ISBN 0–333–27467–9

To
MY PARENTS

who taught me as a boy
the adventure of learning and
spared me nothing that might further that end

Contents

Preface

I

It was my reading and outlining of Frederick Copleston's masterful *A History of Philosophy* during my student days that first sparked off my interest in doing a comprehensive study of the cosmological argument for the existence of God. Copleston's *History* provides the broadest historical survey to date of the cosmological argument, but his expositions of the various versions of the proof are necessarily brief and must be extracted from the wide range of other material presented in his work. Perhaps the finest overall study on the cosmological argument up to this point is R. L. Sturch's unpublished Oxford doctoral thesis 'The Cosmological Argument'. Unfortunately, Sturch's survey of the argument, because it is broader than mine, is much less detailed and sometimes contains positive misunderstandings. What I have sacrificed in breadth, I have attempted to make up in analysis and accuracy. A comprehensive, scholarly history of the cosmological argument still remains to be written. Such a history would include the cosmological arguments of Fakhr al-Dīn al-Razī, Bonaventure, Suarez, Descartes, Locke, Clarke and Wolff, thinkers whom I have not included in this study. But my present work is a step in that direction. In this book I have chosen to analyse in detail the cosmological arguments of thirteen of the proof's greatest proponents; these constitute the peaks in the long history of the argument and are exemplary models of the various forms which the cosmological argument assumes. In the final chapter of this work, I attempt to formulate a typology of the various versions surveyed and to distil what I perceive to be the major critical issues involved in each form of the argument.

II

I hope that this study will help to meet a serious need in the contemporary debate over the argument. For the past thirty years or so, philosophers of religion interested in argumentative theism have been preoccupied with the ontological argument, but interest in that proof now appears to be waning, and there are glimmers of a revival of interest in the cosmological proof, if one can judge by the frequency of articles on the subject in philosophical journals. But contemporary writers have by all indications a woeful ignorance of the historical versions of the argument. I am amazed at the shallow and often grossly inaccurate expositions of the differing forms of the argument given by contemporary authors. As a result of these misunderstandings, many of the purported refutations of the cosmological argument are aimed at straw men. In fact, as a result of my research, I would venture to say that if one were to pick up at random an article on the cosmological argument, it is probably historically inaccurate and focuses on the wrong issues. This makes it indeed a challenge to present and perspicaciously analyse the most significant versions of the cosmological argument, and I approach the task with trepidation. For I am sure that if most of the expositions and critiques I have read are filled with errors evident to me, then the chances are that my own analysis is also in error in places. But the frustration is that I do not know where those places are; so I must beg the reader's indulgence when he discerns instances in which I have unknowingly erred.

III

What exactly constitutes a cosmological argument? Probably the best definition is that the cosmological argument is an *a posteriori* argument for a cause or reason for the cosmos. Three items in this definition deserve emphasis. First, the cosmological argument is an *a posteriori* argument. Unlike the ontological argument, the cosmological argument always contains an existential premiss, that is, it asserts that something exists. The fact that the argument may also employ *a priori* principles, such as the principle of contradiction or the principle of causality, does not negate the fact that the argument as a whole is *a posteriori*, since its truth is dependent on the fact that something exists.[1] Second, the cosmological argument seeks a cause or reason. Some versions of the argument conclude to a being which is the first cause of the universe, either in a temporal sense or in rank. Other versions posit a being which is the sufficient reason for the world. The distinction between cause and reason is an important one that is rarely appreciated but one that must be maintained if we are correctly to understand the different forms of the argument. Third, the cosmological argument seeks to account for the cosmos. Most versions of the cosmological argument and certainly all of the modern ones attempt to account for the existence of the world. But the prime mover arguments do not seek a cause of the world's existence, but a cause of the world's being a cosmos, usually by positing an astronomical system of spheres set in motion by the prime mover. Here a somewhat arbitrary and hazy boundary is drawn between the cosmological and teleological arguments, the latter also seeking a cause of the world's being a cosmos, but with the emphasis on order, design, and the adaptation of means to ends. The cosmological argument, then, does not necessarily have to conclude to a cause of the universe's existence, for its ancient forms were dualistic and sought merely to account for cosmic motion.

The cosmological argument has a long and venerable history, possessing a resilience under criticism that is truly remarkable. Its intersectarian appeal is broad, and it has been propounded by Greek pagans, Muslims, Jews, Christians, both Catholic and Protestant, and even pantheists. Among the catalogue of its supporters are the greatest minds of the Western world: Plato, Aristotle, ibn Sīnā, al-Ghāzālī, ibn Rushd, Maimonides, Anselm, Bonaventure, Aquinas, Scotus, Suarez, Descartes, Spinoza, Berkeley, Locke and Leibniz. The durability of the argument and the stature of its defenders is eloquent testimony to the fact that to man this world is somehow just not sufficient of itself, but points to a greater reality beyond itself.

IV

I should like to thank my wife Jan for her production of the typescript; I consider her a full partner in this enterprise. I am indebted to Professors Anthony Kenny and John Hick for their reading and commenting on the text. I also wish to express my gratitude to the late Mr Hugh Andersen and Mr and Mrs F. C. Andersen of the Baywood Corporation for their generous grant that made this research possible.

München,
Bundesrepublik Deutschland

WILLIAM LANE CRAIG

NOTE

1. For a good statement of this point, see William L. Rowe, *The Cosmological Argument* (Princeton, N. J.: Princeton University Press, 1975), p. 3.

Chapter 1

Plato

Plato (428–7 B.C. – 348–7 B.C.), in introducing natural theology into the subject matter of Western philosophy, has rightly been called the creator of philosophical theism.[1] In his dialogues we can discover the philosophical roots of both the cosmological and teleological arguments for the existence of God. The cosmological proof finds only brief statement in Plato's thought; indeed, it is the presence of teleology in the universe that forms the primary foundation for Plato's theism.[2] But Plato does have a proof for God or gods from motion, and Cicero was correct in pointing to Plato and Aristotle as the originators of the classic prime mover argument.[3]

Plato's proof for a first mover may be found in the tenth chapter of the *Laws*.[4] In this exchange between the Athenian stranger and Cleinas, Plato's specific object is the refutation of atheism. He appears to regard the existence of the gods as crucial for giving to his system of political laws a trans-cultural authority.[5] He wants to prove that the principles of justice are not simply pragmatic inventions of statesmen, but that they exist by nature and are therefore obligatory upon all men. No one, observes the Athenian, ever broke the laws intentionally unless he believed: (1) that the gods do not exist, or (2) that if they do they have no concern for the affairs of men, or (3) that they are easily appeased by prayers and sacrifice.[6] Plato essays to refute each point; his proof for God constitutes the refutation of the first.

When challenged to prove the existence of the gods, Cleinas offers a teleological argument and a proof from universal consent.[7] But the Athenian counsels him that these proofs will not be found convincing by those who would deny the gods' existence. Such persons argue that the heavenly bodies are only earth and stone and that the order we perceive in the universe is merely the product of the interaction of chance and regularity.[8] The heavenly bodies are formed from the basic elements fire, water, earth, and air by chance combination plus internal structural affinities. In this way heaven and all that is in it was formed, as well as animals, plants, and the orderly procession of the seasons; they are not the product of intelligent purpose at all. Gods, like the laws of states, are simply inventions of men and may be disregarded.[9] Hence, neither the teleological argument nor the proof from universal consent will have much force in persuading persons who hold to such opinions.

The Athenian therefore proposes a new proof. The source of the 'vain opinion of those physical investigators' is that they are 'ignorant of the nature and power of the soul'.[10] They do not realise that soul came before the body and is the source of all its changes. The Athenian then offers this proof from motion:

> *Ath.* . . . Someone says to me, 'O stranger, are all things at rest and nothing in motion, or is the exact opposite of this true, or are some things in motion and others at rest?'—To this I shall reply that some things are in motion and others at rest . . . .
>
> . . . there is a motion able to move other things, but never to move itself;—that is one kind; and there is another kind which can always move itself as well as other things . . . ,—that is also one of the many kinds of motion . . . .
>
> . . . when one thing changes another, and that another, of such will there be any primary changing element? How can a thing which is moved by another ever be the beginning of change? Impossible. But when the self-moved changes other, and that again other, and thus thousands upon tens of thousands of bodies are set in motion, must not the beginning of all this motion be the change of the self-moving principle? . . .
>
> . . . If . . . all things were at rest in one mass, which of the above mentioned principles of motion must necessarily be the first to spring up among them? Clearly the self-moving . . . . Then we must say that self-motion being the origin of all motions, and the first which arises among things at rest as well as among things in motion, is the eldest and mightiest principle of change, and that which is changed by another and yet moves other is second . . . .
>
> . . . And what is the definition of that which is named 'soul'? Can we conceive of any other than that which has been already given—the motion which can move itself? . . .
>
> . . . soul is the first origin and moving power of all that is, . . . she has been clearly shown to be the source of change and motion in all things . . . .
>
> . . . In the next place, must we not of necessity admit that the soul is

the cause of good and evil . . . , if we suppose her to be the cause of all things? . . .

. . . And as soul orders and inhabits all things that move, however moving, must we not say that she orders also the heavens? . . .

. . . One soul or more? More than one— . . . at any rate, we must not suppose that there are less than two—one the author of good, and the other of evil . . . .

. . . Shall we say then that it is the soul which controls heaven and earth, and the whole world?—that it is a principle of wisdom and virtue, or a principle which has neither wisdom nor virtue? . . .

. . . If . . . we say that the whole path and movement of heaven, and all that is therein, is by nature akin to the movement and . . . calculation of mind, and proceeds by kindred laws, then, . . . we must say that the best soul takes care of the world and guides it along the good path . . . .

. . . Then, . . . since soul carries all things round, either the best soul or the contrary must of necessity carry round and order and arrange the revolution of the heaven.

Cle. And judging from what has been said, stranger, there would be impiety in asserting that any but the most perfect soul or souls carries round the heavens . . . .

. . . *Ath.* If the soul carries round the sun and moon, and the other stars, does she not carry round each individual of them?

Cle. Certainly . . . .

. . . *Ath.* And this soul of the sun . . . ought by every man to be deemed a god . . . .

. . . And of the stars too, and of the moon, and of the years and months and seasons, must we not say in like manner, that since a soul or souls . . . are the causes of all of them, those souls are gods, . . . whatever be the place and mode of their existence;—and will anyone who admits all this tolerate the denial that all things are full of gods?

Cle. No one, stranger, would be such a madman.[11]

With this proof Plato has introduced argumentative theism into philosophy. The radical novelty which Plato ascribes to this argument is evident from his various descriptions of the proof: a 'singular' argument, 'my unfamiliar argument', 'this most deceptive argument . . . , too much for you, out of your depth and beyond your strength'.[12] There are foreshadowings of his proof from motion among the pre-Socratic philosophers. Alcmaeon had said that the soul is immortal because it is forever in motion like the sun, moon, and stars, and Parmenides had sought a source of Being as Plato seeks a source of motion.[13] Nevertheless, Plato is the first to attempt to prove scientifically that immortal soul is the ἀρχὴ κινήσεως and that this is God.[14] Plato, then, marks the true beginning of the cosmological argument. His proof may be outlined as follows:

1. Some things are in motion.
2. There are two kinds of motion: communicated motion and self-motion.
3. Communicated motion implies self-motion because:
   a. Things in motion imply a self-mover as their source of motion
      i. because otherwise there would be no starting point for the motion
         a. because things moved by another imply a prior mover.
   b. If all things were at rest, only self-motion could arise directly from such a state
      i. because a thing moved by another implies the presence of another moving thing.
      ii. But this contradicts the hypothesis.
4. Therefore, the source of all motion is self-motion, or soul.
5. Soul is the source of astronomical motion because:
   a. The heavens are in motion.
   b. Soul is the source of all motion.
6. There is a plurality of souls because:
   a. There must be at least one to cause good motions.
   b. There must be at least one to cause bad motions.
7. The soul that moves the universe is the best soul because:
   a. The motions of the heavens are good, being regular and orderly like those of the mind.
8. There are many souls, or gods, because:
   a. Each heavenly body is a source of self-motion.

We may now use this outline for a more detailed analysis of Plato's argument.

When Plato asserts that *some things are in motion*, he has more in mind than movement in space. Taylor suggests 'process' as a translation of κίνησις.[15] Plato himself lists ten kinds of motion, including change in size and wasting away.[16] Since self-motion is later declared to be the function of soul, motion must be taken to include mental activities and changes as well as physical movements. Hence, Plato is arguing, in effect, for a first source of change.

Presumably Plato would justify the first step in his argument by appealing to the obvious things in motion all around us. We shall see that he was especially struck by the grandeur of the motions of the stars, the planets, the moon, and the sun. This point of departure marks the proof as an *a posteriori* demonstration for God's existence. A simple look at the world around us is sufficient to convince us that some things are in motion.

Second, *there are two kinds of motion: communicated motion and self-motion.* Of the ten types of motion, explains Plato, self-motion is 'superior to all the others'.[17] For self-motion stands apart from all the other types, which could all be classed as communicated motion. Self-motion is originated from within the mover itself, while all other motion is imparted to the moving thing from another thing. For example, self-motion occurs when I decide and execute the act of writing, but communicated motion occurs when the pen moves across the page, not of its own power, but at the instigation of another, in this case a self-mover. Broadly speaking, then, there are two kinds of motion: communicated motion and self-motion.

Plato's third step is clearly of crucial significance to the cogency of his argument: *communicated motion implies self-motion.* He offers two lines of support. First, things in motion imply a self-mover as their source of motion. In other words, a series of things being moved by another must terminate in a first mover, which will be a self-mover. The reader will recognise this as the well-known infinite regress argument. Plato contends that such a series must end in a first self-mover because if it did not, then there would be no first source, no beginning, no starting point of change. This is because a thing moved by another implies, by definition, that there is something causally prior to it causing it to move. The implicit assumption here is that if motion has no beginning, then it cannot exist now. Plato does not defend this with any argument, however. He simply maintains that either the series of things moved by another begins with a self-mover or it does not begin at all. The latter alternative is taken as self-evidently ridiculous.

There is a fascinating passage in the *Phaedrus* in which Plato attempts to prove the immortality of the soul and upon which the *Laws* argument is based that may shed some light on Plato's reasoning. He writes,

> The soul through all her being is immortal, for that which is ever in

motion* is immortal; but that which moves another and is moved by another, in ceasing to move ceases also to live. Only the self-moving, since it cannot depart from itself, never ceases to move, and is the fountain and beginning of motion to all that moves besides. Now, the beginning is unbegotten, for that which is begotten must have a beginning; but this itself cannot be begotten of anything, for if it were dependent upon something, then the begotten would not come from a *beginning.*† But since it is unbegotten, it must also be indestructible. For surely if a beginning were destroyed, then it could neither come into being itself from any source, nor serve as the beginning of other things, if it be true that all things must have a beginning. Thus it is proved that the self-moving is the beginning of motion; and this can neither be destroyed nor begotten, else the whole heavens and all creation‡ would collapse and stand still, and lacking all power of motion, never again have birth.

* [Or, reading *αὐτο κίνητον* . . . , 'that which moves itself' . . . .]

† [Reading ἐξ ἀρχῆς . . . .]

‡ [According to another reading, 'and the whole earth'.][18]

The question that immediately arises here is whether Plato means by 'beginning' a temporal starting point or an ultimate source. In other words, is he arguing that temporally prior to the series of things moved by another there must have been a self-mover or that in a series of things being moved by another simultaneously there must be an ultimate source of the motion, that is, a self-mover? Reflection on this matter suggests that it is the second alternative that Plato has in mind. Since the soul is ever in motion, Plato would see no problem in a soul's eternally moving a body around in space. But in this case we would have the motion of a thing moved by another (the body moved by the soul), and there would be no beginning to this motion. The motion of the soul is not here temporally prior to the motion of the body; they are co-eternal. Therefore, Plato cannot be arguing that the series of things moved by another must terminate in a self-mover temporally prior to the series, for the first member of the series could be co-eternal with the self-mover. Hence, there would be no beginning to the motion of things moved by another. By 'beginning' Plato must mean an ultimate source, not a temporal starting point. He is arguing that in a series of things being moved by another simultaneously, there must be an ultimate source of this motion, or otherwise there would be no motion at all. So, by 'prior' Plato does not mean temporally prior, but 'logically and causally prior'.[19] He wants to prove that there is an unbegotten, indestructible, first source (or sources) of motion that begets the motion in other things. This interpretation of Plato's argument illuminates his remark that if the self-mover were destroyed, the heavens would come to a standstill. If he were speaking of a temporal regress, the statement would be false, for the original mover could have perished long ago and have been replaced by new movers, or the things moved by another might have just kept on moving after the initial push, though the first mover subsequently perished. One could retort that Plato means to say that if there were no temporally first mover, then there would never have been any motion, and, hence, the heavens would be at a standstill. But it makes more sense to interpret Plato as saying that if one were to remove the ultimate source of motion going on right now, then the motion would cease, and everything would be frozen into immobility. This interpretation is confirmed when one considers how heavily Plato's astronomical system figures in his argument, as we shall see. For Plato accounts for motion by arguing up to an ultimate mover of the heavens. The motion here is entirely simultaneous, and the ultimate mover must be moving at all times for motion to exist. Hence, his remark about the heavens collapsing and ceasing to move supports the idea of the beginning of motion as an ultimate source and not as a temporal starting point.

But if this is the case, what is to be made of Plato's argument? He seems simply to assert as self-evident that what is begotten must have an ultimate source; since motion from another is a begotten motion, there must be a motion unbegotten or self-originated which begets the other motion. Thus, he says, if you destroy the self-moving source of motion, all dependent motion would cease, and everything would be at a standstill. Communicated motion implies a motion from itself, and no matter how many instances of communicated motion one may have, they still imply a motion from itself. Therefore, there must be a first or highest self-mover.

The second argument in support of step three in our outline is that if all things were at rest, only self-motion could arise directly from such a state. This is because communicated motion implies that something else is already moving, and this contradicts the original assumption that all things are at rest. Here Plato is envisaging a situation in which everything is at a complete standstill. Which motion, he asks, will be the first to arise? He is therefore speaking here of 'first' in a temporal sense. Self-motion would be temporally prior to all other motion if everything were at rest. This is, of course, a purely hypothetical situation, and Plato may include the argument to cover both alternatives, that motion is eternal or that motion arises from rest. If motion is eternal, he has argued, there must still be a highest mover as the source of all motion; now he contends alternatively that if motion arises from rest, then self-motion must be the first to arise. Taylor's translation of Plato's conclusion makes this line of reasoning quite clear:

> Consequently as the source of all motions whatsoever, the first to occur among bodies at rest and the first in rank in moving bodies, the motion which initiates itself we shall pronounce to be necessarily the earliest and mightiest of all changes, while that which is altered by something else and sets something else moving is secondary.[20]

For these two reasons, Plato maintains that communicated motion implies self-motion.

The fourth step is to assert that *the source of all motion is self-motion, or soul.* We have seen from the *Phaedrus* that soul is the self-moving entity which is the source of all motion. Plato concludes,

> But whereas the self-moving is proved to be immortal, he who affirms that this is the very meaning and essence of the soul will not be put to confusion. For every body which is moved from without is soul-less, but that which is self-moved from within is animate, and our usage makes it plain what is the nature of the soul. But if this be true, that soul is identical with the self-moving, it must follow of necessity that the soul is unbegotten and immortal.[21]

For Plato, though, soul is not simply a living, self-moving entity, but also mind. Friedrich Solmsen states that for Plato soul combines the qualities of both mind and life, encompassing life, divinity, goodness, and rationality.[22] In the *Phaedo* soul is described as that which apprehends the eternal objects of the intellect, the Forms.[23] Plato's doctrine is that while man's body is perishable, the intellectual part of his soul is immortal. Hence, G. M. A. Grube comments,

> To Socrates and to Plato, as to Aristotle, the activities of the soul culminated in the intellect as its highest function. So much so that 'mind' is at times a far more suitable translation of *ψυχή*.[24]

In arguing to soul as the source of all motion, Plato is arguing to the existence of mind which moves all things.

Fifth, says Plato, *soul is the source of astronomical motion.* We often forget today how awesome the heavens in their constant revolution across the sky must have appeared to the ancients. As Skemp points out, the Academy was 'lavishing' a great deal of time and thought on the subject of astronomy, and this because it was the science which would serve to 'awake man to his divine destiny'.[25] According to Plato, there are two things which 'lead men to believe in the Gods': the argument concerning the soul and the argument 'from the order of the motion of the stars, and of all things under the dominion of the mind which ordered the universe'; hence, he presses these two arguments into service in his case against atheism.[26] Plato reasons here that since all motion is caused by soul, then soul must cause the movements of the vast heavenly system. Thus, Plato attempts to move beyond mere human souls to some sort of soul great enough to move the fixed stars across the sky. This soul will be more easily identifiable as a God.

The sixth step in the argument asserts, *there is a plurality of souls.* Up to this point Plato has merely proved the existence of soul in the world, but not any individual souls. Now he contends that there must be at least two souls, one as the source of good, or regular, motion and one as the source of bad, or erratic, motion. This should not be taken to mean that there exists a sort of dualism between two ultimate principles, one good and one evil, as in Zoroastrianism. Plato simply states that there must be at least two souls to account for the diversity of motion in the universe. Plato may be thinking, on the one hand, of the regular motion of the fixed stars and, on the other, of the motion of the planets, which is virtually inexplicable on a geocentric cosmology.[27] Solmsen, however, on the evidence of *Laws* 7.821a–822c, believes that the irregular motions are in the sublunary world, since Plato declares that all heavenly motion is regular.[28] If all motion were due to the exercise of one soul's power, everything would be presumably moving in perfect harmony. Since there do exist erratic motions, there must be a plurality of souls.

Seventh, Plato asserts that *the soul that moves the universe is the best soul.* This is the nearest Plato gets to monotheism. Although Burnet says that we can hardly doubt that Plato was a monotheist, even he admits that God is not the only self-mover, 'but simply the best of them'.[29] The self-movers may be thought of as hierarchically arranged, with God as the best soul of all.

It is instructive to note that Plato does not identify God with the Good of the *Republic.*[30] The gods are souls, not Forms.[31] Cornford explains,

> As immortal and imperishable, the soul is 'most like the divine, immortal, intelligible, simple, and indissoluble (because incomposite);

whereas the body is most like the mortal, multi-form, unintelligible, dissoluble (because composite) and perpetually changing' (*Phaedo* 78B). To that extent the soul is akin to the unchanging Forms in the eternal world. But the soul is unlike the Forms in that it is alive and intelligent, and life and intelligence cannot exist without change (*Soph.* 248E). All souls, therefore, must partake also of the lower order of existence in the realm of change and time.[32]

Thus, God as the best soul is not the Good or any other Form. And yet, as Burnet remarks, Plato's Good would certainly be God in a modern theistic sense.[33] Grube suggests that for Plato the concept of θεός involved two aspects of reality: the static and the dynamic.[34] God can be thought of as the ultimate reality, the absolute being, or as the creator and source of all activity. To ask for Plato's God is really to ask two questions: what is the ultimate and absolute reality and what is the creator and maker of life?[35] Plato would not have answered the questions in the same way: the Forms correspond to God in the first sense, while the souls are gods in the second sense.[36] Plato never called the Forms gods, but they are his ultimate reality. The best soul is not, then, the source of the being of the universe but simply of its activity. The tension here in Plato's thought is perhaps best left unresolved, for as Gerard Watson emphasises, 'Plato attempted no final systematization of the various theories he put forward'.[37]

Plato calls it the best soul because the orderly movements of the heavens are most like those of mind. It is Reason in the world that is the cause of regularity and order.[38] Without it, chaos would result. The orderly movement of the stars is evidence that the soul that moves the universe is the best soul.

Finally, Plato concludes, *there are many souls, or gods.* Plato's cosmological argument is not a proof for the existence of one God. Though Taylor regards Plato as a monotheist, he nevertheless comments,

> The argument, as it stands, is not necessarily an argument for the existence of only one God. If there is a plurality of perfectly orderly motions, there will be a corresponding plurality of perfectly good souls. Hence Plato speaks all through the reply to the atheist of 'gods' rather than of God. At most the argument would go to prove that there is one soul which is the greatest and best of all, a supreme 'God of gods'.[39]

This is not to say Plato was a simple polytheist. Commentators agree that the categories of polytheism and monotheism are not strictly applicable to Greek philosophical thought about God. Grube suggests that for the Greek, 'god' is primarily a predicative notion.[40] The Greek would not say that God is *x*, but that *x* is a god or is divine. Many things might share such divine status. I. M. Crombie thinks that the adjective 'divine' may simply mean something like 'ultimate'.[41] The ultimate may be one or many; the question of unicity was simply not regarded as important. Noting that Plato shifts 'haphazardly' from *θεός* to *θεοί* in the *Laws*, Crombie asserts that there is no more significance in the use of the singular than the plural.[42] To label Plato as a crass polytheist would thus be somewhat unfair, though it would also be inaccurate to describe him as a strict monotheist. The exchange between Taylor and Cornford is particularly interesting in this regard. When Taylor in his commentary on the *Timaeus* presented a very monotheistic Plato, Cornford indignantly declared in his own commentary on that work,

> There is . . . no justification for the suggestion conveyed by 'God' with a capital letter, that Plato was a monotheist. He believed in the divinity of the world as a whole and of the heavenly bodies. The *Epinomis* recommends the institution of a cult of these celestial gods . . . . It is not fair either to Plato or to the New Testament to ascribe the most characteristic revelations of the Founder of Christianity to a pagan polytheist.[43]

In a *Mind* article, Taylor responded to Cornford's ascription to Plato of pagan polytheism. The Greek thinkers did not regard the question of the unicity of 'God' as primary, states Taylor; but more importantly, Plato's lesser gods are all under the sovereignty of a single, supreme will and intelligence, which constitutes at least an implicit monotheism. To allow Plato to speak of God (with the capital letter) is to run much less risk of falsifying his thought than to call him a pagan polytheist.[44] Nor can such a description be justified on the basis of Plato's use of *θεοί*—compare Plotinus who freely spoke of *θεοί* and allowed the Roman state gods, but could never be described therefore as a polytheist.[45] Apologising for the excessiveness of his language, Cornford subsequently modified his position on Plato's polytheism. Remarking that the plural or singular of *θεός* cannot be determinative, Cornford admitted,

> As for 'polytheist', . . . I do not wish to defend the word, but I now admit that it is, on the whole, truer to say that Plato was at heart a

> monotheist than to say that he was not . . . . This is a case in which I have overstressed one side of Plato's thought in trying to correct too much emphasis on the other.[46]

Thus, Plato retains a dual character to his thought about the divine. On the one hand, according to Gustav Mueller, 'Greek ploytheism pervades Plato's realms . . . . It is never doubted. Plato . . . loves the gods and their festivals and does not attempt to replace them by reason or by a naturalistic being-in-general'; yet on the other hand, 'Plato is a polytheist, but he is not only a polytheist', for he also adheres to an 'absolute monotheism'.[47] Perhaps Taylor's description of Plato's thought as implicit monotheism is the best characterisation that can be made utilising these categories. For, as Verdenius notes, 'Plato admits the existence of personal gods, such as the Olympian gods, but he endows them with only a lesser degree of divinity . . . '.[48] Plato seems to regard any soul as divine, the souls of the heavenly bodies as even more so, and the best soul as primarily so.

We may schematise Plato's argument as follows:

1. Some things are in motion.
2. There are two kinds of motion: communicated motion and self-motion.
   a. Communicated motion is imparted from another.
   b. Self-motion is self-originated.
3. Communicated motion implies self-motion.
   a. Things in motion require self-motion as the ultimate source of their motion.
      i. If there were no ultimate, self-moving source of motion, then there would be no beginning to communicated motion.
      ii. If communicated motion has no beginning, it cannot now exist.
      iii. But motion exists (1).
      iv. Therefore, there must be a beginning of communicated motion in an ultimate, self-moving source.
   b. A temporal origin of motion requires a temporally first, self-moving source of motion.
      i. Communicated motion implies the presence of another moving thing.
      ii. Therefore, communicated motion could not be the first motion to originate.
      iii. Self-motion is self-originated.
      iv. Therefore, self-motion could be the first motion to originate.

4. Soul (Mind) is the cause of all motion.
   a. Communicated motion implies self-motion (3).
   b. Self-motion is caused by the animate power of the souls (minds) of self-movers.
5. Soul (Mind) is the cause of astronomical motion.
   a. The heavens are in motion.
   b. Soul (Mind) is the cause of all motion (4).
6. There are many heavenly souls (minds).
   a. Regular motions require the existence of good soul (mind), while erratic motions require the existence of bad soul (mind).
   b. The motion of each heavenly body requires a soul (mind) as the cause of its motion.
7. The Soul (Mind) which moves the universe is the highest Soul (Mind).
   a. For it imparts rational order and motion to the entire cosmos.

A final question, as interesting as it is complex, is the relationship between the God of the *Laws* and the God of the *Timaeus*. With the *Timaeus* the Platonic 'Trinity' is complete: the Good, the Demiurge, and the World Soul.[49] Which of these is to be identified with the best soul of the *Laws*? As we have seen, it cannot be the Good, for this is Form, not soul. The question, then, is whether the best soul of the *Laws* is identical with the Demiurge or the World Soul.

P. E. More argues that the World Soul is not to be identified with God.[50] Plato, he asserts, avoids all forms of pantheism, which would result if the World Soul were God. Nevertheless, the *Laws* argument does prove that God has the attributes of soul. Burnet explicitly identifies the Demiurge with God.[51] Taylor also calls the Demiurge God and the supreme soul.[52] He argues that the wise and good soul of the *Laws* is the craftsman of the *Timaeus*.[53] Taylor recognises that the creation of the world is part of the mythology of the *Timaeus*, but he asserts that for Plato the physical world has a 'maker', and this doctrine is directly analogous to the Christian doctrine of creation in that it implies that '. . . the physical world does not exist in its own right, but depends on a really self-existing being, the best ψυχή, God, for its existence'.[54] Denying the Neoplatonist doctrine that God is the One or Form of the Good and that the Demiurge is the νοῦς proceeding from it, Taylor concludes,

> . . . the Demiurge of the *Timaeus* is excactly the 'best ψυχή' which is said in the *Laws* to be the source of the great orderly cosmic movements, that is, he is God, and if we are to use the word God in the sense it has in Plato's natural theology, the only God there is.[55]

On the other hand, Grube argues that the World Soul is the logical product of the argument of the *Laws*.[56] The Demiurge is but a mythological figure employed to illustrate the ever-present factors in the organisation of the universe; there never was a literal creation.[57] A literal creation leads to absurdities; the Demiurge is declared to be the creator of all soul, and yet he himself must be soul because he has wisdom, which cannot exist apart from soul. Hence, the Demiurge is only a literary device; souls have always existed. As for the relation between gods, human souls, and the World Soul, Grube asserts that the World Soul is simply the collection of all souls, human and divine.[58] Cornford also identifies the best soul of the *Laws* with the World Soul, but he does not try to reduce the latter to the collection of all souls. He takes Taylor to task for trying to 'Christian-ize' Plato's theism and turn the Demiurge into the God of the Bible.[59] Both the Demiurge and the primordial chaos are mythological symbols, according to Cornford, representing the continual tension between Reason and Necessity in the world.[60] For Plato necessity was not associated with natural law, but with chance.[61] Necessity is the present intractable element in the world that must be persuaded by reason to conform to law-like operation. Chaos is an abstraction, a picture of the universe without reason.[62] The Demiurge is a symbolic figure representing Reason in the World Soul.[63] Cornford notes that the Demiurge is not really a religious figure at all, since he is not an object of worship.[64] He is simply a mythological figure analogous to some primitive religions' 'Maker' who serves to account for the construction of the world but is not an object of religious devotion. The World Soul is the ultimate cause of all motion and becoming since neither the Forms nor the Receptacle nor the Demiurge (being mythological) can account for it. This also means that Necessity must, as the cause of errant motion, be an irrational surd factor within the World Soul itself.[65] Cornford concludes his commentary with an analysis showing a similar train of thought in the Greek tragedian Aeschylus, who found order and peace in the reconciliation of Reason and Necessity by the power of persuasion.[66]

Responding to Cornford's charges, Taylor maintains that the Demiurge of the *Timaeus*, while part of the *pictorial* imagery of that dialogue, is not therefore *mythological* in the sense of unreal; indeed, the Demiurge represents a supreme rational and righteous purposive agent operative throughout the universe.[67] Taylor observes that even Genesis uses obviously pictorial language about God without thereby implying His unreality. Accordingly, Taylor takes the Demiurge to be the 'imaginative symbol' of the 'divine *νοῦς*', and he refuses to reduce the

Demiurge to the World Soul.[68] As for Cornford's contention that the Demiurge is not a religious figure and therefore not God, Taylor rebuts, '. . . is it meant that the feelings betrayed by Plato's language in all these dialogues towards the "maker and father of all", "the King", "the best soul" are not specifically emotions of religious veneration?'[69] To compare the Demiurge to the 'Maker' of the primitive Australians is to evacuate Plato's profoundest meaning and to ignore the moral government of the world prominent in both the *Laws* and the *Timaeus*.[70]

Solmsen contends that the best soul of the *Laws* is the Soul of the World.[71] He argues that νοῦς lacks the necessary contact with the world of becoming and that God must therefore be ψυχή, which is akin to mind but also has the principle of Life. Since the Demiurge of the *Timaeus* is a mythical figure,[72] this means that Plato's Deity must be the World Soul.[73]

Skemp, however, does not regard the Demiurge as mythological. He provides references to Plato's use of the concept of Demiurge in earlier dialogues, including the *Sophistes*, where we are introduced to a *δημιουργῶν θεός* whose activity is a type of *ποιητική*, and the *Philebus*, which is generally not considered mythical in any sense.[74] Referring to the latter work, Skemp disputes the reduction of the Demiurge to the World Soul and considers the Demiurge to be the ultimate source of motion.[75] God is the Demiurge who stands above all lesser souls.[76]

The resolution of the dispute may be left to the Plato scholars. Solmsen rightly cautions with regard to Plato that '. . . none of his approaches to the problem of deity is in any way final or dogmatic'.[77] So the question may be incapable of being settled with finality. Yet the issue raised here is important for the cosmological argument. For it forces upon us the question as to whether the argument may not lead us to a being which is simply the soul of the world and not its creator.[78] The urgency of such a question for philosophy of religion has become obvious since Whitehead and the introduction of process theology. Plato's argument from motion, if cogent, leads no further than the World Soul, whatever the status of the Demiurge is conceived to be. The logical conclusion of the *Laws* argument is simply a soul or souls that move the heavens with everlasting motion. If Plato did believe in a Demiurge God beyond this, he would have to do more than he has done in the *Laws* to prove his existence.

NOTES

1. A. E. Taylor, *Plato: The Man and his Work* (London: Methuen, 1926), p. 493. Taylor elsewhere notes that the phrase 'natural theology' was coined by Cicero's contemporary Marcus Terentius Varro, who utilised the expression to distinguish it from poetical theology, or what we would call classical mythology, and from civil theology, or state religion. Natural theology is the discourse of philosophers about God and is intended to convey truth about reality, according to Varro. 'Natural theology, then, meant originally a doctrine about God which is neither imaginative fiction nor socially useful fiction but science, and such a doctrine was attempted for the first time by Plato . . .' (A. E. Taylor, *Platonism and its Influence* [New York: Longmans, Green, 1932], p. 99).

2. Chung-Hwan Chen, 'Plato's Theistic Teleology', *Anglican Theological Review* 43 (1961): 71–87. John Wild notes that the teleological argument is propounded in many variations throughout the dialogues, especially in *Timaeus* 29, 47 and *Philebus* 28. (John Wild, 'Plato and Christianity: A Philosophical Comparison', *The Journal of Bible and Religion* 17 [1949]: 9.)

3. Cicero, *De natura deorum* Cf. J. Ferguson, 'Theistic Arguments in the Greek Philosophers', *Hibbert Journal* 51 (1953): 156.

4. Plato, *Laws* 10. 884–899d.

5. Ibid., 10. 889e–890d.

6. Ibid., 10. 885b.

7. Ibid., 10. 886.

8. Ibid., 10. 886e, 889b–889e.

9. Ibid., 10. 889e–890.

10. Ibid., 10. 891c, 892. Unless otherwise indicated, all quotations of Plato's works are from Plato, *The Dialogues of Plato*, 4th ed. rev., 4 vols., trans. with Introductions and Analyses by B. Jowett (Oxford: Clarendon Press, 1953).

11. Ibid., 10. 893b–899c.

12. Ibid., 10. 891d, e; 892d, e.

13. J. B. Skemp, *The Theory of Motion in Plato's Later Dialogues* (Cambridge: Cambridge University Press, 1942), pp. 5–6. See Chapters 3 and 4: 'Antecedents of the *κίνησις*-doctrine of the *Timaeus* in Alcmaeon, the Pythagoreans and the medical writers', and 'Antecedents of the *κίνησις*-doctrine of the *Timaeus* in the system of Empedocles'.

14. John Burnet, *Greek Philosophy*, pt. 1: *Thales to Plato* (London: Macmillan, 1914; rep. ed., 1924), pp. 333, 336. It must be admitted that certain pre-Socratics conceived of God as νοῦς or ψυχή respectively, but they did not seek to construct proofs for God's existence. (See Edward Hussey, *The Presocratics* [London: Gerald Duckworth, 1972].)

15. Plato, *The Laws of Plato*, trans. A. E. Taylor (London: Dent, 1934), p. lii.

16. Plato, *Laws* 10. 893c–894. For an enumeration of the ten types, see B. Jowett, Analysis of Plato, *Dialogues*, 4: 142.

17. Plato, *Laws* 10. 894d.

18. Plato, *Phaedrus* 245c–d.

19. Taylor, *Platonism*, p. 101. Skemp would support our interpretation and Tayor's description when he comments with regard to Reason and Necessity, or Mind and the Errant Cause, which are the causes of motion in the *Timaeus*:

Within this Ouranos, however, the interplay of the two *αἰτίαι κινήσεως*, *νοῦς* and *ἀνάγκη*, is more important than the workings of the astronomical system. We have . . . the two *αἰτίαι κινήσεως*, *νοῦς* and the *πλανωμένη αἰτία*. We must remember that *αἰτίαι* never means a previous event related causally to a subsequent, but an active agency of a higher order of reality which is literally 'responsible for' the physical event.*

* Cf. *αἰτία ἑλομένου, ὁ δὲ θεὸς ἀναίτιος*, *Rep.* x 617e. (Skemp, *Theory*, p. 71)

For the view that Plato speaks of a temporal priority, see W. F. R. Hardie, *A Study in Plato* (Oxford: Clarendon Press, 1936), pp. 107–8.

20. Plato, *Laws*, p. 286.
21. Plato, *Phaedrus* 245e–246.
22. Friedrich Solmsen, *Plato's Theology* (Ithaca, N.Y.: Cornell University Press, 1942; reprint ed., Johnson Reprint Corporation, 1967), pp. 89, 92.
23. Plato, *Phaedo* 66b.
24. G. M. A. Grube, *Plato's Thought* (London: Methuen, 1935), p. 122.
25. Skemp, *Theory*, p. 68.
26. Plato, *Laws* 12. 966e. Cf. Taylor, *Plato: Man and Work*, p. 490.
27. For a table of these various motions, see Francis MacDonald Cornford, *Plato's Cosmology* (London: Kegan Paul, Trench, Trubner, 1937), pp. 136–7. Cornford's table is drawn from the *Timaeus*, but he comments that

> . . . in the *Laws* Soul is not merely called the source of motion (as at *Phaedrus* 245D), but more specifically 'the cause of the becoming and perishing of all things' (891E); it 'controls all change and rearrangement' (892A); it is the 'first becoming and change' (896A); it originates all *διάκρισις*, *αὔξη*, *γένεσις* and their opposites (894B). (Ibid., p. 206)

Hence, soul would have to account for all the motions listed in Cornford's table. Plato argues that this requires a plurality of souls.

28. Solmsen, *Theology*, p. 139.
29. Burnet, *Philosophy*, p. 337.
30. This mistake is made, for example, by I. M. Forsyth, who confusedly argues that God is one with the Good and is eternal soul, thus being both the originator of motion in the universe and its final goal (I. M. Forsyth, 'Aristotle's Concept of God as Final Cause', *Philosophy* 22 [1947]: 117). Cf. W. J. Verdenius: 'Plato's God is such a form, an ideal model or system of models' (W. J. Verdenius, 'Plato and Christianity', *Ratio* 5 [1963]: 19).
31. Taylor, *Platonism*, pp. 103–4; cf. Solmsen, *Theology*, pp. 72, 89.
32. Cornford, *Cosmology*, pp. 63–4.
33. Burnet, *Philosophy*, p. 336.
34. Grube, *Thought*, pp. 150–1.
35. Ibid., p. 152.
36. Ibid., p. 162.
37. Gerard Watson, 'The Theology of Plato and Aristotle', *Irish Theological Quarterly* 37 (1970): 60.
38. Cornford, *Cosmology*, p. 203.
39. Taylor, *Platonism*, p. 103.
40. Grube, *Thought*, p. 150. Cf. Watson, 'Theology', p. 56.

41. I. M. Crombie, *An Examination of Plato's Doctrines* (London: Routledge & Kegan Paul, 1962), p. 369.
42. Ibid., p. 371.
43. Cornford, *Cosmology*, p. 35.
44. A. E. Taylor, 'The "Polytheism" of Plato: An Apologia', *Mind* 47 (1938): 183–4.
45. Ibid., p. 184.
46. F. M. Cornford, 'The "Polytheism" of Plato: An Apology', *Mind* 47 (1938): 324.
47. Gustav E. Mueller, 'Plato and the Gods', *Philosophical Review* 45 (1936): 462, 466, 469. Watson writes,

> Plato was evidently a naturally pious man, one who in the normal course of events would have accepted a purified form of the conventional religion of his city which was a religion with personal gods. But Plato was also the culmination of the philosophical tradition in Greece which had attempted to explain the problem of the One and the Many by invoking principles which were essentially impersonal—Water, Air, Fire, Aether, Numbers, the Atoms. Plato united these two streams in himself. (Watson, 'Theology', p. 60)

48. Verdenius, 'Plato', p. 19.
49. The *Timaeus* is usually considered to be one of Plato's latest dialogues, embodying his mature thought. But it has been argued that the *Timaeus* may actually be a middle dialogue and that Plato later abandoned the theory of Forms expounded in the *Phaedo* and the *Republic* and retained in the *Timaeus*. (See, for example, G. E. L. Owen, 'The Place of the *Timaeus* in Plato's Dialogues', *Classical Quarterly* 3 [1953]: 79–95.) If this is true, then the best soul of the *Laws* is all that is left of his earlier 'Trinity'. For a good discussion of the status of the Good, the Demiurge, and the World Soul and for a synopsis of various opinions on this issue, see Ernst Douda, 'Platons Weltbaumeister', *Altertum* 19 (1973): 147–56.
50. Paul Elmer More, *The Religion of Plato* (Princeton: Princeton University Press, 1921), pp. 222–3.
51. Burnet, *Philosophy*, p. 341.
52. A. E. Taylor, *A Commentary on Plato's 'Timaeus'* (Oxford: Clarendon Press, 1928), pp. 75–8.
53. Ibid., p. 64.
54. Ibid., p. 71.
55. Ibid., p. 82. Disagreeing with Taylor on this count is R. Hackforth, who argues that God is pure νοῦς and that soul is caused by νοῦς. Citing *Laws* 10. 892a, c; 10. 896a; 10. 967d in support, he maintains that soul is an originated being. He observes that in both the *Philebus* and the *Timaeus*, the Demiurge causes the World Soul. But he interprets this, not as an origin in time, but as a sort of ontological dependence (R. Hackforth, 'Plato's Theism', *Classical Quarterly* 30 [1936]: 5). Hackforth recognises that *Philebus* 30c and *Timaeus* 30b agree that νοῦς cannot exist apart from soul and that furthermore the *Sophist* 249a states that νοῦς must have *ζωή* and these two can exist together only in a soul, but he rejoins that this is talking only about the universe which *has* νοῦς and not about God, who *is* νοῦς (Ibid., p. 7). But this is a highly contrived response and serves to

expose the artificiality of Hackforth's position. It seems clear that if the Demiurge exists, he would be a soul. Hackforth's references certainly do not prove soul is originated and sometimes even suggest the contrary. His interpretation of the *Phaedrus* takes 'unbegotten' in a temporal sense, which, we have seen, is unlikely. Thus, if the Demiurge is the cause of the World Soul, he must be identical with the best soul of the *Laws*.

56. Grube, *Thought*, pp. 140–9.

57. Ibid., pp. 162–3, 169–71.

58. Ibid., pp. 170–1. Whether *Philebus* 30a–d would warrant this deduction seems questionable.

59. Cornford, *Cosmology*, p. xi. He specifically disagrees with Taylor's comments on 29d–30c and 69c. 3 of the *Timaeus*. For Taylor's response see Taylor, 'Apologia', pp. 180–99. Commenting on Taylor's response, Cornford surrenders the ascription of polytheism to Plato, but defends—successfully, I think—his contention that love and omnipotence cannot be attributed to Plato's God (Cornford, 'Apology', pp. 321–30).

60. Ibid., p. 37.

61. Ibid., p. 167.

62. Ibid., p. 203.

63. Ibid., p. 197.

64. Ibid., pp. 209–10.

65. Ibid., p. 35.

66. Ibid., pp. 361–4.

67. Taylor, 'Apologia', p. 184.

68. Ibid., p. 185.

69. Ibid., pp. 189–90.

70. Ibid., p. 190.

71. Solmsen, *Theology*, pp. 112–13.

72. Ibid., p. 146.

73. Ibid., p. 149.

74. Skemp, *Theory*, pp. 109–10.

75. Ibid., p. 66.

76. Ibid., pp. 113–15.

77. Solmsen, *Theology*, p. 146.

78. G. C. Field, *The Philosophy of Plato* (London: Oxford University Press, 1949), p. 145. It might be asked whether Plato's God is personal. Field says no (Ibid. p. 147). Taylor suggests that for the Greek, the concept of personality has no real meaning and is thus an inadmissible category to impose on Plato's thinking. God is mind that sets all things in order, but 'To ask whether that mind is "personal" is to commit an anachronism' (A. E. Taylor, *Plato* [London: Constable, 1914], p. 142).

Chapter 2

Aristotle

Aristotle of Stagira (384–322 B.C.) moves far beyond Plato in his argumentation for the existence of God. For while Plato first employed the logic of the cosmological argument, it was Aristotle who developed it and argued that even Plato's self-mover must have a cause in an utterly unmoved mover which Aristotle called God.

In order to fully appreciate Aristotle's cosmological argument, we must understand his distinction between potency and actuality. Prior to Aristotle, the Megaric school had denied all becoming and change in the world. In Aristotle's words,

> So they say that none of the things that are either comes to be or passes out of existence, because what comes to be must do so either from what is or from what is not, both of which are impossible. For what is cannot come to be (because it *is* already), and from what is not nothing could have come to be (because something must* be present as a substratum).
>
> * Reading in 1.31 *δεῖν* . . . .[1]

Aristotle solves the dilemma by his distinction between potency and actuality.[2] A thing can be said to be in more than one sense: '. . . "being" and "that which is" . . . sometimes mean being potentially, and sometimes being actually'.[3] For example, a thing may be actually one thing, but potentially many things.[4] We would say in that case that it has the potency to be divided. A potency is a 'principle in the very thing acted on which makes it capable of being changed'.[5] As such, it is the 'source of movement or change'.[6] Actuality, on the other hand, is associated with 'complete reality'; if a thing actually exists, then it exists in complete reality.[7] 'Actuality means the existence of the thing . . . .'[8] Examples serve to elucidate the meaning of the terms: thus, a man may be actually asleep, but he has the potency of being awake; a creature with its eyes shut cannot actually see, but it has the potency of sight. Now change is the actualisation of some potency, or in Aristotle's words, 'the fulfillment of what exists potentially, in so far as it exists potentially'.[9] Change is neither potency nor actuality: it is the *transition* between the two. This solves the problem posed by the Megaric school, for a thing changes, not from being or not-being as such to being, but from potential being to actual being.[10]

With this basic understanding of the actuality/potency distinction in hand, we are now equipped to consider Aristotle's argument for the existence of God. Aristotle's famous proof from motion for the existence of an unmoved mover is fully explicated in both the *Physics* and *Metaphysics*. His views on the necessity of an unmoved mover gradually evolved in his philosophy.[11] His earliest treatise dealing with the subject of the motion of the heavenly bodies, *On Philosophy*, has been lost, but Cicero quoted the essay, and these fragments are instructive. In the first of these, Aristotle ascribes intelligence to the stars.[12] In the second passage, he argues that the heavenly bodies move voluntarily by an exercise of their own will.[13] In the third passage, a critic charges Aristotle with inconsistency in calling the world divine and in stating that only mind is divine and the world has a transcendent mover.[14] According to Ross, the passages are inconclusive, and the safest inference is that Aristotle had not yet made up his mind with regard to the motion of the heavens.[15] When we come to Aristotle's *On the Heavens*, we find no mention of the necessity of an unmoved mover. In this work, he introduces the notion of the ether, a fifth element in addition to earth, water, fire, and air, of which the stars are said to be composed and which moves naturally in a circle.[16] The stars are still conceived as having souls and power of initiating their natural motion.[17]

But when we come to the *Physics*, Aristotle sees the need to explain even the motion of the outermost heavenly bodies by the agency of a mover itself unmoved. There are two versions of the proof from motion in the *Physics*, one in book seven and one in book eight.

The first proof is too lengthy to quote verbatim, but it may be summarised as follows.[18] Everything in motion must be moved by something. If it is not self-moved it is moved by another. And nothing can be self-moved. For if a thing in motion is caused to stop moving because something else stops moving, then the thing in motion cannot be self-moved. Everything in motion is divisible, so let AB represent a thing in motion. Now if B is at rest, then AB must be at rest. This means AB is dependent on B for its motion. But if anything (AB) stops moving because something else (B) stops moving, then it (AB) is not itself self-moved. Therefore, there is no self-mover, and everything in motion must be moved by something.

Furthermore, the series of things moved by another cannot go on to infinity; there must be a first mover. For an infinite series of movers is impossible. In such a series, the motion communicated by each mover is simultaneous: A is moving B, which moves Γ, which moves Δ, and so on, all at the same time. Thus, the members of the whole series move each other in a finite time. Since the series is infinite, there will be infinite motion. But this means there is an infinite motion in a finite time, which is impossible. It might be objected that this is not impossible because each member in the series moves in a finite time, and there is no contradiction in saying an infinite number of things have an infinite motion in a finite time. But in physical motion, all the movers must be in simultaneous contact with one another, so that considered as a whole, they do form one body. But this means that one thing moves with an infinite motion in a finite time, and this is impossible. Therefore, the series of things moved by another must come to an end, terminating in a first mover and a first moved thing.

This proof is not nearly as sophisticated as Aristotle's later ones, so I defer a lengthy discussion of this argument in order to devote more space to the later proofs. I shall restrict myself to a few comments: (1) This is a proof from motion in the sense in which we understand the word today: movement from place to place. This is evident from Aristotle's remark that things 'moved locally and corporeally' must be in contact with one another.[19] He says that we observe this to be 'universally' the case.[20] He goes on to say that a thing may be moved locally by something else pulling, pushing, carrying, or twirling it, all of which require physical contact.[21] (2) The reason that everything in motion is divisible is that in any motion between two termini part of the thing in motion must be at the first terminus and part at the second, for if it were in either one entirely it would not be moving.[22] This argument is capable of two interpretations. On the one hand, it may be understood as an attempt aimed at refuting Plato's doctrine of a self-mover as the source of motion. This would imply that the second proof of the *Physics*, accepting as it does the existence of self-movers, contradicts and reformulates this proof. On the other hand, it may be interpreted to mean that no body can be self-moved and must be moved by another thing, namely, its soul.[23] This interpretation seeks to harmonise the proofs. (3) The series of movers Aristotle has in mind here is not a temporal regress, but a hierarchical series of things being moved by another. The innermost sphere of heavenly bodies is moved by the one enclosing it and that by the one enclosing it, and so on, out to the outermost sphere of the heavens. The movement of one sphere is simultaneous with the movement of the others. (4) Aristotle argues that this series cannot be infinite and so must terminate in a first mover and first moved thing. Presumably the latter would be the outermost sphere. But Aristotle does not specify how the first mover is related to it nor does he call it God.

Aristotle's later proof of the existence of a first unmoved mover is an extended one also, and thus any quotation of the proof as a whole is impracticable.[24] He does, however, provide us with a concise concluding summary of his proof, and this statement may serve as a springboard for our discussion of his argument:

> In the course of our argument . . . we established the fact that everything that is in motion is moved by something,[1] and that the movent is either unmoved or in motion, and that, if it is in motion, it is moved either by itself or by something else and so on throughout the series:[2] and so we proceeded to the position[3] that the first principle that directly[4] causes things that are in motion to be moved is that which moves itself and the first principle of the whole series[5] is the unmoved . . . the necessity that there should be motion continuously requires that there should be a first movent that is unmoved even accidentally,[4] if, as we have said,[5] there is to be in the world of things an unceasing and undying motion, and the world is to remain[6] permanently self-contained and within the same limits: for if the first principle is permanent, the universe must also be permanent, since it is continuous with the first principle.
>
> [1] Chapter 4.
> [2] *ἀεί*. i.e. if a particular *κινοῦν* derives its motion from another *κινοῦν* the same question arises with regard to the second *κινοῦν*, and so on.
> [3] Chapter 5.
> [4] *κινουμενων μέν* in 1.33 can hardly stand. It may have displaced *προσεχὴς μέν* . . . or *κινήσεως*.
> [5] sc. *κινούμενα* and *ὅ αὐτὸ ἑαυτὸ κινεῖ* together.
> [4] Reading in 1.24 *καὶ κατὰ συμβεβηκός* . . . .
> [5] Chapter 1.
> [6] Reading in 1.26 *μενεῖν* . . . .[25]

Aristotle's argument may be outlined as follows:

1. Everything that is in motion is being moved by something.
2. This something is itself either in motion or not in motion.
3. If it is in motion, then it is either self-moved or moved by another.

4. The members of a series of things each being moved by another must ultimately be in motion only by reference to a self-moved thing.
5. The members of the whole series of self-movers and things moved by another must be in motion only by reference to an unmoved mover.
6. This first mover must be utterly unmoved and eternal because:
   a. motion itself is continuous and eternal.

We may fill out this skeleton outline of Aristotle's proof by examining each of its steps separately.

The first step, that *everything that is in motion is being moved by something*, presupposes Aristotle's analysis of the nature of motion. Motion for Aristotle has a connotation much broader than that which we usually understand by the term. Perhaps a better translation would simply be 'change'. But this would obscure Aristotle's true meaning, for he carefully distinguishes between change (*μεταβολή*) and motion (*κίνησις*). Although he uses the terms interchangeably early in the *Physics*,[26] he soon renders them distinct. There are four types of change, each taking place within a category: substantial change involving coming to be and passing away, qualitative change involving alteration of qualities, quantitative change involving increase or decrease in amount, and change of place involving locomotion from place to place.[27] But substantial change cannot truly be said to be motion, for motion involves a subject's moving from a starting point to a goal, whereas in substantial change there is no enduring subject.[28] The subject comes to exist or ceases to exist; it does not itself move from one state to another. Therefore, motion can take place only within the categories of quality, quantity, and place.

For Aristotle the presence of motion in the world is simply a basic datum of sense experience. 'We physicists', he writes, '. . . must take for granted that the things that exist by nature are, either all or some of them, in motion . . .'[29] The argument of Parmenides and Melissus, that Being is one and cannot change, Aristotle considers hardly worth refuting.[30] To contend that motion does not exist is to 'disregard sense-perception' and is an example of intellectual weakness.[31] With regard to theories that all things are in motion or all things are at rest, Aristotle simply retorts, 'We have sufficient ground for rejecting all these theories in the single fact that we *see* some things that are sometimes in motion and sometimes at rest'.[32] Aristotle's firm reliance on sense experience to support this point marks the argument as an *a posteriori* proof.

Aristotle also argued that motion is everlasting. He proffers basically two arguments. First, motion can have neither a beginning nor an end.[33]

Motion cannot exist apart from the objects that are in motion. If motion had a beginning, then either the objects came into being from not-being or they always existed in a state of rest until at some point they began to move. The first alternative is impossible because the generation of objects is itself a change. Presumably Aristotle is arguing that this change must have been caused by a previous motion of something already existing so that a temporal infinite regress of causes of motion is generated. The second alternative is unacceptable because the prior state of rest must have been caused by something, rest being the privation of motion. Thus, again a temporal regress of motions is generated. The second alternative is doubly unreasonable because motion occurs only when two things are brought into proximity with one another; but if everything were at rest, nothing could be brought near something else to move it, and motion would never begin. So at least one thing had to be moving in order to cause motion to begin; but this is self-contradictory. Therefore, motion had no beginning. Nor can motion ever cease. For if motion were destroyed, its destruction would be a change. And the destroyer of motion would then have to be destroyed, and so on, *ad infinitum*.

The second proof for motion's being everlasting is from the nature of time.[34] Time is the measure of motion with respect of 'before' and 'after'.[35] Thus, time cannot exist without motion. Every moment of time is the end of the past and the beginning of the future. Thus, every moment of time is bounded on either side by more time. Therefore, time can have neither beginning nor end. Since time cannot exist without motion, motion, too, must exist without beginning or end. Hence, it is everlasting.

But granted that things are in motion and that motion is everlasting, how can it be proved that everything in motion is being moved by something? Could not motion simply be uncaused, a brute, surd fact? To answer this question we must turn to Aristotle's actuality/potency distinction. Motion or change exists; but change is the actualising of some potency. It is because things have real potencies that they are able to change. To deny the reality of potencies is to land oneself in the Parmenidean absurdity of denying change.[36] Further, the actualisation of any potency demands the action of something already actual: 'For from the potential the actual is always produced by an actual thing, e.g. man by man, musician by musician; there is always a first mover, and the mover already exists actually'.[37] The implicit assumption here is that *the potential cannot actualise itself*. The potential, precisely because it is potential, cannot make itself actual. This is simply to say, something cannot bring itself into existence. Thus, anything in motion must be moved by something. This something need not itself be in motion, but it must actually exist.[38] Aristotle, then, does not simply assume the truth of this first step in his proof; rather its truth is based upon his analysis of being and change. Everything that is in motion is being moved by something.

The second step is that *this something is itself either in motion or not in motion.* If it is not in motion, it is an unmoved mover. The third step is that *if it is in motion, then it is either self-moved or moved by another.*

Aristotle's fourth step is to argue that *the members of a series of things each being moved by another must ultimately be in motion only by reference to a self-moved thing.* Aristotle offers three arguments to prove that any series of things moved by another must terminate in a self-mover.

First, the series of things moved by another cannot be infinite and must end in a thing that moves itself.[39] Aristotle makes it clear by his example that he is speaking of a hierarchical series of simultaneous movers:

> . . . either the movent [mover] immediately precedes the last thing in the series,* or there may be one or more intermediate links: e.g. the stick moves the stone and is moved by the hand, which again is moved by the man: in the man, however, we have reached a movent that is not so in virtue of being moved by something else.
>
> * i.e. the thing that is moved.[40]

Perhaps a more contemporary example of the same nature would be that of a boy rolling a hoop: the hoop is moving because of the stick, and the stick is moving because of the boy, who moves himself as he runs along. The action of all the movers is simultaneous. Aristotle argues that any series of things moved by another must terminate in a self-mover, as in the example, because there cannot be an infinite series of hierarchically arranged things moved by another. Such a series requires a first member because the intermediate movers have no causal efficacy of their own. This is evident from the fact that (1) the first mover truly moves the last intermediate mover but not vice versa, and (2) the first mover will be able to move an object without any intermediaries whatsoever, while the intermediate mover cannot move any object without a first mover. In Aristotle's words, '. . . the first [mover] will move the thing without the last, but the last will not move it without the first: e.g. the stick will not move anything unless it is itself moved by the man'.[41] This second reason is clearly the more important point: it is of the nature of intermediate movers to have no causal efficacy of their own to move; they are merely instruments by which a thing which moves itself moves an object. But an infinite series of such things moved by another can have no first mover, and without a first mover, nothing would be moving. This, of course, contradicts step one of the proof and plunges one back again into the hopeless absurdities of the Megaric school. Therefore, any series of things being moved by another must terminate in a first mover. And since the cause of motion must be either in motion or not in motion (step two), and since, if it is in motion, it is either self-moved or moved by another (step three), and since the series of things moved by another cannot be endless, then the first mover must be self-moved.

Second, the same argument may be stated another way.[42] When a mover moves an object, it moves it with something, either with itself or with another thing. For example, a man may move the stone by himself or with a stick. But every thing that moves an object by the agency of another implies 'that which imparts motion by its own agency'.[43] And the series of such things cannot be infinite:

> Thus, if the stick moves something in virtue of being moved by the hand, the hand moves the stick: and if something else moves with the *hand*, the hand also is moved by something different from itself. So when motion by means of an instrument is at each stage caused by something different from the instrument, this must always be preceded by something else* which imparts motion with itself. Therefore, if this last movent is in motion and there is nothing else that moves it, it must move itself. So this reasoning also shows that, when a thing is moved, if it is not moved immediately by something that moves itself, the series brings us at some time or other to a movent of this kind.
>
> * Reading in 1.31 *ταύτῃ*.[44]

Aristotle makes very plain the *instrumental* character of the intermediate movers. Since they have no power to move anything by themselves, and since all the members of an infinite series would be of this sort, the existence of motion demands that the series be finite, terminating in a first mover that moves others by its own agency.

Aristotle's third argument is somewhat difficult to follow.[45] If everything in motion is being moved by something else, then either (1) its ability to move something else is caused by something's moving it or (2) its ability to move something else is not related to the fact that something is moving it. But the second alternative is impossible. For it implies that what causes motion need not be in motion. But if that is so, then it is possible that at some time, nothing that exists would be in motion. But motion is necessary and eternal, as we have seen, so that the above conclusion is impossible. And, Aristotle asserts, we cannot deduce an impossibility from a possibility. Therefore, alternative two must be rejected. But consider the other alternative: if a thing moves another only because it is itself being moved, then either (a) it is moved with the same kind of motion it causes (e.g. the hand's local motion causes the stick's local motion which causes the stone's local motion) or (b) it is moved by a different kind of motion than it causes (e.g. a change in quality, say, temperature, causes local motion, say, expansion). But both of these are impossible. For (a) would require that a man throwing a ball would himself be in the state of being thrown, which is ridiculous. And (b) fares no better; for the series would have to stop somewhere, since there are only three types of motion. The suggestion that the three types repeat themselves cyclically is of no help, for this reduces to (a). Since a thing is caused by remote as well as immediate causes, we would still have a thing's being caused in the same respect in which it is causing. This also implies that everything that has the capacity to cause, say, increase also has the capacity to be, say, altered, at least indirectly, which is ridiculous. All this goes to prove that the original assumption—everything in motion is being moved by something else—is not true; the series of things moved by something else must end in something either unmoved or self-moved.

Thus, Aristotle, in this version of his proof for a first mover, appears to adopt a position entirely contrary to that of the proof in *Physics* 7, in which he argued that a self-mover is impossible and that everything in motion is, indeed, moved by something else. Contrary to this former position, he now contends that the members of a series of things moved by another must ultimately be in motion only by reference to a self-moved thing.

The fifth step in our outline is that *the members of the whole series of self-movers and things moved by another must be in motion only by reference to an unmoved mover*. The first thing Aristotle wants to prove here is that every self-mover is moved by a part of it which is unmoved. He does this by a process of elimination.

First, a self-mover cannot move itself as a whole.[46] Aristotle apparently alludes to his argument in his earlier version of the cosmological argument that since anything in motion is divisible, therefore there can be no self-mover. But the allusion is not clear, and Aristotle seems to assimilate it to the second point, which he prefers. This is that nothing can be self-moved as a whole because then it would be both in potency and actuality, which is contradictory. For that which is capable of being moved is in potency to movement, while that which is a mover is already in the activity of moving. Hence, a thing would have to be both potential and actual with regard to movement in order to move itself, which is contradictory. The conclusion is that a self-mover cannot be moved of its entirety: one part must move another part.

Second, the parts of a self-mover do not mutually move each other.[47] There are four points to consider here: (a) if the two parts move each other, there is no first mover; (b) that which causes movement need not be moved by anything else; (c) everlasting motion requires a first mover; and (d) a thing cannot be causing and undergoing the same motion. With regard to the first point, Aristotle is not clear; he appears to argue that in any series of movers, there must be higher movers than others until one reaches a first mover, but if the two parts move each other, there would be no first mover, which is impossible. Turning to his second point, Aristotle asserts that there is no necessity that the part that causes motion should be moved itself in return. Thus, one would have an unmoved part and a moved part. Third, Aristotle simply asserts that if motion is to be everlasting, there must be a part that is either unmoved or moved by itself. The fourth point is that if the two parts moved each other, then we would have a thing undergoing the same motion it is causing—it could be causing heat and yet being heated.

Third, a self-mover is not moved by a self-moving part.[48] For if it is moved by a self-moving part, then it is really the part that is the self-mover, not the whole. (Presumably, then, the analysis may begin all over again, directed now at this part.) On the other hand, if the whole thing were self-moving as an entirety, the movement of its parts would be incidental. The only way a thing can be self-moved is to have a part that causes motion and is yet itself unmoved.

Thus, every self-mover—man, animal, or plant—must have a part that is an unmoved mover and a part that is moved. 'Therefore in the whole of the thing we may distinguish that which imparts motion without itself being moved and that which is moved: only in this way is it possible for a thing to be self-moved.'[49] Hence, all motion must have ultimate reference to an unmoved mover or movers.[50]

In the second part of this step of the proof, Aristotle asks what the cause of motion in general must be.[51] Whether there should be one or many of these unmoved movers is irrelevant, he says. He will attempt to prove that there is something unmoved and changeless, whether incidentally or essentially, which is capable of causing motion.

All self-movers must have parts because anything in motion is divisible, as we have seen. Therefore, self-movers that come to be and pass away cannot be the source of eternal motion, for their generation and destruction is a type of change (*μεταβολή*) that must be caused. 'So the fact that some things become and others perish, and that this is so continuously, cannot be caused by any one of those things that, though they are unmoved, do not always exist . . . .'[52] Nor can the eternity and continuity of motion be caused by all of them together. For an eternal and continuous effect demands an eternal and continuous cause, but the members of the series are not such. This means there must be something outside the series that is the ultimate cause of motion:

> It is clear, then, that though there may be countless instances of the perishing of some principles that are unmoved but impart motion, and though many things that move themselves* perish and are succeeded by others that come into being, and though one thing that is unmoved moves one thing while another moves another, nevertheless there is something that comprehends them all, and that as something apart from each of them, and this it is that is the cause of the fact that some things are and others are not and of the continuous process of change: and this causes the motion of the other movents, while they are the causes of the motion of other things.
>
> * Cf. 256a 25n.[53]

Thus Aristotle completes his reduction of all self-movers to unmoved movers and all unmoved movers to the first unmoved mover above them all. We may conclude step four, the members of the whole series of self-movers and things moved by another must be in motion only by reference to an unmoved mover.

The fifth step is the coping stone of the entire proof: *this first mover must be utterly unmoved and eternal.* Aristotle first offers two arguments to prove that the unmoved first mover is one. First, the principle of economy demands it.[54] When the facts can be explained by reference to one unmoved first mover it is unnecessary to posit several. Second, the everlasting nature of motion demands it.[55] If motion is eternal, it must be continuous; for if it always exists, it is continuous, whereas what is successive has discontinuity.[56] But if motion is continuous, it is also one. And it can only be one if it is caused by one mover and in one subject of motion; for if it were caused by one mover after another it would no longer be continuous but successive.

The second argument above also serves to establish the eternity of the first unmoved mover.

Third, the first unmoved mover is changeless, either essentially or incidentally.[57] In self-movers, the unmoved part does not move of itself, but it is moved in an incidental way, or *per accidens*. For when the body of a self-mover moves from place to place, so does its soul. Thus, it, too, moves in a way. Now it is impossible, asserts Aristotle, for anything which is moved accidentally to cause continuous motion. Apparently the assumption is that even an incidental movement in the first unmoved mover would upset the continuity of motion, but Aristotle does not explain how. Hence, Aristotle concludes that this first mover must be utterly unmoved and eternal.

Before we pass on to Aristotle's proof in *Metaphysics* Λ, a few concluding remarks on the version in the *Physics* would be in order. The proof obviously presupposes the ancient Greek astronomical system. Thus, Aristotle proceeds to argue that the first moved thing is as eternal as the first unmoved mover and that, since no motion is continuous except locomotion in a circle, the first moved thing rotates eternally.[58] Moreover, the first unmoved mover is at the circumference of the universe, causing the rotation of the outer sphere of the cosmos.[59] As Ross explains, the concentric spheres of the universe were thought to be connected to one another such that when the first unmoved mover rotated the outermost sphere, all the others rotated as well.[60] This formed a hierarchical chain of simultaneous movers that enabled Aristotle to argue back to a first unmoved mover as the cause of the motion we observe in the world here and now without reference to movers in the past. The question is, of course, whether the proof is so dependent on this pre-Copernican cosmology that the argument is vitiated.

We may also wonder about the theological status of this unmoved first mover. Is it God? Jean Paulus and Joseph Owens think not. They contend that the unmoved mover is the immanent soul of the outermost sphere.[61] But it is very difficult to see how this can be correct. The doctrine of sphere souls plays no part in Aristotle's argument in the *Physics*. The self-movers mentioned are all sublunary. The entire thrust of Aristotle's argumentation in steps four and five is to reduce self-movers to an unmoved mover that causes motion in self-movers. But an ensouled sphere would be a self-mover. Moreover, all self-movers are moved incidentally, and this would also seem to be true of the soul of the first heavenly sphere, since it is in local motion—but this contradicts Aristotle's plain statement that the first mover is unmoved even *per accidens*. Furthermore, Aristotle argues that the first mover is incorporeal and is at the circumference of the first sphere, a description which better fits an extra-mundane being than the soul of the outermost sphere.[62] Owens comments that the unmoved first mover belongs to a class of things whose members are perishable.[63] But the passage he cites—*Physics* 8. 6. 258b16–259a6—is, in the first place, stated hypothetically ('Let us suppose, if any one likes, that . . . it is possible for them at different times to be and not to be . . . .'[64]), is, in the second place, primarily directed to animal souls as perishable unmoved movers, and is, in the third place, designed to prove the very opposite of the first unmoved mover, namely that it is changeless and eternal. On balance, the unmoved first mover of the *Physics* would seem to be a being incorporeal, changeless, and eternal, existing apart from the universe. But at the same time, it must be said that nowhere does Aristotle identify the first unmoved mover as *ὁ θεός*. Nor can the first unmoved mover be said to be personal. It seems to be more like the invisible motor of the universe, turning for infinite time the crank that runs the machine-like system of the spheres.

We might also ask about the uniqueness of the unmoved first mover. There are three passages in the *Physics* that discuss the possibility of a plurality of unmoved movers. In the first passage, Artistotle merely mentions the possibility: '. . . there must necessarily be something, one thing or it may be a plurality, that first imparts motion . . .'.[65] In the second passage, he argues that there can be only one unmoved first mover because the principle of economy and the continuity of motion demand it.[66] But in the third passage, he asserts that the heavenly bodies such as the planets are affected by 'first principles' of motion, which are incidentally moved not by themselves, but by something else.[67] But exactly what these first principles are is not clear. They may be taken to be the spheres or the souls that move the spheres.[68] Or they may be separate unmoved movers that are assigned to each sphere.[69] The difficulty with the first interpretation is that the celestial souls would be incidentally moved by themselves as their sphere rotates, not by something else, as Aristotle specifies.[70] But the problem encountered in the second interpretation is that if the principles are utterly separate, there appears to be no way in which they could be moved even incidentally. Wolfson asserts that these principles are transcendent unmoved movers not residing in the spheres, yet they are incidentally moved because of their 'fixed and constant relation' to their respective spheres.[71] But this really explains nothing. At any rate, if this passage does speak of a plurality of unmoved movers, commentators are agreed that it is a later addition inserted parenthetically by Aristotle into the text and does not represent the original argument of the *Physics*. And the point remains that Aristotle gave a unique status to the first unmoved mover as utterly unmoved, even incidentally, which could not be said of any of the others. The first unmoved mover exists beyond and apart from the universe of which all others are part and parcel.

But at least two unanswered questions still remain about the unmoved first mover of the *Physics*: (1) What is the nature of this incorporeal being and (2) how does it impart motion? For the answers to these questions, we must turn to the pages of the *Metaphysics* and to Aristotle's exposition there of the proof for the unmoved mover.

According to Ross, the argument for the unmoved first mover in *Physics* 8 is retained in *Metaphysics* Λ, not contradicted, though Aristotle here explicates clearly for the first time how God operates in moving the heavens.[72] Aristotle's version of the proof is as follows:

> . . . it is necessary that there should be an eternal unmoveable substance. For substances are the first of existing things, and if they are all destructible, all things are destructible. But it is impossible that movement should ever come into being or cease to be; for it must always have existed. Nor can time come into being or cease to be; for there could not be a before and an after if time did not exist . . . .
>
> But if there is* something which is capable of moving things . . . , but is not actually doing so, there will not necessarily be movement: for that which has a potency need not exercise it . . . if it does not *act*, there will be no movement. Further, even if it acts, this will not be enough, if its essence is potency; for there will not be eternal movement: for that which is potentially may possibly not be. There must, then, be such a principle, whose very essence is actuality. Further, then, these substances must be without matter, for they must be eternal, at least if anything else is eternal. Therefore they must be actuality.†
>
> * 1071b12 read *εἰ ἔστι κινητικόν*.
> † 1071b22 read *ἐνέργεια*.[73]

We may outline the argument as follows:

1. If all substances are perishable, then all things are perishable.
2. But time and motion are not perishable.

3. Therefore, there must be some imperishable substance.
4. This imperishable substance must be an eternal, incorporeal being of pure actuality.

We shall repeat our procedure of examining each step of the outline separately. First, *if all substances are perishable, then all things are perishable*. Since for Aristotle substance is the primary constituent of reality, the argument here is that if substances are all perishable, then everything else is perishable, since they are posterior to and dependent upon substance for their being. But more specifically, Aristotle in book Λ mentions three types of substances: perishable sensible substances (plants, animals), eternal sensible substances (heavenly bodies), and unchangeable substances (forms).[74] Seen in this light, step one is something of a tautology: if all things are perishable, then all things are perishable. Perhaps Aristotle might have argued more effectively, if all things are perishable, then time and motion are perishable . . . . But he does not, and step one remains: if all substances are perishable, then all things are perishable.

Step two continues, *but time and motion are not perishable*. Aristotle's reasoning simply repeats the conclusions of *Physics* 8, including the contention that the only continuous motion is locomotion in a circle. This point forms the springboard for Aristotle's cosmology.

Step three concludes: *therefore, there must be some imperishable substance*. The reasoning here is not that time and motion are substances or 'things' but, as we have seen in our previous discussion, that they cannot exist apart from things. Without things or substances, there can be no motion, and without motion there can be no time. Therefore, since time is imperishable and motion is imperishable, there must be some imperishable substance.

Aristotle spells out the nature of this substance in step four: *this imperishable substance must be an eternal, incorporeal being of pure actuality*. First, it must be eternal because it is imperishable. By 'eternal' Aristotle means everlasting, not timeless, for the imperishable substance is co-eternal with motion and time. Second, it is incorporeal, asserts Aristotle, because it is eternal.[75] This does not appear to follow; what Aristotle probably means to assert is that because the substance is pure actuality (which Aristotle identifies with form), it must be incorporeal, for matter involves potentiality. A being of pure actuality would be a form. Third, it would be a being of pure actuality. Aristotle assumes that this eternal substance is the cause of motion or, in other words, that motion cannot simply be uncaused, a brute fact. But we have seen in our discussion of the *Physics* how he attempted to prove what he simply assumes here. If motion must have a cause, then eternal substance is the only suitable candidate, for motion must be continuous. But in order to cause eternal motion, this substance or substances must be pure actuality. For if it existed with any potency, then it might possibly not exist. And if it were possible for it not to exist, it could not cause eternal (that is, necessary) motion. Therefore, this imperishable substance must be an eternal, incorporeal being of pure actuality.

What can be known of the nature and operation of this being or beings? Aristotle calls it 'a mover which moves without being moved', or an unmoved mover.[76] It is said to move things in the same way that objects of desire and thought do. These are final causes: they move by being something at which action aims. Therefore, the unmoved mover moves the first heaven by being an object of love. Ross comments,

> There has been much controversy over the question whether God is for Aristotle only the final cause, or the efficient cause as well, of change. The answer is that God is the efficient cause by being the final cause, but in no other way . . . He moves directly the 'first heaven'; i.e., He causes the daily rotation of the stars round the earth. Since He moves by inspiring love and desire, it seems to be implied that the 'first heaven' has soul. And this is confirmed by statements elsewhere that the heavenly bodies are living beings.*
>
> * [*De Caelo*] 285a29, 292a20, b1.[77]

This provides the solution to the unanswered question of the *Physics* as to how the unmoved mover can produce physical motion.

Since it is incorporeal, the first unmoved mover can have no physical activities, but Aristotle does give it a mental life and begins at this point to call the unmoved mover 'God'.[78] God, says Aristotle, is 'a living being, eternal, most good, so that life and duration continuous and eternal belong to God; for this *is* God'.[79] Aristotle proceeds to argue that the divine thought is 'a thinking on thinking'.[80] This is because God's thoughts must be directed toward the best and his thinking is the best. Aristotle's God is thus turned in upon himself in eternal self-contemplation. Finally, Aristotle ascribes goodness to God.[81] The Good exists primarily in God, and he is the source of goodness in the world. From the foregoing, it seems quite clear that Aristotle's unmoved mover is, indeed, the God of theism: an eternal, unchanging, incorporeal, most good, self-thinking mind. On the other hand, God is in no sense the creator of the universe: it is co-eternal and, moreover, not dependent on him for its continued existence. And Aristotle's God is of no value for religious devotion, for he is entirely unaware of all save himself. He causes motion in the world only in the way in which a statue inspires admiration in its viewer.

We must ask at this point whether Aristotle believed there to be only one God. This appeared to be so in the *Physics*, as we have seen, and our exposition of Λ seems to lead to the same conclusion. But we have skipped book eight of Λ, which is a late addition to the treatise and interrupts the flow of thought found in books seven and nine. In book eight, Aristotle posits a plurality of unmoved movers. It is here that his full-blown astronomical system comes clearly into view. He argues that the eternal motion of each of the planets and other heavenly bodies demands an eternal, unmoveable substance as their respective cause of motion.[82] He turns to Greek astronomy for an estimation of the required number of unmoved movers. Ross's description of Aristotle's cosmology is well worth quoting:

> The universe consists of a series of concentric spheres. The earth is a sphere of no great relative size,[3] at rest at the centre of the universe.[4] The outer shell of the universe—the 'first heaven'—is a finite sphere containing what we now call the fixed stars.[5] These stars have no motion of their own but are carried round by the uniform rotation of the first heaven once in twenty-four hours.[6] With regard to the more complex movements of the sun, the moon, and the planets Aristotle adopts with a modification the theory of Eudoxus as it had been developed by his own friend Callippus[7] . . . .
>
> . . . Aristotle assigns reagent spheres moving in directions contrary to those of the original spheres and allowing only the movement of the *outermost* sphere of each system (the daily rotation from east to west) to be carried through to the system inside it. He thus gets 55 spheres in all . . . .
>
> The movement of the first heaven is due to the action of God, operating as an object of love and desire . . . . But the proper motions

[3] . . . Aristotle's opinion, expressed in this connexion (298a9–15), that there may be no great distance between Spain and India . . . was one of the chief causes that sent Columbus on his voyage . . . .

[4] [*De Caelo*] II. 13, 14 . . . .

[5] I. 5, II. 4.

[6] II. 6, 8.

[7] *Met.* Λ. 8.

of the sun, moon, and planets involve spheres rotating in directions different from that of the first heaven, and this movement he explains by the action not of God but of a separate motive agent for each sphere—the 'intelligences' of the schoolmen.[1] He certainly means to reach a monistic system; he adopts as his own the Homeric maxim 'the rule of many is not good; one ruler let there be.'[2] The intelligences must be inferior to the prime mover, but their actual relation to God is quite obscure, as is also their mode of operation on the spheres. As they are incorporeal beings, presumably they too act not as physical agents but as objects of desire.

[1] *Met.* 1073a 26-b1; *De Caelo* 279a18–22.
[2] *Met.* 1076a4.[83]

Such is Aristotle's cosmology; but the status of God in all this is not clear. Owens argues strongly that Aristotle does *not* wish to reach a monistic system.[84] He contends that Aristotle required an unmoved mover for every eternal movement and that the unicity or plurality of these separate substances was a matter of indifference to him. For Aristotle the fundamental unity of things is a problem of *order*, not of *derivation*. Thus, the first unmoved mover is primary because it moves the first heaven; the others are second, third, and so forth, according to the order of the stellar motions. Owens argues that Λ. 8. 1074a31–38 teaches, not that there is only one unmoved mover, but that there can be only one *first* unmoved mover. But it is first in order, not in being.

Hence, it would seem that in the evolution of his thought Aristotle eventually came to believe in many unmoved movers, though these are hierarchically ordered such that one is supreme over the others. If pressed for consistency, it would seem that his system would have to collapse back into one unmoved mover because the unmoved movers are all the same in form, and form cannot be individuated without matter, which the unmoved movers lack.[85] Be this as it may, it nevertheless raises a very important issue for the cosmological argument: can it be proved that only *one* God exists? Most subsequent proponents of the argument thought that it could, but Aristotle forces them to confront the question squarely.

We could schematise the composite Aristotelian argument for the existence of God thus:

1. There is motion in the world.
   a. This is evident from sense perception.

2. Motion is eternal.
   a. Motion cannot have a beginning or end.
      i. Motion cannot have been created from nothing nor can it be destroyed.
         a. The creation of objects in motion is a change requiring a prior motion, *ad infinitum.*
         b. The destruction of objects in motion requires a destroyer which would have to be destroyed, *ad infinitum.*
      ii. Motion cannot have begun from a prior state of rest.
         a. Rest, as a privation of motion, must be caused, and this cause caused, *ad infinitum.*
         b. Motion's generation out of rest is self-contradictory.
   b. The eternity of time requires eternal motion.
      i. Time is eternal.
         a. Every moment of time is the end of the past and the beginning of the future.
         b. Thus, every moment of time is bounded by time.
      ii. Time cannot exist without motion.
         a. Time is the measure of motion.
      iii. Therefore, motion is eternal.
3. Everything in motion is being moved by something actual.
   a. Motion is the actualisation of a potency.
   b. No potency can actualise itself.
   c. Therefore, a potency can be actualised only by something already actual.
4. Things in motion are either self-moved or being moved by another.
5. The series of things being moved by another must terminate in either a self-mover or an unmoved mover.
   a. In a hierarchically ordered causal series, the intermediate movers all move because of the agency of a first mover.
      i. The intermediate movers are by nature only instruments of a first mover.
         a. The first mover can move an object without the presence of intermediates, but intermediates cannot move the object without the presence of a first mover.
   b. But in an infinite series, there is no first mover.
   c. Therefore, there would be no motion.
   d. But this contradicts (1): There is motion in the world.
   e. Therefore, the series of things being moved by another must be finite and terminate in a first mover.
   f. This first mover may be either self-moved or unmoved.

6. Self-movers reduce to unmoved movers.
   a. Nothing can move itself as a whole.
      i. It would be potential and actual in the same respect at the same time.
      ii. But this is contradictory.
   b. Self-movers must be moved by an unmoved part.
      i. Since it is not moved as a whole, it must be moved by its parts.
      ii. The parts cannot move each other.
         a. Things being moved by another require a first mover. (5.e.)
         b. But if the parts move one another, there is no first mover.
      iii. Therefore, it must be moved by an unmoved part, an unmoved mover.
7. There must be a first unmoved mover that is the cause of eternal motion.
   a. Perishable unmoved movers cannot cause eternal motion.
      i. Their coming to be and passing away is a change that must be caused.
      ii. They cannot cause this eternal process because they do not always exist.
   b. The whole series of perishable unmoved movers cannot cause eternal motion.
      i. Motion is eternal and continuous.
      ii. An eternal and continuous effect requires an eternal and continuous cause.
      iii. But perishable unmoved movers are not eternal or continuous.
      iv. Therefore, they cannot be the cause of motion.
   c. Embodied unmoved movers, even if eternal, cannot cause eternal motion.
      i. All such unmoved movers are moved incidentally when their bodies move.
      ii. This would interrupt eternal and continuous motion.
   d. There must be a first unmoved mover, eternal, changless, incorporeal, one, pure actuality, as the cause of eternal motion.
      i. It must be eternal.
         a. It must cause eternal motion.
      ii. It must be changeless.
         a. It must cause continuous motion.
      iii. It must be incorporeal.
         a. Corporeal things are moved incidentally, which it is not.
      iv. It is one.

a. The principle of economy demands only one first unmoved mover to cause motion.

b. Continuous motion demands only one first unmoved mover.

(*i*) Motion can be continuous only if there is one first mover and one first moved thing.

v. It is pure actuality.

a. If it had any potency, it might not exist.

b. Then it could not cause eternal motion.

This schema brings out several interesting features of the argument. First, it is noteworthy that the argument does not merely assume the eternity of motion for the sake of argument, but is actually dependent upon it. To carry his case Aristotle must *prove* there exists an infinite temporal regress. As for the hierarchical regress, which Aristotle argues could not be infinite, it must be remembered that he had no concept of inertia, such that a thing might be moving without being in contact with a mover. For Aristotle, all causes of motion are simultaneous. Things being moved by another are never arranged in a temporal regress. Someone might argue that things moved by another do not reduce to self-movers because they were moved by another thing in the past which was moved by another thing in the past, and so on. But on Aristotle's principles such a situation could not arise; mover and moved are simultaneous.[86] Aristotle's basic argument is that since motion is eternal, there must exist a being or beings capable of causing such an effect.

One cannot also help being struck by the fantastic astronomical system implicit in the proof. Portions of the argument make little sense unless one keeps this cosmology in mind. In fact, one might say that this entire proof is an attempt to account, not for the motion we observe in daily, earthly affairs, but rather for the majestic sweep of that glittering host across the night sky of ancient Greece. Philosophy, observes Aristotle, begins with a sense of wonder about the world:

> For it is owing to their wonder that men both now begin and at first began to philosophize; they wondered originally at the obvious difficulties, then advanced little by little and stated difficulties about greater matters, e.g. about the phenomena of the moon and those of the sun, and about the stars and about the genesis of the universe.[87]

Anyone who has studied modern star-charts of the heavens will lend a sympathetic ear to these men of antiquity, who gazed up into the night sky, as yet undimmed by pollution and the glare of city lights, and watched the slow but irresistible turn of the cosmos, replete with its planets, stars, and familiar constellations, across their view and *wondered*—what is the cause of all this? In a fragment of *On Philosophy*, Aristotle imagines the impact of such a sight on men who had never beheld the sky,

> When thus they would suddenly gain sight of the earth, seas, and the sky; when they should come to know the grandeur of the clouds and the might of the winds; when they should behold the sun and should learn its grandeur and beauty as well as its power to cause the day by shedding light over the sky; and again, when night had darkened the lands and they should behold the whole of the sky spangled and adorned with stars; and when they should see the changing lights of the moon as it waxes and wanes, and the risings and settings of all these celestial bodies, their courses fixed and changeless throughout all eternity—when they should behold all these things, most certainly they would have judged both that there exist gods and that all these marvellous works are the handiwork of the gods.[88]

This same line of thought is still found in the *Metaphysics*, where Aristotle observes that his metaphysical philosophy is empirically confirmed: the unceasing movement of the first heaven is not only plain 'in theory' but also 'in fact'.[89] Aristotle's proof for God from motion thus seems to be essentially a proof from the motion of the heavens. It is rooted in a sense of wonder about the universe and the propensity of men to ask, 'Why?' Aristotle almost reminds one of Leibniz who, two thousand years later, was to say, '. . . the first question which should rightly be asked, will be, *Why is there something rather than nothing*?'[90]

But lest a misunderstanding arise, it must quickly be added that Aristotle, unlike Leibniz, is not seeking *reasons*, but *causes* of the universe. Owens explains,

> The starting point [of Aristotelian philosophy] is located in the things of the sensible universe; the procedure is the explanation of these things through their causes; the goal is the ultimate causes that provide the final and fully satisfactory answer to the problems about which men wonder.* In a word philosophy seeks the causes that explain the things of the sensible universe . . . .
>
> * . . . .

> The causes sought by Wisdom are established as the four causes of the *Physics*. These are definitely not abstractions. They are physical principles found as such in the material universe. They are either the components of sensible things, or else the producers or corresponding ends of physical change. Clearly, what Aristotle has in mind as the first causes sought by Wisdom are not abstract 'grounds' or 'reasons.'[91]

Hence, Aristotle is not seeking to render ultimately intelligible in an abstract sense the presence of motion in the universe; he is trying to account for it by designating its cause. He observes the motion of the vast stellar systems and asks, what could the cause of this be?

Finally, we might note that in addition to the argument from motion, Aristotle's cosmological argument also contains the germ of the argument from contingency. This is evident when he argues, in effect, that if time and motion are perishable, all things are perishable; time and motion are not perishable; therefore, not all things are perishable, that is to say, some thing is imperishable.[92] Or again we find the same sort of thought when he calls the unmoved mover a necessary being.[93] But these are only glimmers of an argument that is to become even more significant than Aristotle's proof from motion for the first unmoved mover.

NOTES

1. Aristotle, *Physica* 1. 8. 191a25–30. All quotations of Aristotle's works are taken from W. D. Ross, ed., *The Works of Aristotle*, 12 vols. (Oxford: Clarendon Press, 1908–52).
2. Ibid., 1. 8. 191b25. The notion of potency supplants that of privation, which is discussed just prior to the reference to the present distinction.
3. Aristotle, *Metaphysica* Δ. 7. 1017a35.
4. Aristotle, *Physica* 1. 3. 186a1.
5. Aristotle *Metaphysica* Θ. 1. 1046a10.
6. Ibid., Δ. 12. 1019a15.
7. Ibid., Θ. 3. 1047a30–1047b1.
8. Ibid., Θ. 6. 1048a30.
9. Aristotle, *Physica* 3. 1. 201a10.
10. Aristotle, *Metaphysica* Θ. 3. Aristotle remarks,

> Therefore it is possible that a thing may be capable of being and not *be*, and capable of not being and yet *be*, and similarly with the other kinds of predicate; it may be capable of walking and yet not walk, or capable of not walking and yet walk.*
>
> * 1047a23 read *καὶ μὴ βαδί ειν δυνατὸν εἶναι βαδί ον* . . . (Ibid., Θ. 3. 1047a20)

11. W. K. C. Guthrie enumerates three stages in Aristotle's thought: (1) he begins with the doctrine of *Laws* 10, heavenly bodies self-moved by their souls; (2) he then holds that the ether of the outer sphere moves naturally in a circle, and the doctrine of the soul tends to recede; (3) he finally arrives at the doctrine of the prime unmoved mover as the source of all motion. (W. K. C. Guthrie, 'Development of Aristotle's Theology', *Classical Quarterly* 27 [1933]: 162–71.) On the other hand, Easterling goes so far as to argue that even the passages which speak of an unmoved mover in *Physics* B and Γ are later insertions. He contends that while the notion of God as final cause was conceived early by Aristotle, it was not linked to the idea of the unmoved mover (H. J. Easterling, 'The Unmoved Mover in early Aristotle', *Phronesis* 21 [1976]: 252–65).
12. Cicero, *De natura deorum* 2. 15. 42.
13. Ibid., 2. 16. 44.
14. Ibid., 1. 13. 33.
15. W. D. Ross, *Aristotle's Physics* (Oxford: Clarendon Press, 1936), p. 96. Cf. Guthrie, 'Development', pp. 164–5.
16. Aristotle, *De caelo* 1. 2. 268b15–3.270b30.
17. Ibid., 2. 6. 288a25–288b10, 292a15–20, 292b1–5.
18. Aristotle, *Physica* 7. 1. 241b21–243a1.
19. Ibid., 7. 1. 242b20–25.
20. Ibid., 7. 1. 242b20.
21. Ibid., 7. 2. 243a15.
22. Ibid., 6. 4. 23410–20.
23. This interpretation was suggested by Alexander of Aphrodisias and is accepted by Joseph Owens (Joseph Owens, 'The Conclusion of the *Prima Via*', *Modern Schoolman* 30 [1952]: 39). For more on this interpretation see W. A. Wallace, 'The Cosmological Argument: A Reappraisal', *Proceedings of the Catholic Philosophical Association* 46 (1972): 46–7.
24. Aristotle, *Physica* 8. 1–6. 250b5–260a15; 8. 10. 266a10–267b25.
25. Ibid., 8. 6. 259a25–259b25.
26. Ibid., 3. 1. 201a5.
27. Ibid., 3. 1. 201a10.
28. Ibid., 5. 1. 225a20–225b5.
29. Ibid., 1. 2. 185a10.
30. Ibid.
31. Ibid., 8. 3. 253a30.
32. Ibid., 8. 3. 254a35.
33. Ibid., 8. 1. 251a10–251b5, 251b25–252a1.
34. Ibid., 8. 1. 251b10–25.
35. Ibid., 4. 2. 219b1.
36. Aristotle, *Metaphysica* Θ. 3. 1046b30.
37. Ibid., Θ. 8. 1049b20–25.
38. Aristotle, *Physica* 3. 1. 201a25.
39. Ibid., 8. 5. 256a5–20.
40. Ibid., 8. 5. 256a5. Michael J. Buckley comments,

The series in question here is not the . . . causal chain of antecedents in time. It is the series of causes, essential and particular, actually at work to effect this particular movement. It is not a search for a temporal principle, into the 'after' and 'before' sequence from which an origin in time will emerge. The question is rather about the causal influences actually responsible for, joined to, and simultaneous with a particular motion. Can one proceed endlessly through moved movers or must one reach a first mover unmoved? (Michael J. Buckley, *Motion and Motion's God* [Princeton: Princeton University Press, 1971], p. 47)

41. Aristotle, *Physica* 8. 5. 256a10. Buckley's comment is worth noting:

The infinite series is a denial of a first, and would, thus, be a denial of any causality—for whatever causality is possessed by these secondary causes is derived from the first. Without a first, independent cause, there would be nothing upon which the other causes depend and by which they would be used. Causality would be intelligible without instrumentality or without dependent causes—if such a case *de facto* exists; it would be absurd however without a first cause (Buckley, *Motion*, p. 61).

42. Aristotle, *Physica* 8. 5. 256a20–256b1.
43. Ibid., 8. 5. 256a25.
44. Ibid., 8. 5. 256a30–256b1.
45. Ibid., 8. 5. 256b1–257a30.
46. Ibid., 8. 5. 257a30–257b10.
47. Ibid., 8. 5. 257b10–257b25.
48. Ibid., 8. 5. 257b25–258a1.
49. Ibid., 8. 5. 258a1.
50. Ibid., 8. 5. 258b1–5.
51. Ibid., 8. 6. 258b10.
52. Ibid., 8. 6. 258b25.
53. Ibid., 8. 6. 258b30–259a5.
54. Ibid., 8. 6. 259a10–15.
55. Ibid., 8. 6. 259a10–15.
56. Cf. ibid., 5. 3. 227a5–10. For Aristotle things are continuous only if their touching extremities are 'one and the same' and 'contained in each other'; thus, they are essentially one thing, whereas something 'that is in succession and touches is "contiguous"', like two billiard balls in juxtaposition (ibid.).
57. Ibid., 8. 6. 259a20–259b30.
58. Ibid., 8. 6. 260a1–8. 9. 266a5.
59. Ibid., 8. 10. 267b5.
60. Ross, *Physics*, pp. 707–8.
61. Jean Paulus, 'La théorie du premier moteur chez Aristote', *Revue de philosophie* 33 (1933): 259–94, 394–424; Joseph Owens, *The Doctrine of Being in the Aristotelian 'Metaphysics'*, 2nd ed. (Toronto, Canada: Pontifical Institute of Mediaeval Studies, 1963), pp. 438–9. Buckley disagrees (Buckley, *Motion*, p. 72). He supports our argumentation and underlines the fact that the unmoved mover cannot be 'a world soul for it is moved neither accidentally nor essentially nor is it in any way possessive of magnitude . . . . The Unmoved Movers of *Physics* viii and of *Metaphysics* xii must identify because they are unmoved' (Ibid., pp. 84–5).
62. Aristotle, *Physica* 8. 10. 266a10–267b5. In proving that the unmoved first mover is incorporeal, Aristotle's basic argument is that nothing finite can cause motion for an infinite time. If a finite thing were moving another thing for infinite

time, then a part of the finite thing would be moving a part of the other thing for a finite time. But if one adds up the parts, the finite things would soon be complete, whereas finite times added to one another would not equal infinite time. This means the finite thing must move the other thing in a finite time, or in other words, nothing finite can cause motion for an infinite time. To move something for an infinite time would require a thing of infinite magnitude. But according to Aristotle, an actually existing infinite magnitude is not possible (ibid., 3. 5–8). Therefore, the unmoved mover must be without magnitude, that is, must be incorporeal (ibid., 8. 10. 266a10–20).

Aristotle also argues that an infinite force cannot reside in a finite magnitude. An infinite force could do a task in time t; but a finite force will do it in time $t + x$. But if one increases indefinitely the magnitude of power in the finite thing, eventually it will do the task in time t. But then an infinite force and a finite force would be equal, which is absurd. Thus, infinite force cannot reside in a finite thing. Since eternal motion presumably requires infinite force, the unmoved mover cannot be a finite thing. Because an infinite thing is impossible, the unmoved mover must be incorporeal (ibid., 8. 10. 266a25–266b5).

63. Owens, *Being*, p. 439.

64. Aristotle, *Physica* 8. 6. 258b15.

65. Ibid., 8. 6. 258b10.

66. Ibid., 8. 6. 259a10–15.

67. Ibid., 8. 6. 259b25–30.

68. See Ross's comment in Ross, *Physics*, pp. 707–8.

69. See Philip Merlan, 'Aristotle's Unmoved Movers', *Traditio* 4 (1946): 26–7; H. A. Wolfson, 'The Plurality of the Immoveable Movers in Aristotle and Averroes', *Harvard Studies in Classical Philology* 63 (1958): 237.

70. The difficulty is compounded by the fact that Aristotle holds that only perishable self-movers are incidentally moved by themselves (Aristotle, *Physica* 8. 6. 259b15–30). But the spheres are not perishable. Hence, on the one hand the celestial souls would have to be moved by themselves, but on the other they could not be moved by themselves.

71. Wolfson, 'Plurality', p. 237.

72. Ross, *Physics*, p. 100.

73. Aristotle, *Metaphysica* Λ. 6. 1071b4–20.

74. Ibid., Λ. 1. 1069a30.

75. Ibid., Λ. 6. 1071b20.

76. Ibid., Λ. 7. 1072a20–25.

77. W. D. Ross, *Aristotle*, 5th ed. (London: Methuen, 1949), p. 181. Although in his study of the efficient cause in Aristotle, Francis Meehan disputes Ross's judgement, he completely gives away his case when he admits,

> Nothing . . . prevents the prime immaterial unmoveable mover from moving as final cause and simultaneously as efficient cause. Finality, far from excluding efficient causality, rather embraces it as the superior embraces the inferior causes . . . . in God the two are inseparable and indistinct. What Aristotle excludes from the concept of God as cause is any exercise of efficiency outside of finality. In Him the final cause implies and absorbs the efficient (Francis X. Meehan, *Efficient Causality in Aristotle and St. Thomas* [Washington, D.C.: Catholic University of America Press, 1940], pp. 96–7).

Ross's view is upheld by I. M. Forsyth, 'Aristotle's Concept of God as Final Cause', *Philosophy* 22 (1947): 120. For a discussion of the difficulties and possibility of reconciling the *Physics* and the *Metaphysics* on this score, see Marcel De Corte, 'La causalité du premier moteur dans la philosophie aristotélicienne', *Revue d'histoire de la philosopie* 5 (1931): 105–46.

78. Aristotle, *Metaphysica* Λ. 7. 1072b20–25.

79. Ibid., Λ. 7. 1072b25.

80. Ibid., Λ. 9. 1074b30.

81. Ibid., Λ. 10. 1075a10–20.

82. Ibid., Λ. 8. 1073a30.

83. Ross, *Aristotle*, pp. 96–8. Cf. W. D. Ross, *Aristotle's Metaphysics*, 2 vols. (Oxford: Clarendon Press, 1924) 2: 384–7. For a comprehensive study see Friedrich Solmsen, *Aristotle's System of the Physical World* (Ithaca, N.Y.: Cornell University Press, 1963).

84. Owens, *Being*, pp. 444–50.

85. Aristotle, *Metaphysica* Λ. 8. 1074a31–38. The scholastic solution to the problem of the plurality of angels will not work for Aristotle because though each angel was thought to be the single member of his species (there being no matter to individuate the form), the angels could have different forms and thus be differentiated by specific differences within their genus. Both Wolfson and Merlan fail to fully appreciate the fact that because Aristotle's movers are all alike in form, no plurality of species can exist; hence, lacking the individuating principle of matter, they would be one (Wolfson, 'Plurality', p. 241; Merlan, 'Movers', pp. 7–12).

86. It must be said that Aristotle's views on inertia are inconsistent with the bulk of his principles.

87. Aristotle, *Metaphysica* Λ. 1. 982b10–15.

88. Cicero, *De natura* 2. 37. 95–6. A. H. Chroust believes this to be Aristotle's first cosmological argument, but strictly speaking, it is an example of a teleological argument (Anton-Hermann Chroust, 'Aristotle's *On Philosophy*', *Laval théologique et philosophique* 29 [1973]: 19). For a fuller and thoroughly documented account of the same, see Chroust's two chapters, 'A Cosmological (Teleological) Proof for the Existence of God in Aristotle's *On Philosophy*' and 'The Concept of God in Aristotle's *On Philosophy*', in Anton-Hermann Chroust, *Aristotle: New Light on His Lost Works*, 2 vols. (London: Routledge & Kegan Paul, 1972), 2: 159–74, 175–93.

89. Aristotle, *Metaphysica* Λ. 7. 1072a20. The philosopher here makes explicit what, according to Ross, is only implicit in the *Physics*:

> . . . [Aristotle] has not proved that there is continuous change in the strict sense, continuous change of one single subject of change. His certainty that such change exists arises from a reason which has never been mentioned in the argument, viz. the observation of the never-ceasing rotation of the heavens. He has not proved, as he claims,[1] that there *must* be continuous change, but he has a strong reason for believing that there is.
>
> * 259a16, b23. (Ross, *Physics*, p. 92)

90. G. W. Leibniz, 'The Principles of Nature and of Grace, Based on Reason', in *Leibniz Selections*, ed. Philip P. Wiener, The Modern Student's Library (New York: Charles Scribner's Sons, 1951), p. 527.

91. Owens, *Being*, pp. 172, 74.

92. See J. A. Bernardette, 'Aristotle's Argument from Time', *Review of Metaphysics* 12 (1959): 361–9.

93. Aristotle, *Metaphysica* Λ. 7. 1072b10.

Chapter 3

Arabic Theologians and Philosophers

Probably no chapter in the history of the cosmological argument is as significant—or as universally ignored—as that of the Arabic theologians and philosophers. Although we find in them the origin and development of two of the most important versions of the cosmological argument, namely the argument from temporal regress and the argument from contingency, the contribution of these Islamic thinkers is virtually ignored in anthologies and books on the subject.[1] Furthermore, until quite recently the only articles on them had to be ferreted out of esoteric orientalist or Near Eastern journals. A paucity of English translations of primary sources exists; moreover, those works that have been translated are often available only through obscure publishing houses in far-off places, making it all the more difficult to obtain material. These obstacles notwithstanding, anyone desiring a basic knowledge of the history of the cosmological argument cannot afford to overlook the contribution of these Muslim theologians and philosophers.

Most philosophers today probably have a passing knowledge of the principal Arabic philosophers, having read a chapter on Islamic philosophy in a secondary source such as Copleston's *History*.[2] If so, then they are aware that the Muslim philosophers may be divided into two groups, the eastern and the western. The former encompasses the Middle Eastern nations, and its most famous representative is Avicenna (ibn Sīnā); the latter is centred in Muslim Spain, and its most well-known thinker is Averroes (ibn Rushd). The eastern group flourished from about the ninth to the twelfth century, while the western group, enjoying in Spain a culture vastly superior to that of medieval Christian Europe, arose about the tenth century and reached its height in the second half of the twelfth.

For our purposes, however, there is a much more significant distinction within Muslim thought than that between eastern and western. Muslim thought on the cosmological argument may be divided into two schools, each of which contributed one of the proofs: *kalām*, which developed various forms of the argument from temporal regress, and *falsafa*, which originated the argument from contingency, from possible and necessary being. *Kalām* may be simply defined as 'natural theology' or philosophical theism, while *falsafa* is the Arabic word used to denote philosophy, a new intruder into Islamic culture.[3]

Taken literally, *kalām* is simply the Arabic word for 'speech'.[4] It came to denote the statement of points of theological doctrine, and was later used to mean the statement of an intellectual position or the argument upholding such a statement. Ultimately, *kalām* became the name of the whole movement within Arabic thought that might best be called Arabic scholasticism.[5] A scholastic theologian, or a practitioner of *kalām*, was called a *mutakallim*. Richard Walzer described them as 'dialectical or speculative theologians' and noted that they are methodologically distinct from the philosophers in that they 'take the truth of Islam as their starting point'.[6] The original *mutakallimūn* were the Mu'tazilites. This school of Islamic theology came into being through controversies involving the interpretation (*ta'wīl*) of the *Qur'ān* in its anthropomorphic descriptions of God and denial of free will. The Mu'tazilites denied literal interpretation of these *Qur'ānic* passages and affirmed man's free will, while the orthodox traditionalists adhered to literalism and determinism. Thus involved as they were in speculative theology, the Mu'tazilites soon confronted Greek philosophical thought and the challenge it posed to faith. Rather than adopt the traditionalist attitude that one knows his faith to be true without knowing *how* it can be true, the Mu'tazilites chose to defend the faith by the use of reason and to thus render their beliefs intellectually respectable. The defence of the faith was taken up by Abū al-Ḥudhayl al-'Allāf (d. 840/50), who in so doing, introduced into Islamic theology many of the Greek metaphysical notions that were to characterise later *kalām*. According to Peters, the Mu'tazilite debt to Greek philosophy is best seen in their belief in the autonomy of human reason and in their metaphysical atomism.[7] With regard to the first, they maintained that man could come to know God through reason alone, unaided by revelation. With regard to the second, the Mu'tazilites adopted the metaphysicis of substance and accidents, but with an atomist twist, for they identified substance with the atoms of which everything is constituted.[8] Not all the *mutakallimūn* were atomists, but all did agree on the nature of the accidents, that the accidents could not endure for two instants of time. Therefore, the atoms were radically contingent and had to be continuously re-created by God in every successive instant.[9] The theological motive behind this was to make God not only the creator of the world but its constant ground of being as well.[10]

W. D. Ross has commented that the advantage of the Aristotelian distinction of actuality and potency is that it conceives of change as a continuous process instead of a catastrophic re-creation of new states of being after former states of being.[11] In opting for a metaphysics of atoms and accidents which are continually being re-created by God, the Islamic theologians necessarily had to reject Aristotle's actuality/potency distinction and its attendant analysis of causuality. For Aristotle, causation occurs when an actual being actualises some potency. But the *mutakallimūn*, with their metaphysics of atoms and accidents, could allow no such action of one being upon another.[12] Any change in being could not be due to the atoms, for they do not endure through time. Change would occur only when God re-created the atoms in new states of being at each successive instant.[13] Thus, the metaphysics of atoms and accidents inevitably lead the Islamic theologians to deny the presence of any secondary causality in the world. God is the only cause there is, and everything that occurs is the result of His direct action in re-creating the atoms in different states of instantaneous being. Later *mutakallimūn*, such as al-Ghāzālī, argued fervently against the notion of secondary casuality, contending that all we perceive is the succession of events, not any causal connection between them.[14] In this he has often been compared to David Hume, who denied that we perceive any necessary connection between events, which are given to us in atomic, separated sense impressions.[15] This comparison, however, can be very misleading. For Ghāzālī actually did not believe in secondary causality at all, God being the prime and only cause of all that takes place.[16] Hume, on the other hand, firmly *believed* in secondary causality, denying only that one could *prove* its existence or necessity.[17] The position of Ghāzālī and the *mutakallimūn* is much more akin to the occasionalism of Nicolas Malebranche than to the scepticism of Hume.[18] In the evolution of Islamic occasionalism, this resulted in a denial of man's free will on the part of the most rigid theologians. Fakhry notes that the metaphysical system of the *mutakallimūn* was therefore just as responsible as the doctrine of the *Qur'ān* for the fatalism that characterises the religion of Islam.[19] But this is to jump ahead a few centuries to the culmination of *kalām*. The Mu'tazilites, as we have seen, adhered to the notion of man's free will, so naturally many felt quite uncomfortable with the incipient determinism implicit in the repudiation of secondary causality which was necessitated by their metaphysical atomism. Therefore, some of them sought to modify the nature of the accidents in order to allow man the responsibility for his acts.[20] Apparently, however, the Mu'tazilites could not unravel this self-contradiction, and their successors whole-heartedly embraced the determinism which they so earnestly wished to avoid.

Bound as it was to political considerations, the fortunes of Islamic theology changed with the Caliphs. Thus, the Mu'tazilites predominated the theological world of Islam from about 833 to 848, when in that year the Caliph al-Mutawakkil repudiated Mu'tazilitism. The forces of traditionalism, led by Aḥmad ibn Ḥanbal (d. 855), sought to restore conservative orthodoxy with a vengeance, severely repressing the Mu'tazilites. In 912, Abū al-Ḥasan 'Ali al-Ash'ari announced his defection from the Mu'tazilite cause and became the pioneer of a movement that took middle ground between the Ḥanbalites and the Mu'tazilites.[21] The Ash'arites and Ḥanbalites vied for power for over a century until the ascendancy of the Seljuk regime in 1055. This guaranteed the victory of the Ash'arites, and in 1063, the Caliph promulgated an edict of toleration, thus giving the Ash'arites the freedom necessary for the propagation of their doctrines. Very little is known about the development of *kalām* from the time of al-Ash'ari to that of al-Ghāzālī. Ash'aritism eventually came to be identified as Islamic orthodoxy. The term '*mutakallim*', which had earlier denoted a Mu'tazilite, was now used to designate an Ash'arite as opposed to a Ḥanbalite traditionalist. *Kalām* had become the argumentative theism employed by the Ash'arites to defend moderate orthodoxy. Although the Mu'tazilite threat to orthodoxy was met successfully by the Ash'arites, during the years that followed a much more ominous threat arose in the brilliant intellect of ibn Sīnā and the philosophy he propounded. This threat was also met, in this instance by Ghāzālī, whose philosophical theism marks a high point of *kalām*. But though *kalām* was to triumph over *falsafa* in the end, it was itself shaped by its opponent. For in every contest with *falsafa*, *kalām* itself became more imbued with the leaven of philosophy. Hence, Peters remarks,

> When the polemic finally abated Islam found that the experience of al-Ash 'ari had been repeated: *falsafah* as such was further weakened, but in its place stood the scholastic *kalām*, faithful in principle to the revelation of the *Qur'ān*, but unmistakably the product, in shape and procedure, of the Hellenic tradition in philosophy, orthodox and at the same time Aristotelian.[22]

What were the principal arguments employed by the *mutakallimūn*, both Mu'tazilite and Ash'arite, for the existence of God?[23] Certainly the major thrust of the *kalām* arguments for divine existence was the demonstration that the universe is a created thing. Fakhry rightly calls this 'the classical argument for the existence of God in Islam',[24] and its development in the hands of the *mutakallimūn* forms one half of the legacy that the Arabians gave to the history of the cosmological argument, the other half being contributed by the philosophers. Al-Alousī lists six arguments employed by the exponents of *kalām* to prove the temporality of the world.[25] (1) The argument from the contrary nature of the simple bodies: the basic elements of the universe (earth, air, and so forth) and their elementary qualities (hot and cold, light and heavy, and so forth) are mutually opposed to one another, yet in the world we find them combined; such combination requires a cause, which is the Creator. (2) The argument from experience: *creatio ex nihilo* is not unlike our experience, for in change the old form of the being vanishes, while a new form appears *ex nihilo.* (3) The argument from the finitude of motion, time, and temporal objects: motion cannot be from eternity, for an infinite temporal regress of motions is impossible, since finite parts can never add up to an infinite whole; therefore, the world and motion must have had a beginning. Or again, motion cannot be from eternity, for an infinite temporal regress of motions is impossible, since an infinite cannot be traversed. Or again, if at any given point in time, an infinite series has transpired, then at an earlier given point only a finite series has transpired; but the one point is separated from the other by a finite interval; therefore, the whole time series must be finite and created. (4) The argument from the finitude of the world: since the world is composed of finite parts, it is finite; everything finite is temporal; therefore, the world must be temporal, that is, have had a beginning and been created. (5) The argument from contingency: the world does not have to exist; therefore, there must be something that determines it to exist. (6) The argument from temporality: bodies cannot be devoid of accidents, which are temporal; whatever cannot exist without the temporal is temporal; therefore, the whole world is temporal and must have been created.

The first and second arguments are primitive and not nearly so influential as the remaining four. There is general agreement that the third and fourth arguments stem from the last great champion of *creatio ex nihilo* in the pre-Islamic era, the Alexandrian commentator and Christian theologian, John Philoponus (d. 580?), known in the Arab world as Yahyā al-Nahwī. Hardly a household word, Philoponus's name is nonetheless well known among Islamicists as the source of much of the *kalām* argumentation against the Aristotelian conception of the eternity of the world. Philoponus's *Contra Aristotelem*, in which he refutes the philosopher's proofs for the eternity of the universe, has been lost, but quotations of the work are cited in Simplicius's commentaries on Aristotle's *On the Heavens* and *Physics*.[26] Fortunately, a similar work of Philoponus's against the Neoplatonist Proclus has been preserved.[27] That the Islamic theologians knew of his works is evident from their bibliographical references.[28] These also give indication that the Arabs knew of a shorter treatise by Philoponus on the creation of the world.[29] Davidson provides this convenient summary of Philoponus's arguments:

> A. Proof of the generation of the universe from the finiteness of the power contained within it: . . .
>
> . . . First supporting argument: The heavens are composed of matter and form. Consequently they are not self-sufficient, and what is not self-sufficient does not have infinite power . . . .
>
> Second supporting argument: The nature of matter is such that matter cannot retain any form indefinitely. Therefore, nothing composed of matter and form can be indestructible . . . .
>
> Third supporting argument: The heavens are composite. Whatever is composite contains the grounds of its dissolution and therefore does not contain infinite power . . . .
>
> The fourth supporting argument . . . any mass can be divided into minimal particles, and those particles can be shown to have finite power . . . .
>
> B. Proofs of the generation of the universe from the impossibility of eternal motion:
>
> First argument: If the universe were eternal, the generation of any object in the sublunar world would be preceded by an infinite series of generations. But an infinite cannot be traversed. Therefore, if the universe were eternal, none of the objects presently existing in the sublunar world could ever have been generated . . . .
>
> Second argument: The eternity of the universe would imply an infinite number of past motions that is continually being increased. But an infinite cannot be added to . . . .
>
> Third argument: The number of the revolutions of the heavenly bodies are multiples of one another, and therefore eternity would imply infinite numbers of past motions in varying multiples. But infinite numbers cannot be multiplied . . . .[30]

Anxious as they were to vindicate the *Qur'ānic* doctrine of creation, the denial of which they considered tantamount to atheism, the *mutakallimūn* eagerly employed Philoponus's arguments in various versions.[31] The first set of the above proofs correspond with the fourth argument listed by al-Alousī, the argument from the finitude of the world. The second set of proofs correlate with the third argument, the proofs from time and motion. The fifth and sixth *kalām* arguments for the temporality of the universe are based on the atomism of the *mutakallimūn*. The universe as a whole is contingent and temporal and needs God to sustain it in time instant by instant.

The overriding aim of these proofs is to demonstrate that the world had a beginning at a point of time. Having demonstrated the temporality of the world, the theologian may then ask why it exists. To account for the existence of the world the *mutakallimūn* invoked the *principle of determination*.

> With the temporality of the world as a premiss, the Mutakallims proceeded to prove that the world being created (ḥadīth) must necessarily have a Creator (muḥdith), by recourse to the so-called 'principle of determination'. In its barest form, this principle meant that since prior to the existence of the universe it was equally possible for it to be or not-to-be, a determinant (murajjiḥ) whereby the possibility of being could prevail over the possibility of not-being was required; and this 'determinant' . . . was God.[32]

Now this raises an extremely interesting and intricate problem: just what did the *mutakallimūn* mean by the principle of determination? It appears to be a genuine anticipation of Leibniz and his celebrated principle of sufficient reason. But what makes the question so perplexing is that the principle of the Islamic thinkers seems to involve the same sort of ambiguity as the principle invoked by Leibniz. That is to say, it is not at all clear whether the *mutakallimūn* mean by 'determinant' a *cause* or a *reason*. In other words, are they arguing that the equal possibility of the world's existing or not existing necessitates an efficient cause which creates the world in being or a sufficient reason, that is, a rationale, for the world's existence? The problem is complicated by the fact that the Muslim thinkers, again like Leibniz himself, do not always use the word in one sense only, but employ 'determinant' to mean 'cause' on one occasion and 'reason' on another. For example, Ghāzālī uses the two terms *murajjiḥ* and *takhsīs* in three different senses, according to Simon Van Den Bergh:

> In the argument given by Ghazali we find the term مرجح ('determining principle', or more literally 'what causes to incline'; the Greek word is τὸ ἐπικλῖνον . . .), which is used by the Muslim theologians in their proof . . . for the existence of God: the possible existence of the world needs for its actual existence a مرجح, a determining principle which cannot itself have a cause, for an infinite series of causes is impossible . . . .
>
> . . . The confusion lies in the term مخصص ('differentiating principle'), which can mean as used by Ghazali (like مرجح *praeponderans*, determining principle or principle giving preponderance) (1) a principle which, determining or choosing without any motive one of two *similar objects*, establishes a distinction between them through this choice, (2) a principle which determines or chooses, without the motive being known, the existence of one of two opposites which seem *equally purposeful*, (3) the dissimilarity which is the motive for the choice.[33]

In the above enumeration, (1) and (2) would be classed as efficient causes, while (3) would be a sufficient reason. The question is, in which sense do the *mutakallimūn* take 'determinant' when discussing the origin of the world? To answer this question we must examine the basis of the principle itself.[34] From information provided by al-Ash'ari, it appears that the Mu' tazilites used the word 'cause' (*'illa*) in at least two senses: (1) that which necessarily accompanies its effect, (2) that which is free and precedes its effect. God could only be called a cause in the second sense. But from the end of the third century A.H., the term *'illa* came to be used exclusively in the first sense. The term *sabab* was reserved for cause in the second sense. Thus, al-Suyūṭī states, '. . . that which necessitates is called *'illa* and that which permits is called *sabab*'.[35] Thus arose the problem of God as the 'perfect cause' (*'illa tāmma*). For if God is the perfect cause, then either His effects must be eternal or He must never act, for if He came to effect something at some point in time, He would not then be perfect and all-sufficient. Thus, the world must be eternal or it could never exist. It is in this context that the principle of determination arises. Al-Alousī explains,

> As to the idea of the determining principle (*al-murajih*); this arises out of the problem of the perfect cause, and its content is in brief that God is eternally perfect, and His will encompasses all potential objects; but why then does His will specify that the world shall be created at one particular time, rather than bring about its existence from eternity?

> Clearly there must be a temporal determinant (*murajih*) responsible for the activation of the will at on [*sic*] particular time. But all times are equivalent in respect of God's ability to create the world; either God must create the world in eternity, in which case there is no need for a determinant; or God did not create the world in eternity, but created it after the passage of ages, in which case a temporal determinant is necessary . . . .[36]

Employed in this sense, the principle demands a sufficient reason as to why God created when He did. The *mutakallimūn* were divided in their response; for example, al-Khaīyāt attempted to give a reason by saying that God knew which time would be most conducive to the good of man,  but al-Ash'ari repudiated the principle by stating that God's will acts freely without need of motive or object.[37] The school of Ash'ari was more influential, and Ghāzālī follows his lead in this. According to Ghāzālī, the principle of determination in the sense of sufficient reason is simply invalid with regard to God. Hence, we find him putting the principle of determination into the mouths of his objectors.[38] Then he commences an elaborate two-step refutation: (1) the world is willed from eternity to appear at a particular time, and (2) that the world began in time is demonstrable through the cosmological argument from temporal regress.[39] The second step is Ghāzālī's proof for God which we shall examine later, but a word on his first contention will aid us in dealing with the present conundrum. Ghāzālī's first point is a clear repudiation of the notion of perfect cause. God is not the 'cause' of the world in the sense that a cause is that which necessarily accompanies its effect. But God is a cause in the second sense mentioned above, a free agent that precedes its effect.[40] Thus, the effect (the universe) need not follow upon the heels of the cause (God), but can appear a finite number of years ago when God willed from eternity that it should. As to the riddle of why God did not choose to create sooner, Ghāzālī, like Ash'ari, responds that God's will needs no determinant to choose; rather, '"Will is an attribute of which the function—rather, nature—is to distinguish something from its like"'.[41] He illustrates this by imagining a man confronted with two delectable, absolutely identical dates, of which he may choose one to eat. If the will cannot distinguish like from like, then 'the excited man will keep fondly and helplessly gazing on for ever, and will not be able to take either date by mere will or choice which is devoid of purpose'.[42] But the absurdity of this is self-evident. For it is of the very nature of will to simply choose, even when the options are identical. Thus, Ghāzālī rejects the use of the principle of determination in the sense of sufficient reason

But as Van Den Bergh noted, Ghāzālī does use the principle in two other senses, each of which is akin to efficient causality. Thus, he would agree that the equal possibility of the world's existing or not existing requires a determinant to achieve its existence; but this determinant is not a reason, but a cause, and the cause is God himself. This corresponds to Van Den Bergh's sense (1) of 'differentiating principle'. Sense (2) arises when one asks why *this* world rather than another?[43] This is the problem of specification, which arises out of the principle of determination, as al-Alousī explains,

> . . . by this was meant the specification by the creator that the world should possess the various properties, dimensions, etc. that it has, rather than others which it might equally have had. This question is closely related to that of determination but it differs from it in the fact that the possibilities from which the specification is made are not alike, . . . as in the case of occasions for creation.[44]

This problem also bedevilled the *mutakallimūn*, and the answer given to this problem is the same as that given to the question of the differentiating principle. God specifies what the world shall be like without the necessity of motivating reasons. Thus, according to Ghāzālī, God is the cause of both the world and all its particular specifications.[45] Certain aspects of the world—such as whether the spheres should rotate east to west or vice versa or where the poles of the spheres should be placed—have no sufficient reason why they are that particular way. God simply specified them in that way without a sufficient reason. There is no principle of specification immanent in the structure of the spheres themselves that demands that they should exist in the particular way they do; as Davidson points out, 'To refute Ghazālī, it would be necessary to show that a *rational* purpose is in fact served by the movements of the heavens in their present directions and by the present locations of the poles . . .'.[46] The only principle of specification that exists is God himself as he specifies without sufficient reasons.

To summarise, then: there are three applications of the principle of determination. (1) When the *mutakallimūn* demand a determinant for the world's existence, they are demanding an agent who chooses to create the world. (2) When it is asked what differentiating principle caused God to create at one moment rather than another, the answer is that no such principle exists. (3) And when it is asked what is the principle of specification that caused God to create this world rather than another, the answer is simply His will. Thus, we have separated out three principles—the principle of determination, the principle of differentiation, and the principle of specification—but, in the Arab writers themselves, the principles are often used interchangeably.

Only the first principle, however, plays a direct role in the cosmological argument. This becomes quite evident when we consider the *kalām* proof for God. Ghāzālī's statement of the proof makes it clear that he is demanding a determining agent who is the cause of the world:

> It is an axiom of reason that all that comes to be must have a cause to bring it about. The world has come to be. *Ergo* the world must have a cause to bring it about. The proposition that 'What comes to be must have a cause' is obvious, for everything that takes place occupies a certain span of time, yet it is conceivable that it come about earlier or later. Its confinement to the particular time span it actually fills demands some determinant to select the time.[47]

Therefore, it seems that despite similarities the principle of determination is not the Leibnizian principle of sufficient reason. Rather the principle of determination in its application to the problem of the origin of the world demands an efficient cause of the existence of the universe.

But this does not mean that the principle of determination is simply the principle of efficient causality. For the cause of the world to which the argument concludes is conceived by the Muslim thinkers to be, not just the mechanically operating, necessary and sufficient condition for the production of an effect, but a personal agent who by an act of will chooses which equally possible alternative will be realised. God is the *sabab* of the world, but not its '*illa*. Otherwise, the universe would exist from eternity. Goodman defines 'determinant' as 'selecting agent' and remarks that

> The notion of God as a Determinant, although related to that of God as Actualizor (and . . . as Creator, or even as prime mover), is conceptually distinct, and its development as an argument for divine existence may well be Islamic.[48]

Thus, when the *mutakallimūn* demand a determinant for the world's existence, they are demanding an agent who chooses to create the world.

This survey of the *kalām* arguments for the existence of God will serve as a basis for a more detailed analysis of the cosmological argument of one of *kalām*'s greatest figures: al-Ghāzālī. But we must also say an introductory word about that second great movement within Islamic thought: *falsafa.* Walzer has described Islamic philosophy as

> . . . that trend of Muslim thought which continues the type of Greek philosophy which the later Neoplatonists had created: a blend of Aristotelian and Platonic views as understood by philosophers in the later centuries of the Roman Empire.[49]

In these philosophers we find a strange blend of Plotinus and Aristotle, an amalgam aptly described as a 'synthesis of Neoplatonic metaphysics, natural science, and mysticism: Plotinus enriched by Galen and Proclus'.[50] For Arabic philosophy sprang out of the translation movement, which imported Greek philosophy ready-made to the Arabs; as Peters so nicely puts it, 'There was no Arab Thales pondering the possibility of reducing all things to the principle of sand'.[51] Rather, Arabic thought was shaped by the Hellenism mediated to it through Syria. Syrian converts to Christianity at Antioch, Edessa, and other seats of learning, after having learned Greek to read the New Testament, turned to classical studies to provide an underpinning for their theological discussion.[52] When Islam superseded Christianity, the translation of Greek works into Syriac and Arabic was encouraged by the Caliphs, thus preserving in the Muslim world what was lost in the West, until the Arabs should return it again via the Jews. The translation movement had disadvantages that were to have a marked impact upon Arabic philosophy. For example, the famous *Theology of Aristotle* was actually a translation of Plotinus's *Enneads* 4–6, wrongly ascribed to the Stagirite. And the *Liber de causis* was actually excerpted from Proclus's 'Elements of Theology'. The Arabians firmly believed that Aristotle and Plato were in agreement on the one true philosophy, which is understandable when one realises that they were under the impression that these Neoplatonic works were authored by Aristotle himself.

Perhaps the most marked aspect of Plotinian influence on the Arabic philosophers is in their emanationism. God is the One from which emanate all multiplicity and matter. But reflecting Aristotelian influence, they did not want their First Principle to be beyond Being, for metaphysics is the study of Being as Being and of the One as well. Thus, they brought the One into Being, and brought the world out of the One in a series of successive emanations, which correspond to the system of Aristotelian spheres. In order to avoid a pantheism inimical to Islam, they sought to make the One a necessary being in whom essence and existence are not distinct, whereas in all other beings, such a distinction holds. Nevertheless, the universe is in a sense necessary, for it emanates inevitably from the One. Thus, what the Arabic philosophers gave with one hand, they took back with the other, and this produced a system of continual tension. Arnaldez remarks,

> Thus, this *falsafa* unites seemingly contradictory concepts of the universe; on the one hand there is a First Principle in whose unity are rooted both the essences and the existences of all beings, and in consequence a continuity is postulated between the Being and beings, which is not interrupted by any creative act; on the other hand, there is an absolute discontinuity between the modes of being of the Principle and of that which proceeds from the Principle. Thus it is possible to speak of a cosmological continuity between the universe and its source (theory of emanation), tending to a form of monism, and of an ontological discontinuity between the necessary and possible, tending to re-establish the absolute transcendence of God. Furthermore, the possible beings, in whom essence is distinct from existence, are only possible if considered in themselves. But they are necessary if considered in relation to the Principle: granted a Being necessary *on its own account*, everything else is necessary *because of it* . . . . Hence, we return to monism.[53]

As for the philosophers themselves, they may be distinguished from their theological counterparts, the *mutakallimūn*, in several ways: (1) their more systematic use of more technical terms derived from Greek philosophy, (2) their wholehearted endorsement of Aristotelian logic, (3) their study of the natural sciences, such as astronomy, physics, chemistry, and medicine, (4) their metaphysical system as a theory of necessary and possible being, (5) their doctrine that God knows particulars insofar as He is the source of their essence and existence, and (6) their insistence that the ethical life can be attained by the guidance of reason.[54] A main difference between a *mutakallim* and a *failasuf* lies in the methodological approach to the object of their study: while the practitioner of *kalām* takes the truth of Islam as his starting point, the man of philosophy, though he may take pleasure in the rediscovery of *Qur'ānic* doctrines, does not make them his starting point, but follows a 'method of research independent of dogma, without, however, rejecting the dogma or ignoring it in its sources'.[55]

We may credit the Arabian philosophers with the origin of the modern cosmological argument based on contingency. For though Aristotle hinted at it and the *mutakallimūn* called the world contingent because of their metaphysical atomism, it was the Arabian philosophers who spelled out the distinction between necessary and possible being on the basis of the essence/existence distinction. They therefore deserve to be credited with the origin of this important version of the cosmological argument.

In this study we shall analyse the arguments for God's existence as propounded by the greatest Arabian philosophers: al-Kindī, al-Fārābī, ibn Sīnā, and ibn Rushd. I have chosen to examine their arguments in chronological order; hence, we shall treat Ghāzālī following ibn Sīnā and preceding ibn Rushd.

Al-Kindī

Universally recognised as the first true philosopher of the Islamic world, Abū Yūsuf Ya'qūb b. Isḥāq al-Kindī (c. 801–c.873) is known as 'the Philosopher of the Arabs'.[56] Taking his theological stance in the Mutazilite tradition, Kindī proceeds to develop a philosophy that can best be characterised as a Neoplatonised Aristotelianism. Kindī stands historically as the bridge between *kalām* and *falsafa*, and it was his conviction that revelation and philosophy attain identical truths, albeit in different ways.[57] Therefore, it is not surprising to find in him a strange blend of philosophical and theological doctrines not to be seen in the more purely philosophical thinkers who followed him. While his concept of God is thoroughly Neoplatonic,[58] he nevertheless sided with the theologians with regard to his argument for the existence of God. For unlike his philosophical successors, Kindī argued that God's existence may be demonstrated by proving that the universe was created in time. Indeed, the 'most important argument for God's existence in the philosophy of al-Kindi' is his argument for creation, and he stands apart as the only Arabian philosopher not believing in the eternity of the universe and matter.[59] Despite the influence of Aristotle and Plotinus upon his thought, he consistently upheld *creatio ex nihilo*: God creates the universe out of nothing (*al–mubdi'*), and Kindī uses the word '*ibdā'*' to specifically denote God's action as a creation in time out of nothing.[60] He reasons that if it may be proved that the universe began to exist a finite number of years ago, then the existence of a Creator may be legitimately inferred. Kindī's argument for creation may be found in his treatise *On First Philosophy*.[61] Here he utilises three arguments for the creation of the universe: an argument from space, time, and motion, an argument from composition, and another argument from time.

The first argument, too lengthy to quote verbatim, may be summarised as follows:[62] There are several self-evident principles: (1) two bodies of which one is not greater than the other are equal; (2) equal bodies are those where the dimensions between their limits are equal in actuality and potentiality; (3) that which is finite is not infinite; (4) when a body is added to one of two equal bodies, the one receiving the addition becomes greater than it was before and, hence, the greater of the two bodies; (5) when two bodies of finite magnitude are joined, the resultant body will also be of finite magnitude; (6) the smaller of two generically related things is inferior to the larger. Given these premisses, it may be shown that no actual infinite can exist. For if one has an infinite body and removes from it a body of finite magnitude, then the remainder will be either a finite or infinite magnitude. If it is finite, then when the finite body that was taken from it is added back to it again, the result would have to be a finite magnitude (principle (5)), which is self-contradictory, since before the finite body was removed, it was infinite. On the other hand, if it remains infinite when the finite body is removed, then when the finite body is added back again, the result will be either greater than or equal to what it was before the addition. Now if it is greater than it was, then we have two infinite bodies, one of which is greater than the other. The smaller is, then, inferior to the greater (principle (6)) and equal to a portion of the greater. But two things are equal when the dimensions between their limits are the same (principle (2)). This means the smaller body and the portion to which it is equal have limits and are therefore finite. But this is self-contradictory, for the smaller body was said to be infinite. Suppose, then, on the other hand, that the result is equal to what it was before the addition. This means that the two parts together make up a whole that is equal to one of its parts; in other words, the whole is not greater than its parts—which, according to Kindī, is hopelessly contradictory. All this goes to show that no actual infinite magnitude can exist. This has two consequences: (1) The universe must be spatially finite. For it is impossible for an actually infinite body to exist. (2) The universe must be temporally finite. For time is quantitative and thus cannot be infinite in actuality. Time must have had a beginning. Now time is not an independent existent, but is the duration of the body of the universe. Because time is finite, so is the being of the universe. Or, to put it another way: time is the measure of motion; it is a duration counted by motion. Now motion cannot exist without a body—this is obvious, for change is always the change of some *thing*. But it is equally true that a body cannot exist without motion.[63] It is said that perhaps the body of the universe was originally at rest and then began to move. But this is impossible. For the universe is either generated from nothing or eternal.

If it is generated from nothing, then its very generation is a type of motion. Thus, body would not precede motion. On the other hand, if the universe is eternal and was once at rest, motion could never arise. For motion is change, and the eternal does not change. The eternal simply is and does not change or become more perfect. It is fully actual and thus cannot move. Therefore, it is self-contradictory to say the universe is eternal and yet motion has a beginning. Motion and the universe are thus coterminous; body cannot exist without motion. The upshot of all this is that body implies motion and motion implies time; therefore, if time had a beginning, then motion and body must have had a beginning as well. For it is impossible for body or motion to exist without time. We have shown that time must be finite. Therefore, the being of the universe must be finite as well.

Al-Kindī's second argument may be summarised as follows:[64] Composition involves change, for it is a joining and organising of things. Bodies are composed in two ways: (1) They are composed of the substance which is its genus and of its three dimensions, which are its specific difference. (2) They are composed of matter and form. Composition involves motion from a prior uncomposed state. Thus, if there were no motion, there could be no composition, and if there were no composition, there could be no bodies. Now time is the duration counted by motion. Body, motion, and time thus occur simultaneously in being. Therefore, since time is finite, motion is finite; and since motion is finite, composition is finite; and since composition is finite, bodies are finite, too.

We may summarise the third argument as follows:[65] It must be the case that before every temporal segment there is another segment of time until we reach a beginning of time, that is, a temporal segment before which there is no segmented duration. For if this were not the case, then any given moment in time would never arrive. The duration from the past infinity to the given moment is equal to the duration from the given moment regressing back into infinity. And if we know what the duration is from past infinity to the given moment, then we know what the duration from the given moment back to infinity is. But this means the infinite is finite, an impossible contradiction. Moreover, any given moment cannot be reached until a time before it has been reached, and that time cannot be reached until a time before it has been reached, and so on, *ad infinitum*. But it is impossible to traverse the infinite; therefore, if time were infinite, the given moment would never have arrived. But clearly a given moment has arrived; therefore, time must be finite. Bodies, then, do not have infinite duration, and, as bodies cannot exist without duration, the being of body is finite and cannot be eternal. (Nor can future time be infinite in actuality. For past time is finite, and future time consists of adding consecutive, finite times to the time already elapsed. And two things quantitatively finite added together produce a finite thing [principle (5)]. Thus, future time never reaches the actually infinite. If someone were to assert that a definite past added to a definite future produces an infinite whole, this can be shown to be false. For time is a continuous quantity, divided by the present into past and future. Every definite time has a first limit and a last limit; in this case, the past and the future share a common limit: the present. But if we know one limit of each of the times, the other limit is also definite and knowable. Thus, the whole continuous quantity of time—past, present, and future—must be definite and limited. Therefore, the future can never be actually infinite.)

We have already mentioned the influence of John Philoponus upon Arabian cosmological thought, and al-Kindī is no exception to the rule. According to Walzer, Kindī was familiar with either Philoponus's actual works or, more probably, a summary of his main tenents.[66] According to Davidson, there were different sets of Philoponus's arguments being circulated, and Kindī's three proofs from creation suggest that he used such a set as the springboard for his own formulation of the case for temporal creation.[67] The second proof in particular shows the influence of the Christian philosopher. He had contended that composition of matter and form and of tri-dimensionality was sufficient to prove the finitude of the universe, and Kindī, with some modifications, follows him in this.[68] The third proof also derives directly from Philoponus, who had reasoned that an infinite number of motions would have had to occur before present motions can take place, if the world were eternal.[69] The significant difference between this and Kindī's version of the proof is that Kindī substitutes time for motion, arguing that an infinite number of temporal segments would have had to elapse before any given moment could arrive. As for the first proof, which is Kindī's most important, Philoponus's influence is at best only indirect. He argued against the infinitude of the body of the universe and employed arguments showing the absurdity of infinites of different sizes, but he did not use Kindī's deductive reasoning against the possibility of the existence of the actual infinite. This would appear to be the argument in which Kindī's own contribution is most marked.

Kindī's three proofs may be outlined in this way:

1. There are six self-evident principles:
   a. Two bodies of which one is not greater than the other are equal.

b. Equal bodies are those where the dimensions between their limits are equal in actuality and potentiality.
c. That which is finite is not infinite.
d. When a body is added to one of two equal bodies, the one receiving the addition becomes greater than it was before and, hence, the greater of the two bodies.
e. When two bodies of finite magnitude are joined, the resultant body will also be of finite magnitude.
f. The smaller of two generically related things is inferior to the larger.

2. No actual infinite can exist because:
   a. If one removes a body of finite magnitude from a body of infinite magnitude, the remainder will be a body of either finite or infinite magnitude.
   b. It cannot be finite
      i. because when the finite body that was removed is added back to the remainder, the resultant body would be finite
         a. because of principle 1.e.
      ii. The body would then be both infinite and finite.
      iii. But this is self-contradictory
         a. because of principle 1.c.
   c. It cannot be infinite
      i. because when the finite body that was removed is added back to the remainder, the resultant body would be either greater than or equal to what it was before the addition.
         a. It cannot be greater than it was before the addition
            (*i*) because then we would have two infinite bodies, one of which is greater than the other.
            (*ii*) The smaller would be inferior to the greater
               (*a*) because of principle 1.f.
            (*iii*) And the smaller would be equal to a portion of the greater.
            (*iv*) Thus, the smaller body and the portion would be finite
               (*a*) because they must have limits
                  α. because of principle 1.b.
            (*v*) The smaller body would then be both infinite and finite.
            (*vi*) But this is self-contradictory
               (*a*) because of principle 1.c.
         b. It cannot be equal to what it was before the addition
            (*i*) because the whole body composed of the greater

portion and the smaller portion would be equal to the greater portion alone.

(*ii*) Thus, a part would be equal to the whole.

(*iii*) But this is self-contradictory.

3. Therefore, the universe is spatially and temporally finite because:
   a. The universe is spatially finite
      i. because an actually infinite body cannot exist.
   b. The universe is temporally finite
      i. because time is finite.
         a. Time is finite
            (*i*) because time is quantitative,
            (*ii*) and an actually infinite quantity cannot exist.
         b. Time is the duration of the body of the universe.
         c. Therefore, the being of the body of the universe is finite.
      ii. because motion is finite.
         a. Motion cannot exist prior to body
            (*i*) because motion is the change of some *thing*.
         b. Body cannot exist prior to motion
            (*i*) because the universe is either generated from nothing or eternal.
               (*a*) If it is generated from nothing, body would not precede motion
                  α. because its very generation is a motion.
               (*b*) If it is eternal, body would not precede motion
                  α. because motion is change,
                  β. and the eternal cannot change
                     (α) because it simply *is*, in a fully actual state.
         c. Thus, body and motion can only exist in conjunction with each other.
         d. Motion implies time
            (*i*) because time is a duration counted by motion.
         e. Time is finite
            (*i*) because of 3.b.*i.a*.
         f. Therefore, motion is finite.
         g. Therefore, the being of the body of the universe is finite.
      iii. because the universe is composed.
         a. Composition involves change (motion)
            (*i*) because it is a joining of things together.
         b. Bodies are composed
            (*i*) because they are made up of substance and of three dimensions,

(*ii*) because they are made up of matter and form.

c. Motion involves time

(*i*) because time is a duration counted by motion.

d. Time is finite

(*i*) because of 3.b.*i*.*a*.

e. Therefore, motion is finite.

f. Therefore, composition is finite.

g. Therefore, the being of body is finite.

iv. because time must have a beginning.

a. Otherwise, any given moment in time would never arrive

(*i*) because infinite time is self-contradictory.

(*a*) The duration from past infinity to any given moment is equal to the duration from the given moment regressing back into infinity.

(*b*) Knowledge of the former duration implies a knowledge of the latter duration.

(*c*) But this makes the infinite to be finite.

(*d*) This is self-contradictory

α. because of principle 1.c.

(*ii*) because infinite time could not be traversed.

(*a*) Before any given moment could be reached, an infinity of prior moments would have to have been reached.

(*b*) But one cannot traverse the infinite.

(*c*) So any given moment could never be reached.

(*d*) But moments are, in fact, reached.

b. Moreover, future time cannot be actually infinite.

(*i*) The future consists of consecutive additions of finite times.

(*ii*) Past time is finite

(*a*) because of 3.b.*iv*.*a*.

(*iii*) Therefore, future time is finite

(*a*) because of principle 1.e.

A brief examination of each of these steps will be worthwhile. First, *there are six self-evident principles*. Kindī actually refers to them as 'true first premisses which are thought with no mediation'.[70] In his subsequent argumentation, he only employs the second, third, fifth, and sixth principles. In fact, he could dismiss point 2.c.*i*.*b*. at once as a violation of the fourth principle, but he does not. Hence, the first and fourth principles need not concern us. The remaining principles are easy enough to understand, whether one agrees with them or not. Principle 1.c is clearly what we would call an analytic statement. Judging by Kindī's use of principle 1.f., the same could be said of it; 'inferior' carries here no judgement of worth. One might argue that Kindī is unfair in principle 1.b., for one can imagine equal bodies that would not involve limits. For example, one might imagine two infinite parallel planes in space or two parallel planes that start at the same place and extend infinitely in one direction. Under principle 1.a., they could be called equal, for one is not greater than the other. Indeed, it might be argued that principle 1.a. contains the better definition of 'equal' and that principle 2.a. is question-begging. Principle 1.e. appears true enough; the real questions arise when one asks whether finites can ever add up to an infinite, or what happens when one adds a finite to an infinite. But for now, we may let that pass and agree with Kindī for argument's sake that there are six self-evident principles.

Principles in hand, Kindī next desires to demonstrate that *no actual infinite can exist*. His use of the word 'actual' is of paramount importance. Kindī's use of this term as well as the word 'body' in step 2.a. makes it quite clear that he is arguing that no ininite quantity can exist *in reality*. He is quite willing to grant that an infinite quantity may exist *potentially*. He explains,

> As it is possible through the imagination for something to be continually added to the body of the universe, if we imagine something greater than it, then continually something greater than that—there being no limit to addition as a possibility—the body of the universe is potentially infinite, since potentiality is nothing other than the possibility that the thing said to be in potentiality will occur. Everything, moreover, within that which has infinity in potentiality also potentially has infinity, including motion and time. That which has* infinity exists only in potentiality, whereas in actuality it is impossible for something to have infinity . . . .
>
> * Reading فان الذي . . . .[71]

Kindī grants that space and time are both potentially infinite, but he denies that such a potentiality could ever be fully instantiated in reality. Though we can imagine the infinite, it is impossible for it to actually exist. The point is, of course, Aristotle's,[72] but al-Kindī turns the Greek philosopher's own principle back upon him and argues that a consistent application of the principle would prohibit Aristotle's doctrine of eternal motion and infinite time. Al-Kindī's use of the word 'body' also deserves comment. We have already remarked that this underlines the fact that he is talking about extra-mentally existing entities, and not just abstract magnitudes. He never speaks of magnitudes in a conceptual way; he is arguing about the real world and always speaks of *bodies* of finite or infinite magnitude. On the other hand, it is clear that by 'body', Kindī does not mean only an extended thing, for he applies his analysis to time as well. In speaking of time, he makes it evident that his analysis of the actual infinite applies to any extra-mentally existing quantitative entity:

> It has now been explained that it is impossible for a body to have infinity, and in this manner it has been explained that any quantitative thing cannot have infinity in actuality. Now time is quantitative, and it is impossible that time have infinity in actuality, time having a finite beginning.[73]

In this way time as well as space will fall within the pale of his argument.

As for the argument itself, it is easy enough to follow. He presents a hypothetical involving a dilemma. This seems to be his favourite form of argument, for he employs it repeatedly throughout the course of his proof. His reason for denying the first disjunct seems obvious enough, but a comment on the second may be helpful. Here he posits a second hypothetical and dilemma. It is interesting that he does not regard step 2.c.*i.a.*(*i*), which establishes two actually existing infinities of which one is greater than the other, as an obvious absurdity. He argues that the smaller infinite body must be equal to a portion of the larger infinite body, and, on his definitions, equal bodies have limits. Therefore, they must be finite. Now besides questioning the validity of his definition of 'equal', one might also wonder if having limits is synonymous with finitude. This is the problem of the infinitesimal, and one might ask if one could not have two bodies of nearly equal length each containing an infinite number of atoms. Such speculation was at the heart of Muʿtazilite atomism and could hardly have been unknown to al-Kindī. Yet he simply takes it for granted that a body with limits is finite. As for step 2.c.*i.b.*, we have already noted that this disjunct could be dismissed as a violation of principle 1.d., which holds that when a body is added to another body, the one receiving the addition becomes greater than it was before. Instead of this, Kindī refutes the point utilising a principle that should have been added to his six: the whole is greater than a part. Having now refuted all the consequents, Kindī may now deny the ground: no actual infinite can exist.

Kindī then applies this reasoning to the universe: *therefore, the universe is spatially and temporally finite.* Step 3.a. is really extraneous to his proof, since what Kindī is really about is to prove the universe began in time—its physical dimensions are interesting but irrelevant. As our outline reveals, Kindī's three proofs for the temporal finitude of the universe actually break down into four. This may be because the second argument appears to be a sort of afterthought on the first and serves to answer a possible objection to the first; so Kindī treats them as one. An actually infinite magnitude cannot exist, he reasons; therefore, time must be finite. The argument regards time as a magnitude, since it is capable of being measured. Since time is the duration of the body of the universe, the being of that body must be as finite as time itself. This reasoning depends upon Kindī's definition of time. This is not the Aristotelian definition, which links time to motion, not just to duration in being. In this first proof, Kindī seems to anticipate the idea of space–time, a nexus in which space and time are inextricably bound up together.[74] He says,

> Time is the time, i.e., duration of the body of the universe. If time is finite, then the being* of [this] body is finite, since time is not an [independent] existent.
>
> * انية . . . .[75]

But someone might object that since, according to Aristotle, time is the measure of motion, it would be possible to have finite time, but at the same time an eternal universe. One might imagine an absolutely still, eternal universe, which then began to move so many years ago. Therefore, Kindī leaves his first definition and hastens to add,

> Nor is there any body without time, as time is but the number of motion, i.e., it is a duration counted by motion. If there is motion, there is time; and if there were not motion, there would not be time.[76]

This serves to introduce his argument from motion, which proceeds according to the Aristotelian concept of time. Step 3.b.*ii.a.* is extraneous to his proof, since he wants to prove that if motion had a beginning, the universe had a beginning. Therefore, he must demonstrate 3.b.*ii.b.*, that body cannot exist prior to motion. He posits a disjunction and proceeds to show how either disjunct proves his case. The first argument we encountered in Aristotle: the very generation of the universe is a motion.[77] (Kindī considers generation and corruption to be motions, whereas Aristotle would technically refer to them as change, not motion.) Besides this, the very point al-Kindī is out to prove is the generation of the universe, so that it does the opponent no good to yield it to him here. The second disjunct is clearly the crucial one: can the universe be eternal and begin to move at a point a finite number of years ago? Kindī says no; the eternal cannot change. Unfortunately, his proof is little more than assertion:

> Motion is change, and the eternal does not move, for it neither changes nor removes from deficiency to perfection. Locomotion is a kind of motion, and the eternal does not remove* to perfection, since it does not move.
>
> * لاينتقل . . . .[78]

This appears to be circular: the eternal cannot change because it is perfect; it is perfect because it cannot change. But he later gives us a clue to his reasoning:

> If . . . the body [of the universe] is eternal, having rested and then moved, . . . then the body of the universe . . . will have moved from actual rest to actual movement, whereas that which is eternal does not move, as we have explained previously. The body of the universe is then moving and not moving, and this is an impossible contradiction and it is not possible for the body of the universe to be eternal, resting in actuality, and then to have moved into movement in actuality.[79]

The terminology here immediately calls to mind the Aristotelian distinction of actuality and potentiality. Al-Kindī appears to reason that anything existing eternally at rest must be a being of complete actuality, with no potential for movement. Having no potentiality, it could never change; it simply *is*. Therefore, it would be impossible for motion to arise in it. Body and motion can only exist in conjunction with one another. Aristotle would have accepted all this and agreed that it is impossible for motion to have a beginning, though for other reasons, as we have seen. But he would have argued that motion is therefore eternal. Kindī now turns his attack on this stronghold of Aristotelianism. Motion implies time; time is finite; therefore, motion is finite. Since body cannot exist without motion, the being of the body of the universe has to be finite.

Kindī then turns to the third argument for the temporal finitude of the universe, a proof from composition. He will not admit the possibility of anything's being composed from eternity; composition involves change that joined the uncomposed entities together. Bodies are composed in two ways; we have seen al-Kindī's debt to Philoponus on this score. Hence, all bodies must be bound up with change, the condition of their composition. But motion or change involves time, as we have seen, and time is finite, as we have seen; therefore, change cannot have been going on eternally. Since composition requires change, it also must have had a beginning. But bodies cannot exist without composition; therefore, the being of the body of the universe must have had a beginning. This proof only serves to underline the earlier proofs. It is different in that it tries to tie bodies to time without referring to the question of whether the universe was generated or is eternal.

The final proof for an origin of the universe breaks some new ground. Al-Kindī gives two reasons why any given moment could never arrive if time were infinite. First, he attempts to reduce the notion of infinite time to self-contradiction. This really has nothing to do with the *arrival* of any given moment; the argument ought to stand alone. His reasoning appears to be this: in order to select any given moment in time, we must know what time it is. But if we know what time it is, then we know how long it has been from that moment back to eternity. So time is not infinite at all, since we know how much has transpired. The assumption, of course, is that to select any given moment, we must know that moment in relation to the past time before it instead of in relation to the present moment in time. The second reason is more to the point. Any moment, such as the present, could never be reached if time were infinite. Before the present moment could be reached, an infinite number of former times would have to have elapsed. For example, if we were to divide time up into, say, hours, then before this present moment could be reached an infinite number of hours would have to have elapsed. But the infinite cannot be traversed. That means the present moment could never arrive, which is absurd. Kindī does not argue here that time is finite because an actual infinite is impossible, and in that sense, this fourth proof stands apart. Rather the proof depends on the notion of traversing the infinite. Kindī's discussion of future time is extraneous to his proof for God, although it is interesting as an example of a potential infinite. For these reasons, then, al-Kindī contends that the universe is spatially and temporally finite.

Kindī does not immediately infer from this conclusion that God exists, however. He has proved that the universe has a beginning in being, but that does not prove that it did not somehow bring itself into being. Hence, he argues,

> An investigation whether it is or is not possible for a thing to be the cause of the generation of its essence, shall now follow the previous [discussion]. We say that it is not possible for a thing to be the cause of the generation of its essence.[80]

We may ask what Kindī means by 'essence'. He explains, 'I mean by "the generation of its essence" its becoming a being, either from something or from nothing . . .'.[81] He later asserts, '. . . the essence of every thing is that thing'.[82] Hence, we should not look in al-Kindī for some sort of ontological essence/existence distinction. His thought is much closer to Aristotle than to Thomas Aquinas. The essence of a thing seems to be what a thing is, but a thing and its essence are only conceptually distinct.[83] Kindī is really asking if a thing can be the cause of itself.

We may summarise his argument as follows: If a thing is the cause of itself, then either (1) the thing may be non-existent and its essence non-existent, (2) the thing may be non-existent and its essence existent, (3) the thing may be existent and its essence non-existent, or (4) the thing may be existent and its essence existent. Number (1) is impossible because then there would be absolutely nothing, and nothing cannot be the cause of anything. Number (2) is impossible because the thing is nothing and nothing cannot be the cause of anything. Number (3) is impossible because a thing and its essence are the same being, so that one could not be existent and the other non-existent. Number (4) is impossible because then the thing would be the cause and the essence the effect, and cause and effect are two different things, whereas a thing and its essence are the same. Basically Kindī is arguing that a thing cannot cause itself to come into being because (1) nothing cannot cause something to be, and (2) to cause itself, a thing would have to be different from itself.

But even at this point, Kindī does not conclude to God's existence. Instead he plunges into an elaborate Plotinian discussion of unity and multiplicity and concludes that the association of unity and multiplicity in the world cannot be due to change, but must be caused.[84] This cause he calls, in good Neoplatonic nomenclature, the True One, and by abstracting all multiplicity from it, Kindī, by use of this *via negativa*, is able to tell us,

> The True One, therefore, has neither matter, form, quantity, quality, or relation, is not described by any of the remaining intelligible things, and has neither genus, specific difference, individual, property, common accident or movement; and it is not described by any of the

things which are denied to be one in truth. It is, accordingly, pure and simple unity, i.e., [having] nothing other than unity, while every other one is multiple.[85]

It is only at this juncture that Kindī now identifies the True One as the cause of the universe. We may schematise Kindī's total proof, omitting the inessential details of the argumentation, thus:

1. There are several self-evident principles.
2. The universe had a beginning in time.
   a. Time is finite.
      i. Argument from infinite quantity.
         a. No actual infinite quantity can exist.
         b. Time is quantitative.
         c. Therefore, infinite time cannot exist.
      ii. Argument from the selection of the given moment.
         a. To select a given moment in time, we must know what time it is.
         b. If we know what time it is, then we know how long it has been from the given moment back to eternity.
         c. Thus, we know how much time has transpired.
         d. Therefore, time must be finite.
      iii. Argument from the arrival of the given moment.
         a. Before any given moment in time could arrive, an infinite number of prior times would have to be traversed if time were infinite.
         b. But the infinite cannot be traversed.
         c. Therefore, no given moment could arrive.
         d. But this is absurd.
   b. The universe cannot exist without time.
      i. If time is simply duration, then the universe could not exist without duration.
      ii. If time is the measure of motion, the universe could not exist without time.
         a. The universe cannot exist without motion.
            (*i*) If the universe were fully at rest from eternity, it could not begin to move.
            (*ii*) Therefore, there would now be no motion.
            (*iii*) But this is absurd.
   c. Therefore, the universe must have had a beginning in time.
3. The universe could not cause itself to come into existence.

a. Nothing cannot cause something to exist.
b. To cause itself, a thing would have to be something other than itself.

4. Multiplicity in the universe must be caused.
5. The cause of multiplicity in the universe is the cause of the universe itself, and it is the True One.

The True One is the source of all unity and coming to be.[86] Kindī declares,

> As the True One, the First, is the cause of the beginning of the motion of coming to be, . . . it is the creator of all that comes to be. As there is no being except through the unity in things, and their unification is their coming to be, the maintenance of all being due to its unity, if [things which come to be] departed from the unity, they would revert and perish . . . . The True One is therefore the First, the Creator who holds everything He has created, and whatever is freed from His hold and power reverts and perishes.[87]

In concluding to the existence of God, al-Kindī has made a Plotinian move to supplement his argument from creation. The source of the being of the universe is also the ultimate source of its multiplicity.

God is thus declared to be the ultimate cause. Kindī takes this notion quite seriously, and it involves him in a rigorous determinism. As Fakhry explains, for Kindī causal action is primarily a process of bringing things forth out of nothing into being, and this action belongs to God alone.[88] Even so-called secondary causes are merely recipients of God's sovereign action who in turn pass it on successively.[89] God is therefore the only real agent or cause in the world.

This serves to point up an important final issue. Kindī's argument from the temporal finitude of the world has at its heart the presupposition of the principle of efficient causality. But it is important to see exactly how this is so. Al-Kindī does not argue that every event has to have a cause and that the series of causes cannot be infinite. The use of the causal principle is not to be found here, for Kindī's arguments are based simply on the notion of the succession of temporal segments. One could hold (as al-Ghāzālī did) that causal connection is only a psychological disposition habitually formed from observation of constant conjunction and yet argue that there cannot be an infinite temporal regress of such successive states because of reasons revolving around the impossibility of an actually existing infinite. The use of the causal principle arises after al-Kindī has proved that the universe began to exist a finite number of years ago. Having proved that the universe came into being from nothing and that it could not cause itself to come into existence, he then infers that it and the multiplicity in it must have a Creator cause. Now this may be a natural and entirely justified inference, but it is important to point out that it does presuppose the validity of the causal principle; that is to say, it assumes that the universe could not come into existence wholly uncaused, as David Hume was to later assert that it might have. Al-Kindī assumes that having proven that the universe began and that it could not cause itself to begin, then it must have an efficient cause to make it begin. In the words of El-Ehwany, 'The Kindian arguments for the existence of God depend on the belief in causality . . . . Given that the world is created by the action of *ibda*' in no time, it must be in need of a creator, i.e., God'.[90]

Al-Fārābī

The Neoplatonic tendencies in the philosophy of al-Kindī come to full fruition in the metaphysical system of Muḥammed b. Muḥammad b. Ṭarkhān al-Fārābī (d. 950; known in the Latin West as Abunaser), who has been hailed as 'the first outstanding logician and metaphysician of Islam'.[91] Fārābī was the 'founder of Arab Neoplatonism and the first major figure in the history of that philosophical movement since Proclus'.[92] To him we may credit the first exposition of the modern cosmological argument from contingency.

An understanding of that argument requires a prior knowledge of Fārābī's important distinction between essence and existence. According to E. L. Fackenheim, it is Fārābī who introduces into philosophy the concept of possibility defined in terms of essence and existence.[93] The distinction itself, however, has roots that go further back.[94] We have already seen how al-Kindī utilises the distinction. Nor were the earlier Mu'tazilites unaware of the conceptual difference between the two, as Arnaldez explains:

> The Mu'tazila, in order to preserve the absolute transcendence of the divine unity, had distinguished essence from existence in created beings. For them, there was in God no paradigm (*mat͟hal*) for the essence of the creature, and creation consisted simply in bestowing existence on essences which were in 'a state of nothingness'. The creative act was conceived in a positive sense as what causes essences to

> pass from non-existence to existence (*lam yakun fayakūnu*). God, whom nothing resembles, was therefore beyond the essence and the existence of creatures here below.[95]

In fact, the distinction itself can easily be read into Aristotle, as is clear from a passage such as the following:

> He who knows what human—or any other—nature is, must know also that man exists; for no one knows the nature of what does not exist—one can know the meaning of the phrase or name 'goat-stag' but not what the essential nature of a goat-stag is. But further, if definition can prove what is the essential nature of a thing, can it also prove that it exists? And how will it prove them both by the same process,* since . . . what human nature is and the fact that man exists are not the same thing? Then too we must hold that it is by *demonstration* that the being of everything must be proved—unless indeed to be were of its essence; and since being is not a genus,[†] it is not the essence of anything. Hence the being of anything as fact is matter for demonstration, and this is the actual procedure of the sciences, for the geometer assumes the meaning of the word triangle, but that it is possessed of some attribute[‡] he proves. What is it, then, that we shall prove in defining essential nature? Triangle? In that case a man will know by definition what a thing's nature is without knowing whether it exists. But that is impossible.
>
> * ....
> † ....
> ‡ ....[96]

The distinction between the essence of a thing and the existence of a thing probably arose out of the remarks of later commentators on passages such as the above. But what does Fārābī himself understand by the distinction between essence (*māhiyyah*) and existence (*huwiyyah*)? In his *Gems of Wisdom* Fārābī asserts that essence is that whereby a thing is what it is, while existence is that whereby the essence is an actuality in being.[97] In other words, essence is the very nature of a thing, while existence is the state of being real or actual in the world. Gilson remarks that the Arab philosopher evidently had in mind a passage from Aristotle like the one cited above: 'In order to formulate this distinction technically, Alfarabi resorted to a logical remark made by Aristotle: the notion of *what a thing is* does not include the fact *that is it*'.[98] Thus, Fārābī writes,

> A real distinction occurs here and . . . existence is one thing and essence is another. If essence and existence were one thing, then we should be unable to conceive the one without conceiving the other. But, in fact, we are able to conceive essence in itself. If it is true that man has existence by essence, this would be like saying that to conceive man's essence is to imply his existence . . . .
>
> . . . If existence should enter into composition with the essence of a man like one entering into the essence of two, this would mean that it is impossible to conceive perfectly the essence of a man without his existence as part of the essence. Just as the essence of two would be destroyed by taking away a unity from it, so would the essence of man be destroyed by taking away existence from it. But this is not true, because existence does not enter into composition with the essence of a thing, for it is possible to understand the essence of a man, and not to know whether it exists in reality. On the other hand, if there was no distinction between essence and existence in created beings, then these could be said to exist by their essence. But there is one being alone whose essence is His very existence, and that is God.[99]

The question immediately arises as to whether Fārābī conceived this distinction to be a logical, conceptual one or an ontological, metaphysical one. According to Gilson, Fārābī held the distinction to be a real, that is, an ontological one:

> . . . the logical distinction introduced by Aristotle between the conception of essence and the affirmation of existence became the sign of their metaphysical distinction. The new doctrinal position thus defined is made up of three moments: a dialectical analysis of the notion of essence, which shows that the notion of existence is not included; the affirmation that, since it is so, essence does not entail actual existence; the affirmation that existence is adventitious to essence.[100]

It seems to me that it is the third point that is crucial here, for the other two could be explained on the basis of a conceptual distinction alone. Thus, one might believe that man's essence does not entail either the concept of existence or actual existence itself, just as Aristotle apparently did. But this does not mean that there are real essences; they are simply mental abstractions, the conception of which does not involve existence in any way.[101] Nor is a real distinction implied in saying that in God alone are essence and existence identical. This could mean that in God alone the conception of His essence includes the idea of existence, whereas in all other beings, the idea of existence does not enter into the definition of the essence. To deny the real distinction does not imply that essence and existence are identical; they are conceptually distinct from one another and it is possible to mentally abstract the essence of something without assuming its existence. But when Fārābī says that existence is an accident added to the essence of something, then the case for a real distinction would seem to be confirmed, for the substance/accident distinction is not merely mental, but characteristic of reality itself.[102]

A question closely related to this is whether Fārābī regarded existence as a predicate. Let us hear from Fārābī himself on this:

> *Question*: Does the proposition 'Man exists' have a predicate, or not?
>
> *Answer*: This is a problem on which both the ancients and the moderns disagree; some say that this sentence has no predicate, and some say that it has a predicate.* To my mind both of these judgments are in a way correct, each in its own way. This is so because when a *natural scientist* who investigates perishable things considers this sentence . . . it has no predicate, for the existence of a thing is nothing other than the thing itself, and [for the scientist] a predicate must furnish information about what exists and what is excluded from being.† Regarded from this point of view this proposition does not have a predicate. But when a logician investigates this proposition, he will treat it as composed of two expressions, each forming part of it, and it [i.e. the composite proposition] is liable to truth and falsehood.‡ And so it does have a predicate from his point of view.
>
> * . . . .
>
> † . . . .
>
> ‡ . . . .[103]

If Fārābī regards existence as metaphysically distinct from essence and therefore as an accident, he would say that 'exists' is a predicate, for it is an attribute added to what a thing is. And this is, in fact, what he says. Logically, 'exists' is a predicate. His denial of this for the natural scientist means only that a sentence like 'This plant exists' tells the scientist nothing about the plant before him on his specimen table; the existent plant is there in front of him, and to say it exists furnishes no information about it. In this sense, 'exists' is not a predicate. But logically speaking, 'exists' is a predicate of any subject. Rescher's remarks on this passage appear to be mistaken; he comments,

> Al-Fārābī, followed in this regard by Ibn Sīnā (Avicenna), wants clearly to distinguish the existence (*huwiyyah*) of a thing from its essence (*māhiyyah*).* But if 'exists' is a predicate, then the existence of a thing would seem to become one of its properties, and could thus be held to be among the attributes constituting its essence. To preserve a clear distinction between essence and existence, Al-Fārābī denies that existence is a predicate (i.e., an *informative* predicate) . . . .
>
> * On their view these coincide only in God.[104]

It is true to state that if 'exists' is a predicate, then existence becomes a property, in this case an accident, of a thing. But to say that this in turn constitutes its essence is entirely mistaken. The essence of a thing would be ontologically distinct from its accident of existence; the attribute of existence, just like those of tall, thin, blue-eyed, and so forth, would be added to an essence to make an actually existent thing. In creating things, God would conjoin the accident 'existence' with some essence; in God alone does existence constitute the essence itself. That is why Fārābī affirms that 'exists' is a predicate.[105] In Gilson's words, 'Not for an instant is there any doubt that existence is a predicate of essence, and because it is not essentially included in it, it is considered an "accident"'.[106] Thus, it seems clear that for Fārābī, existence is both a predicate and an accident, and the distinction between essence and existence is not merely mental, but real.

In my opinion, however, the strongest evidence for the real distinction in Fārābī, ibn Sīnā, and others is the use made of this distinction in their cosmological arguments for God's existence. They will argue that because a being's essence does not involve its existence, this being requires an efficient cause, a ground of its continued existing, which constantly conjoins existence with its essence. It is difficult to see how this argument could even begin to work without presupposing a real distinction between essence and existence. If the distinction were only mental, then no existential, sustaining cause of existence would seem to be needed. But this is precisely the sort of cause their cosmological arguments require. Fackenheim also seems to grasp this point; he regards the essence/existence distinction in Fārābī and ibn Sīnā as metaphysical, not mental, because it is the basis of their distinction of possible and necessary being, which is a metaphysical distinction.[107] We shall now turn to an examination of that distinction.

Fārābī uses his essence/existence distinction to formulate a second distinction crucial to our understanding of his cosmological proof, that between necessary and possible being. He states,

> Everything that is belongs to one of two kinds. In the case of beings of the first kind, existence is not involved in their essence. These are called 'of possible existence'. In the case of a being of the second kind, its essence does involve existence. This is called 'necessarily existent'.[108]

In other words, a being is possible if the conception of its essence does not necessitate the conception of its existence; for example, I can think of the essence of 'man', 'tree', 'unicorn', or 'centaur' without involving the notion of existence. But a being is necessary if the conception of its essence involves existence as a part of that very essence; for example, the essence of God would, presumably, involve some reference to existence, for God is the absolutely necessary being or self-existent being or some such existent such that being or existence constitutes at least part of what it is, that is, its essence. Fārābī has not yet proved that such a being exists; at this point all beings could be merely possible beings, for all we know. But Fārābī is not content with so simple a distinction. Hence, he adds a third category: 'The first divisions are three: (a) what cannot not exist; (b) what cannot at all exist; and (c) what can exist and not exist'.[109] The first category is the necessary being, the third is the possible being, and the second we might call the impossible being, for it is impossible for it to exist. Perhaps the impossible being would be that whose essence involves a logical contradiction, such as a square circle, for this could not at all exist. Fārābī, however, is still not satisfied and makes yet another distinction: 'The first divisions are four: (a) what cannot at all not exist; (b) what cannot at all exist; (c) what cannot not exist at a particular time; (d) what can exist and not exist'.[110] Here he has made a distinction within the category of necessary being: a necessary being either (a) cannot at all not exist or (b) cannot at a particular time not exist. With regard to (b), it is clear that Fārābī is here contemplating a type of being that is in some sense necessary, but does not partake of the absolute necessity of (a). His thought appears to be this: a being whose essence involves existence would be absolutely necessary or necessary *per se*, while a being whose essence does not involve existence is derivatively necessary or necessary *ab alio*, once its cause is given. Thus, he writes of this second sort of being,

> And if it *is* necessary, it has become necessarily existent through something outside itself. It follows therefore that this being is *per se* never other than of possible existence, and that it is necessarily existent *ab alio* . . . .[111]

The being that is derivately necessary is a possible being *per se* because its essence does not involve existence. Fārābī states,

> The existence of a thing which is due to a cause outside itself is neither impossible *per se*, —for then it could not exist—, nor is it *per se* necessary, —for then it could not owe its existence to an external cause—: the existence of such a thing is *per se* possible.

According to Fackenheim, the category of beings which are possible *per se* but necessary *ab alio* has reference primarily to the eternal and immaterial beings: although they require a cause outside themselves in order to exist, they nevertheless exist eternally and necessarily through their Cause.[112] There are thus two different ways of viewing Fārābī's categories of beings. (1) With regard to essence and existence, there are two types of being: necessary and possible, but within the realm of the possible, there are eternal possible beings and temporal possible beings. (2) With regard to eternity, there are two types of being: necessary and possible, but within the realm of the necessary, there are being(s) which are absolutely necessary and beings which are derivatively necessary. The confusion in this categorisation results from the beings which are possible *per se*, but are nevertheless eternal. Fārābī wants to give them a status midway between possible beings and absolutely necessary being, so he calls them necessary *ab alio* and in so doing changes the meaning of 'necessary' from self-existent to eternal. This reflects Aristotelian influence, since for Aristotle, 'necessary' and 'eternal' are interchangeable terms, as is evident in his remark,

> For what is 'of necessity' coincides with what is 'always', since that which 'must be' cannot possibly 'not-be'. Hence a thing is eternal if its 'being' is necessary: and if it is eternal, its 'being' is necessary.[113]

By this move, Fārābī makes room for his Neoplatonic emanationism. Thus, he writes, 'If one thing makes another, this means that the other necessarily follows from the thing, and the making by a thing of another is the necessitation of that other by the thing'.[114] Accordingly, he argues that the universe is the co-eternal creation of God.[115] The world emanates out of God with inevitable necessity.[116] Fackenheim remarks,

> The intelligible world emanated from the One can neither 'not-be' nor be other than it is: it is as necessary as the One itself . . . . Because of the necessary nexus between the One and the beings of the immaterial world, the Aristotelian convertibility between necessity and eternity remains unimpaired.[117]

This doctrine is the product of Fārābī's second categorisation of beings: there are two types of necessary being, God and the system of the spheres which necessarily emanates from Him. But in arguing for the existence of God, this distinction is only secondary. For our purposes the categorisation according to the essence/existence distinction will be of primary importance.

When arguing for the existence of God, Fārābī disdained the use of the *kalām* argument from creation. Not only was this argument antithetical to his emanationist doctrine, but it was, thought Fārābī, invalid as well. In his work *On Changeable Beings*, Fārābī contends that because time and motion do not exist all at once, but progressively come to be, they do not involve the absurdities attendant on an actually existing infinite multitude of things.[118] Fārābī employs instead the argument from motion,[119] the argument from causality,[120] and the argument from necessary and possible being. It is the third proof that marks al-Fārābī's distinctive contribution to the cosmological argument. He argues,

> Contingent beings . . . have had a beginning. Now that which begins to exist must owe its existence to the action of a cause. This cause, in turn, either is or is not contingent. If it is contingent, it also must have received its existence by the action of another cause, and so on. But a series of contingent beings which would produce one another cannot proceed to infinity or move in a circle. Therefore, the series of causes and effects must arrive at a cause that holds its existence from itself, and this is the first cause (*ens primum*).[121]

The proof may be outlined:

1. Contingent beings begin to exist.
2. Anything that begins to exist has a cause of its existence.

3. This cause is contingent or not.
4. A series of contingent beings each caused by another cannot be infinite or circular.
5. Therefore, the series of contingent beings must end in a cause that is self-existent and first.

In the first premiss, that *contingent beings begin to exist*, Fārābī is evidently thinking of what we have called his second way of categorising being. For if he were thinking of beings necessary *per se* and possible *per se*, it is not true that possible beings must begin to exist. But in terms of necessary and possible with regard to eternity, it is true that all possible beings begin to exist. Fārābī begins with possible beings in the sense of temporal beings, but he will shift mid-course, as Aquinas does in the third way (of which this proof is the root), to arguing concerning beings possible *per se*.

When Fārābī asserts in the second point that *anything that begins to exist has a cause of its existence*, he is not thinking of a temporally prior cause. If this were the case, one could have an infinite regress of causes. Only if the causes are hierarchically arranged will the Aristotelian argument against an infinite regress be applicable. What Fārābī has actually done is introduce his essence/existence distinction at this point. If a thing begins to exist, then its essence cannot involve its existence; otherwise it would have always existed. Therefore, it must have an existential cause, that is to say, a cause that continually conjoins existence to its essence to sustain it in being.

Hence, when Fārābī maintains in his third point that *this cause is contingent or not*, the meaning of 'contingent' has now shifted to 'possible *per se*'. He is asking whether the existential cause of the temporal being in question is itself composed of essence and existence. This is more evident in a similar statement of the proof:

> Transition from not-being to being demands an actual cause. This cause either has its essence identical with its existence or not. If it does then being is uncaused. If it does not, then existence must be from another, and that from another, and so on until we arrive at a First Cause, whose essence differs in no way from its existence.[122]

Fārābī is arguing that temporal beings must be caused by an existential cause; this being is in turn either possible *per se* or necessary *per se*. If it is possible *per se*, then even if it is eternal, it, too, must have a cause of its existing.

When Fārābī contends in his fourth point that *a series of contingent beings each caused by another cannot be infinite or circular*, he is doubtlessly thinking of the traditional Aristotelian arguments against an infinite causal regress. Such a regress would have no causal efficacy and so would produce no effect, which is contrary to the senses. A circular chain of causes will involve a cause that ultimately causes itself to exist, which is absurd.

Therefore, he concludes, *the series of contingent beings must end in a cause which is self-existent and first*. This being will not be self-caused, but uncaused, for its very essence will be existence. Hence, it requires no cause of the composition of essence and existence in its being, since it simply *is* existence. We shall explore this concept further when we discuss Aquinas's third way.

We may schematise Fārābī's proof in this way:

1. Contingent beings begin to exist.
2. Anything that begins to exist must have an existential cause of its existing.
   a. There is a real distinction between essence and existence.
   b. In beings that begin to exist, their essence does not involve existence.
      i. For if their essence involved existence, they would exist eternally.
   c. Therefore, such beings require a cause which conjoins existence with their essence.
3. This existential cause is composed of essence and existence or it is not.
4. A hierarchically ordered series of existential causes each composed of essence and existence cannot be infinite or circular.
   a. Such series would either have no self-existent member and, hence, no existential causal efficacy or involve an absurd self-caused being.
5. Therefore, the series of existential causes must end in a cause which is self-existent and first.
   a. Its essence is existence.
   b. It is the source of existence for all other beings.

Fārābī goes on to argue that such a being is infinite, immutable, one, intelligence, truth, and life; but his arguments need not concern us at this point, for we shall encounter them again in ibn Sīnā and Aquinas. What Fārābī has accomplished that is of lasting historical and philosophical importance is founding a new cosmological argument upon the notions of possible and necessary being, an argument that would have widespread and lasting significance, but whose founder would be lost in obscurity and not receive the credit due to him.[123]

Ibn Sīnā

The greatest of the eastern philosophers in the Arab world, Abū 'Alī al-Husain ibn Sīnā (980–1037; known to the West as Avicenna) brought Fārābī's Neoplatonism to full bloom, and from that point on *falsafa* was equivalent to ibn Sīnā, the open target of the *mutakallimūn*, who readily discerned the unorthodox nature of his philosophy. His debt to Fārābī is great, as is evident even in his remark that he had read the *Metaphysics* of Aristotle forty times and never understood it until he came upon Fārābī's commentary.[124]

Like Fārābī, ibn Sīnā employed the essence/existence distinction and the necessary/possible distinction in his proof for God's existence.[125] With regard to the first distinction, ibn Sīnā held everything has a particular reality (*ḥaqīqa*) which is its essence (*mākīyya*) and which is distinct from its existence (*wujūd*). For ibn Sīnā, the essence of a thing is given in response to the question, 'What is it?' The answer given will be a definition of the thing including its genus, its species or specific difference within the genus, and all other differences necessary for a complete description of its essence. The existence of a thing is posited according to the response to the question, 'Is it?', that is to say, 'Does it exist?' Like Fārābī, ibn Sīnā understands the distinction to be ontological in nature. He writes, 'Everything having quiddity is caused. Other things, with the exception of the necessary being, have quiddities which are possible through themselves; to such quiddities being does not accrue except extrinsically . . .'.[126] Says Afnan: '. . . Avicenna transforms a logical distinction which Aristotle had drawn between essence and existence into an ontological distinction of great import'.[127] Ibn Sīnā conceived of essences in three ways, as Gilson explains,

> Essences are to be found in three different conditions: in themselves, in concrete things, or in our intellect. Considered such as they are in themselves, they constitute the proper object of metaphysics; considered such as they are in singular things, they constitute the proper object of natural science, or physics; considered such as they are in our intellect, they constitute the proper object of logic.[128]

Thus, essences exist not merely in the mind, but also instantiated in reality in individual beings. It is important to note that the essence of a thing is not the same as Aristotle's form of a thing. The essence of a thing is the essence of the entire form/matter composite; we are given the essence of this composite when we ask what it is. Thus, ibn Sīnā writes,

> Everything except the One who is by His essence One and Existent acquires existence from something else . . . . In itself it deserves absolute non-existence. Now it is not its matter alone without its form or its form alone without its matter which deserves non-existence but the totality (of matter and form).[129]

One may conceive of the essence of any form/matter composite without positing the existence of that thing. Hence, existence must be added to the essence in order for the thing to be instantiated in reality. As Gilson comments, 'Since existence is never included in the definition of any essence, but is added to it as a separable concomitant, to ascertain the identity of an essence is to define a pure "possible"'.[130] For this possible to become actual, existence must be added to it. Thus, existence, according to ibn Sīnā, is an accident.[131] The essence/existence distinction was, as we shall see in our discussion of Aquinas, to have a profound influence on the West, which received it from ibn Sīnā through William of Auvergne.[132]

The second distinction requisite to an understanding of ibn Sīnā's cosmological argument is that of possible and necessary being, which he founds on the essence/existence distinction. Nasr explains, 'Only in the Necessary Being (*wājib al-wujūd*), or God, are essence and existence inseparably united, while for all other beings unity and existence are only accidents added to their essence or quiddity'.[133] It is of further interest that ibn Sīnā also defines this in terms of *logical* necessity. He writes,

> The necessary being is that which, if assumed to be non-existent, involves a contradiction. The possible being is that which may be assumed to be non-existent or existent without involving a contradiction.[134]

In defining necessity of being in terms of logical necessity, ibn Sīnā clearly anticipates the ontological argument. For if it is logically self-contradictory to say, 'Necessary being does not exist', one could argue as Anselm did that a necessary being must exist. Ibn Sīnā does not proceed along that path; but in light of his definition of possible and necessary, it is easy to understand Kant's criticism that the cosmological argument reduces to the ontological. Ibn Sīnā follows Fārābī in drawing further distinctions within the realms of the necessary and possible:

> The necessary being may be so either *per se* or not *per se*. In the former case a contradiction is involved if it is assumed to be non-existent . . . . As for the being which is necessary but not *per se*, this is a being which is necessary, provided a certain being other than it is given . . . . Everything that is necessarily existent *ab alio* is possibly existent *per se* . . . . Considered in its essence it is possible; considered in actual relation to that other being it is necessary, and, the relation to that other being considered as removed, it is impossible.[135]

Here we find what we previously encountered in Fārābī: 'necessary' is now used in the sense of eternal, and there are two types of such beings, of which only the necessary *per se* is logically necessary. The other type of being is only derivatively necessary; in terms of essence and existence it is still possible *per se*. Derivatively necessary beings are such because of their relation to a cause of which they are the effect;[136] should the cause be removed, they become impossible beings, not in the usual sense of logically impossible, but more in the sense of actually impossible.[137] Hence, for ibn Sīnā, 'necessary being' can mean either logically necessary being (necessary *per se*) or actually necessary being (eternal being). God is both logically and actually necessary, while the Intelligences which emanate from Him are actually necessary.[138]

With these two distinctions in hand, we may turn to ibn Sīnā's argument for the existence of God. Because he believes in the necessary emanation of the world from God, he, like Fārābī before him, rejects the *kalām* argument from creation, and develops instead his argument from contingency.[139] In his *al-Risālat*, ibn Sīnā formulates the argument in this fashion:

> Whatever has being must either have a reason for its being or have no reason for it. If it has a reason, then it is contingent, equally before it comes into being (if we make this mental hypothesis) and when it is in the state of being—for in the case of a thing whose being is contingent the mere fact of its entering upon being does not remove from it the contingent nature of its being. If on the other hand it has no reason for its being in any way whatsoever, then it is necessary in its being. This rule having been confirmed, I shall now proceed to prove that there is in being a being which has no reason for its being.
>
> Such a being is either contingent or necessary. If it is necessary, then

the point we sought to prove is established. If on the other hand it is contingent that which is contingent cannot enter upon being except for some reason which sways the scales in favour of its being and against its not-being. If the reason is also contingent, then there is a chain of contingents linked one to the other, and there is no being at all; for this being which is the subject of our hypothesis cannot enter into being so long as it is not preceded by an infinite succession of beings, which is absurd. Therefore, contingent beings end in a Necessary Being.[140]

The origins of the proof are not difficult to discern. We find Fārābī's distinction between possible and necessary being, the *mutakallimūn* insistence on the need for a determinant, and the Aristotelian argument against an infinite regress. We may outline the proof so:

1. Definitions:
   a. Every being has either a reason for its existence or no reason for its existence.
   b. A being which has a reason for its existence is contingent, both before it exists and after it exists
      i. because its actually coming to exist does not remove the contingent nature of its existence.
   c. A being which has no reason for its existence is necessary.
2. Every being is either contingent or necessary.
3. If it is necessary, then a necessary being exists.
4. If it is contingent, then a necessary being exists because:
   a. A contingent being cannot come into existence without a reason.
   b. If this reason is also contingent, then there is a series of contingent beings linked together.
   c. Such a series cannot be infinite
      i. because then there would be no being at all
         a. because the being in question could come into existence only if it were preceded by an infinite succession of beings, which is absurd.
   d. Therefore, the series must terminate in a necessary being.
5. Therefore, a necessary being exists.

The argument is much more profound than it appears at face value, and we would be apt to misinterpret it if we did not keep in mind the metaphysical distinctions just discussed. We have called the first step in the proof *definitions* because it does not appear that ibn Sīnā is here *arguing* that a being without a reason for its existence is contingent;

rather he is simply letting us know what he means by the term. Thus, when we come to step 2., we understand what a contingent being is and what a necessary being is because those expressions have been previously defined. Thus, step 1.a. and step 2. are really identical. The argument proper really begins at step 2., as ibn Sīnā acknowledges; what goes before are merely assertions. The only point he tries to argue for in step 1. is that once a contingent being, always a contingent being. We shall return to this point later; the definitions of contingent and necessary being must first merit our attention. The most striking aspect of ibn Sīnā's definitions is obviously their resemblance to Leibniz's conception of necessary and contingent being. Leibniz, following his principle of sufficient reason, argues that every contingent being must have a reason outside itself for its existence, whereas a necessary being contains within itself its reason for existence. Although ibn Sīnā maintained that the necessary being need have no reason at all for its existence, it is the demand for a *reason* for the existence of contingent being that so closely parallels Leibniz. The question immediately arises, does this mean that ibn Sīnā's argument, like Leibniz's, presupposes the principle of sufficient reason? The answer to this question depends upon what ibn Sīnā means by the term 'reason'. Does he mean with Leibniz that there must be some ground of intelligibility for the existence of contingent things or does he speak of the need for an efficient cause of the existence of contingent things? Rahman contends that it is the former:

> His argument which . . . became the cardinal doctrine of the Roman Catholic dogmatic theology after Aquinas, is . . . like the Leibnizian proof of God as the *ground* of the world, i.e., given God, we can understand the existence of the world. Here cause and effect behave like premises and conclusion, i.e., instead of working back from a supposed effect to its cause, we work forward from an indubitable premise to its conclusion. Indeed, for Ibn Sīnā, God creates through a rational necessity . . . .[141]

On the other hand, Afnan summarises ibn Sīnā's argument in such a way as to make it clear that a cause, not a reason, is being sought:

> . . . every existing being could be either necessary or possible. If it is necessary, then it would be what we seek; if it is possible, it would be for us to show that it originated from a being that must be necessary. There cannot be for an essentially possible being, essentially possible causes without end at one time. The chain of causation cannot be

retraced indefinitely. So long as it is a possible being unable to produce itself, there must be some original being that was able to give it existence.[142]

This argument is not at all the Leibnizian proof for the existence of God as the sufficient reason for the world. There are several reasons to accept Afnan's interpretation as the true meaning of ibn Sīnā's argument. (a) Both Fārābī and ibn Sīnā regarded necessary being as uncaused and possible being as caused. Ibn Sīnā writes,

> . . . The being necessary *per se* has no cause, while the being possible *per se* has a cause . . . .
>
> That necessary being has no cause is evident. For, if the necessary being had a cause for its existence, its existence would be by that cause. But whenever the existence of a thing is by something [else], if it is considered *per se* without another thing, an existence is not necessary for it; and whenever a thing is considered *per se* without another thing, and an existence is not necessary for it, it is not a being necessary *per se*. It is clear, therefore, that if the being necessary *per se* had a cause it would not *be* a being necessary *per se*. So now it is evident that the necessary being has no cause . . . .
>
> Further, whenever anything considered *per se* is a possible being, both its existence and its non-existence are by a cause. For, if it exists, existence has happened to it in distinction from non-existence, and if it does not exist non-existence has happened to it in distinction from existence. Now inevitably each one of the two states happens to it either from another thing or not from another thing. But if it is from another thing this other thing is the cause, while if it does not happen from another thing [it is a being necessary *per se*, not a being possible *per se* as we had supposed].[143]

Thus, when ibn Sīnā says here that a contingent being requires a reason for its existence, whereas a necessary being does not, it seems probable that he is speaking of the need for a cause. (2) Ibn Sīnā appears to follow the *mutakallimūn* in demanding a cause for contingent being. We have already examined the relationship between the principle of determination and the principle of sufficient reason, and concluded that the Islamic theologians posited the need for a cause of contingent being, not a reason. Ibn Sīnā seems to follow them in this: he makes the mental hypothesis of a time before the existence of contingent being (a hypothesis only, for he believes in the eternal emanation of contingent from necessary being) and asserts there must be some reason which tips the scales in favour of its existence. 'Reason' here is used in the sense of 'cause', just as the *mutakallimūn* used 'determinant' for 'cause'. This is confirmed by ibn Sīnā's statement that if this reason is contingent, then one has a series of contingents. For it does not make much sense to speak of contingent 'reasons' for existence, and, indeed, the Leibnizian form of the argument involves no reference to infinite regress at all. It is much more plausible to regard ibn Sīnā as here referring to contingent causes, that is, causes which are themselves only possible beings, so that a series of possible beings is established in which each member causes the existence of the one subsequent to it. (3) Ibn Sīnā's conception of the agent cause makes it clear that he is seeking a cause, not a reason, for the existence of contingent being. Aristotle had specified the four types of causes: efficient, formal, final, and material. Ibn Sīnā, while accepting this typology, makes within the category of efficient cause a sub-division, distinguishing between the causality of the *mover* and the causality of the *maker*. The moving cause sets things in motion (change), but the agent cause actually produces the being of its effect, as Gilson explains,

> The new type of causality distinguished by Avicenna is that of the 'agent cause' . . . . Its proper effect is the very being of the thing caused. What is here meant by being, is existence. The agent, Avicenna says, 'is the cause that gives to the thing an existence (*esse*) distinct from its own' (*Metaph.* VI, 1).[144]

When describing God's relationship to the world, ibn Sīnā speaks of God as the agent cause; that is to say, God produces the very existence of the universe.[145] This appears to decisively confirm Afnan's rendering of the argument. As we noted earlier, ibn Sīnā does not clearly distinguish *sabab*, which Arberry translates 'reason', from *'illa*, or cause.[146] What then may be said concerning Rahman's treatment of the proof? (1) He appears to have confused the order of creation with the order of our knowledge of God. Because the universe flows irresistibly from the being of God, Rahman assumes that our knowledge of God follows the same order, beginning with God and then deductively proceeding to the world. But these two orders must not be assimilated; though God is ontologically prior to the universe, epistemologically the universe as His effect is prior, and we reason back to Him as the cause of the contingent world we perceive. (2) Rahman grossly misrepresents Aquinas's version of the argument by equating it with Leibniz's proof. It is true that Aquinas's argument is basically ibn Sīnā's, but neither of these employs an argument for the existence of God as the sufficient reason for the world. Hence, although we find a surface similarity to Leibniz, ibn Sīnā's argument is not at all the same as that of the German philosopher. So by 'necessary' and 'contingent', ibn Sīnā means 'uncaused' or 'caused'. This is of interest because it means that in the proof itself the notion of logical necessity does not enter in; the necessary being at the argument's terminus will not have been proved to be logically necessary, but simply uncaused.

We ought to say a word about point 1.b.*i*., that a contingent being remains contingent after it exists. This brief phrase veils ibn Sīnā's essence/existence distinction. At face value, the point might be taken simply to mean that once a thing comes to exist it is still contingent because it originally had a cause at its inception so many years ago. Thus, we might say that an antique desk is contingent because it was caused, even though its maker has since ceased to exist. But this cannot be ibn Sīnā's meaning. For we have seen that he regarded something that exists as in a sense necessary; given its prior causes, it is necessary that this effect exist. The only way in which it is still contingent is that it is possible *per se*. But this introduces the essence/existence distinction. Ibn Sīnā is not arguing that the being is contingent because it once was caused; he is maintaining that it is contingent because it is being caused right now. In other words, because its essence does not require existence, in order to exist this contingent being must have existence continually given to its essence. It requires a continual, sustaining ground of being. This becomes clear from reflection upon ibn Sīnā's argument in the *al-Shifa'*:

> . . . everything that has not existed and then exists is determined by something admissable other than itself. And the case is the same for non-existence.
>
> This is because either the quiddity of the thing is sufficient for this determination or a quiddity is insufficient for it. Now if its quiddity is sufficient for either one of the two states so that it . . . happens, and that thing is necessary in its quiddity through itself, and yet it was supposed not necessary, this is absurd. And if the existence of its quiddity is insufficient for it, but [it is] something to which the existence of itself is added, so that its existence must be due to the existence of another thing not itself, then this thing is its cause; therefore it has a cause. So, in sum, one of the two states is necessary for it not through itself but through a cause. The factor of existence comes by a cause which is a cause of existence, while the factor of non-

existence comes by a cause which is the non-existence of the cause for the factor of existence, as you know.[147]

This is why ibn Sīnā says that '. . . the mere fact of its entering upon being does not remove from it the contingent nature of its being'.[148] Contingent being is contingent because its existence is distinct from its essence. Actually coming into existence does not remove a thing's contingency because its essence is no more disposed to exist after the thing is than before it comes to be. The tacit implication of this is that in a necessary being, which is uncaused, the essence and existence must be somehow inseparably united. Thus, beneath a few lines of a couple of definitions, ibn Sīnā conceals quite a store of metaphysical subtleties that must be surfaced for a proper appreciation of his arguments.

The second step formulates a disjunction: *every being is either contingent or necessary*. What this means, we have seen, is that every being is either caused or uncaused. Step 3. affirms one disjunct: *if it is necessary, then a necessary being exists.*

Step 4. affirms the other disjunct: *if it is contingent, then a necessary being exists.* Thus, ibn Sīnā is out to show that given any existent thing, its very being requires the existence of a necessary being. Any thing one selects is either necessary or contingent; if it is necessary, then a necessary being exists, and if it is contingent, then a necessary being exists; choose either disjunct—a necessary being must exist. One important facet of this reasoning is that ibn Sīnā cannot be accused of committing any fallacy of composition, for he nowhere asserts that the whole universe is contingent because the parts of it are. He does not even speak of the universe at all. Ibn Sīnā believes that the existence of one contingent being is sufficient to necessitate the existence of necessary being.

In 4.a. he reasserts his earlier definition: a contingent being cannot come into existence without a reason. This really means: a caused being cannot come into existence without a cause. This is, of course, tautological, but it is nonetheless noteworthy, for it serves to draw our attention to ibn Sīnā's notion of causation. At face value, one might think ibn Sīnā is here referring to temporal causes: a son caused by the father caused by the grandfather caused by the great-grandfather, and so forth. But this would be mistaken. As we discovered in step 1., a being is contingent, not because it was once caused to be, but because it is constantly and continually caused to be. In the above example, the progenitors each cause their immediate descendants to come into existence; but they do not sustain them in existence, for the son continues to exist after the father dies. Granted that the father is the cause of the son's coming to exist, what is the cause of the son's existing, even after the father no longer exists? Because the essence of the son does not entail existence, there must be some cause for the continued existing of the son. Thus, the consideration of temporal causes is not really to the point at all. What ibn Sīnā is seeking is, so to speak, existential causes. It would be entirely possible for a being to have no temporal causes at all, to be eternal, but it would not thereby be uncaused in the existential sense. Since its essence does not entail existence, its existing must be caused. It is therefore contingent. In one sense, then, a being may be uncaused (temporally) and yet contingent.[149] On the other hand, if a being is temporally caused then it must be existentially caused as well and, hence, must be contingent. For if it is temporally caused, then its essence does not entail existence; otherwise it would have always existed. Thus, anything temporally caused must be contingent, but not every contingent thing need be temporally caused. Hence, when ibn Sīnā asserts that a being which has a cause for its existence is contingent and a being which has no cause for its existence is necessary, he is talking about existential, not temporal causes. So in step 4.a., when he says that a contingent being's coming into existence requires a cause, he is talking about an existential cause, which conjoins existence with its essence.

This is confirmed by 4.b. and 4.c. For here ibn Sīnā argues against the possibility of an infinite regress of contingent causes. Since he also believed in the eternity of the universe, it is clear that he cannot have in mind a temporal regress of causes. He must, then, be arguing against a regress of existential causes. The argument is that any being which is composed of essence and existence is existentially caused. This cause itself is either contingent or necessary. If it is contingent, then it, too, requires an efficient cause of its existing, and so on. We are thus constructing a 'vertical', existential series of agent causes, not a 'horizontal', temporal series of moving causes. This sort of series cannot go on without end, contends ibn Sīnā. For then there would be no being at all. For the being in question could come into existence only if it were preceded by an infinite succession of beings, which is absurd. This is clearly reminiscent of the Aristotelian argument from motion. Aristotle had argued that motion could not occur if there were no first mover; ibn Sīnā contends there would be no existence if there were no first being. As he explains elsewhere:

> . . . the argument would go on to infinity. But [even] if it went on to infinity, in spite of that its existence would never have been determined for it, so an existence would never have happened to it. And this is

> impossible, not only because of the infinite series of causes (for in this context it is doubtful whether such an extension is impossible), but more because there does not exist any extension by which it can be determined, after it has been assumed as existing already.[150]

So just as Aristotle had maintained that the intermediate causes in a hierarchically arranged series of causes are merely instruments of the first cause, so ibn Sīnā argues that the existence of a contingent being cannot be caused by an infinite series of contingent beings hierarchically arranged. What we have called an existential or hierarchical series, ibn Sīnā calls, in language to be adopted by Duns Scotus, an *essential* series as distinguished from an *accidental* one. An essentially ordered series of causes of existence must end in a necessary being, that is, a being which is uncaused and whose existence is involved in its essence. In this way ibn Sīnā argues that given any being at all, if it is contingent, then a necessary being exists.

Step five concludes that since both disjuncts lead to the same conclusion, *therefore, a necessary being exists.* We may schematise ibn Sīnā's argument thus:

1. Definitions:
   a. Contingent being: a being composed of essence and existence, which therefore requires an existential cause.
   b. Necessary being: a being not composed of essence and existence, which therefore does not require an existential cause.
2. Every being is either contingent or necessary.
3. If it is necessary, then a necessary being exists.
4. If it is contingent, then a necessary being exists.
   a. A contingent being requires an existential cause.
   b. If this cause is also a contingent being, then an existential causal series is formed.
   c. An existential causal series cannot be infinite.
      i. An infinite series has no first cause.
      ii. Therefore, there would be no cause of existence.
      iii. Therefore, contingent being could not exist.
      iv. But this is absurd.
   d. Therefore, the existential causal series must terminate in a necessary being.
5. Therefore, a necessary being exists.

Having proved that a necessary being exists, what can be known of its nature? First, there is only one necessary being.[151] If there were two necessary beings, they would have to differ in some respect. This difference would be either accidental or essential. If they differ accidentally, this is either because they have different accidents or because one has some accident not present in the other. If the former, neither are necessary beings, for they would have to be caused, since accidents are added to the essence of a thing. If the latter, then the one without the accidental element is the true necessary being. In effect, ibn Sīnā argues that necessary being cannot have accidents; every property it has it has essentially. Thus, if two necessary beings are to differ, they must differ essentially. But this is also impossible. For if they differ essentially at least one or both of them must have a compound essence, since they are alike in one respect and different in another. But all compounds are caused; therefore, the being lacking a simple essence cannot be necessary.

Second, the necessary being has no cause.[152] This is obvious, since a necessary being is an uncaused being. But it also means, says ibn Sīnā, that God's essence is the same as His being. His existence cannot be caused by some external being, for then He would not be necessary. Can His existence be caused by His essence, then? No, for then the essence itself must become a complete being in order to cause the existence of another. But essence without existence is nothing and cannot, therefore, cause being. This means that God's essence does not just *involve* existence; rather it *is* existence. In fact, it can even be said that God in a sense has no essence. Now this is a very odd way of speaking, indeed, but it is ibn Sīnā's conclusion, and we shall see its effect upon the Christian scholastics as well.

Third, God is pure actuality.[153] God must have all perfections, since all perfections in the universe come from His essence, and all imperfections must be negated of Him. Since He is perfect, He can have no potentiality to receive anything; His perfection exists in full actuality. He cannot have matter, therefore, since matter involves potentiality. Moreover, He must be absolutely one and simple. For if His attributes were added to His essence, His essence would be the reason for the attributes, and the attributes would be potential in respect to the essence. If His attributes were said to constitute His essence, then He would be compound. Since, then, He is absolutely one, He cannot change, for change is the replacement of one attribute by another.

In this way ibn Sīnā attempts to demonstrate that his necessary being is, in fact, the God of Islam. We need not follow him further in his discussion of the attributes, for the above is sufficient to indicate the direction of his thought. His proof presupposes two important principles: (1) The real distinction between essence and existence and (2) the causal principle. His argument from contingency was to have far-reaching influences, and though the Thomistic third way has become more well-known than the version propounded by ibn Sīnā, in the words of Rahman, 'Aquinas' own metaphysics (and theology) will be unintelligible without an understanding of the debt he owes to ibn Sīna'.[154]

Al-Ghāzālī

Jurist, theologian, philosopher, and mystic, Abu Ḥāmid Muḥammad ibn Ṭā'ūs Aḥmad al-Ṭūsi al-S̲h̲āfi'i, generally known simply as al-Ghāzālī (1058–1111; known in the West as Algazel), has been acclaimed the Proof of Islam, the Ornament of Faith, and the Renewer of Religion.[155] For in him we find the 'final triumph of Ash'arite theology' and the victory of *kālam* over *falsafa*.[156] Ghāzālī was 'the greatest figure in the history of the Islamic reaction to Neo-Platonism',[157] and, despite ibn Rushd's attempted refutation of Ghāzālī's objections, he dealt a blow to Islamic philosophy from which it would never recover. Ghāzālī struck this blow with the publication in 1095 of his *Incoherence of the Philosophers*, a withering attack on Arabic philosophy, particularly as exemplified in Aristotle, Fārābī, and especially ibn Sīnā. It was only after he had thoroughly immersed himself in the teachings of the *falasifa* and even published an exposition of their tenets in the *Intentions of the Philosophers* that he felt equipped to defeat the philosophers on their own grounds.

Nearly a quarter of the *Incoherence* is devoted to the issue of whether the universe had a beginning in time, and on this question Ghāzālī ardently upholds the traditional *kalām* argument. It is with this argument that we shall be occupied, but it ought to be noted that this is not the only argument for God's existence employed by Ghāzālī; in his excellent treatment of Ghāzālī's argument from creation, Goodman lists citations for the teleological argument, the argument from self-authenticating authority, and the *kalām* argument from the temporal character of the universe.[158] Ghāzālī also hints at the Prime Mover argument from motion.[159] Interestingly, he at one time even propounded the contingency argument used by the Neoplatonists.[160] But he came to discard the proof because he believed it to be ultimately counterproductive, as Goodman explains,

> If it is possible to reason from a contingent world to a necessary God, it may equally be thought possible to reason from a necessary God to

> the contingent world. If the world's contingent existence is attributable to a necessary Being whose nature is to impart being to all that exists besides Him, then it might well be claimed that the world's existence itself is no longer contingent, but necessary in relation to its Cause* . . . . God is the ground of being, but nothing more; the world remains 'dependent' on God, but hangs only by the most tenuous metaphysical thread, vaguely characterized as 'ontological dependence'.
>
> Ghazâlî's suspicion is that 'ontological dependence' may prove a vacuous relation. By Aristotelian standards, what always exists must exist: if the world is eternal then, it is its own necessary being . . . . *Ex hypothesi* there must be some self-sufficient being; but, as Ghazâlî puts it, if the world is eternal, that being has already been reached. There is no need that it be God. The contingency argument, then, is self-undermining . . . . If the world is eternal, it is Ghazâlî's firm belief, neither the contingency argument nor any other argument can establish the need for the existence of God.†
>
> * . . . .
>
> † . . . .[161]

This explains the urgency with which Ghāzālī pursued the proof that the universe has a beginning in time, for to his mind the thesis of an eternal universe was quite simply equivalent to atheism.[162]

In the *Incoherence*, Ghāzālī's position is one of attack, not construction.[163] His faith had gone through a crisis period of scepticism, and in the *Incoherence*, according to W. Montgomery Watt, Ghāzālī 'is trying to show that reason is not self-sufficient in the field of metaphysics and is unable out of itself to produce a complete world-view'.[164] Therefore, we should not expect to find him setting forth a reasoned case for theism. But he does argue for the temporal beginning of the universe, and, placed within the context of his total thought as expressed elsewhere, this does constitute an argument for God's existence. The logical context for the arguments in the *Incoherence* may be found in the *Iqtiṣād* and 'The Jerusalem Letter' of Ghāzālī. In the first of these two works, Ghāzālī presents this syllogism: 'Every being which begins has a cause for its beginning; now the world is a being which begins; therefore, it possesses a cause for its beginning'.[165] Defining his terms, Ghāzālī states, 'We mean by "world" every being except God; and by "every being which begins" we mean all bodies and their accidents'.[166] Ghāzālī regards the first premiss as indubitable, calling it 'an axiom of reason' in his 'Jerusalem Letter'.[167] But he does supply a supporting argument: anything that comes to be does so in a moment of time; but since all moments are alike prior to the existence of the thing, there must be 'some determinant to select the time' for its appearance.[168] Thus, the cause demanded in the first premiss is really the determinant, as Beaurecueil explains,

> The first premiss of his syllogism furnishes a starting point which, in his eyes, presents no difficulty at all . . . . we must understand by *a being which begins* that which did not exist at one time, which was nothing, and which finally came to existence; as for the *cause* which he requires, it is precisely that which gives preference to the existence of one being over its non-existence. The coming to existence, established by the senses in the world of bodies, demands the intervention of a determinant principle among the possibles . . . .[169]

Ghāzālī now essays to prove in the second premiss that the world has come to be. This is the logical juncture at which the arguments in the *Incoherence* fit in, for it is evident that his argument from temporal regress is designed to prove that the world must have had a beginning.[170] We noted earlier that Ghāzālī mounts two lines of attack on the thesis of the world's eternity: (1) that the philosophers fail to demonstrate the impossibility of the creation of a temporal entity from an eternal being and (2) that the beginning of the universe is demonstrable. It is to the second point that we shall now turn our attention. Ghāzālī summarises his proof as follows:

> You reject as impossible the procession of a temporal from an eternal being. But you will have to admit its possibility. For there are temporal phenomena in the world. And some other phenomena are the causes of those phenomena. Now it is impossible that one set of temporal phenomena should be caused by another, and that the series should go on *ad infinitum*. No intelligent person can believe such a thing. If it had been possible, you would not have considered it obligatory on your part to introduce the Creator (into your theories), or affirm the Necessary Being in whom all the possible things have their Ground.
>
> So if there is a limit at which the series of temporal phenomena stops, let this limit be called the Eternal.
>
> And this proves how the possibility of the procession of a temporal

from an eternal being can be deduced from their fundamental principles.[171]

We have already commented on the origin of this popular *kalām* argument for God's existence. Ghāzālī's terse summary may be outlined as follows:

1. There are temporal phenomena in the world.
2. These are caused by other temporal phenomena.
3. The series of temporal phenomena cannot regress infinitely.
4. Therefore, the series must stop at the eternal.

We shall now fill out the structure of this outline by a step-by-step analysis. The first point, that *there are temporal phenomena in the world* is straightforward. We experience in the world of the senses the coming to be and the passing away of things around us. Ghāzālī takes the point as obvious.

Secondly, *these are caused by other temporal phenomena.* This step assumes the principle of secondary causation, which, we have seen, Ghāzālī thoroughly repudiates. It is therefore odd for him to be propounding the principle here himself. Probably the best explanation is that it is a concession to his opponents. The argument is addressed to the philosophers, who believed in the existence of real causes in the world.[172] Rather than raise here an extraneous issue that could only sidetrack the discussion, he gives the philosophers their four Aristotelian causes operating in the world. Ghāzālī himself did not believe in the efficacy of secondary causes, and his argument for a beginning of the universe does not depend on their presence. For he could just as easily have argued that there are temporal phenomena in the world, these temporal phenomena are preceded by other temporal phenomena, and so forth. The proof is not dependent at this point upon the causal principle, and it seems likely that Ghāzālī admits it simply for the sake of his opponents, who would not think to dispute it.[173] Thus, he willingly acknowledges of temporal phenomena that these are caused by other temporal phenomena.

The third premiss, *the series of temporal phenomena cannot regress infinitely*, is the crux of the argument. Ghāzālī supports the premiss by showing the absurdities involved in the supposition of the eternity of the world, that is, in an infinite regress of temporal phenomena. For example, it leads to the absurdity of infinites of different sizes.[174] For Jupiter revolves once every twelve years, Saturn every thirty years, and the sphere of the fixed stars every thirty-six thousand years. If the world were eternal, then these bodies will each have completed an infinite number of revolutions, and yet one will have completed twice as many or thousands of times as many revolutions as another, which is absurd. Or again, there is the problem of having an infinite composed of finite particulars.[175] For the number of these revolutions just mentioned is either odd or even. But if it is odd, the addition of one more will make it even, and *vice versa.* And it is absurd to suppose that the infinite could lack one thing, the addition of which would make the number of the total odd or even. If it is said that only the finite can be described as odd or even and that the infinite cannot be so characterised, then Ghāzālī will answer that if there is a totality made up of units and this can be divided into one-half or one-tenth, as we saw with regard to the different ratios of revolutions per year on the part of the planets, then it is an absurdity to state that it is neither odd nor even.[176] If it is objected to this that the revolutions do not make up a totality composed of units, since the revolutions of the past are non-existent and those of the future not yet existent, Ghāzālī will reply that a number must be odd or even, whether it numbers things that now exist or not.[177] Hence, the number of the revolutions must be odd or even. Or again, there is the problem of souls.[178] If the world is eternal then there will be an infinite number of actually existing souls of deceased men. But an infinite magnitude cannot exist. Ghāzālī implicitly assumes here the truth of Aristotle's analysis of the infinite, knowing that his opponents also accept it. Ghāzālī's arguments may appear rather quaint, presupposing as they do the constancy of the solar system and the life of man upon earth. But the problems raised by the illustrations are real ones, for they raise the question of whether an infinite number or numbers of things can actually exist in reality. Ghāzālī argues that this results in all sorts of absurdities; therefore, the series of temporal phenomena cannot regress infinitely.

The conclusion must therefore be: *the series must stop at the eternal.* The series of temporal phenomena must have a beginning. Therefore, according to the principle of determination (premiss one in the *Iqtiṣād*), an agent must exist who creates the world. Ghāzālī states,

> . . . the people of the truth . . . hold that the world began in time; and they know by rational necessity that nothing which originates in time originates by itself, and that, therefore, it needs a creator. Therefore, their belief in the Creator is understandable.[179]

This also means for Ghāzālī that time itself had a beginning and was created.[180] As Michael E. Marmura points out, Ghāzālī does not challenge the Aristotelian definition of time as the measure of motion, nor does he question the legitimacy of the inference of the eternity of motion from the eternity of time.[181] For him if temporal phenomena, or things changing in time, have an origin, then time, as the measure of such change, must have an origin as well. Prior to the beginning of the world was simply God and no other being. Time came into existence with the universe. It is only through the weakness of our imagination that we think there must be a 'time' before time:

> . ... all this results from the inability of the Imagination to apprehend the commencement of a being without supposing something before it. This 'before', which occurs to the Imagination so inevitably, is assumed to be a veritable existent—viz., time. And the inability of the Imagination in this case is like its inability to suppose a finite body, say, at the upper level, without something above its surface. Hence its assumption that beyond the world there is space—i.e., either a plenum or a void. When therefore it is said that there is nothing above the surface of the world or beyond its extent, the Imagination cannot accept such a thing—just as it is unable to accept the idea that there is nothing in the nature of a verifiable being before the existence of the world.[182]

So just as we realise the universe is finite and nothing is beyond it, though we cannot imagine such a thing, so we know that time, too, is finite and nothing is before it. Similarly, to suppose that God could have created the world earlier is simply 'the work of the Imagination'.[183] Ghāzālī is fond of emphasising that it is the imagination that leads one astray with regard to questions of time and space; we must accept the conclusions of reason despite the problems the imagination might confront. So with regard to the problem of God's creating the world earlier, this is obviously nonsensical since no time existed before the universe. Thus, it could not have been created sooner in time, and to think it might have is only to be deceived by the imagination.

Now placing this argument within the logical context of Ghāzālī's thought, we can see why Ghāzālī concludes that the world must have a cause: the universe had a beginning; while it was non-existent, it could either be or not be; since it came to be, there must be some determinant which causes it to exist. And this is God. Thus, Ghāzālī says, 'So either the series will go on to infinity, or it will stop at an eternal being from which the first temporal being should have originated.[184] Ghāzālī assumes that the universe could not simply spring into existence without a determinant, or cause. We may schematise his argument as follows:

1. Everything that begins to exist requires a cause for its origin.
2. The world began to exist.
   a. There are temporal phenomena in the world.
   b. These are preceded by other temporal phenomena.
   c. The series of temporal phenomena cannot regress infinitely.
      i. An actually existing infinite series involves various absurdities.
   d. Therefore, the series of temporal phenomena must have had a beginning.
3. Therefore, the world has a cause for its origin: its Creator.

In conclusion, it is significant to note that Ghāzālī does not, like al-Kindī, base his argument on the finitude of time. Rather he argues from temporal *phenomena*, not time itself. These phenomena cannot regress infinitely, for this is absurd. We might also note that Ghāzālī, like Kindī, argues against the *real* existence of an infinite quantity. This is especially clear when in the *Iqtiṣād* Ghāzālī states that God's knowledge of infinite possibles does not refute his case against the infinite magnitude, for these 'knowables' are not real, existent things, to which his argument is confined.[185] Finally, we should reiterate that the role of the causal principle is not in the relation between phenomena, but in the demand for a determinant which causes the phenomena to be. This fact alone serves to clearly demark Ghāzālī's proof from arguments relying upon the reality of secondary causes, for example, the first three ways of Aquinas. Since God is the only cause, a causal series of any sort cannot exist. In sum, Ghāzālī's cosmological argument is squarely based on two principles, as pointed out by Beaurecueil:

> 'There remain . . . to the scepticism of Ghāzāli two great limits, which appear now with a majestic clarity: one, the impossibility of the infinite number, and the other, the necessity of a principle of determination amongst the possibles.'*
>
> These are the two pillars of all Ghāzāli's reasoning in his proof for the existence of God: the impossibility of the infinite number permits him to establish that the world has a beginning; on the other part, if it has begun, it is necessary that one being should give preference to its existence over its non-existence: this being is God, its creator.
>
> * Carra de Vaux, *Gazali*, p. 80–81.[186]

Ibn Rushd

The greatest philosopher produced by Muslim Spain, Abu'l-Walīd Muḥammad b. Aḥmad b. Rushd (1126–1198), known in the Latin West as Averroes, or more simply, the Commentator, became renowned for his extensive commentaries on Aristotle. As a faithful Aristotelian, he severely scolds Ghāzālī for his attempts to prove the temporality of the universe, and he chastises the errant ibn Sīnā for his lack of fidelity to true Aristotelianism. Ibn Rushd re-supports the philosophers in arguing for the eternity of the world,[187] but his fairness to Aristotle prevents him from embracing the real distinction between essence and existence introduced by Fārābī and ibn Sīnā. Accordingly, he regards ibn Sīnā's version of the contingency proof as invalid. He himself believes that the best arguments for God's existence for the common man are simply *Qur'ānic* ones, the proof from providence and the proof from the wonders of creation.[188] As a commentator on Aristotle's metaphysics, he also reproduced the prime mover argument from the motion of the spheres.[189] But in the *Incoherence of the Incoherence*, he does provide what he considers to be a valid form of ibn Sīnā's contingency argument. This argument is of interest because it does not rely on the real distinction between essence and existence. He writes,

> If one wanted to give a demonstrative form to the argument used by Avicenna one should say: Possible existents must of necessity have causes which precede them, and if these causes again are possible it follows that they have causes and that there is an infinite regress; and if there is an infinite regress there is no cause, and the possible will exist without a cause, and this is impossible. Therefore, the series must end in a necessary cause, and in this case this necessary cause must be necessary through a cause or without a cause, and if through a cause, this cause must have a cause and so on infinitely; and if we have an infinite regress here, it follows that what was assumed to have a cause has no cause, and this is impossible. Therefore, the series must end in a cause necessary without a cause, i.e. necessary by itself, and this necessarily is the necessary existent. And when these distinctions are indicated the proof becomes valid.[190]

Ibn Rushd acknowledges the proof to be ibn Sīnā's; the other influence is Aristotelian, as we shall see further. We may outline the argument in this way:

1. Possible beings must be caused.
2. There cannot be an infinite series of possible beings each caused by another because:
   a. In an infinite series there is no cause.
   b. So the possible being would be uncaused.
   c. But this contradicts (1): *Possible beings must be caused.*
3. Therefore, the series must end in a necessary cause, which is either caused or uncaused.
4. There cannot be an infinite series of caused necessary causes because:
   a. in an infinite regress there is no cause.
   b. So caused necessary causes would not be caused.
   c. But this is self-contradictory.
5. Therefore, the series must end in an uncaused necessary cause, which is the necessary being.

Ibn Rushd's differences with ibn Sīnā appear in the very first step, *possible beings must be caused*, for he does not define 'possible' in terms of essence and existence. Rather a possible being is a thing that comes into existence and passes away and that is caused. A necessary being is any eternal thing, as is evident from this passage:

> . . . what has a cause can be divided into what is possible and what is necessary.* If we understand by 'possible' the truly possible † we arrive at the necessary – possible ‡ and not at the necessary which has no cause; and if we understand by 'possible' that which has a cause and is also necessary . . . it has not yet been proved that their infinite number is impossible, in the way it is evident of the truly possible existents . . .
>
> * Averroës here means, I think, by 'possible' the transitory, sub-lunary things, and by 'necessary' the separate Intellects, the eternal celestial bodies, or the world as a whole.
>
> † i.e. matter, or rather the transient individual.
>
> ‡ i.e. everything eternal with the exception of God; in this argument there is implied a trichotomy of reality into the absolutely necessary (i.e. the prime mover), the necessary – possible or hypothetically necessary (i.e. everything eternal, with the exception of the prime mover), and the possible (i.e. actualized matter) . . . .[191]

Here the truly possible is any caused, perishable thing; the necessary – possible retains the caused nature of the perishable being but not its susceptibility to generation or corruption; and the necessary being is both uncaused and eternal. This definition evidences clear Aristotelian influence. All possible beings, then, must be caused.

Second, he argues that *there cannot be an infinite series of possible beings each caused by another*. Again the argument belongs to Aristotle. In a hierarchical or essential series, there is no true cause except the first; remove this, as in an infinite series, and all causal efficacy will disappear. He explains the point at length:

> . . . the infinite regress of causes is according to philosophical doctrine in one way impossible, in another way necessary; impossible when this regress is essential and in a straight line and the prior cause is a condition of the existence of the posterior, not impossible when this regress is accidental and circular, when the prior is not a condition for the posterior and when there exists an essential first cause—for instance, the origin of rain from a cloud, the origin of a cloud from vapour, the origin of vapour from rain. And this is according to the philosophers an eternal circular process . . . . And similarly the coming into existence of one man from another is an eternal process, for in such cases the existence of the prior is not a condition for the existence of the posterior . . . . This kind of cause leads upwards to an eternal first cause which acts in each individual member of the series of causes at the moment of the becoming of its final effect; for instance, when Socrates engenders Plato, the ultimate mover, according to the philosophers, is the highest sphere, or the soul, or the intellect,* or all together, or God the Creator. And therefore Aristotle says that a man and the sun together engender a man,† and it is clear that the sun leads upwards to its mover and its mover to the First Principle. Therefore the past man is not a condition for the existence of the future man. Similarly, when an artisan produces successively a series of products of craftsmanship with different instruments, and produces these instruments through instruments and the latter again through other instruments.‡ the becoming of these instruments one from another is something accidental, and none of these instruments is a condition for the existence of the product of craftsmanship except the first‖ instrument which is in immediate contact with the work produced.¶ Now the father is necessary for the coming into existence of the son in

* The soul, i.e. the soul as totality, the Platonic or Neoplatonic World-Soul; the intellect, i.e. the νοῦς as a supramundane entity.

† Aristotle, *Met.* Λ 5. 1071a13 . . . , *Phys.* B 2. 194b13.

‡ . . . .

‖ First, i.e. nearest to the product of art, but, in fact, last in the series of instruments.

¶ . . . .

> the same way as the instrument which comes into immediate contact with the product of craftsmanship is necessary for its coming into existence. And the instrument with which this instrument is produced will be necessary for the production of this instrument, but will not be necessary for the production of the product of craftsmanship unless accidentally . . . . Those, however, who regard an infinite series of essential causes as possible are materialists, and he who concedes this does not understand the efficient cause.[192]

This passage is of considerable interest, since ibn Rushd goes to great pains to describe and illustrate an essential causal series. Such a series is earmarked by two characteristics: (1) it is in a straight line, that is to say, the causes stand one above the other in a non-repetitive fashion, and (2) each cause is a condition for the existence of its effect, that is to say, each cause not only causes the effect to come into existence, but it causes the continuous existing of the effect as well. In other words, it causes not only the becoming of the effect but the being of the effect. Thus, a father or a carpenter's tool do not cause the continued existing of the son or cabinet they produce, for they may perish while the son or cabinet continues to exist. They are therefore only accidental causes; in an essential causal series, such as things being moved simultaneously by another, if one of the members perishes, the effect, in this case the motion, ceases.

So it is in a series of possible beings being caused by another. Each member in the series depends for its existence immediately on its predecessor and ultimately upon the first cause. What sort of series ibn Rushd has in mind is perhaps indicated by his example of the sun's causing the generation of a man. Following Aristotle, he believed that all generation and corruption and all change had to be referred ultimately to the heavenly spheres and thence to God. He argues here that not only movement must be so ascribed, but existing as well. All beings derive their existence ultimately from God and mediately through the system of Intelligences. We would perhaps speak today of the contemporaneous conditions for the existence of, say, myself at this moment. My existence depends on the existence of other factors which depend in turn on others for their existence. This would seem to be an essential series of possible beings caused by another. Ibn Rushd maintains that such a series cannot be infinite because then there would be no first cause and without a first cause, none of the other causes would have any efficacy. Hence, the final effect would not be caused, which contradicts our notion of possible being. Now it is not quite clear whether ibn Rushd is arguing that in an infinite series the final effect would be uncaused and this is impossible because it contradicts what we mean by the word 'effect' or that in an infinite series the final effect would be ultimately uncaused and therefore could not exist, which contradicts our experience that it does exist. Certainly, the latter would be the stronger argument, and one would have little doubt that this is ibn Rushd's meaning were it not for the fact that he will later use the former argument in contending against an infinite series of necessary beings. Whichever is the case, the conclusion remains: there cannot be an infinite series of possible beings each caused by another.

The third step proceeds, *therefore, the series must end in a necessary cause, which is caused or uncaused.* By 'necessary', he means eternal. Transitory beings must depend on some eternal being which sustains the perishable beings in existence. Ibn Rushd has clearly in mind the system of spheres and Intelligences. Now this necessary being is itself either sustained in existence by some other necessary being (say, a higher sphere) or it is not so sustained, but exists uncaused. Because there must be some first cause of the series of possible beings, the series must end in a necessary cause, which is caused or uncaused.

Fourth, *there cannot be an infinite series of caused necessary causes.* In other words, the enclosing spheres cannot go out and out infinitely; they must stop at an outermost sphere. Ibn Rushd's proof of this is rather odd: since in an essential infinite series there is no cause, the members of such a series would not be caused. But then the caused necessary causes would not be caused, which is self-contradictory. He does not say they could not exist, but only that they would be uncaused. If this is his argument, it does not prove the existence of a terminus to the series in an uncaused necessary cause, but only that possible beings are caused by necessary causes, which may or may not be infinite in number. For 'uncaused' could mean either self-existent or dependent upon an infinite regress of causes. Either of these would be an uncaused necessary being. It seems ibn Rushd should have argued that there cannot be an infinite series of caused necessary causes because without a first cause, nothing at all could exist. Perhaps this is what he meant to say, but in that case the distinction between possible and necessary, or perishable caused and eternal caused, beings is utterly superfluous. The argument would then be simply that all caused beings depend ultimately upon a first cause.

Finally, he concludes, *therefore, the series must end in an uncaused necessary cause, which is the necessary being.* We have already noted the ambiguity of the phrase 'uncaused necessary cause'. Ibn Rushd, however, equates this with the necessary being which is self-existent. Standing at the head of the essential series of causes of existence, it is the source of the existence of the universe. We could schematise the argument thus:

1. Contingent beings, that is, perishable and caused beings, exist.
2. There cannot be an infinite essential series of contingent beings which are caused by another.
   a. An infinite series has no first cause.
   b. Therefore, contingent beings would be uncaused.
   c. But this contradicts (1): contingent beings, that is, perishable and caused beings exist.
3. Therefore, the series must end in a necessary, that is, eternal, being, which is either caused or uncaused.
4. There cannot be an infinite essential series of caused necessary beings.
   a. An infinite series has no first cause.
   b. Therefore, caused necessary beings would be uncaused.
   c. But this is self-contradictory.
5. Therefore, the series must end in an uncaused necessary cause, which is the self-existent necessary being.

The argument of ibn Rushd is important because it is an example of ibn Sīnā's proof without the metaphysical foundations of the essence/existence distinction and because its influence has been widespread, from Aquinas's second way and onward.

With passing of ibn Rushd the exotic flower of *falsafa* in the Islamic world faded quickly, never to reappear. The Golden Age of *kalām* ended soon afterward with the death of Fakhr al-Dīn al-Rāzī (1149–1209), who was considered to be the reviver of Islam in the twelfth century just as Ghāzālī had been in the eleventh. But the *falsafa* and the *kalām* cosmological arguments did not die with them. The Arabic theologians and philosophers bequeathed their developments of the cosmological argument along with the legacy of Aristotle to the Latin West, with whom they rubbed shoulders in Muslim Spain.[193] Christians lived side by side with Muslims in Toledo, and it was inevitable that Arabic intellectual life should become of keen interest to them. The medium of this transmission was the Jews, whose own language was close to Arabic.[194] The Jewish thinkers fully participated in the intellectual life of the Muslim society, many of them writing in Arabic and translating Arabic works into Hebrew.[195] And the Christians in turn read and translated works of these Jewish thinkers. The *kalām* argument for the beginning of the universe became a subject of heated debate, being opposed by Aquinas, but adopted and supported by Bonaventure.[196] The *falsafa* argument from necessary and possible being was widely used in various forms and eventually became the key Thomist argument for God's existence. Thus it was that the cosmological argument came to the Latin-speaking theologians of the West, who receive in our Western culture a credit for originality that they do not fully deserve, since they inherited these arguments from the Arabic theologians and philosophers, whom we tend unfortunately to neglect.

NOTES

1. For example, Burrill makes no mention of the Arabic contribution (Donald Burrill, *The Cosmological Argument* [New York: Doubleday & Co., 1967]). On the other hand, Sturch devotes three chapters exclusively to Arabic developments of the cosmological argument (R. L. Sturch, 'The Cosmological Argument' [Ph.D. thesis, Oxford University, 1970], pp. 59–120a).

2. Frederick Copleston, *A History of Philosophy*, vol. 2, *Mediaeval Philosophy: Augustine to Scotus* (London: Burns, Oates & Washbourne, 1950), pp. 186–200. See also his chapter in Frederick Copleston, *A History of Medieval Philosophy* (London: Methuen & Co., 1972), pp. 104–24. For an overview of the principal philosophers of the eastern group (al-Kindī, al-Rāzī, al-Fārābī, ibn Sīnā) and of the western group (ibn Bājjah, ibn Tufayl, ibn Rushd), see M. Mahdi, 'La philosophie islamique: les écoles orientale et occidentale', *Cultures* 4 (1977): 37–50.

3. F. E. Peters, *Aristotle and the Arabs: The Aristotelian Tradition in Islam* (New York: New York University Press, 1968; London: University of London Press, 1968), pp. 135–6. See also De Lacy O'Leary, *Arabic Thought and its Place in History*, rev. ed. (London: Kegan Paul, Trench, Trubner & Co., 1939; New York: E. P. Dutton & Co., 1939), p. 135.

4. *Encyclopaedia of Islām*, 1st ed., s.v. 'Kalām', by D. B. Macdonald.

5. According to T. J. De Boer,

> An assertion, expressed in logical or dialectical fashion, whether verbal or written, was called by the Arabs–generally but more particularly in religious teaching—a *Kalam* (λόγος) . . . . The name was transferred from the individual assertion to the entire system, and it covered also the introductory, elementary observations on Method, —and so on (T. J. De Boer, *The History of Philosophy in Islam*, trans. Edward R. Jones [London: Luzac & Co., 1933], pp. 42–3).

For a history of the origin and development of this movement, see Peters, *Arabs*, pp. 135–55; Majid Fakhry, *A History of Islamic Philosophy* (New York & London: Columbia University Press, 1970), pp. 56–81.

6. Richard Walzer, 'Early Islamic Philosophy', in *The Cambridge History of Later Greek and Early Mediaeval Philosophy*, ed. A. H. Armstrong (Cambridge: Cambridge University Press, 1970), p. 648.

7. Peters, *Arabs*, p. 140.

8. For a fine synopsis of the origin and development of Islamic atomism, see

Husâm Muhî al-Alousî, *The Problem of Creation in Islamic Thought: Qur'an, Hadith, Commentaries, and Kalam* (Baghdad: National Printing and Publishing Co., 1965), pp. 269–97.

9. See D. B. Macdonald, 'Continuous re-creation and atomic time in Muslim scholastic theology', *Isis* 9 (1927): 326–44.

10. Fakhry, *History*, p. 70.

11. W. D. Ross, *Aristotle*, 5th ed. (London: Methuen & Co., 1964; New York: Barnes & Noble, 1964), p. 177.

12. They thus arrived at a metaphysical system not dissimilar to G. W. F. Leibniz's monadology. But Leibniz's monads were 'windowless' because of his doctrine that every predicate is contained in the analysis of its subject, whereas the atoms of the *mutakallimūn* could not affect each other because each one ceased to exist the instant it was created. Moreover, Leibniz's conclusion was that everything operates according to a pre-estalished harmony infused in each monad, while the *mutakallimūn* concluded that God is the only and ever-present cause of all that happens. Whether Leibniz's system is in the end any less deterministic than that of the Islamic theologians is a matter of some controversy.

13. Majid Fakhry, *Islamic Occasionalism and its Critique by Averroës and Aquinas* (London: George Allen & Unwin, 1958), p. 30.

14. Al-Ghazali, *Tahafut al-Falasifah* [*Incoherence of the Philosophers*], trans. Sabih Ahmad Kamali (Lahore: Pakistan Philosophical Congress, 1958), pp. 185–96.

15. David Hume, *Enquiries Concerning the Human Understanding and Concerning the Principles of Morals*, 2d ed., ed. L. A. Selby-Bigge (Oxford: Clarendon Press, 1902), pp. 17–24, 42–7, 79; David Hume, *A Treatise of Human Nature*, 2 vols., with an Introduction by A. D. Lindsay (London: Dent, 1968; New York: Dutton, 1968), pp. 11, 81–5. Ghāzāli is compared to Hume by, for example, A. F. M. Hafeezullah Bhuyan, 'The Concept of Causality in Al-Ghazzali', *Islamic Culture*, April 1963, pp. 88–9.

16. In the *Tahafut*, he responds to an objector who urges that fire alone is the cause of burning in cotton and that the fire cannot but burn the cotton, since it is its nature to burn a flammable object brought into contact with it:

> This is what we deny. We say that it is God who . . . is the agent of the creation of blackness in cotton, of the disintegration of its parts, and of their transformation into a smouldering heap or ashes. Fire, which is an inanimate thing, has no action. How can one prove that it is an agent? The only argument is from the observation of the fact of burning at the time of contact with fire. But observation only shows that one is *with* the other, not that it is *by* it and has no other cause than it (Al-Ghazali, *Tahafut*, p. 186).

In his greatest religious work, Ghāzālī asserts, '. . . everything is from God. That is, God is the primal, first Cause of all (musabib-ülasbāb)', and he expounds a rigorous determinism in which everything, even man's 'free' acts are from God (Al-Ghazāli, *The Revival of Religious Sciences*, trans. Bankey Behari [Farnham, England: Sufi Publishing Co., 1972], p. 129).

17. Hume fled from what he called Pyrrhonic scepticism to a more workable mitigated scepticism. He realised that a consistent application of his sceptical

principles would be completely unliveable; he therefore appealed to Nature as the guarantor of the reasonableness of our causal inferences based on experience. Thus, beneficient Nature establishes our *belief* in causation, which we cannot prove by reason. The contrast of Hume's faith in the causal principle with Ghāzālī's denial of secondary causality is clearly seen in Hume's attack on just the sort of occasionalism espoused by Ghāzālī (Hume, *Enquiries*, pp. 158–65, 70–3; Hume, *Treatise*, pp. 178–9, 254).

18. Nicolas Malebranche, *Dialogues on Metaphysics and on Religion*, trans. Morris Ginsberg (London: George Allen & Unwin, 1923), pp. 177–201. For Malebranche God is the true and only cause of every event, so-called secondary causes being the mere occasions on which God acts (ibid., pp. 185–6, 189–90). See also Fakhry, *Occasionalism*, pp. 9–14.

19. Fakhry, *Occasionalism*, pp. 14, 56–57; Macdonald, 'Recreation', pp. 328, 333.

20. See Peters, *Arabs*, pp. 144–5; Fakhry, *History*, pp. 69–70.

21. On the issue of divine attributes, the Ash'arites believed that God did possess the attributes ascribed to him in the *Qurān*, but that these ascriptions are entirely equivocal so that they do not mean the same thing when predicated of man. As for determinism, the Ash'arites adhered to strict determinism by God, but also believed that God creates in man an accident whereby an act can be imputed to the alleged agent. For a discussion of these and other issues, see al-Ash'ari's *Kitāb al-Luma'* and *Risālat Istiḥsān al-Khawḍ fī 'Ilm al-Kalām* which are translated in Richard J. McCarthy, *The Theology of al-Ash'ari* (Beyrouth: Imprimerie Catholique, 1953).

22. Peters, *Arabs*, p. 187.

23. Writing in the twelfth century, ibn Rushd distinguishes three schools of thought within Islam concerning the problem of God's existence: (1) The literalists who disdain rational argument altogether and claim that God's existence is known on the basis of authority alone, (2) the Ash'arites (and implicitly, the Mu'tazilites) who contend that the existence of God may be rationally demonstrated from temporality (*ḥuduth*) or contingency (*jawāz*), and (3) the Sufis who believe in a direct apprehension of God apart from speculative argument (Ibn Rushd, *Al-Kashf 'an Manāhij al-Adillah*, cited in Majid Fakhry, 'The Classical Islamic Arguments for the Existence of God', *Muslim World* 47 [1957]: 133–4). We are considering the argumentation employed by the second group. For a good overview, see in addition to Fakhry 's article A. J. Wensinck, 'Les preuves de l'existence de Dieu dans la théologie musulmane', *Mededeelingen der Koninklijke Academie van Wetenschappen* 81 (1936): 41–67. According to Fakhry, prior to the rise of the Mu'tazilites, the question of the demonstrability of God's existence did not arise; belief in God was based on revelation or authority (Fakhry, 'Arguments', p. 135).

24. Ibid.

25. Al-Alousî, *Creation*, pp. 298–320.

26. Simplicius, *In Aristotelis de caelo commentaria*; Simplicius *In Aristotelis physicorum libros quattuor posteriores commentaria.*

27. Joannes Philoponus, *De aeternitate mundi contra Proclum.*

28. Ibn al-Khammār, ibn Rushd, and al-Suhrawardi all mention that Yahyā al-Nahwī argued for the temporality of the world on the basis of its finitude (Al-Alousî, *Creation*, p. 311). Al-Fārābī also knew Philoponus, perhaps in a direct

Arabic translation, as his quotations differ from those of Simplicius (Herbert A. Davidson, 'John Philoponus as a Source of Medieval Islamic and Jewish Proofs of Creation', *Journal of the American Oriental Society* 89 [1969]: 359–60). According to Davidson, references to Philoponus also occur in Sijistānī, ibn al-Haytham, and ibn Sīnā (ibid., pp. 360–1).

29. Ibid., p. 361.

30. Ibid., pp. 362–3. See also Schmuel Sambursky, 'Note on John Philoponus' Rejection of the Infinite', in *Islamic Philosophy and the Classical Tradition*, ed. S. M. Stern, Albert Hourani, and Vivian Brown (Columbia, S.C.: University of South Carolina Press, 1972), pp. 351–3. For a general overview of the Islamic–Jewish treatment of the problem of infinity, see Louis-Émile Blanchet, 'L'infini dans les pensées Juive et Arabe', *Laval théologique et philosophique* 32 (1976): 11–21.

31. See Al-Alousî, *Creation*, pp. 304, 310–11; Davidson, 'Philoponus', pp. 376–7.

32. Fakhry, 'Arguments', p. 139.

33. Simon Van Den Bergh, Notes to *Tahafut al-Tahafut* [*The Incoherence of the Incoherence*], 2 vols., by Averroes, trans. by Simon Van Den Bergh (London: Luzac & Co., 1954) 2: 2, 17–18.

34. See Al-Alousî, *Creation*, pp. 224–68.

35. Al-Suyūṭi, cited in *The Encyclopaedia of Islām*, 1971 ed., s.v. '*illa*', by H. Fleisch and L. Gardet. This distinction was apparently not shared by the philosophers, for both al-Fārābī and ibn Sīnā use *sabab* as a synonym of '*illa* (ibid.; A.-M. Goichon, *Lexique de la langue philosophique d'Ibn Sīnā* [Paris: Desclée de Brouwer, 1938], pp. 149, 237–8). As a result they argued for the eternity of the universe. A cause in actuality cannot exist without its effect; therefore, as eternal First Cause God cannot but produce the world from eternity.

36. Al-Alousî, *Creation*, pp. 238–9. Note that al-Alousī is using 'determinant' exclusively in the third sense listed by Van Den Bergh above. The argument is that if the world is not eternal, then there must be sufficient reason why God chose one moment to create rather than another, which is impossible because all moments are alike.

37. Al-Alousî, *Creation*, pp. 247–8.

38. Al-Ghazali, *Tahafut*, pp. 14–15, 23–4. One passage reads:

> The procession of a temporal (being) from an eternal (being) is absolutely impossible. For, if we suppose the eternal at a stage when the world had not yet originated from Him, then the reason why it had not originated must have been that there was no determinant for its existence, and that the existence of the world was a possibility only. So, when later the world comes into existence, we must choose one of the two alternatives (to explain it)—namely, either that the determinant has, or that it has not, emerged. If the determinant did not emerge, the world should still remain in the state of bare possibility, in which it was before. But if it has emerged, who is the originator of the determinant itself? And why does it come into being now, and did not so before? . . . In fine since all the states of the Eternal are alike, either nothing shall originate from Him, or whatever originates shall continue to originate forever (Ibid., p. 14).

39. Ibid., pp. 16, 32.

40. This fact seems to elude Fakhry, who struggles to explain away the 'flagrant contradiction' of how Ghāzālī could deny the concept of causality and yet maintain that since the universe had a beginning, before its existence there must have been a determinant which caused it to exist (Fakhry, 'Arguments', p. 141). Fakhry attempts to resolve the contradiction by stating that what the world needs is not a cause, but a determinant. But this, of course, explains precisely nothing, for Ghāzālī repudiates the need for a determinant in the sense of a reason, but affirms the need for a cause. This involves no contradiction, for Ghāzālī does not deny the causal principle; he denies *secondary* causality (Peters, *Arabs*, p. 190; Fakhry, *History*, p. 257). God is the only cause of all there is (De Boer, *History*, pp. 160, 62; Bhuyan, 'Causality', pp. 89–91). Hence, Ghāzālī is perfectly consistent in demanding a cause for the world's existence.

41. Al-Ghazali, *Tahafut*, p. 25.

42. Ibid., p. 27. This the Arabic version of the more famous Buridan's ass, the helpless animal which starved to death as it wavered indecisively between two equally appetising bundles of straw. The original problem is from Aristotle, *De caelo* B 13. 295b32, where a man equally hungry and thirsty is caught between food and drink at an equal distance. According to Leibniz's principle of sufficient reason, *everything*, even God's choices, must have a reason; therefore, Buridan's ass would have certainly starved (G. W. Leibniz, *Theodicy: Essays on the Goodness of God, the Freedom of Man, and the Origin of Evil*, trans. E. M. Huggard [London: Routledge & Kegan Paul, 1951], pp. 149–50; cf. Gottfried Martin, *Leibniz: Logic and Metaphysics*, trans. K. J. Northcott and Lucas [Manchester: Manchester University Press, 1960], pp. 9–10.), though such a situation could never occur in reality, Leibniz cautions, for two alternatives are never absolutely identical.

43. Cf. Leibniz's principle of the best, which serves to solve the same problem in a different way (G. W. Leibniz, 'Mr. Leibniz's Fifth Paper: Being an answer to Dr. Clark's Fourth Reply', in G. W. Leibniz, *The Philosophical Works of Leibnitz*, trans. George Martin Duncan [New Haven, Conn.: Tuttle, Morehouse & Taylor, 1890], pp. 255–6). Leibniz argued that God must always choose the best and that this is therefore the best of all possible worlds. Although some *mutakallimūn* would have agreed, most would have said that God's will chooses without necessarily choosing the best and why He chooses one alternative rather than another is that it is simply His choice.

44. Al-Alousî, *Creation*, p. 252. See also Herbert A. Davidson, 'Arguments from the Concept of Particularization in Arabic Philosophy', *Philosophy East and West* 18 (1968): 299–314.

45. Al-Ghazali, *Tahafut*, pp. 83–4.

46. Davidson, 'Particularization', p. 314.

47. Al-Ghāzāli, 'The Jerusalem Tract', trans. and ed. A. L. Tibawi, *The Islamic Quarterly* 9 (1965): 98. Ghāzālī's statement of the proof is simply the culmination of the thinking of the Ash'arite school, which argued in a similar fashion: 'The world is contingent. Every contingent thing must have a cause, therefore, the world must have a cause, and as no contingent thing can be the cause, that cause must be God' (M. Abdul Hye, 'Ash'arism', in *A History of Muslim Philosophy*, ed. M. M. Sharif [Wiesbaden: Otto Harrassowitz, 1963], p. 238).

48. Lenn E. Goodman, 'Ghazâlî's Argument from Creation', *International*

Journal for Middle East Studies 2 (1971): 76, 83. Cf. Fakhry, *History*, pp. 258–9.

49. Walzer, 'Philosophy', p. 648.

50. *Encyclopaedia of Islām*, 1st ed., s.v. 'Falsafa', by R. Arnaldez.

51. Peters, *Arabs*, p. 157.

52. See Etienne Gilson, *History of Christian Philosophy in the Middle Ages* (London: Sheed & Ward, 1955), pp. 181–3; Fakhry, *Occasionalism*, pp. 22–4.

53. *Encyclopaedia of Islām*, 1st ed., s.v. 'Falsafa'.

54. *Encyclopaedia of Islām*, 1st ed., s.v. 'Falāsifa', by R. Arnaldez.

55. *Encyclopaedia of Islām*, 1st ed., s.v. 'Falsafa'.

56. D. M. Dunlop, *Arab Civilization to A.D. 1500* (London: Longman, 1971), p. 175.

57. Ahmed Fouad El-Ehwany, 'Al-Kindi', in *History*, ed. Sharif, pp. 425–7.

58. Ya'qūb ibn Isḥāq al-Kindi, *Al-Kindi's Metaphysics: A Translation of Ya'qūb ibn Isḥāq al-Kindī's Treatise 'On First Philosophy'*, with an Introduction and Commentary by Alfred L. Ivry (Albany, N.Y.: State University of New York Press, 1974), pp. 12–16; Alfred L. Ivry, 'Al-Kindi as Philosopher: The Aristotelian and Neoplatonic Dimensions', in *Philosophy*, ed. Stern, Hourani, and Brown, pp. 117–24.

59. George N. Atiyeh, *Al-Kindi: The Philosopher of the Arabs* (Rawalpindi: Islamic Research Institute, 1966), p. 49. Kindi accepted the Mu'tazilite creed (Richard Walzer, 'Islamic Philosophy', in *History of Philosophy, Eastern and Western*, 2 vols., ed. S. Radhakrishnan [London: Allen & Unwin, 1953], 2: 131). However, even some of the Mu'tazilites before him, such as Abū Ḥudhayl, had tried to reconcile Aristotle's statements concerning the eternity of the world with the doctrine of creation found in the *Qur'ān* by maintaining that '. . . the universe . . . existed eternally, but in perfect quiescence and stillness, as it were latent and potential, rather than actual . . . . Creation meant that God brought in movement so that things began to exist in time and space . . .' (O'Leary, *Arabic Thought*, p. 125). But al-Kindī clearly rejects any such compromise and argues strongly for a genuine creation of the universe from nothing. In fact, Fakhry credits al-Kindī with the earliest statement of the argument from creation for the existence of God (Fakhry, 'Arguments', p. 140). For a helpful discussion of Kindī's relationship to the Mu'tazilites, see Ivry's introduction in al-Kindi, '*On First Philosophy*', pp. 22–34.

60. Atiyeh, *Al-Kindi*, p. 52. On the significance of Kindi's use of the term '*ibdā'*', see Richard Walzer, 'New Studies on Al-Kindi', in Richard Walzer, *Greek into Arabic: Essays on Islamic Philosophy*, Oriental Studies (Oxford: Bruno Cassier, 1962), pp. 187–90. Walzer cites references to Kindı's definitions of the term: 'to make a thing appear out of nothing'; 'to produce real things from nothing'. (ibid., p. 187.) Contrast this with ibn Sīnā's use of *ibda'* to mean creative emanation of being as opposed to temporal creation (*Encyclopaedia of Islām*, 1971 ed., s.v. '*ibda'*', by L. Gardet).

61. Al-Kindi, '*On First Philosophy*', pp. 67–75. See two other treatises by al-Kindī which are translated in N. Rescher and H. Khatchadourian, 'Al-Kindi's Epistle on the Finitude of the Universe', *Isis* 57 (1966): 426–33; F. A. Shamsi, 'Al-Kindi's Epistle on What Cannot Be Infinite and of What Infinity May Be Attributed', *Islamic Studies* 14 (1975): 123–44.

62. Al-Kindi, '*On First Philosophy*', pp. 67–73.

63. We here omit Kindī's attempt to prove motion must exist, as it is not really to the point and is poorly reasoned.
64. Al-Kindi, '*On First Philosophy*', pp. 73–4.
65. Ibid., pp. 74–5.
66. Walzer, 'Studies', p. 191.
67. Davidson, 'Philoponus', pp. 370–1.
68. Ibid., pp. 371–2.
69. Ibid., pp. 372–3.
70. Al-Kindi, '*On First Philosophy*', p. 68. In his treatise 'On the Unity of God and the Finiteness of the Body of the World', Kindī calls them the evident first premisses. Ivry comments, '"which are thought with no mediation": . . . i.e., as intellectual intuitions, free of prior logical, as well as physical, mediation . . .' (Alfred L. Ivry, Commentary to '*On First Philosophy*', by al-Kindi, p. 147).
71. Al-Kindi, '*On First Philosophy*', p. 70.
72. For Aristotle on the impossibility of an actually existing infinite, see Aristotle *Physica* 3. 4–8. 202b30–208a20. It is his view that the infinite can exist only potentially, as, for example, in infinite divisibility.
73. Al-Kindi, '*On First Philosophy*', p. 69.
74. Cf. H. Minkowski, 'Space and Time', in *Problems of Space and Time*, ed. with an Introduction by J. J. C. Smart, Problems of Philosophy Series (New York: Macmillan, 1964; London: Collier-Macmillan, 1964), pp. 297–312.
75. Al-Kindi, '*On First Philosophy*', p. 70.
76. Ibid.
77. I think Ivry misunderstands Kindī's argument here. Ivry says that Kindī tries to show that both *creatio ex nihilo* and infinite temporal regression are impossible, and therefore the problem of the origin of the universe is an irresolvable antimony (Ivry, 'Al-Kindi', p. 120). But this runs contrary to the whole thrust of the treatise. What Kindī is arguing here is that body cannot exist apart from motion, whether body came into being from nothing or is eternal. In the first case, its coming to be would be a motion; therefore, body does not exist without motion. Kindī does not object (as does Aristotle) to designating this as the first motion.
78. Al-Kindi, '*On First Philosophy*', p. 68.
79. Ibid., p. 72.
80. Ibid., p. 76.
81. Ibid.
82. Ibid., p. 77.
83. Ibid.
84. Ibid., p. 94.
85. Ibid., p. 112.
86. Ibid., p. 113.
87. Ibid., p. 114.
88. Fakhry, *History*, p. 95.
89. El-Ehwany, 'Al-Kindi', p. 429.
90. Ibid., pp. 429–30.
91. Fakhry, *History*, p. 125.
92. Ibid., p. 147. See also Miriam Galston, 'A Re-examination of Al-Farabi's Neoplatonism', *Journal of the History of Philosophy* 15 (1977): 13–32.
93. Emil L. Fackenheim, 'The Possibility of the Universe in Al-Farabi, Ibn

Sina and Maimonides', *Proceedings of the American Academy for Jewish Research* 16 (1946–47): 39.

94. Cf. A. -M. Goichon, *Le distinction de l'essence et de l'existence d'apres ibn Sīnā* (Paris: G. -P. Maisonneuve & Larose, 1937), pp. 130–1.

95. *Encyclopaedia of Islām*, 1st ed., s.v. 'Falsafa'.

96. Aristotle, *Analytica posteriora* 92b3–18.

97. Alfarabi, *The Gems of Wisdom*, in *Collection of Various Treatises of Alfarabi*, ed. Muhammed Ismail (Cairo: 1907), pp. 115–25.

98. Gilson, *History*, p. 185.

99. Alfarabi, *Gems*, pp. 115–25 (trans. in Robert Hammond, *The Philosophy of Alfarabi and its Influence on Medieval Thought* (New York: Hobsen Book Press, 1947], p. 14). See also Gilson, *Philosophy*, p. 186. Hamui provides this analysis of the Fārābī text:

> . . . alfarabi holds that a real distinction obtains here and that the essence and the existence of creatures differ as different entities. The principal arguments in favour of his view may be summarized as follows: (a) if essence and existence were but one thing, we should be unable to conceive the one without conceiving the other. But we are as a fact able to conceive of essence by itself. In other terms were it true that man had existence by essence, this would be equivalent to saying that to conceive man's essence is to imply his existence. So he continues with the same idea: if existence ought to enter into the essential constitution of man like one which enters into the essence of two, this would mean the impossibility of perfectly conceiving the essence of man without the essential element 'Existence', namely, just as the essence of two would be destroyed by taking away a unity from it, so would the essence of man by taking away existence from him. But it is not so. Existence does not enter into the essential composition of a thing, for it is possible to conceive the essence of man, and to ignore whether he exists in reality. (b) If there be no real distinction between the two, then the essence is identical with the existence. But in God alone are these identical (Robert Hamui, *Alfarabi's Philosophy and its influence on Scholasticism* [Sydney, Australia: Pellegrini & Co., 1928], pp. 44–5).

100. Gilson, *Philosophy*, p. 186.

101. For this view, see Francis A. Cunningham, 'Averroes *vs.* Avicenna on Being', *New Scholasticism* 48 (1974): 185–218. 'If these men were not talking about the real distinction, what, then, were they talking about? A mental difference' (ibid., p. 202). For a refutation of Cunningham's case, see Beatrice H. Zedler, 'Another Look at Avicenna', *New Scholasticism* 50 (1976): 504–21. See also note 131.

102. Fārābī accepted the Aristotelian categories of being, or substance and its accidents. See Hamui, *Philosophy*, p. 31.

103. Al-Fārābī, 'Treatise on answers to questions asked of him', in *Alfārābī's Philosophische Abhandlungen*, ed. F. Dieterici (Leiden: Brill, 1890), p. 90.

104. Nicholas Rescher, *Studies in the History of Arabic Logic* (Pittsburgh: University of Pittsburgh Press, 1963), pp. 40–1.

105. Rescher explains this by saying that Fārābī really means 'grammatical predicate' (ibid., p. 40); but this move is wholly unnecessary and leads to a

misunderstanding of Fārābī's position.

106. Gilson, *History*, p. 186.

107. Fackenheim, 'Possibility', p. 54.

108. Al-Fārābī, *Philosophische Abhandlungen*, p. 57.

109. Al-Fārābi, *Fuṣūl al-Madanī* [*Aphorisms of the Statesman*], ed. and trans. with an Introduction and Notes by D. M. Dunlop (Cambridge: Cambridge University Press, 1961), p. 58.

110. Ibid.

111. Al-Fārābi, *Philosophische Abhandlungen*, p. 57.

112. Fackenheim, 'Possibility', p. 40.

113. Aristotle *De generatione et corruptione* 337b35. Cf. Aristotle, *Metaphysica* 1026b25–30; Aristotle *Ethica Nicomachea* 1139b23.

114. Al-Fārābi, *Fusūl*, p. 65.

115. Ibid., p. 66.

116. Al-Fārābī spins out a metaphysical emanationism in which the spherical cosmology of Aristotle is blended with the Plotinian account of multiplicity. Hamui summarises the process:

> . . . From the First Being (The One) comes forth the First Intellect, Pure Soul, which is called the First Caused. From the First Intellect thinking of the First Being flows forth a second Intellect, and a Sphere. From the second Intellect comes forth a third Intellect, and a Sphere. From the third Intellect flows forth a fourth Intellect and a Sphere. And so the process goes on in necessary succession, down to the lowest Sphere, that of the Moon, from which flows forth a pure Intellect, which is the Active Intellect, and herewith end the separate intellects . . . . These ten Intellects with the nine Spheres together form the second principle of Being. The Active Intellect, bridge of conjunction between heaven and earth, constitutes the third principle. From the third principle . . . proceeds the Cosmical Soul, forming the fourth principle. Lastly appear Form and Matter, as being of the fifth and sixth principles; and with them the series of Spiritual existences is closed (Hamui, *Philosophy*, pp. 51–2).

The reason for the emanation of the First Intellect is explained by Fakhry, 'The crux of the argument . . . is that the First—owing to the superabundance of his being and perfection—generates the whole order of being in the universe by a "necessity of nature". . .' (Fakhry, *History*, p. 137). Each successive Intellect is generated by the act of its contemplation upon its predecessor (ibid.). All these beings are possible *per se*, in that their essences do not involve existence, but they are necessary *ab alio* in their eternal procession from the being of God.

117. Fackenheim, 'Possibility', p. 44.

118. Davidson, 'Philoponus', pp. 380–1.

119. Alfarabi, *The Sources of Questions*, in *Collection*, pp. 70–1.

120. Alfarabi, *Gems*, pp. 115–25. Compare the cosmological argument of ibn Rushd and Aquinas's second way.

121. Alfarabi, *Sources*, p. 66 (trans. in Hammond, *Philosophy*, p. 21).

122. Alfarabi, *Sources*, p. 65 (trans in Hammond, *Philosophy*, p. 20).

123. Aquinas usually receives the credit for developing this cosmological argument, but as both Hamui and Hammond emphasise, all of Aquinas's first

three ways are to be found in Fārābī (Hamui, *Philosophy*, pp. 40, 45; Hammond, *Philosophy*, p. 21.)

124. Fakhry, *History*, p. 147.

125. Seyed Hossein Nasr states,

> There are two major distinctions which underlie the philosophy of Ibn Sīnā, one an ontological distinction between quiddity, or essence (*māhīyāh*), . . . and existence (*wujūd*), and the other the tripartite division between the Necessary (*wājib*), possible (*mumkin*) and impossible (*mumtani'*) beings (Seyyed Hossein Nasr, *An Introduction to Islamic Cosmological Doctrines* [Cambridge, Mass.: Belknap Press of Harvard University Press, 1964], p. 198).

126. Avicenna, *Metaphysica* 8.4.

127. Soheil M. Afnan, *Avicenna: His Life and Works* (London: George Allen & Unwin, 1958), p. 117. Zedler concurs: 'What begins explicitly as a logical analysis of essence becomes in Avicenna's system a metaphysical composition of essence and existence in "created being"' (Zedler, 'Another Look', pp. 509–10).

128. Gilson, *History*, p. 189. But see note 131 below.

129. Avicenna, *Metaphysica* 8.5.

130. Gilson, *History*, p. 192.

131. But there is considerable dispute over exactly what ibn Sīnā meant by the accidentality of existence. According to Gerard Smith, it implies that essences themselves are 'stiff and spiky with reality' and that these are set over against God, who grants existence to them (Gerard Smith, 'Avicenna and the Possibles', *New Scholasticism* 17 [1943]: 346–7). God is not the ground of the possibility of possible beings or essences; rather they confront God as possible in their own right. Thus, if no universe existed, the realm of essences would even then have some measure of quasi-reality, 'dangling in the metaphysical void' between God and the non-existent universe (ibid., p. 348). More recently, however, many writers insist that such an understanding seriously misrepresents the thought of ibn Sīnā. Beatrice Zedler argues that because existence comes to a thing from without, from its cause, ibn Sīnā calls it an accident. But this is not to be taken in a literal, metaphysical sense of accident, but only in a logical sense (Beatrice H. Zedler, 'Saint Thomas and Avicenna in the "De potentia Dei"', *Traditio* 6 [1948]: 153–4.) This does not mean that ibn Sīnā's distinction between essence and existence is merely logical; the accidentality of existence makes it clear that it is a real distinction that is here conceived (Zedler, 'Another Look', pp. 504–21). Rahman and Fackenheim point out that existence is not part of the constituents of a thing like ordinary accidents; Rahman describes it as 'a relation to God', Fackenheim as a 'concomitant' of the whole (Fazlur Rahman, 'Ibn Sīna', in *History*, ed. Sharif, p. 484; Fackenheim, 'Possibility', p. 53). Parviz Morewedge maintains that for ibn Sīnā the accidentality of existence does not mean there is a ghostly, independently existing realm of essences awaiting existence. An essence has existence only 'when there is an actual individual existent of which such an essence is predicated or in which it subsists (*īstādan*)' (Parviz Morewedge, 'Ibn Sina [Avicenna] and Malcolm and the Ontological Argument', *Monist* 54 [1970]: 236). What then is existence, if not an accident? According to Rahman, ibn Sīnā took the word 'exists' in two senses: (1) the purely mental existence of ideas of objects that have no extra-mental reality, and (2) the real instantiation of

such an essence in reality (F. Rahman, 'Essence and Existence in Avicenna', *Mediaeval and Renaissance Studies* 4 [1958]: 8). It is in the second sense only that existence is added to essence:

> Hence, 'existence', or, as it should be better put, 'instantiation' of the quiddity, being something more than the quiddity itself is said by Avicenna to be 'a further fact about it', or 'to be something added to it'. Since the right meaning of 'existence' as instantiation was not understood, philosophers . . . have been led to think that existence is an 'accident' of the quiddity or essence (Ibid., pp. 8–9).

A proper understanding of ibn Sīnā's use of the term 'existence' would be a happening by which the essence actually comes to be: '. . . existence is not an element in a "thing" of the order of matter and from . . . . It is an *'araḍ*, a "happening", an event which actualizes the potentiality of form and matter' (ibid., p. 15; the same judgement is made by Parviz Morewedge, 'Philosophical Analysis and ibn Sīnā's "Essence–Existence" Distinction', *Journal of the American Oriental Society* 92 [1972]: 429). Such an interpretation would make ibn Sīnā's concept of existence very close to that of Thomas Aquinas.

132. William of Auvergne, *De trinitate* 7. See also Copleston, *Augustine to Scotus*, p. 195; Albert Judy, 'Avicenna's "Metaphysics" in the Summa contra Gentiles', *Angelicum* 52 (1975): 340–84, 541–86; esp. 554–86.

133. Nasr, *Introduction*, p. 198.

134. Ibn Sīnā, *Al-Najāt Fi al-Hikmah al-Manṭiqīyyah wa al-Tabī'ah al-Ilāhīyyah*, 2nd ed., ed. Muhie al-din Sabri al-Kurdi (Cairo: al-Saada Press, 1938), p. 224.

135. Ibid.

136. Ibn Sīnā states, '. . . the necessary being by His essence cannot be a necessary being through another . . . for what is made necessary through something else is posterior to that something else and depends upon it' (Ibn Sīnā, *al-Najāt*, p. 227).

137. Normally, impossible being is defined in terms of an essence that involves a self-contradiction. But a thing could be logically possible, but actually impossible, since if its necessary and sufficient conditions are lacking, it is actually impossible for it to appear.

138. They are necessary *ab alio*; but even this phrase can be troublesome, as Fackenheim notes,

> There is in both al-Farabi and Ibn Sina a certain ambiguity in the use of the term 'necessary *ab alio*' (الوجود بغيره واجب): (i) its first meaning is well expressed in *an-Najjāh* p. 226 . . . : 'It is evident . . . that everything that is necessary *ab alio* is *per se* possible. But this is convertible . . . Everything possible *per se*, when it exists actually, is necessary *ab alio*'. . . . In this sense, the term 'necessity *ab alio*' signifies the full determination toward existence of any being, temporal or eternal. In this sense, any substance which actually exists has 'become' necessary; the full presence of its causes has necessitated its existence . . . . (ii) The second meaning of the term 'necessary *ab alio*' is that 'impossibility of being otherwise' . . . which is possessed by such beings as exist unchangeably through an eternal and necessary nexus with the First

> Cause. In this sense, only the eternal and immaterial beings beyond the lunar sphere are 'necessary *ab alio*' in addition to being possible *per se*, whereas the sublunary temporal beings are simply possible . . . . These two meanings are not always clearly distinguished (Fackenheim, 'Possibility', pp. 40–1).

Copleston comments,

> In effect, therefore, we can say that even trees, animals, and men are hypothetically necessary, provided that we allow for the difference between such beings, which come into existence and pass away, and the immaterial intelligences which, though proceeding from God, do so eternally (Copleston, *Augustine to Scotus*, p. 114).

139. See Davidson, 'Philoponus', p. 381. Ibn Sīnā argued for the idea of eternal creation. For him creation is simply the bestowal of being to something by an efficient cause; the temporal factor is wholly irrelevant. God is the creator of the world by constantly giving it its being, and whether its being was preceded by non-being is purely accidental. The world may be eternal and yet created, utterly dependent upon God moment by moment for its continued existence (Fakhry, *History*, pp. 170–1). The universe originates in an eternal emanation or procession from God, just as the rays of the sun proceed from it. Nasr describes the generation of the universe:

> The Plotinian cosmogony which Ibn Sīnā follows . . . derives the hierarchy of creatures from Pure Being itself without in any way destroying the absolute transcendence of Being with respect to the Universe which it manifests . . . . The First Intellect . . . is possible in essence and necessary by virtue of the 'Cause of Causes', . . . or the Necessary Being itself. But because the First Intellect is possible, it generates multiplicity within itself. By intellection of the Divine Essence, it gives rise to the Second Intellect, and by intellection of its own essence to two beings which are the soul of the first heaven and its body . . . . The Second Intellect through intellection generates in a similar manner the Third Intellect, the Soul of the second heaven and its body. This process continues until the ninth heaven and the Tenth Intellect, which governs the sublunary region, are generated . . . . The heavens, therefore, are generated by a series of intellections, each Intellect actually giving being to that which it generates . . . . The ontological degree of the Intelligences is clearly distinguished from the Celestial Souls, and the Intelligences who are the angels are made definitely separate substances and the source of all forms . . . (Nasr, *Introduction*, pp. 203–4).

Thus, ibn Sīnā somewhat complicates Fārābī's scheme by distinguishing between Intelligences and the Souls of the spheres. The equation of the Intelligences with angels is probably an attempt to placate Islamic orthodoxy (cf. ibid., p. 238).

140. Ibn Sīnā, *al-Risālat al-'Arshīya*, in Arthur J. Arberry, *Avicenna on Theology* (London: John Murray, 1951), p. 25. Cf. translation of the same as well as a translation of ibn Sīnā's version of the proof from the *al-Najāt* in George F. Hourani, 'Ibn Sīnā on Necessary and Possible Existence', *Philosophical Forum* 4 (1972–3); 77, 81–2.

141. Rahman, 'Ibn Sīna', p. 482.
142. Afnan, *Avicenna*, pp. 130–1.
143. Ibn Sīnā, *al-Shifā*: *al-Ilāhiyyāt*, (I), ed. G. C. Anawati and Sa'id Zayed (Cairo: Organisation Générale des Imprimeries Governmentales, 1960), pp. 37–9. (Basically Hourani's trans.). Cf. Gilson, *History*, p. 207; Fackenheim, 'Possibility', pp. 39–40.
144. Gilson, *History*, p. 210.
145. Ibid., pp. 211–12.
146. Hourani agrees (Hourani, 'Ibn Sīnā', p. 85).
147. Ibn Sīnā, *al-Shifā'*, pp. 38–9. (Hourani's trans.).
148. Ibn Sīnā, *al-Risālat*, p. 25.
149. For example, the world; Rahman states, 'For ibn Sīnā . . . the world is an eternal existence, but since it is in itself contingent, in its entirety it needs God and is dependent upon Him eternally' (Rahman, 'Ibn Sīna', p. 503). Thus, Gilson lauds ibn Sīnā's God as truly transcendent (Etienne Gilson, *The Spirit of Mediaeval Philosophy*, trans. A. H. C. Downes [London: Sheed & Ward, 1936], p. 80). But it must be questioned whether ibn Sīnā succeeds in preserving that transcendence. Nasr points out the 'contradiction' between ibn Sīnā's ontology in which he 'clearly separates Being from all particular beings' and his cosmogeny in which he 'considers the Universe as an effusion (*faiḍ*) of Being' (Nasr, *Introduction*, p. 212).
150. Ibn Sīnā, *al-Shifa'*, p. 40 (Hourani's trans.). Gilson comments,

> . . . Avicenna shows that in any causal series of three terms, there must be a cause that is not caused, a cause that is being caused, and an effect that does not cause. The fact that there is only one intermediate cause, or many, between the first cause and the last effect, is irrelevant to the problem. In all such cases, the existence of the last effect is necessary by reason of the first cause, whose efficacy accounts for the whole series of causes and effects (Gilson, *History*, p. 212).

In his *al-Najāt*, Ibn Sīnā employs a different argument against an infinite regress of hierarchical causes. He reasons that the total series of causes, be it finite or infinite, is either necessary *per se* or possible *per se*. If it were necessary, then one would have a necessary being composed entirely of possible units, which is absurd. If it is possible, then it needs a cause, either outside the series or within the series. If it is caused by a unit within the series, this unit must be either necessary or possible. It cannot be necessary, for every unit was agreed to be possible. But if it is possible, then in causing the series to exist it causes itself to exist, which is impossible. Therefore, the cause of the total series must be outside the series. Since all possible beings were included within the series, that cause must be a necessary being. In this case, the series terminates in this being, so that the number of possible beings in the series cannot have been infinite after all (Ibn Sīnā, *al-Najāt*, p. 235). This argument is echoed in Duns Scotus's cosmological proof.
151. Ibn Sīnā, *al-Risālat*, pp. 25–6.
152. Ibid., p. 26–7.
153. Ibid., pp. 29.
154. Rahman, 'Ibn Sīna', p. 505.

155. M. Saeed Sheikh, 'Al-Ghazāli: Metaphysics', in *History*, ed. Sharif, p. 581.
156. O'Leary, *Thought*, p. 219.
157. Fakhry, *History*, p. 244.
158. Goodman, 'Creation', pp. 68–75.
159. Al-Ghazāli, *Revival*, p. 237.
160. Goodman, 'Creation', p. 75. Ghāzālī does not, however, employ the essence/existence distinction in his version.
161. Ibid., p. 77.
162. Al-Ghazali, *Tahafut*, pp. 89, 140. Cf. Goodman, 'Creation', pp. 80–1.
163. Al-Ghazali, *Tahafut*, p. 8.
164. W. Montgomery Watt, *Muslim Intellectual: A Study of Al-Ghazali* (Edinburg: Edinburgh University Press, 1963), p. 58.
165. Al-Ghāzāli, *Kitāb al-Iqtiṣād fi'l-I'tiqād*, with a Foreword by Îbrahim Agâh Çubukçu and Hüseyin Atay (Ankara: University of Ankara Press, 1962), pp. 15–16; cf. p. 20. For a detailed analysis of the *Iqtiṣād* proof, see S. de Beaurecueil, 'Gazzālī et S. Thomas d'Aquin: Essai sur la preuve de l'existence de Dieu proposee dans l'*Iqtiṣād* et sa comparison avec les "voies" Thomistes', *Bulletin de l'Institut Français d'Archaeologie Orientale* 46 (1947): 203–12. Fakhry comments on the terminology of this proof:

> The syllogism runs as follows: Everything temporal (*ḥadīth*) must have a cause. By *ḥadīth*, Al-Ghazālī tells us, he means 'what did not previously exist and then began to exist'. Prior to its existence, this 'temporal world' was 'possible' (*mumkin*) i.e. 'Could equally exist or not exist', To tilt the balance in favour of existence a 'determinant' (*murajjiḥ*) was necessary—since otherwise this possible universe would have always remained in a state of non-being.*
>
> * [*Kitāb al-Iqtiṣād fi'l-'Itiqād*], Cairo, n.d., p. 14 (Fakhry, 'Arguments', p. 141).

166. Al-Ghāzāli, *Iqtiṣād*, p. 24.
167. Al-Ghāzāli, 'Jerusalem Tract', p. 98.
168. Ibid.
169. Beaurecueil, 'Ġazzālī et S. Thomas', pp. 212–13.
170. In the *Iqtiṣād* and 'The Jerusalem Letter' Ghāzālī employes a somewhat different line of reasoning. Taking as his point of departure the existence of motion and rest, he argues: (1) bodies cannot exist without motion or rest; (2) motion and rest both have a beginning; (3) therefore, bodies (of which the world is a collection) must have had a beginning. In 'The Jerusalem Letter' he employes the typical *kalām* argument that since motion and rest are accidents, and accidents are temporal, the substance in which they inhere must be temporal. The *Iqtiṣād* also includes an involved discussion of the nature of bodies and accidents, but contains as well arguments against the possibility of an infinite temporal regress. Such a regress would be absurd because: (1) the arrival of the present moment would mean that the infinite has an end; (2) the heavenly spheres would have completed an infinite number of resolutions which must be either odd or even; and (3) infinites of different sizes would exist, all of which are absurd. The second and third arguments are found in the *Incoherence*. For analyses of these, see Goodman, 'Creation', pp. 72–5; Beaurecueil, 'Ġazzālī et S.

Thomas', pp. 203–12; Wensinck, 'Preuves', pp. 48–54.

171. Al-Ghazali, *Tahafut*, p. 32.

172. Nasr, *Introduction*, p. 230.

173. In the same way, Ghāzālī assumes for the sake of argument Aristotelian, not atomistic, metaphysics in the *Incoherence* (Davidson, 'Particularization', p. 309).

174. Al-Ghazali, *Tahafut*, p. 20.

175. Ibid., pp. 20–1.

176. Ibid., p. 21.

177. Ibid., pp. 21–2.

178. Ibid., p. 22.

179. Ibid., p. 89.

180. Ibid., p. 36.

181. Michael E. Marmura, 'The Logical Role of the Argument from Time in the Tahāfut's Second Proof for the World's Pre-Eternity', *Muslim World* 49 (1959): 306.

182. Al-Ghazali, *Tahafut*, p. 38.

183. Ibid., p. 43.

184. Ibid., p. 33

185. Beaurecueil, 'Gazzālī et S. Thomas', p. 211.

186. Ibid., p. 222.

187. See George F. Hourani, 'The Dialogue between al-Ghazālī and the Philosophers on the Origin of the World', *Muslim World* 48 (1958): 183–91.

188. Samuel Nirenstein, *The Problem of the Existence of God in Maimonides, Alanus, and Averroes: A Study in the Religious Philosophy of the Twelfth Century* (Philadelphia: Dropsie College for Hebrew and Cognate Learning, 1924), pp. 46–7.

189. Averroes, *Die Epitome der Metaphysik des Averroes*, trans. S. Van Den Bergh (Leiden: E. J. Brill, 1970), pp. 104–46; cf. Averroes, *Tahafut*, 1:34, 237–8; Gilson, *History*, pp. 221–2.

190. Averroes, *Tahafut*, 1: 165.

191. Ibid., 1: 164, 2: 104.

192. Ibid., 1: 58–9, 2: 101.

193. See O'Leary, *Thought*, pp. 275–94.

194. Ibid., p. 269.

195. De Boer, *History*, pp. 208–13.

196. Bonaventure argued that the existence of God is incompatible with the eternity of the universe and marshalled several arguments to demonstrate that the universe had a beginning (Bonaventure, 2 *Sententiarum* 1.1.1.2.1–6): (1) because it is impossible to add to the infinite, the number of days elapsed till the present cannot be infinite; (2) because it is impossible to order an infinity of terms according to beginning, middle, and end, the series of temporal events in the world could not exist from eternity; (3) because an infinite cannot be traversed, the present day could never have arrived if celestial revolutions have been going on eternally; (4) because since the Intelligences know the revolutions of their respective spheres, an infinite number of revolutions would mean that the finite could comprehend the infinite, which is impossible; and (5) infinite time would necessitate an infinite number of souls of the deceased, which is impossible because an actual infinite cannot exist. (See Etienne Gilson, *The Philosophy of St.*

Bonaventure, trans. Dom Illtyd Trethowan and F. J. Sheed [London: Sheed & Ward, 1938], pp. 190–4.) See also Francis J. Kovach, 'The Question of the Eternity of the World in St. Bonaventure and St. Thomas—A Critical Analysis', *Southwestern Journal of Philosophy* 5 (1974): 141–72; Bernardino Bonasea, 'The Impossibility of Creation from Eternity according to St. Bonaventure', *Proceedings of the American Catholic Philosophical Association* 48 (1974): 121–35; Bernardino Bonansea, 'The Question of an Eternal World in the Teaching of St. Bonaventure', *Franciscan Studies* 34 (1974): 7–33. In March of 1974 a conference at the Catholic Institute of Paris devoted itself to the relation between Bonaventure and Aristotle and Aquinas; the results of the conference include several papers on Bonaventure's argument for creation which have been published in *Miscellanea Franscescana* 75 (1975): 745–55, 757–66, 843–59, 883–92. One should also draw attention to the works of Van Steenberghen on Bonaventure, which are listed in Fernand Van Steenberghen, 'Le mythe d'un monde éternel', *Revue philosophique de Louvain* 76 (1978): 157–79.

Chapter 4

Jewish Philosophers of Religion

Standing in the gap between the Arabic philosophers of Muslim Spain and the Christian theologians of the West, the Jewish philosophers were instrumental in the transmission of Aristotelian and Arabic philosophy to medieval Europe. These Jewish thinkers were themselves to exercise considerable influence upon Christian scholasticism, so their formulations of the cosmological argument deserve our attention.[1] Spawned within Islamic culture, Jewish philosophy was to a considerable extent dependent upon Arabic philosophical thought.[2] Often writing in Arabic rather than their native tongue, Jewish philosophers tended to adopt the Arabic treatment of philosophical issues. The peculiar feature of medieval Jewish philosophy is that it preoccupied itself with specifically religious issues; accordingly, it might be more properly described as philosophy of religion, as Julius Guttmann observes:

> Even more than Islamic philosophy, it was definitely a philosophy of religion. Whereas the Islamic Neoplatonists and Aristotelians dealt with the full range of philosophy, Jewish thinkers relied for the most part on the work of their Islamic predecessors in regard to general philosophic questions, and concentrated on more specifically religio-philosophic problems . . . . the great majority of Jewish thinkers made the philosophic justification of Judaism their main subject, dealing with problems of metaphysics in a religio-philosophic context.[3]

Jewish philosophy was thus a more specialised discipline than Arabic philosophy, but for all that, it was still cast in the same mould as its Islamic predecessor. Jewish philosophy of religion was the offspring of the Muslim *kalām*, and, as Guttman remarks, the same needs that brought about the development of Islamic philosophy of religion on the part of the Mu'tazilites produced its Jewish counterpart, with the result that the 'Islamic background determined the character of medieval Jewish philosophy from beginning to end'.[4] In fact, with specific regard to the arguments for the existence of God, we find within Jewish thought the same bifurcation between *kalām* and *falsafa* that we encountered in Muslim speculation about God.[5] Thus, some Jewish philosophers employ with alacrity the *kalām* arguments from creation for the existence of God, while others disdain them, preferring to utilise arguments from motion and from necessary and possible being. But it is interesting to note that, whether their arguments were derived from the *mutakallimūn* or from the philosophers, the only argument for the existence of God employed by the Jewish thinkers was the cosmological argument. Therefore, Wolfson calls the cosmological argument based on the principle of causality 'the standard proof of the existence of God is Jewish philosophy'.[6]

Saadia

The chief exponent of the *kalām* argument from creation for the existence of God was Saadia ben Joseph (882–942), the 'first important Jewish philosopher'.[7] Although Saadia repudiated the metaphysical atomism of the Mu'tazilites, he remained dependent upon them for his proofs for God's existence.[8] Saadia presents four *kalām* arguments for creation: a proof from the finitude of the world, a proof from composition, a proof from the temporality of accidents, and a proof from the finitude of time.[9] Only the fourth argument is of real interest, however. There Saadia attempts to reduce the hypothesis of infinite time to absurdity:

> The fourth proof is [based] on [the conception of] time. That is to say, I know that there are three [distinct] periods of time: past, present, and future. Now even though the present is shorter than any moment of time, I assumed . . . that this present moment is a point and said . . .: 'Let it be supposed that a person should desire mentally to advance in time above this point. He would be unable to do it for the reason that time is infinite, and what is infinite cannot be completely traversed mentally in a fashion ascending [backward to the beginning]'.
>
> Now this same reason makes it impossible for existence to have

> traversed infinity in descending fashion so as to reach us. But if existence had not reached us, we would not have come into being . . . . Since, however, I find that I do exist, I know that existence has traversed the whole length of time until it reached me and that, if it were not for the fact that time is finite, existence could not have traversed it.[10]

Davidson demonstrates at some length Saadia's dependence on Philoponus for this proof.[11] But there are differences: for example, Saadia transforms Philoponus's argument against an infinite temporal regress of causes into an argument against an infinite regress of moments of time. According to Davidson, these changes reflect Arabic influence, indicating that Saadia received the proofs only after they had been reformulated by *kalām*.[12] We may outline Saadia's argument thus:

1. It is impossible to mentally regress through time to reach the beginning of time because:
   a. the infinite cannot be traversed,
   b. and time is, *ex hypothesi*, infinite.
2. It is impossible for existence to progress through time to reach the present moment because:
   a. existence must traverse exactly the same series that our thoughts traversed,
   b. but the traversal of such a series has been shown to be impossible.
3. Therefore, we do not now exist, which is absurd.
4. Therefore, time must be finite because:
   a. otherwise existence could never have traversed it and reached the present moment.

Saadia's first point is that *it is impossible to mentally regress through time to reach the beginning of time.* He actually speaks of ascending through time. In medieval terminology an ascending series was one that regressed from effect to cause, while a descending series was one that progressed from cause to effect.[13] Thus, Saadia contends that we cannot mentally ascend through the entire series of past moments of time since time is *ex hypothesi* infinite. No matter how far back in time our thoughts regress, an infinity of prior time always remains.

For the same reason, Saadia continues, *it is impossible for existence to progress through time to reach the present moment.* As Diesendruck points out, Saadia is arguing that the series which our thoughts traverse and the series which existence traverses are one and the same series.[14] Existence must reach the present by traversing in the opposite direction the same infinite series of temporal moments that our thoughts proved incapable of traversing. If the series of moments cannot be traversed one way, Saadia asks, why should we think that it can be traversed the other way? Saadia speaks as though time were spatialised and existence were a thing moving from one point to another along the time line. The problem with such a conception is that there is no occult entity 'existence' that moves through time as a body moves through space. But although the imagery may be defective, the point of the argument remains clear: things existing at the present moment cannot come to exist until an infinite number of prior moments and existents have elapsed. But such a series cannot elapse (be traversed). Therefore, the present moment with its existents could never arrive. Stated in this way, the argument foreshadows the thesis of Kant's first antinomy of pure reason.

It is most interesting that Saadia immediately discerns the relevance of the Zeno paradoxes to the problem of traversing past infinity, a point that modern writers on the paradoxes have failed to notice. For subsequent to the statement of the proof itself, Saadia goes on to urge that the traversal of a finite spatial distance does not actually involve traversing an infinite because in this case no actual infinite exists, only an infinitely divisible finite distance.[15] In this case infinity exists only potentially, not actually. But in contrast to this, an infinity of past time would be an actual infinity, and no actual infinity can be traversed. It might be thought that this involves Saadia in an atomistic view of time as composed of discrete moments, but this is not necessarily so. For he could admit that any finite time segment is infinitely divisible and yet traversable just as a finite distance is, but maintain that an actually infinite duration of time could no more elapse than could an actually infinite distance be traversed. In this case the present moment and its existents could never come to be.

Therefore, we do not now exist, which is absurd, Saadia concludes. The present moment has obviously arrived and existence has obviously traversed the time series. *Therefore, time must be finite*; for only if time is finite could existence reach the present moment. In this way Saadia proves that the world and time must have had a beginning. He then proceeds to argue that since nothing can cause itself to come into existence, the world must have a Creator.[16]

These further arguments need not concern us, and a schematisation of Saadia's proof would virtually reproduce our outline, so I omit it here. The most interesting portion of his proof is his case against infinite time, which, like all problems concerning the infinite, is extremely fascinating and possesses such allure that even Kant adopted a nearly identical argument, which he regarded as cogent in itself, for proving the thesis of his first antimony.

Maimonides

By far and away the most significant Jewish philosopher of the Middle Ages is Moses ben Maimon (1135–1204), or Maimonides, affectionately referred to by the Latin scholastics as Rabbi Moses. With Maimonides we reach 'the high water mark of medieval Jewish philosophy'.[17] He argues the case for God's existence from the standpoint of the philosophers, not the *mutakallimūn*, and he eschews the *kalām* arguments for creation.[18] In the light of Leo Strauss's insistence that the *Guide* is 'under no circumstances a philosophic book',[19] it might be questioned whether our categorising Maimonides as a representative of the philosophical tradition of theistic argumentation is quite accurate. But while it is true that Maimonides, like the Christian scholastics after him, was really at heart a theologian, his proofs for the existence of God grow exclusively out of the philosophic tradition, not out of *kalām*, and, hence, he may be classed as a philosopher in this sense. Moreover, even Strauss himself points out that

> . . . Maimonides insists on the necessity of starting from evident presuppositions, which are in accordance with the nature of things, whereas the *kalâm* proper starts from arbitrary presuppositions, which are chosen not because they are true but because they make it easy to prove the beliefs taught by the law.[20]

We observed in the preceding chapter that one of the earmarks of philosophy as opposed to *kalām* was that it did not use religious doctrinal positions for its point of departure. In proving God's existence, Maimonides strictly follows this procedure, for he lays down twenty-six propositions proven by the philosophers as foundational to his arguments.[21] Thus, in proving the existence of God, Maimonides proceeds as a philosopher.

He opens his proofs for the existence of God by positing twenty-six propositions.[22] These principles have been 'fully established', and their correctness is 'beyond doubt', states Maimonides, since 'Aristotle and the Peripatetics who followed him have proved each of these propositions'.[23] But the twenty-sixth proposition, the one which posits the eternity of the universe, Maimonides does not accept, but will admit for the sake of argument.[24]

Maimonides then introduces his first argument, the proof from motion. Too lengthy to quote verbatim, we may summarise the proof in this way: There must be a cause of the change in the transient sublunary world. This cause is itself caused by another. The series of moving causes cannot be infinite; it must ultimately derive from the heavenly sphere which causes all motion by its rotary locomotion. There must be a cause of the motion of this sphere, either within the sphere or without it. If the cause is without the sphere, it is either corporeal or incorporeal. It is incorporeal, it is not properly 'without' the sphere, but 'separate' from the sphere. If the cause is within the sphere, it may be extended throughout it and be divisible, or it may be indivisible. Thus, we have four alternatives: the motion of the sphere may be caused by (1) a corporeal object without the sphere, (2) an incorporeal object separate from the sphere, (3) an internal force extended throughout the whole sphere, or (4) an indivisible force within the sphere. The first alternative is impossible because this cause would require another cause and so on, *ad infinitum*. But this would involve an infinite number of spheres, which is impossible. The third alternative is impossible because the sphere, being corporeal, must be finite. Therefore, the force it contains must be finite, and a finite force cannot cause eternal motion. The fourth alternative is impossible because then the soul of the sphere would be moved accidentally, and a thing moved accidentally must come to rest. Thus, it could not cause eternal motion. This means only the second alternative can be affirmed; Maimonides proclaims triumphantly, 'This Prime Motor of the sphere is God, praised be His name!'[25] The reader will recognise the Aristotelian origin of the proof. According to Husik, the proof from motion was first introduced into Jewish philosophy by Abraham ibn Daud (d. 1180?), and Maimonides's version differs from that of his Jewish predecessor primarily in being more elaborate.[26] But Maimonides's thoughtful formulation of the argument historically marks him as the third great champion of the proof for God from motion; for, amazing as it may seem, during the nearly fourteen long centuries separating Maimonides and Aristotle, no truly great proponent of the prime mover argument except ibn Rushd ever arose.[27] Neoplatonic arguments for the One were much more in vogue, and the nearly millenium and a half between the Greek and Jewish philosophers saw only incidental use of the proof from motion. It must seem no less astounding to moderns to find Maimonides confidently expounding the same astronomical system of spheres as that propounded by Aristotle in the fourth century B.C. But this is testimony both to the overpowering influence of Aristotle's intellect and to the sluggish progress of a world lacking the scientific method of experimentation.

We may outline Maimonides's proof as follows:

1. There must be a cause for the motion or change of transient things in the sublunary world because:
   a. prop. 25.
2. There must be a cause of the motion of the cause.
3. This causal series of motions cannot be infinite and will cease at the first heavenly sphere, which is the source of all sublunary motion, because:
   a. prop. 3.
4. There must be a cause for the motion of this sphere because:
   a. prop. 17.
5. This cause may reside without the sphere or within it.
6. If it resides without the sphere it may be corporeal or incorporeal (in which case it is really separate from, not without, the sphere).
7. If it resides within the sphere, it may be extended throughout the sphere and be divisible, or it may be an indivisible force.
8. Therefore, the cause for the motion of this sphere must be either a corporeal object without the sphere, an incorporeal object separate from the sphere, a divisible force extended throughout the sphere, or an indivisible force within the sphere.
9. It cannot be a corporeal object without the sphere because:
   a. a corporeal object is itself moved when it sets another object in motion,
   b. and this corporeal object would need another corporeal object to set it in motion, and so on, *ad infinitum*;
   c. but this is impossible
      i. because of prop. 2.
10. It cannot be a divisible force extended through the sphere because:
    a. the sphere is finite
       i. because of prop. 1,
    b. and therefore the force it contains must be finite
       i. because of prop. 12;
    c. but a finite force cannot produce an eternal motion.
11. It cannot be an indivisible force within the sphere because:
    a. as the sphere moves, the force would be moved accidentally
       i. because of prop. 6,
    b. and things that move accidentally must come to rest

i. because of prop. 8;

c. therefore, it could not cause eternal motion.

12. Therefore, the cause for the motion of this sphere must be an incorporeal object separate from the sphere, or God.

Let us briefly analyse the proof step by step. First, *there must be a cause for the motion or change of transient things in the sublunary world.* Like Aristotle, Maimonides selects as his point of departure an empirically observable facet of experience, namely change. This marks the *a posteriori* character of the proof. The support for the first step is the twenty-fifth proposition, which is the Aristotelian analysis of change in terms of matter and form. Whenever change occurs, it is because the primary matter has been imbued with a new form. The proposition asserts that every such change requires a cause which moves the matter to receive the form. The analysis here ultimately reduces to Aristotle's actuality/potentiality distinction, for the form is the actuality that causes the pure potentiality of matter to be a certain thing. Being purely potential, matter cannot actualise itself; therefore, there must be some cause. Hence, there must be a cause for the motion or change of transient things in the sublunary world.

Second, *there must be a cause of the motion of this cause.* Maimonides assumes that the cause of motion in step 1 is itself in motion. For if it were an unmoved mover, his point would be proved. Therefore, he takes it to be in motion just like its effect. He adds that the motion of this cause will be either the same as the kind it causes or different, but he does not develop the point. Aristotle, it will be remembered, had argued that the kinds of motion are finite in number, and therefore there could not be infinite movers. But Maimonides has no need of this argument and lets it lie. Unlike Aristotle, Maimonides also includes substantial change, or generation and corruption, as a kind of motion right from the start of his proof. The same analysis of actuality and potentiality that required a cause of the motion in step 1 also requires that there must be a cause of the motion of this cause.

Step 3 asserts that *this causal series of motions cannot be infinite and will cease at the first heavenly sphere, which is the source of all sublunary motion.* Maimonides supports the step by use of proposition 3, that an infinite number of causes and effects is impossible, this being so because any infinite magnitude cannot actually exist (propositions 1 and 2). Now this is extremely interesting because it marks a sharp departure from the Aristotelian argument from motion. It will be remembered that Aristotle's *tour de force* against the infinite regress is that in a hierarchically arranged series of simultaneous causes of motion, the intermediate causes have no causal efficacy of their own, being mere instruments, and, thus, a first cause must exist to produce the given effect. Maimonides completely abandons this line of reasoning: he makes no mention of the impossibility of a so-called essential series of causes, arguing instead that an infinite number of actual existents cannot exist. He believed that an infinite series of causes and effects could exist extending back into the past, for it was his opinion that the eternity of the world is philosophically possible, even if not plausible. But in that case, the infinite number of entities do not co-exist, for they appear successively; it is the co-existence of an infinite number of finite things that is impossible. In arguing against an infinite series of causes of motion, Maimonides thus makes it evident that he, like Aristotle, is thinking of simultaneous causes of motion, for these all co-exist. The causes of motion cannot be infinite, not because of any analysis of the nature of essential causality, but because an actual infinite cannot exist. This step of the proof also brings into full view the Aristotelian system of the spheres. Maimonides asserts that the causes of sublunary motion can only go so far until they reach the motion of the fifth element, by which he apparently means the ether of which the spheres are composed in contrast to the four elements of the sublunary world, earth, water, air, and fire. The spheres are the source of all motion on earth, according to Maimonides, and he furnishes an exceedingly instructive example:

> The motion of the fifth element is the source of every force that moves and prepares any substance on earth for its combination with a certain form, and is connected with that force by a chain of intermediate motions. The celestial sphere [or the fifth element] performs the act of locomotion which is the first of the several kinds of motion (Prop. XIV.), and all locomotion is found to be the indirect effect of the motion of this sphere; e.g., a stone is set in motion by a stick, the stick by a man's hand, the hand by the sinews, the sinews by the muscles, the muscles by the nerves, the nerves by the natural heat of the body, and the heat of the body by its form. This is undoubtedly the immediate motive cause, but the action of the immediate motive cause is due to a certain design, e.g., to bring the stone into a hole by striking against it with a stick in order to prevent the draught from coming through the crevice. The motion of the air that causes the draught is the effect of the motion of the celestial sphere. Similarly it may be shown that the ultimate cause of all generation and destruction can be traced to the motion of the sphere.[28]

One of the key moves in the prime mover argument is to get away from sublunary motion to astronomical motion. Otherwise, the human soul takes on the character of an unmoved mover. Here again Maimonides leaves Aristotle, referring to the Greek philosopher's argument in the passing mention of generation and destruction as ultimately assignable to the sphere. Maimonides instead argues that the soul (which is the form of the body) does indeed have a cause for its causal activity. The causes of the soul's activity are its motives, and its motives are determined by external factors. Thus, Maimonides moves from the world into the soul and back into the world again, which allows him to move up to the heavenly sphere as the cause of certain environmental factors. What is so interesting about this is that Maimonides seems to have unwittingly involved himself in total determinism for, as his example illustrates so clearly, even the 'free' acts of man are determined by purely physical factors. If he denies this, then every human soul may be an unmoved mover. For even if the soul causes certain effects because of determining external influences, it is nonetheless *unmoved*. We might say it is moved to action by some cause, but that is an equivocal use of the word 'moved', meaning 'motivated', for the soul does not move *per se.*[29] In what sense, then, does Maimonides contend that the sphere is the source of all sublunary motion, when clearly the soul is the unmoved source of at least some motion? The answer is that the sphere is the source of all sublunary motion in that it causes the external factors that determine the purposes of the soul. Thus, even the motion caused by the soul is ultimately caused by the sphere. Therefore, what Maimonides is really about is the demonstration of cosmic determinism. His argument is not a simple proof from motion, that *z* is moved by *y*, and *y* by *x*, and so on, back to *a*. This sort of chain is broken when one reaches the soul, for it is not moved at all. But Maimonides wants to show that when the soul causes motion, it does so because of the factors determined by the motion of the sphere.

The fourth step asserts that *there must be a cause for the motion of this sphere*. Maimonides cites preposition 17 as the basis of this step. The root analysis is the same as that found in step 1, the Aristotelian distinction of actuality and potentiality. Step 5 asserts a disjunction: *this cause may reside without the sphere or within it*. Step 6 posits a further disjunction within the first disjunct above: *if it resides without the sphere, it may be corporeal or incorporeal* (*in which case it is really separate from, not without, the sphere*). Step 7 posits a disjunction within the second disjunct of step 5: *if it resides within the sphere, it may be extended throughout the sphere and be divisible, or it may be an indivisible force*. The disjunction is based on proposition 11, which asserts that things existing through a material object may be extended and divisible (like colour or heat) or it may be indivisible (like the intellect or soul). This means that there exist four alternatives: *the cause for the motion of this sphere must be either a corporeal object without the sphere, an incorporeal object separate from the sphere, a divisible force extended throughout the sphere, or an indivisible force within the sphere.* Maimonides now proceeds to eliminate three of the alternatives.

He argues in the ninth step that *it cannot be a corporeal object without the sphere.* Proposition 9 requires that when one corporeal object moves another, it can do so only by setting itself in motion. That means that if the sphere were set spinning by another enclosing sphere, this latter would also have to be revolving. But then it would require some cause of its motion as well. Thus, the initial problem is only encountered again at a later step. Because of the impossibility of an infinite number of actual existents, there cannot be an infinite number of spheres. Maimonides makes no reference to the Aristotelian argument against an infinite series in this step any more than he did in step 3. The argument here does not prove that there is only one heavenly sphere directly moved by God; Maimonides would have to admit that this sphere could be moved immediately by a corporeal object without the sphere, that is, another sphere, but he insists that this only delays the problem and cannot settle it.[30] Because no actual infinite can exist, the motion of the sphere cannot ultimately be caused by another sphere—there must be an outermost sphere not moved by another. Therefore, the cause of the motion of the sphere cannot be a corporeal object without the sphere.

Maimonides skips down to the third alternative and argues that *it cannot be a divisible force extended throughout the sphere.* The sphere being corporeal, it must also be finite, since proposition 1 declares that no actual infinite can exist. Since the sphere is finite, the force it contains must also be finite, for, according to proposition 12, a force that occupies all parts of a corporeal object is finite. And according to this alternative, the force does occupy all parts of the sphere, being extended throughout. No doubt Maimonides is reasoning that if each part contains a determinate quantum of force, then a finite number of parts will produce a finite quantum of force. But a finite force cannot produce an infinite, eternal motion, such as was assumed according to proposition 26. The argument harks back to Philoponus's proofs of the temporality of the universe, as we saw in the last chapter, and ultimately to Aristotle himself. It assumes that a finite force cannot do a finite amount of work for an infinite time. For these reasons, the cause of the sphere's motion cannot be a divisible force extended throughout the sphere.

Maimonides in step 11 dismisses the fourth alternative: *it cannot be an indivisible force within the sphere.* In other words, the sphere is not a self-mover moved by its own soul. Here Maimonides does employ the Aristotelian argument concerning the soul's accidental motion, but he does so with a twist. As the sphere turns, its soul would be moved accidentally, according to proposition 6. Maimonides illustrates accidental motion by the example of a nail in a boat; the nail itself is firmly fixed, but as the boat moves, so does the nail. A more modern example might be that of a stationary man standing in a lift; though he himself does not move, as the lift moves to the top floor, the man moves in a secondary or accidental sense. So also when a body/soul composite moves about, the body moves essentially, but the soul only accidentally.[31] Therefore, the soul of the sphere would be moved accidentally by the sphere's rotation. But according to proposition 8, things moved accidentally must come to rest. This is so because a thing moved accidentally 'does not move of its own accord';[32] for example, the soul moves only because of the body's motion. But since the soul causes the body's motion, could not the soul cause the body to move eternally, and so itself be moved accidentally forever? Here again, Maimonides's determinism comes to the fore; this is impossible, he contends, for the soul only moves the body at the instigation of external causes, and, according to this alternative, there are no external causes superior to the soul of the sphere.[33] Since there are no eternal entities other than the sphere, there would be nothing to move the sphere from eternity. The reasoning is reminiscent of Aristotle's unmoved mover, which eternally moves the spheres by acting as the eternal object of desire for their respective souls. If the sphere were moved by its soul, then either there must be some more ultimate cause of its motion in terms of external determining factors existent from eternity, or it would come to rest. In either case, the sphere does not ultimately cause its own motion. Thus, the cause of the sphere's motion cannot be an indivisible force within the sphere.

The conclusion is that alternative two must be affirmed and that *therefore, the cause for the motion of this sphere must be an incorporeal object separate from the sphere, or God.* There must exist a source of all motion which is incorporeal, separate from the material universe, unmoved either essentially and accidentally, and eternal. This, proclaims Maimonides, is God.

We may schematise Maimonides's first proof as follows:

1. There must be a cause for the motion of things in the sublunary world.
2. This causal series of motion cannot be infinite and will cease at the

first heavenly sphere, which is the source of all sublunary motion.

a. It cannot be infinite.
   i. In a series of the causes of motion, all the causes exist simultaneously.
   ii. An infinite number of things cannot actually exist.
   iii. Therefore, the number of causes and effects must be finite.

b. It will cease at the first heavenly sphere.
   i. Things in motion are either moved by another or self-moved.
   ii. Things moved by another are ultimately moved by the sphere.
      a. Things moved by another ultimately derive their motion from environmental factors determined by the sphere.
   iii. Things self-moved are ultimately moved by the sphere.
      a. Self-movers move only at the stimulus of external factors.
      b. These factors are determined by the sphere.
      c. Thus, self-movers ultimately are caused to move by the sphere.
   iv. Therefore, all sublunary motion is ultimately caused by the sphere.

3. There must be a cause for the motion of this sphere.
4. This cause may be either a corporeal object without the sphere, an incorporeal object separate from the sphere, a divisible force extended throughout the sphere, or an indivisible force within the sphere.
5. It cannot be a corporeal object without the sphere.
   a. A corporeal object is itself moved when it sets another object in motion.
   b. This corporeal object must have another corporeal object as a cause of its motion, and so on.
   c. This causal series cannot be infinite (2.a.).
   d. Therefore, a corporeal object without the sphere cannot be the ultimate cause of motion of the sphere.
6. It cannot be a divisible force extended throughout the sphere.
   a. The sphere must be finite.
      i. For no actual infinite can exist.
   b. Therefore, the force it contains must be finite.
   c. And a finite force cannot cause eternal motion.
   d. But motion is eternal, according to the hypothesis.
   e. Therefore, a divisible force extended throughout the sphere cannot be the ultimate cause of the motion of the sphere.
7. It cannot be an indivisible force within the sphere.
   a. As the sphere moves, the soul of the sphere would move accidentally.

b. Things that move accidentally must come to rest.
   i. They do not move of their own accord, but are caused to move by the stimulus of external factors.
   ii. But no external factors are eternal.
   iii. Therefore, things moved accidentally cannot be in motion forever.
c. Therefore, the soul of the sphere could not cause eternal motion.
d. But motion is eternal, according to the hypothesis.
e. Therefore, an indivisible force within the sphere cannot be the ultimate cause of the motion of the sphere.

8. Therefore, the cause for the motion of the sphere must be an incorporeal object separate from the sphere, or God.

What can be known of the nature of God? Maimonides has already in the proof itself called attention to God's incorporeality, separateness, utter immobility, and eternity. In addition to that, he argues, God must be indivisible and unchangeable. For according to proposition 7, whatever moves is divisible, and since God cannot move, he must be indivisible. And according to proposition 5, motion implies actuality and potentiality; God, not being able to move, must not possess any potentiality to change. Moreover, there is only one God, for, according to proposition 16, incorporeal beings cannot be counted. Finally, God transcends time because, according to proposition 15, things which do not move have no relation to time, as time cannot exist apart from motion. Thus, from the prime mover argument alone, Maimonides seeks to establish a God characterised by some of the traditional theistic attributes.

Maimonides's second argument, a more simple argument from motion, he ascribes to Aristotle:

> If there be a thing composed of two elements, and the one of them is known to exist also by itself, apart from that thing, then the other element is likewise found in existence by itself separate from that compound. For if the nature of the two elements were such that they could only exist together—as, e.g., matter and form—then neither of them could in any way exist separate from the other. The fact that the one component is found also in a separate existence proves that the two elements are not indissolubly connected and that the same must therefore be the case with the other component. Thus we infer from the existence of honey-vinegar and of honey by itself, that there exists also vinegar by itself. And after having explained this Proposition

> Aristotle continues thus: We notice many objects consisting of a *motor* and a *motum*, i.e., objects which set other things in motion, and whilst doing so are themselves set in motion by other things; such is clearly the case as regards all the middle members of a series of things in motion. We also see a thing that is moved, but does not itself move anything, viz., the last member of the series; consequently a *motor* must exist without being at the same time a *motum*, and that is the Prime Motor, which, not being subject to motion, is indivisible, incorporeal, and independent of time, as has been shown in the preceding argument.[34]

The argument may be outlined as follows:

1. Given a thing composed of two elements, if one of the elements exists separately, then the other element does so as well because:
   a. the separate existence of one element proves that the two elements are not so indissolubly united that they cannot exist separately.
2. We see in experience objects that are in motion and move others and objects that are in motion but do not move others.
3. Therefore, there must be something that moves other things but is not itself in motion.
4. This is the Prime Mover, or God.

The argument is straightforward enough. Step 1 tells us that *given a thing composed of two elements, if one of the elements exists separately, then the other element does so as well.* Maimonides recognises that not all composites are capable of being divided. Primary matter, for example, cannot exist alone, but only in conjunction with form. But, he argues, when we see one of the two elements existing alone and that same element existing in combination with another, it is a valid inference that when this element is extracted from the composite, the other element will continue to exist.

Step 2 continues: *we see in experience objects that are in motion and move others and objects that are in motion but do not move others.* Maimonides views motion and causing motion as a sort of composition in a being. For example, the stick is set in motion by the hand and moves the stone. The stone is in motion but moves nothing else. Thus, the stick has a combination of two elements, while in the stone only one element exists alone.

The conclusion is that *therefore, there must be something that moves other things but is not itself in motion.* Maimonides simply applies the reasoning of step 1 to motion. Since the element of being in motion can exist alone, then the element of causing motion can exist by itself.

This is the Prime Mover, or God. This assumes the cogency of the foregoing proof. For the human soul would fit quite nicely the description given in step 3. But Maimonides presupposes the ascription of sublunary motion to the causal efficacy of the spheres and the motion of the spheres themselves, which no one could seriously believe to be caused by the human soul.

Any schematisation of the proof would be the same as the outline. The only real point of interest in the argument is that it is unusual in employing an analogical form of reasoning, which is more commonly associated with the teleological argument. There one argues that in the same way that we assume that products evidencing the adaptation of means to ends imply a designer, so we assume that the universe must have a designer; here Maimonides maintains that in the same way that we assume that the existence of a separate element from a composite implies that the other element can also exist alone, so we assume there must be a mover which is not in motion. Hence, this is a cosmological argument using analogical reasoning.

Maimonides's third proof is an extremely important version of the cosmological argument and may be summarised as follows: Many things actually exist, as is evident by the senses. There are three alternatives concerning these: (1) all things are without beginning and end, (2) all things have a beginning and end, or (3) some things have a beginning and end. The first is clearly refuted by the testimony of the senses. The second is inadmissable, because then everything could cease to exist, and that which is said of a whole class of things must actually happen. Everything, then, would cease to exist, and, since something cannot come from nothing, nothing would ever exist. But since we see things existing and we ourselves exist, we may conclude that since transitory things exist, there must be an eternal being not capable of ceasing to exist and whose existence is real, not just possible. This being is necessary, either on its own account or on account of some external force. If it is the latter, then its existence or non-existence is equally possible in itself, but its existence is made necessary through the external force. That force, then, is the absolutely necessary being. This being possesses absolutely independent existence and is the source of the existence of all things. We may outline Maimonides's third proof in this way:

1. Many things exist because:
   a. we perceive them with the senses.
2. There are three alternatives: all things are without beginning and end,

all things have beginning and end, or some things have beginning and end.

3. It is impossible that all things are without beginning and end because:
   a. we clearly perceive objects that come into and pass out of existence.
4. It is impossible that all things have beginning and end because:
   a. then all things might cease to exist,
   b. and whatever is said to be possible of a whole class of things must actually happen.
   c. Therefore, everything would cease to exist.
   d. But then nothing would exist now
      i. because there would be no being to cause things to exist.
   e. But this is not true
      i. because we perceive existing things,
      ii. and we ourselves exist.
5. Therefore, there must be an eternal, indestructible being, whose existence is real, not merely possible.
6. This being is necessary on its own account or on account of some external force.
7. If it is necessary on account of some external force, then it would be necessary because of that force, though it would be possible in itself.
8. The external force, therefore, is the absolutely necessary being, the source of the existence of all things.

Though Maimonides gives Aristotle the credit for this proof, the reader will immediately recognise the work of al-Fārābī and ibn Sīnā. According to Husik the argument from possible and necessary being is introduced into Jewish philosophy by Abraham ibn Daud.[35] Maimonides is too great a thinker, however, to simply parrot his Arabic and Jewish predecessors, and therefore a thorough analysis of his version of the proof should be rewarding.

The first step is characteristic of the cosmological argument from contingent being: *many things exist*. The justification is entirely *a posteriori*; we know things exist because we perceive them with our senses.

Second, *there are three alternatives: all things are without beginning and end, all things have beginning and end, or some things have beginning and end*. Maimonides states the alternatives poorly, for the compound predicate makes the statements confusing. We might ask why all things or something might not have a beginning but no end, or have an end but no beginning. But if all things had one of the conjuncts but not the other, then alternative 1 would cover it, since it can be stated, 'no things have beginning and end'. And if some things possessed just one of the conjuncts, alternative 3 would cover it, 'some things have beginning and end'. It is clear that Maimonides is taking the predicate as a unity, 'beginning-and-end'. Either no things have beginning-and-end, all things have beginning-and-end, or some things have beginning-and-end. A more simple way of putting it is to use the word 'eternal'. Thus, the alternatives would be: all things are eternal, no things are eternal, or some things are eternal. This clearly covers all the possibilities. For consistency's sake, it is best for now to retain the original language of the proof: there are three alternatives: all things are without beginning and end, all things have beginning and end, or some things have beginning and end.

The first alternative is easily eliminated: *it is impossible that all things are without beginning and end* because we see objects in the world which come to exist and then are destroyed.

Next *it is impossible that all things have beginning and end.* In other words, not every thing can be transitory in existence, coming to be and passing away. He states,

> The second case is likewise inadmissible, for if everything had but a temporary existence all things might be destroyed, and that which is enunciated of a whole class of things as possible is necessarily actual. All things therefore must come to an end, and then nothing would ever be in existence, for there would not exist any being to produce anything. Consequently, nothing whatever would exist [if all things were transient]; but as we see things existing, and find ourselves in existence, we conclude as follows:—Since there are undoubtedly beings of a temporary existence, there must also be an eternal being that is not subject to destruction, and whose existence is real, not merely possible.[36]

In this very interesting argument, Maimonides contends that if no thing were eternal, then it would be possible for everything to simply lapse into non-existence. And once absolutely nothing existed, something could never re-appear, for nothing would exist to bring it into being. In other words, out of nothing, nothing comes. If there were nothing—no matter, no space, no time, no God—then nothing could ever come into existence, he argues. Maimonides must be assuming in the third proof that time is infinite, just as he did in the first proof. For he maintains that if nothing were eternal, then it would be possible that all things might cease to exist. But if time is not infinite, this is not necessarily so. For it is possible that the universe began *ex nihilo* at some point a finite number of years ago and will continue to exist indestructibly into the future. Similarly, Christianity holds that the human soul is immortal, but not eternal, unlike Plato, who believed in the pre-existence and eternity of soul. Hence, it is not strictly true to say that if no thing were eternal, then everything could lapse into non-existence: for a thing may be indestructible, but not eternal.[37] This realisation would not be damaging, however, for it would simply force the insertion of an extra clause into the argument. Maimonides could have argued that if no things were eternal then either (1) all things came into existence from nothing or (2) it is possible that all things might cease to exist. In either case, the refutation is the same: out of nothing, nothing comes.[38] Hence, nothing would exist now. And this is absurd on two counts: (1) we clearly perceive existing things all around us, and (2) we are aware of our own individual existence. Now the crucial premiss in this argument is 4.b. For certainly 4.a. appears true enough: it must be remembered that even matter would be included in the 'things' Maimonides is talking about. If every thing had a beginning and an end (or even just an end), then it is possible that everything could simply cease to exist. The real problem concerns the existence of transitory beings whose life-spans overlap, such that before one ceases to be another comes into being. Could not such a series be eternal? Maimonides argues that it cannot: whatever is said to be possible of a whole class of beings must actually happen. In a letter to ibn Tibbon, Maimonides elucidates the point:

> When the possible is said of a species, it is necessary that it exists in reality in certain individuals of this species: for if it never existed in any individual, it would be *impossible* for the species, and what right would one have to say that it is *possible*? If, for example, we say that writing is a thing possible for the human race, it is necessary then that there be men who write at a certain time: for if one held that there is never any man who writes, that would be saying that writing is impossible for the human race. It is not the same for the *possible* which is said of an individual: for if we say that it is possible that this child writes or does not write, it does not follow from this possibility that the child must necessarily write at one particular moment. Therefore, the *possible* said of a species is not, properly speaking, in the category of the possible, but is in some ways *necessary*.[39]

Maimonides is arguing that every possible that really deserves the name must, if it is enunciated of a whole class of things, be actualised at some time. Therefore, given an infinite time, which would be presupposed by a beginning-less series of overlapping transitory beings, the possibility of everything's vanishing would have to be actualised. The root of this is probably grounded in Aristotle's contention that the possible is that which can be other than it is, and every possible *must* at some time be actual.[40] Thus, if it is possible for nothing to exist, then at some point in infinite time, nothing will exist. And, asserts Maimonides, that point having been reached nothing would ever exist again. Thus, because in infinite time everything would cease to exist if no eternal thing exists, it is impossible that all things have beginning and end.

Maimonides concludes, *therefore, there must be an eternal, indestructible being whose existence is real, not merely possible.* It is interesting that he contrasts the real with the possible; it is evident that he is speaking in terms of actual necessity and possibility, not logical necessity and possibility. It ought also to be kept in mind that he has not concluded to God, but simply to some eternal thing(s), whether it be matter, or the spheres, or the Intelligences.

In the sixth step, Maimonides states that *this being is necessary on its own account or on account of some external force.* In this step Maimonides uses 'necessary' in the sense of eternal, just as Fārābī and ibn Sīnā do on occasion. It is further evident that the external force is the cause of the necessary being. Thus, we have the familiar distinction between necessary *per se* and necessary *ab alio* here repeated. Maimonides is inquiring whether the eternal being discovered in the first five steps is absolutely necessary or it is derivatively necessary, that is, eternal but nonetheless dependent upon a cause for its existence.

Step 7 proceeds, *if it is necessary on account of some external force, then it would be necessary because of that force, though it would be possible in itself.* Maimonides puts it this way: '. . . its existence and non-existence would be equally possible, because of its own properties, but its existence would be necessary on account of the external force'.[41] This brings to mind the essence/existence distinction of Fārābī and ibn Sīnā. For in what sense can this being's existence and non-existence be said to be equally possible, when it has been proved to exist necessarily? The answer can only be that its existence is possible in itself; its essence does not involve existence, or as Maimonides says, its properties, that is, its essential attributes, do not require that it exist. Hence, it must have what we have called an existential cause which causes its existing by continually conjoining existence to its essence.[42] Although it is derivatively necessary on account of its existential cause, it is nonetheless possible in itself because its essence does not involve existence.

Maimonides then concludes in step 8, *the external force, therefore, is the absolutely necessary being, the source of the existence of all things.* This is the being whose essence involves existence and is therefore not merely necessary in the sense of eternal, but is absolutely necessary, that is, it possesses 'absolutely independent existence' and is 'the source of the existence of all things, whether transient or permanent'.[43] It is necessary *per se* whereas all other beings are possible *per se*. It is of interest to note that for Maimonides the existence of a contingent being is apparently immediately caused by the absolutely necessary being, for he has no argument here against an infinite regress of contingent causes of existence. He proceeds without intermediary from the contingent being to the absolutely necessary external force. We may schematise Maimonides's proof in this fashion:

1. Many things exist.
   a. The testimony of our senses makes this undoubtable.
2. There are three alternatives concerning the existence of these things: all things are eternal, no things are eternal, or some things are eternal.
3. It is impossible that all things are eternal.
   a. We clearly perceive some things that come into and pass out of existence.
4. It is impossible that no things are eternal.
   a. If no thing were eternal, then it is possible that all things could cease to exist.
   b. What is said to be possible of a whole class of things must eventually actually happen, given sufficient time.
   c. Therefore, everything would have ceased to exist.
      i. Given infinite past time, all possibilities would have to have been actualised.
      ii. The existence of nothing is a possibility (4.a.).
      iii. Therefore, the possibility of the existence of nothing would have to have been actualised.
   d. But then nothing would exist now.
      i. Out of nothing, nothing comes.
   e. And this is absurd.
      i. We clearly perceive existing things.
      ii. We are aware of our own individual existence.
5. Therefore, some things are eternal.
6. This thing is eternal on its own account or on account of an external cause.
   a. If its essence includes existence, it is eternal on its own account.

b. If its essence does not include existence, it is eternal on account of an external cause.
   i. There is a real distinction between essence and existence.
   ii. Thus, if the essence does not include existence, existence must be added to the essence in order for the thing to exist.
   iii. The being that adds existence to the essence is therefore the existential cause of that thing.

7. If this thing is eternal on account of some external cause, then this thing is contingent in itself, though eternal on account of its cause.
   a. If its essence does not include existence, it depends for its existence on a cause (6.b.).
   b. It is therefore contingent in itself, though it exists eternally.
8. The external cause is therefore the absolutely necessary being.
   a. Its essence includes existence.
      i. All things which have existence added to their essences are caused by a being whose essence involves existence.
   b. It is therefore necessary in itself and causes the existence of all other things.

Again we may ask what can be known of the nature of such a being. We have already seen that this being is eternal and utterly independent in existence. It is therefore uncaused (proposition 10); it does not include any plurality (proposition 21), that is, it is a simple being without composition; thus, it cannot be material or reside in a material object (proposition 22), for all corporeality involves composition. Hence, concludes Maimonides,

> It is now clear that there must be a being with absolutely independent existence, a being whose existence cannot be attributed to any external cause, and which does not include different elements; it cannot therefore be corporeal, or a force residing in a corporeal object; this being is God.[44]

Moreover, there is but one God. First, if there were two absolutely independent beings, they would share the property of absolute existence. This property would thus be added to their respective essences. But that means that their essences do not involve existence, and they are not therefore absolutely necessary beings. Second, a being whose essence involved existence would be absolutely simple. It would therefore be the only member of its species and have nothing in common with other beings. Thus, there can only be one being whose essence involves existence, or only one God.

This is a sophisticated version of the cosmological argument and one destined to exercise great influence. Maimonides himself held it in high esteem: 'This is a proof the correctness of which is not doubted, disputed, or rejected, except by those who have no knowledge of the method of proof'.[45] The foundation stone of the argument is the real distinction between essence and existence.

Finally, we may turn to Maimonides's fourth argument, the proof from potentiality and actuality. He states,

> We constantly see things passing from a state of potentiality to that of actuality, but in every such case there is for that transition of a thing an agent separate from it (Prop. XVIII.). It is likewise clear that the agent has also passed from potentiality to actuality. It has at first been potential, because it could not be actual, owing to some obstacle contained in itself, or on account of the absence of a certain relation between itself and the object of its action; it became an actual agent as soon as that relation was present. Whichever cause be assumed, an agent is again necessary to remove the obstacle or to create the relation. The same can be argued respecting this last-mentioned agent . . . . This series of causes cannot go on *ad infinitum*; we must at last arrive at a cause of the transition of an object from the state of potentiality to that of actuality, which is constant, and admits of no potentiality whatever.[46]

The argument is clearly Aristotelian in character, and, when one remembers that motion is the transition from potentiality to actuality, it also becomes apparent that the proof is another version of the argument from motion. We may outline it as follows:

1. We see things passing from potentiality to actuality.
2. Every such transition requires a separate cause because:
   a. prop. 18.
3. This cause in turn requires a separate cause for its transition from potentiality to actuality.
4. This series of causes cannot be infinite.
5. Therefore, there must be a being which is wholly actual and causes constantly the transition from potentiality to actuality.

The first step, that *we see things passing from potentiality to actuality*, is based on sense experience. The change here referred to is all types of change mentioned in proposition 4.

Second, *every such transition requires a separate cause*. Here again Maimonides's implicit determinism pervades the argument. He wants to prove that nothing can be self-moved, that is, that it cannot bring itself from potentiality to actuality. For example, we might say that a man is self-moved and that his soul is unmoved. But then the soul becomes an unmoved mover, which is not the conclusion Maimonides seeks. Therefore, he argues in proposition 18 that even the soul is caused to act by external factors.[47] Maimonides informs us that in cases where the soul is the cause of the change, there are two alternatives with regard to that change: (1) If there is no external obstacle to the change, then there would be no change, but only the effected actual state. This clearly denies the exercise of free will. Maimonides argues that when we choose to effect some change, this causal activity takes place only because of external determining factors. Otherwise, we would have always effected the change. This presupposes that new motives cannot appear in the soul wholly of its own accord. (2) If the change occurs when an obstacle is removed, then it is this removal that is the true cause of the change. In other words, our choices are not the causes of our activities; our actions are wholly determined by causes outside ourselves, and our exercise of free will is entirely illusory. It is difficult to see how Maimonides can avoid complete determinism. In effecting a transition from potentiality to actuality, the soul is determined to do so, and thus every such transition requires a separate cause.

But this still does not solve the difficulty. For even if the soul is determined to act as it does, it still is unmoved and would be a purely actual being. So in step 3 Maimonides asserts, *this cause in turn requires a separate cause for its transition from potentiality to actuality*. Maimonides is endeavouring to prove that even the soul in effecting change itself changes. He must prove that the soul changes when effecting change, or it could be the purely actual being. Hence, he argues that any cause of change, in effecting change, itself changes. It does so in changing from a potential cause to an actual cause. Before it effects the change, it is only a potential cause; but as it effects the change, it is an actual cause. Hence, it has moved from potentiality to actuality. Again Maimonides emphasises that it does not change itself from potential to actual cause (i.e. by its own free will). Rather this change occurs when another external agent either removes the obstacle to change that exists in the potential cause itself or brings the potential cause into a relation that brings the potentiality of the cause to actuality. For example, perhaps a man cannot sleep because he is worried about losing his employment; but when the boss informs him that his job is secure, the internal obstacle to sleep (namely, the worry) is removed, and the change from waking to slumbering is blissfully effected. Or again, a captured solider may be the potential cause of the signing of a false confession to his crimes; but he does not become the actual cause of such until he is brought into relation with the gun at his head. Thus, even the soul is not purely actual, for in effecting changes it moves from being a potential cause to being an actual cause, and it does this not on its own initiative but only at the instigation of some external cause. Therefore, every transition from actuality to potentiality requires a cause, and this cause in turn requires a separate cause for its transition from potentiality to actuality.

Fourth, *this series of causes cannot be infinite.* Presumably this is because an actual infinite cannot exist.

Finally, *therefore, there must be a being which is wholly actual and causes constantly the transition from potentiality to actuality.* The being in which this series terminates must be a being that constantly causes the same eternal effects, otherwise it would change from being a potential cause to being an actual cause. Now this is obviously not the conclusion Maimonides wants, for it would necessitate, among other things, an eternal creation. For God could not change from being potential creator to actual creator. God would cause the eternal rotation of the spheres, and these would cause certain specific effects that would mechanically occur like the motion of the gears of a clock as they are moved by the spring. We may provide the following schema of the proof:

1. We see things passing from potentiality to actuality.
2. Every such transition requires a separate cause.
   a. Nothing can cause itself to pass from potentiality to actuality.
      i. If a thing could change itself, then, given no obstacle to change, the change would have always already occurred; that is, there would be no change, only the actual effected state.
      ii. If a thing could change itself and does so when a given obsctacle is removed, then the cause of the change is not the thing itself, strictly speaking, but the cause of the removal of the obstacle.
   b. Therefore, it must be caused to pass from potentiality to actuality by some external cause.
3. This separate cause in turn requires a separate cause for its transition from potentiality to actuality.
   a. In becoming a cause, it passes from potentiality to actuality.

    i. It changes from being a potential to an actual cause.
  b. Such a transition requires a separate cause (2.).
4. This series of causes cannot be infinite.
  a. An actual infinite cannot exist.
5. Therefore, the series must terminate in a being that is wholly actual and causes constantly the transition from potentiality to actuality.

What can we know about this being? First, it has no potentiality in its essence, that is, it cannot not-exist (proposition 23). Second, it cannot be corporeal because potentiality, which it lacks, is inextricably bound up with matter (proposition 24). At this point Maimonides announces that '. . . the immaterial being that includes no possibility whatever, but exists actually by His own essence, is God'.[48] Third, since He is incorporeal, there can be only one God (proposition 16).[49]

Maimonides concludes his four proofs for the existence of God by stating: 'Even if we were to admit the Eternity of the Universe, we could by any of these methods prove the existence of God; that He is One and incorporeal, and that He does not reside as a force in a corporeal object'.[50] Although Maimonides believes we can prove that God exists, he does not think that this means that we have any positive knowledge of God's essence. Maimonides is a champion of the *via negativa* which accords us only knowledge of what God is not.[51] In his systematic presentation of arguments for God's existence and for the negative knowledge of God, Maimonides greatly influenced the Christian scholastics who drew upon his work. The *Guide* was translated from Arabic to Hebrew during Maimonides's lifetime and into Latin within ten years of his death. His thought was thus readily available to Latin-speaking theologians, and Thomas Aquinas in particular used Maimonides as his 'guide and model' in his systematic harmonisation of Aristotle and Christianity.[52] This is especially significant for our purposes because, as J. O. Riedl explains, the greatest influence of Maimonides on Aquinas is precisely in the Five Ways, in which Thomas follows Maimonides closely, even utilising identical phraseology in his arguments.[53] As we now turn in the following chapter to the Christian formulations of the cosmological argument, we shall often find ourselves casting a backward glance to the philosophers of Islam and Judaism in order to understand the proofs in their proper historical setting.

NOTES

1. Though not as widely ignored as the Arabic philosophers, these Jewish

thinkers are nevertheless largely neglected in favour of Christian writers; I have never seen a selection from even Maimonides included in a philosophy of religion reader, and his proofs for the existence of God are sometimes grossly misrepresented (as in Jacob B. Agus, *The Evolution of Jewish Thought from Biblical Times to the Opening of the Modern Era* [London and New York: Abelard-Schuman, 1959], p. 185).

2. Frederick C. Copleston, *A History of Medieval Philosophy* (London: Methuen & Co., 1972), p. 105.

3. Julius Guttmann, *Philosophies of Judaism: The History of Jewish Philosophy from Biblical Times to Franz Rosenzweig*, with an Introduction by R. J. Z. Werblowsky, trans. David W. Silverman (London: Routledge & Kegan Paul, 1964), p. 55.

4. Ibid.

5. See G. Vajda, 'Le "kalām" dans la pensée religieuse juive du Moyen Age', *Revue de l'histoire des religions* 183 (1973): 143–60; Louis-Émile Blanchet, 'L'infini dans les pensées juive et arabes', *Laval théologique et philosophique* 32 (1976): 11–21.

6. Harry Austryn Wolfson, 'Notes on Proofs of the Existence of God in Jewish Philosophy', in *Hebrew Union College Annual* 1 (1924): 584.

7. Isaac Husik, *A History of Medieval Jewish Philosophy* (Philadelphia: The Jewish Publication Society of America, 1940), p. 23. Saadia was the first to 'set up a comprehensive system of religious philosophy' demonstrating 'the superiority of Judaism' over other religious systems and over the doctrines of the philosophers [Henry Malter, *Saadia Gaon: His Life and Works*, the Morris Loeb Series (Philadelphia: The Jewish Publication Society of America, 1921), p. 175.]; accordingly, he 'deserves to be considered the father of medieval Jewish philosophy of religion' (Guttmann, *Philosophies*, p. 61).

8. See Martin Schreiner, 'Sa'adja b. Josef al-Fajjûmî', in *Dreizehnter Bericht über die Lehranstahlt für die Wissenschaft des Judenthums in Berlin* (Berlin: 1895), pp. 59; Guttmann, *Philosophies*, p. 62; Husik, *History*, pp. 25–6.

9. Saadia Gaon, *The Book of Beliefs and Opinions*, trans. Samuel Rosenblatt (New Haven, Conn.: Yale University Press, 1948), pp. 41–4. For a discussion of Saadia's first three proofs, see Harry Austryn Wolfson, 'The Kalam Arguments for Creation in Saadia, Averroes, Maimonides and St. Thomas', in *Saadia Anniversary Volume*, Texts and Studies, vol. 2 (New York: American Academy for Jewish Research, 1943), pp. 197–207; Herbert A. Davidson, 'John Philoponus as a source of Medieval Islamic and Jewish Proofs of Creation', *Journal of the American Oriental Society* 89 (1969): 362–70.

10. Saadia, *Book*, p. 44.

11. Davidson, 'Philoponus', pp. 362–70.

12. Ibid., p. 370.

13. Cf. Aristotle, *Analytica Posteriora* 1. 22. 83b6–7.

14. Z. Diesendruck, 'Saadya's Formulation of the Time-argument for Creation', in *Jewish Studies in Memory of George Alexander Kohut, 1874–1933*, ed. S. W. Baron and A. Marx (New York: Bloch, 1935), p. 154.

15. Saadia, *Book*, p. 45.

16. Ibid., pp. 46–7.

17. Husik, *History*, p. 236. In the words of J. H. Hertz, 'The popular Jewish estimate of him is reflected in the contemporary saying . . . , "From Moses to

Moses, there never arose a man like Moses"; while to the non-Jewish world, he has ever been *the* Jewish philosopher and *the* Jewish theologian' (J. H. Hertz, 'Moses Maimonides: A General Estimate', in *Moses Maimonides: VIIIth Centenary Volume*, ed. I. Epstein [London: Socino Press, 1935], pp. 3–4).

18. Moses Maimonides, *The Guide for the Perplexed* 1. 74. Guttmann states,

> He proved the existence of God by purely Aristotelian arguments . . . . Taking his stand upon strict science—that is, the metaphysics of Aristotle—Maimonides repudiates the proof of the Kalam as superficial and tendentious' (Guttmann, *Philosophies*, p. 157).

19. Leo Strauss, 'The Literary Character of the *Guide for the Perplexed*', in *Essays on Maimonides: An Octocentennial Volume*, ed. Salo Wittmayer Baron (New York: Columbia University Press, 1941), p. 44.

20. Ibid., p. 39.

21. Maimonides, *Guide* 2. intro.

22. The propositions may be summarised:

1. An infinite magnitude cannot exist.
2. An infinite number of finite magnitudes cannot co-exist.
3. An infinite number of causes and effects cannot exist.
4. Change may be in substance, quantity, quality, or place.
5. Motion implies change and transition from potentiality to actuality.
6. Motion is either essential or accidental, the former being due to an external force, the latter to its participation in the motion of another thing.
7. Changeable things are divisible and, hence, corporeal.
8. A thing moved accidentally must come to rest.
9. A thing that moves something else does so by setting itself in motion.
10. Anything in a corporeal body is either an accidental or essential property.
11. Some properties of a corporeal object (e.g. colour) are divisible; others (e.g. soul) are not.
12. A force occupying all parts of a corporeal, finite object is finite.
13. Only circular locomotion can be continuous change.
14. Locomotion is the most basic motion.
15. Time and motion are inseparable.
16. Incorporeal beings cannot be numbered, unless they inhabit a corporeal body.
17. Everything in motion is moved by an agent, either external or internal.
18. Everything that passes from potentiality to actuality is caused to do so by an external agent.
19. A caused being is a possible being.
20. A necessary being has no cause.
21. The essence of a composed being does not necessitate existence, since its composition is the cause of its existence.
22. Material bodies are composed of substance and form and are subject to accidents.
23. Every possible being may at some time be without actual existence.
24. Potentiality implies corporeality.

25. Every composed being consists of matter and form and requires a cause for its existence.
26. Time and motion are eternal.

This wholesale borrowing on the part of Maimonides perfectly illustrates the point made earlier that the Jewish philosophers concentrated on religious problems, being content to simply adopt the philosophical backdrop of their Arabian predecessors.

23. Maimonides, *Guide* 2. intro. All quotations from the *Guide* will be from Moses Maimonides, *The Guide for the Perplexed*, 2nd ed. rev., trans. M. Friedländer (London: George Routledge & Sons, 1928).

24. Ibid. Maimonides believed that the doctrine of *creatio ex nihilo* was both religiously superior and philosophically more probable than the eternity of the universe (ibid., 2. 22, 23). But all his proofs for God's existence take for granted the eternity of the universe. For more on this, see E. L. Fackenheim, 'The Possibility of the Universe in Al-Farabi, Ibn Sina and Maimonides', *Proceedings of the American Academy for Jewish Research* 16 (1946–47): 57–70; Mājid Fakhry, 'The "Antinomy" of the Eternity of the World in Averroes, Maimonides and Aquinas', *Le Museon* 66 (1953): 139–55; Georg Wieland, 'Die Gottesbeweise des Moses Maimonides und die Ewigkeit der Welt', *Philosophisches Jahrbuch* 82 (1975): 72–89. For a good overall discussion of Maimonides's four proofs, see George C. Papademetriou, 'Moses Maimonides' Doctrine of God', ΦΙΛΟΣΟΦΙΑ 4 (1974): 306–29; Wieland, 'Gottesbeweise', pp. 77–84.

25. Maimonides, *Guide* 2. 1.

26. Husik, *History*, p. 253; cf. 217.

27. See R. L. Sturch, 'The Cosmological Argument' (Ph.D. thesis, Oxford University, 1970), pp. 19–27.

28. Maimonides, *Guide* 2. 1.

29. Maimonides might say, with Aristotle, as he indeed later does, that the soul is moved accidentally, but he does not argue the point here.

30. In point of fact, Maimonides does accept a system of multiple spheres, souls, and Intelligences. See Friedländer, Analysis to *Guide*, by Maimonides, p. 1.

31. Maimonides, *Guide* 2. 1.

32. Ibid.

33. Ibid.

34. Ibid.

35. Husik, *History*, pp. 218–19, 253.

36. Maimonides, *Guide* 2. 1.

37. This raises yet another fascinating question: could the converse be true, that a thing could have an end and yet no beginning? It would not be eternal, yet it would exist for infinite time in the past, a sort of mirror-image of immortality. This would not damage Maimonides's case, however, for he would argue that in infinite time, this being would cease to exist, just like beings that have both beginning and end, and thus there would be nothing. The *mutakallimūn*, of course, would have said it is nonsensical to speak of a being's actually existing for infinite time and yet having an end to its existence. Thus, we can imagine them asking Maimonides why could not tomorrow or next year be the point at which the possibility of the non-existence of the world be realised? Should he counter that in the infinite time that has passed, all possibilities would have been actualised, they might rejoin that at *any* point on the series of past events, an

infinite time would have already elapsed, and thus one could never reach a point at which the universe would have collapsed into non-being. What this really goes to show, they might conclude, is the absurdity of positing infinite past time, for at *any* point all previous possibilities would have been already realised, given that in infinite time every possible will be actualised.

38. Maimonides himself alludes to this additional clause which we have added to the argument when he later says,

> If the spheres were transient, then God is their Creator, for if anything comes into existence after a period of non-existence, it is self-evident that an agent exists which has effected this result. It would be absurd to contend that the thing itself effected it (Maimonides, *Guide* 2.2).

39. Moses Maimonides to R. Samuel ibn Tibbon, cited in S. Munk, Commentary to *Le Guide des Égares* (Paris: A. Franck, 1861), p. 39.

40. Aristotle, *Metaphysica* Θ. 8. 1050b5–25. In his commentary on ibn Rushd's *Tahafut*, Simon Van Den Bergh encounters the same line of reasoning and traces it to Aristotle:

> . . . every potentiality will realise its actuality . . . . Averroës refers here to one of the problems most discussed in Islam, whether there can be possibles that are never realized. According to Aristotle, *Met.* Θ and init., you cannot say that a certain thing may possibly bc but will never be, for this would destroy the definition of the impossible, since 'impossible' means what will never be . . . a possible cannot be infinitely unrealized . . . (Simon Van Den Bergh, Notes to *Tahafut al-Tahafut* [*The Incoherence of the Incoherence*], 2 vols., by Averroes [London: Luzac & Co., 1954] 2: 36).

41. Maimonides, *Guide* 2. 1.

42. Cf. ibid., 1. 57. According to Copleston, Maimonides follows al-Fārābī in designating existence as an accident or accidental determination (Copleston, *Medieval Philosophy*, p. 139). But Fackenheim disputes this, asserting that although Maimonides calls existence an accident in all beings other than God, this only means that existence in created beings is given to them by God; accordingly, existence is 'each being's mediated participation in the creative act of God' (Fackenheim, 'Possibility', p. 68).

43. Maimonides, *Guide* 2. 1. According to Wolfson,

> In Jewish philosophy the assertion that in God essence and existence are identical . . . was merely another way of saying that God is necessary existence out of which arises the eternity, unity, simplicity, and unknowability of God, and in fact all those negations which tend to make God an absolute and infinite being. It did not however mean that thereby God becomes a 'real' being (*ens reale*) as opposed to a being of reason or a fictitious being (*ens rationis, ens fictum*). Or, in other words, the fact that in the idea of God essence involved existence was not used to prove the actual existence of God, for in Jewish as well as in Arabic philosophy that mode of reasoning was not followed (Harry Austryn Wolfson, *The Philosophy of Spinoza*, 2 vols. [Cambridge, Mass.:

Harvard University Press, 1934], p. 122). Hence, we find no ontological argument in Maimonides.

44. Maimonides, *Guide* 2. 1.
45. Ibid.
46. Ibid.
47. Ibid., 2. intro.
48. Ibid., 2. 1.
49. Ibid.
50. Ibid.
51. For a further discussion on this aspect of Maimonides's thought, see T.-L. Penido, 'Les attributs de Dieu d'apres Maimonide', *Revue Néo-Scholastique de Philosophie* 26 (1924): 137–63; H. A. Wolfson, 'The Amphibolous Terms in Aristotle, Arabic Philosophy, and Maimonides', *Harvard Theological Review* 31 (1938): 151–73; H. A. Wolfson, 'Maimonides on Negative Attributes', in *Louis Ginzberg Jubilee Volume* (New York: Jewish Publications, 1945), pp. 419–46; Joseph A. Buijs, 'Comments on Maimonides' Negative Theology', *New Scholasticism* 49 (1975): 87–93; Clyde Lee Miller, 'Maimonides and Aquinas on Naming God', *Journal of Jewish Studies* 28 (1977): 65–71.
52. Husik, *History*, p. 306.
53. John O. Riedl, 'Maimonides and Scholasticism', *New Scholasticism* 10 (1936): 27–8.

Chapter 5

Thomas Aquinas

Underrated by non-Thomists and overrated by Thomists, Thomas of Aquino (1225–1274) is one of those philosophers whom nearly everybody quotes but whom few understand. Probably more ink has been spilled over his celebrated Five Ways for proving the existence of God than over any other demonstrations of divine existence, and yet they remain largely misunderstood today. No doubt this is because these five brief paragraphs are so often printed in anthologised form and are therefore read in isolation from the rest of Aquinas's thought. To take these proofs out of their context in Aquinas's thought and out of their place in the history of the development of these arguments will tend only to obscure the true nature of the proofs. A proper understanding of Thomas's proofs necessitates reading them in their immediate context, ferreting out of his other works the basic epistemological and metaphysical principles they presuppose, comparing them to similar versions which Aquinas formulated elsewhere, and relating them to their historical context, particularly to the proofs propounded by Aristotle, the Arabic philosophers, and Maimonides. Few modern philosophers of religion who are not already committed Thomists seem to have sufficient interest in the thought of a medieval theologian for such an admittedly arduous task. But this can only result in neglect of Aquinas's important contributions to the philosophy of religion or to shallow expositions of his thought, mingled with positive misunderstandings.[1]

Thomas's cosmological proofs are found in a number of his writings, and an expositor must decide how he will approach these various arguments. While it would constitute a valuable and no doubt very interesting study to examine each of the proofs as they appeared chronologically in Aquinas's works and to attempt to discover how Thomas's thought evolved in his efforts to prove God's existence, I have chosen a different approach to these arguments.[2] We shall examine each of the proofs in the form in which it appears in the *Summa theologiae* and then utilise the other versions to shed further light on and to round out the terse statement of the arguments in the *Summa*. Thomas's proofs for the existence of God encompass the whole of 1a. 2–11 in the *Summa theologiae*. Modern readers, used as they are to anthologised versions of Aquinas's Five Ways, all too often fail to grasp this important point. Aquinas is sometimes criticised for what is thought to be his over-hasty conclusion:'. . . and this is what everybody understands by God';[3] but this misunderstanding arises only by tearing Aquinas's proofs out of their proper context. It is not until the finish of question 11 that the existence of what we mean by 'God' has been demonstrated.[4] The organic unity of question 2 with questions 3 to 11 is borne out in Aquinas's own words: in the *Summa contra gentiles* he effects the transition by saying, 'Accordingly having proved that there is a first being which we call God, it behoves us to inquire into his nature';[5] in the *Summa theologiae* he writes, 'Having recognized that a certain thing exists, we have still to investigate the way in which it exists, that we may come to understand what it is that exists'.[6] Especially noteworthy are the modest conclusions drawn from the preceding proofs: a first being or certain thing called God exists; now it remains to explicate His nature. Thus, any consideration of these brief proofs apart from their total context necessarily truncates and misrepresents the thought of Aquinas.

With regard to the arguments themselves, Aquinas considered each to be a distinct and demonstrative proof of God's existence. He explicitly states, 'There are five ways in which one can prove that there is a God'.[7] Earlier he had addressed the question of whether God's existence can be made evident, and he concluded that it can:'. . . we can demonstrate what in itself is not evident to us, namely, that God exists'.[8] We can know the existence of God by our 'natural powers of reasoning'; '. . . God's effects . . . serve to demonstrate that God exists . . . .'[9] Nor did Aquinas regard these as probability arguments only: we must use, says Thomas, 'demonstrative arguments whereby we can convince our adversaries', leaving 'certain probable arguments' for the 'practice and help of the faithful, but not for the conviction of our opponents' who would be confirmed in their error when they see that Christian belief is based on proofs that are less than demonstrative.[10] This is why Aquinas never sought to demonstrate the existence of the Trinity: 'For when someone wants to support faith by unconvincing arguments, he becomes a laughing stock for the unbelievers, who think that we rely on such arguments and believe because of them'.[11] Hence, it is clear that Aquinas believes that these five arguments are *proofs* in the strongest sense of that word. Moreover, he regarded each as a *distinct* demonstration of God's existence. The reasoning in each is similar, but the point of departure for each proof is unique, as we shall see in greater detail when we examine each argument.

Therefore, the view of a writer like Mascall that the Five Ways should be considered as neither proofs nor distinct arguments, but as an expression of the 'radically un-self-sufficient character of finite beings' that leads us to 'see them as dependent on a transcendent self-sufficient creative Cause',[12] is simply out of the question. One may wish to advance such a position, but it does not represent Aquinas in any way. For he clearly considered each argument to be a distinct and demonstrative proof of God's existence.

Of the Five Ways only the first three are cosmological arguments. In each of the first three proofs Aquinas reasons from a particular datum of experience in general—change, causation, contingent beings—to an ultimate Being which is the cause of these in the world. The fourth argument is not usually classed as cosmological, but is based on degrees of being and is the most Platonic of Aquinas's proofs. The fifth argument is clearly the teleological argument. Therefore, we shall restrict our attention to the first three ways. Each of these three ways is an *a posteriori* argument. This is apparent, first, when we consider Aquinas's empirical epistemology: what we know we come to know only through sense data.[13] Therefore, if we are to know that God exists, it is only because we can reason back to Him from His effects in the world.[14] According to Etienne Gilson, underlying Aquinas's criticism of the Anselmian *a priori* argument is his empirical epistemology, 'namely that all our knowledge originates from sensory intuitions'.[15] Any proof for God is thus necessarily *a posteriori*. Secondly, Aquinas explicitly refutes *a priori* proofs for God's existence.[16] Whether his reasoning is correct or not is beside the point; he argues that *a priori* proofs are not cogent and that the proper way to prove God's existence is through His effects. Third, each proof itself is clearly *a posteriori*. As Aquinas looks out at the world, he sees that some things are changing, some things are being caused, and some things are coming into being and passing away. Each proof begins with some aspect of empirical reality and reasons to a transcendent ground for that aspect of reality. The first three ways, then, are all *a posteriori*.

With these observations behind us, we may now turn to an exposition of Aquinas's first way. He writes,

> The first and most obvious way is based on change. Some things in the world are certainly in process of change: this we plainly see. Now anything in process of change is being changed by something else. This

is so because it is characteristic of things in process of change that they do not yet have the perfection towards which they move, though able to have it; whereas it is characteristic of something causing change to have that perfection already. For to cause change is to bring into being what was previously only able to be, and this can only be done by something that already is: thus fire, which is actually hot, causes wood, which is able to be hot, to become actually hot, and in this way causes change in the wood. Now the same thing cannot at the same time be both actually *x* and potentially *x*, though it can be actually *x* and potentially *y*: the actually hot cannot at the same time be potentially hot, though it can be potentially cold. Consequently, a thing in process of change cannot itself cause that same change; it cannot change itself. Of necessity therefore anything in process of change is being changed by something else. Moreover, this something else, if in process of change, is itself being changed by yet another thing; and this last by another. Now we must stop somewhere, otherwise there will be no first cause of the change, and, as a result, no subsequent causes. For it is only when acted upon by the first cause that the intermediate causes will produce the change: if the hand does not move the stick, the stick will not move anything else. Hence, one is bound to arrive at some first cause of change not itself being changed by anything, and this is what everybody understands by God.[17]

It is interesting to note that of all the proofs, Aquinas calls this one the most obvious way (*manifestior via*). It also seems clear that this is Aquinas's favourite argument, for he expounds it numerous times elsewhere, often in quite elaborate forms.[18] In the *Summa contra gentiles* he openly acknowledges that the proof is Aristotle's;[19] we have seen that it was employed by Maimonides and the Arabic philosophers as well. So the argument had a long and venerable history behind it, and Aquinas gladly inherited it, employing the proof often and with enthusiasm. The argument may be outlined in this way:

1. Some things in the world are in a process of change.
2 Anything in a process of change is being changed by something else because:
   a. things in a process of change do not yet actually possess the characteristic into which they are changing, though they have the potentiality to possess it, while things that are causing change have that characteristic already,

i. because causing change is actualising some potential, and this can be done only by something already actual.

b. Something cannot be potential and actual with respect to the same quality at the same time.

c. Therefore, anything in a process of change cannot change itself; it must be changed by something else.

3. But this something else, if it is in a process of change, is also being changed by something else, and so on.
4. This series of things being changed by something else cannot be endless because:
   a. then there would be no first cause of change and hence no subsequent causes of change,
      i. because the subsequent causes are only operative if there is a first cause.
5. Therefore, there must be a first cause of change which is itself unchanging; this we understand to be God.

We would do well to consider each step in the above outline. The first point, that *some things in the world are in a process of change*, raises the question as to what Aquinas regards as change. The problem arises over an ambiguity of translation of the word 'change': both *motus* and *mutatio* describe what we would today call change. But for Aquinas, as for Aristotle, there was a difference between motion (*motus*) and change (*mutatio*). *Motus* could be properly said to take place in only three of the ten categories: quantity, quality, and place.[20] Substantial change is technically speaking *mutatio*: when a substance comes into being (is generated) or perishes (is corrupted), it does not move from one terminus of change to another—it simply begins or ceases to exist.[21] Hence, *mutatio* encompasses all forms of *motus* plus substantial change. Now undoubtedly the most controversial issue surrounding the first way is whether Aquinas intended it to be taken as a proof from *motus* in a *physical* or *metaphysical* sense. If it is concerned with purely physical motion only, then Aquinas has little to say that has not already been said by Aristotle, Maimonides, and ibn Rushd before him. On the other hand, it is the contention of some Thomists such as Gilson and Joseph Owens that the first way is of a metaphysical character and that Aquinas meant it to be understood in terms of his essence/existence distinction.[22] Two principal lines of support are adduced in favour of such a metaphysical interpretation: (1) statements by Aquinas in other versions of the same proof that evidence a metaphysical perspective and (2) conclusions drawn by Aquinas from the argument that necessitate a metaphysical reading of the proof. Each point warrants critical examination.

Owens argues with regard to the first point that the first way points beyond a merely Aristotelian, physical proof from motion. For Aristotle's argument in the *Physics* reaches only the soul of the first heaven and the argument of the *Metaphysics* posits a plurality of unmoved movers.[23] In neither case is the Christian concept of God attained; yet Thomas confidently concludes his argument, '. . . this is what everybody understands by God'.[24] Exploring the historical development of the proof in the hands of Aquinas, Owens turns first to Thomas's comments on chapter 7 of Aristotle's *Physics*. The question here is whether anything can be self-moved. Aristotle's explanation is wholly physical, but Aquinas's is 'highly metaphysical'.[25] Aquinas employs a principle extracted from Aristotle's *Metaphysics* to prove the point: the highest instance of any characteristic is the one which is the cause of that characteristic in other things which are designated by the same name.[26] But things in motion cannot have a primary instance in their own genus because things in motion depend for their motion upon the movement of their parts. Thomas is already beginning to depart from a simply physical understanding of the proof.

Turning next to Aquinas's comments on the eighth chapter of the *Physics*, Owens notes that whereas Aristotle bases the proof on the eternity of motion, Aquinas does not. Instead Aquinas is exercised with the question of the *being* of motion; Owens claims that he shifts the starting point of the proof from the eternity of motion to the *esse* of motion and that the conclusion of this 'highly metaphysical' reasoning will be a cause of the *esse* of motion.[27]

In his commentary on book Λ of the *Metaphysics*, Aquinas again alters the basis of the proof from the eternity of motion to the *esse* of motion. Aristotle's unmoved movers were pure act, but that only meant that they were pure forms; they are still finite substances. But Aquinas interprets the argument in terms of *esse*, and he concludes to a being which produces the act of existing in other beings and exists itself *per se*. Owens does not hesitate to read into the passage Aquinas's doctrine that God is the pure act of existing: '. . . the act which is finally reached is accordingly the act of existing per se'.[28]

Owens then examines each of the versions of the proof as formulated by Aquinas. Although Aquinas's *Commentary on the Sentences* does not contain a proof from motion, it does have other proofs of a similar character, such as the proofs from causality and from degrees of perfection. These two arguments, says Owens, conclude to God as the 'primary cause of the *esse* of creatures and as the immobile being which is presupposed by all mobile and changeable natures which have their *esse* from another'.[29]

With regard to the two proofs from motion in *Summa contra gentiles*, Owens observes that the first does not presuppose the eternity of the world or the animation of the heavens, both of which were part of Aristotle's original. In the second way, these notions appear, but at the root of this proof is the 'notion of the passage from *non esse* to *esse* . . . coupled with that of the passage from potency to act'.[30]

In his *De potentia*, Thomas explains that later philosophers posited a universal cause from which all other things came into being. This can be proved by Aristotle's argument for an utterly unmoved mover. Such a mover would be the most perfect being, and all other things, since they are less perfect, must receive their existence from this unmoved mover. Owens comments, 'The notions of "being moved" and of "receiving *esse*" seem to coincide, as far as the conclusion of the argument is concerned, in leading to the entirely immobile movent'.[31]

The *Compendium theologiae* contains only one proof for God: the proof from motion. Owens argues that the nature of God reached by this proof is only attainable if the proof is understood metaphysically.[32] This is the second line of defence for the metaphysical interpretation, and we shall examine it shortly.

Finally, in the *Summa theologiae* Aquinas distils the demonstration from his earlier *Summa* into its pure form. The general structure of the first way as well as the critical proof for each of its two propositions are retained in the *prima via*. 'But in this way the *via* has been completely detached from its Aristotelian basis, the eternity of cosmic motion. It reaches an entirely different conclusion; namely, the . . . God of Christian revelation.'[33] 'This conclusion,' states Owens, 'is radically different from the conclusion of the Aristotelian argument, which was a plurality of finite entities.'[34] Why then does Aquinas attribute the proof to Aristotle and claim that it is the Greek philosopher who has concluded to the existence of the specifically Christian God? The answer, says Owens, is that Aquinas reads his own metaphysical doctrines back into Aristotle in such a way so as not to falsify what Aristotle said, but nevertheless to shape it to his own way of thinking.[35]

The second line of defence for the metaphysical interpretation is pressed by Stephen L. Weber.[36] He states,

> That St. Thomas is interested not simply in a cause of movement, but in a cause of being, is evident in the use to which he puts the conclusions of Aristotle in this summary of the first way: 'Also it was

shown in Book I, by the argument of the same author [Aristotle], that there is a first immoveable mover, which we call God. But the first mover in any order of movements is the cause of all the movements in that order. Since, then, many things are brought into existence by the movements of the heaven and since God has been shown to be the first mover in the order of those movements, it follows necessarily that God is the cause of being to many things.' . . . Notice that he begins with 'cause of movements' (Aristotle) and concludes with 'cause of being'.[37]

Owens contends that the context of the Five Ways in the *Summa theologiae* also makes it clear that the first way is not simply a physical proof. For example, in the fourth article of the immediately following question, God's essence is proved to be His existence. The second supporting argument for this is from act and potency. Since God has no potentiality, He cannot have *esse* added to His essence; His essence and existence are identical. Concludes Owens: 'The act and potency envisaged in the *prima via*, accordingly, include essence as potency to the act of *esse*'.[38] Such conclusions are thought to necessitate a metaphysical interpretation of the proof from motion.[39] Because Aquinas's earlier versions of the proof import metaphysical concepts and because his conclusions could be drawn only from a metaphysical proof, it is concluded by some Thomists that the first way must be taken metaphysically.

On the other hand, two immediate factors weigh in favour of a purely physical interpretation of the proof: (1) the proof is at face value a proof from motion, and (2) the historical context of the proof suggests a purely physical argument. With regard to the first, the proof itself simply purports to be a proof from *motus*. Moreover, the examples used by Aquinas all refer to instances of Aristotelian motion: the sun's movement across the sky, the movement of the elements and the heavenly bodies, the fire producing heat, the hand and the stick.[40] These examples provide a thread of continuity throughout the earlier and later versions of the proof from change, and give strong indication that Thomas is restricting his proof to Aristotelian motion. Bryar rightly points out that 'The literal development, the words and statements, are not about composition of essence and existence nor do they speak about creation'.[41] If we are to take the proof in this new sense, there must be compelling reasons for doing so. The burden of proof, then, rests with those who would suggest an interpretation that goes beyond the natural sense of the words. Second, the historical proponents of the argument had always taken the proof in a physical sense, and later scholastics such as Scotus were to reject it for this very reason. Aquinas openly acknowledges that the proof is Aristotle's.[42] The influence of Maimonides is unmistakable as well.[43] The proof had always been a physical argument, and Aquinas gives no indication to the reader that he intends his version to be taken in any different light than those of his predecessors. As for Owen's contention that the Aristotelian proof did not lead to the God of the Bible, it must be said that Maimonides thought it did. There is no *prima facie* evidence that Thomas thought differently. Indeed, he concludes his commentary on the *Physics* with these words: 'And thus the Philosopher ends his general discussion of natural things with the first principle of the whole of nature, who is over all things, God, blessed forever, Amen'.[44] Of course, Thomas thought that God must be both separate and one, unlike Aristotle, but that does not mean that he did not think the proof could be formulated along Aristotelian lines to yield the desired results. When Aquinas concludes to a first unmoved mover and says that this is what everybody understands by God, he was simply stating a fact. That is what these medieval Aristotelians—whether Muslims, Jews, or Christians—did understand by God. It might be said that Aquinas was reading back his metaphysics into Aristotle—but then is this also true of Maimonides, ibn Rushd, and others? They believed that a purely physical, Aristotelian-type argument (even if not identical with the original) could conclude to God, and if Aquinas is said to have broken with this historical tradition, that will have to be clearly proved.

Have the exponents of the metaphysical interpretation provided compelling reasons to take the proof in terms of essence and existence? To answer this question we must examine each line of their defence. First, are Aquinas's reformulations of the Aristotelian argument such as to transform the physical proof into a metaphysical proof? Generally speaking, it is quite correct to say that Aquinas understood the actuality/potentiality distinction in a way more 'metaphysical' than did Aristotle.[45] For he regarded every creature as composed of actuality and potency in that its essence is in potency to its act of existing. Hence, a being with no potency in the Aristotelian sense would still have potency in the Thomistic sense. Now the question is, when Aquinas argues from the actuality/potentiality distinction in the first way, is he arguing in the Aristotelian sense or in the Thomistic sense? An examination of Aquinas's comments cited by Owens on the proof of *Physics* 7 reveals that Aquinas remains in the realm of physics with regard to motion.[46] Aquinas is still arguing about purely physical change; he refers to book 6 of the *Physics* for support that there can be no primary instance of motion because things in motion are divisible. Even if his reasoning is 'highly metaphysical', Aquinas in no wise transports the proof itself out of the realm of simply physical change. Turning to Thomas's comments on *Physics* 8, we must say that Owens has here greatly exaggerated the scope of Aquinas's differences with Aristotle. To say that Aquinas has shifted the basis of the proof from the eternity of motion to the *esse* of motion does not seem to be true at all. Aquinas inquires with Aristotle whether motion has always existed or 'whether at some time there may have been nothing in motion';[47] he also deals with the logically prior question of whether motion exists at all, since some (like Parmenides) have denied it.[48] Owens certainly overstates his case when from this he concludes that '. . . what primarily seems to interest St. Thomas in this argument is how the mobile things originally acquired their *esse*, their "to be" from the principle of *esse*'.[49] Nor has Aquinas shifted the basis of the proof: all he says is that if one can prove God exists assuming the eternity of the world, one's proof is stronger than if one denies the eternity of the world, since if the world had a beginning, then it must have had a cause.[50] It seems to be Owens who is reading in metaphysical doctrines, not Aquinas. Finally, looking at Aquinas's commentary on the *Metaphysics*, we again find Owens drawing unwarranted inferences. Aquinas states that given the world's eternity, the first mover must have no potentiality in its essence, for otherwise it might cease to exist, and then motion would not be necessary and eternal. It is difficult to see any advance on Aristotle here. Aquinas also notes that the argument for the world's eternity is not demonstrative, and that if the world is not eternal, Aristotle's conclusions on the immateriality and eternity of the first substance still follow. For if the world is not eternal, then its existence must have been caused by a prior being. If this being is not eternal, then its existence was also caused, and so forth. One cannot regress infinitely, so one must reach 'an eternal substance whose essence contains no potentiality and is therefore immaterial'.[51] The argument is really Aquinas's version of the *kalām* argument mentioned above; he shows how it can be proved that God exists if the world is *not* eternal. Owens has no grounds for reading in here the essence/existence distinction and concluding that the being of pure act is the act of existing *per se* that bestows *esse* on all other beings.

Now we shall examine each of the versions of the proof from motion cited by Owens. In the first place, the proofs from the commentary on the *Sentences* are not versions of the first way at all. Owens himself states, 'The first reason, the *via* of causality, is that there must be something from which creatures derive their *esse*, since creatures have *esse ex nihilo*'.[52] But this is clearly an embryonic form of Aquinas's second or third ways in the *Summa theologiae*, which are not proofs from motion. Nor is the second reason a proof from motion: 'The second argument . . . is that the imperfect presupposes the perfect'.[53] This proof is more closely related to the fourth way of the *Summa theologiae* than to the first. We know beings are imperfect because they are moved, among other things, but it is not their motion that proves God exists. The fact of motion is only secondary to this proof, and, hence, like the first it is not an example of the first way.

The proof in the *Summa contra gentiles* is Aquinas's fullest exposition of the proof from motion, and it merits a more detailed examination. If this proof can be proved to be metaphysical, Owens will have carried his case; if not, the other versions, based on this one, will most probably be simply physical proofs. If we compare the first argument from motion in this *Summa* to the cosmological argument of Aristotle, we shall find that it is wholly lifted out of the pages of the *Physics*. The three proofs of the principle that whatever is in motion is being moved by another are from *Physics* 6. 4; 8. 5; 8. 4 respectively. The three supporting arguments for the impossibility of an infinite regress are from *Physics* 7. 1; 8. 5; 8. 5 respectively. Aquinas contributes virtually nothing of his own to the exposition of this proof. It is Aristotle's and he clearly restricts it to the realm of physical change. Owens is hard-pressed to find anything metaphysical in this proof. He observes that Aquinas has altered the order of the arguments from their order in the *Physics*. But they are still the same arguments. He asserts that Aquinas makes no mention of the eternity of motion or the animation of the heavens. But, in fact, neither does Aristotle in the proof in *Physics* 7, which Aquinas is following here, though rounding it out with Aristotelian arguments from other contexts as well. Owens also notes that Aquinas preserves only the argument from act and potency and the arguments from the instrumentality of intermediate causes when he formulates the proof in the *Summa theologiae*. He drops the arguments that are purely physical. Whether this is significant we shall discuss when we look at the later *Summa*. At this point, it seems clear that the proof is simply physical.

What about the second proof from motion in the *Summa contra gentiles*? In this proof Aquinas refers to all three types of Aristotelian motion: quality, quantity, and place. This is made clear by comparing it to the commentary on the *Physics*, where it follows upon the heels of the first proof.[54] He says the argument is 'particularly clear in local motion',[55] but refers as well to motion with respect to place, increase, and alternation (one quality to another).[56] Indeed, the whole thrust of one part of the argument is that the types of motion are not infinite, and therefore there must exist a first mover. Thomas is, then, dealing with all aspects of Aristotelian motion mentioned earlier. This is also made clear by his examples, all of which are copied from Aristotle: he speaks of healing, teaching, increasing in size, digestion and atmospheric change, as well as change of place.[57] But there is no indication that he intends the proof to be taken in other than a physical sense. Owens admits that the proof 'takes account' of the eternity of the world and the animation of the heavens, but he insists that the proof 'is stronger' without these tenets.[58] But that is not what Aquinas says.[59] Aquinas always chooses the more difficult of two alternatives so that his proof will be all the stronger. In this case that means assuming the eternity of the world. It seems clear, then, that Aquinas has faithfully formulated an Aristotelian proof. All that remains is to see whether in revising the proof for his final *Summa*, he has radically altered its nature.

Before we do, however, a word may be said on the argument in *De potentia*. Here, as in the commentary on the *Sentences*, Aquinas does not prove that God bestows *esse* because He is the prime mover, but because He is the most perfect being. And in no way does Aquinas equate God's bestowal of motion with His bestowal of existence. Owens has seriously misrepresented the argument.

Turning then to the *Summa theologiae*, we need to ask if Aquinas has here produced a metaphysical proof. The answer would seem to be negative. The fact that Aquinas has dropped the more physical arguments (only 'more' physical because the others were also physical) cannot be of much weight, for Thomas has excised most of what he wrote in the *Summa contra gentiles*, not because he has changed his position, but because the proofs in this final *Summa* are schematic outlines designed for novice theological students.[60] This is why the abbreviated proof in the *Summa theologiae* appears to conclude only to an unmoved mover such as the human soul.[61] In the second proof in the *Summa contra gentiles*, Aquinas faithfully reproduces Aristotle's argument that perishable unmoved movers must have a cause of their generation and corruption. Bryar comments,

> First St. Thomas establishes the existence of something which imparts motion through its own agency. This something may be one of many self-movers. Secondly, St. Thomas argues to a first movent which contains a self-mover in continuous motion to account for the eternal generation and corruption of the self-movers . . . .
>
> The arguments in the *Summa Theologiae* and the *Compendium Theologiae*, while not diverging in appearance from the approach and

> language of the *Summa Contra Gentiles*, terminate with what was only the first part of the proof in the last mentioned work.[62]

Hence, the fact that Aquinas has dropped several arguments is of little significance so far as the character of the proof is concerned. His examples display the continuity between the different versions of the proof. Thomas continues, as in all his proofs, to use the same Aristotelian examples of change. And in the *Compendium theologiae*, which we shall examine in a moment, Aquinas still uses the example of the astronomical motion of the spheres. Thomas's use of examples has been much neglected in the discussion of his proofs, but they are very significant because they show us that the versions remain basically the same throughout his writings. Another equally significant reason for regarding the version of the *Summa theologiae* as a simply physical proof is that Thomas does not, in fact, overdraw the conclusion of the proof. He does not claim to have proved that God is pure actuality, for that will be shown later on *another* basis. He simply concludes that there is an unmoved first mover, whom we understand God to be. But I shall discuss more of this later.

I have reserved a discussion of the proof in the *Compendium theologiae* until last. This work was written in the last two years of Aquinas's life at the height of his powers; the *Summa contra gentiles* was already complete and the *Summa theologiae* mostly so. The argument for God's existence in the *Compendium* was written after the Five Ways and should represent the mature thought of Aquinas. He employs only one proof for God's existence in this brief work; the proof from motion:

> We observe that all things that move are moved by other things, the inferior by the superior—as the elements are moved by heavenly bodies, and among the elements, the stronger moves the weaker, and even among the heavenly bodies, the inferior are set in motion by the superior. This, however, cannot proceed to infinity. For everything that is moved by another is a sort of instrument of the first mover. Hence, if there is no first mover, all things that move will be instruments . . . . But even to the untaught it is ridiculous to suppose that instruments are moved unless they are put into motion by some principal agent. This would be like imagining that, when a chest or bed is being built, the saw or hatchet performs its functions without a carpenter. Therefore, there must be a first mover that is above all the others, and this being we call God.[63]

This proof is clearly a physical proof from motion, and Aristotle's system of heavenly spheres is still in full bloom. Owens attempts to show that Aquinas draws conclusions from this proof that would only be warranted by a metaphysical understanding of it. But that is the second line of defence, which we shall examine in a moment. But for now, it seems clear that in all the versions of the proof, we are confronted with a purely Aristotelian argument from *motus* and that no compelling reasons exist to regard this proof as metaphysical.

The second line of defence proposed by the exponents of a metaphysical interpretation of the first way is that Aquinas's conclusions far outstrip a purely physical proof. In light of our previous discussion, one might say that this point, even if valid, only goes to show that Aquinas confounded the Aristotelian act/potency distinction with the Thomistic and so overdrew his conclusions.[64] But does he in fact do so? A close examination of the *Summa theologiae* 1a. 3–11 reveals that practically all of the attributes of God are deduced from nature of the being concluded to in the other four ways, not from the nature of the unmoved first mover. For example, Thomas concludes that God's essence is the same as His existence because God has no potentiality, as Owens pointed out.[65] But the fact that God contains no potentiality is proved not from the first way, but from the second.[66] The first way comes into play only in proving God's incorporeality; Aquinas argues that God cannot be a body for three reasons: (1) Bodies are changed when causing change, so God, as the unchanging first cause of change (*primum movens immobile*), cannot be a body; (2) Since actual existence takes precedence over potential existence, God, as the first existent, must be wholly actual and therefore could not be a body, which always involves potentiality; (3) God is the most excellent of beings, but no body can be the most excellent being.[67] It seems clear that the first reason is deduced from the first way, the second reason from the second, or possibly third, way, and the third from the fourth way. Thus, Aquinas, in proving that God is pure actuality, does not refer to the first way—the first way only proves that God is not a body. Therefore, Aquinas's conclusions from the first way are really quite modest and perfectly tailored to fit a purely physical proof.

In fact it might be charged that the metaphysical interpretation, far from elucidating Aquinas's later conclusions, actually makes nonsense of them. For Weber argues that Aquinas is trying to prove a cause of the being of things in the first way; but Owens qualifies this, asserting, 'In saying that the *prima via* is metaphysical and therefore deals with *being*, one should keep in mind that the *being* so meant is the *esse* of motion and its terminus'.[68] But this notion appears to be unintelligible.[69] Owens treats motion as though it were itself composed of essence and existence,[70] but this distinction applies to *things*, not processes.[71] However, if Owens's interpretation is unacceptable, so is Weber's, for in the first way Aquinas is clearly contemplating a cause of motion, as Owens rightly sees, not a cause of things. Weber has assimilated the second way and the first way. This is more intelligible than Owens's view, but it is not a correct exposition of the *prima via.*

Therefore, the most probable interpretation of the first way would appear to be that Aquinas has followed Aristotle, just as he says, in expounding a physical proof from motion for an unmoved first mover. According to Anton Pegis, Aquinas never abandoned the proof of *Physics* 7 and 8, which he regarded as concluding to the existence of God, not any lesser being.[72] As for the metaphysical interpretation of this proof, O'Brien charges that Owens is guilty of 'misappropriation of the words and teachings of St. Thomas'.[73] Only the third way involves the *esse* of things; the texts cited by Owens to show this is also true of the first way are 'unconvincing' and do not support such an interpretation.[74] Therefore, when Aquinas begins his proof by asserting that some things in the world are in a process of change, he is choosing as his point of departure Aristotelian *motus.*

The second step in our outline of Aquinas's proof was that *anything in a process of change is being changed by something else.* The proof of this premiss is the analysis of change via the actuality/potentiality distinction. In step 2.a. he argues that in change, the thing changing does not yet possess the characteristic into which it is changing. This seems obvious enough: if it already possessed that characteristic, it would not be in change, but would be actualised. Further, a thing causing change already has the characteristic which it is causing in another. At this point Aquinas seems to have been led into a digression that is not essential to his proof. His example of the fire and the wood, introduced at this point, is bound to be misleading and is irrelevant to the main line of the argument. For Thomas does not want to prove that a cause must actually possess the very quality it is causing in its effect; this would be utterly counter-productive, since then the unmoved first mover would have to actually possess all the qualities that it causes, which is absurd. What he wants to prove is that anything in change is being actualised by a being already actual. This is clear by step 2.a.*i.* in our outline: causing change is actualising some potential, and this can be done only by something already actual. What this point proves is not that to cause, say, something to turn black, the cause must itself be black or possess the quality of blackness in order to impart blackness to something else,[75] but rather that a cause must be an actual being to produce an effect—it cannot be a mere potential being; in other words, the potential for blackness in a thing does not actualise itself, nor is it actualised by a potential cause, but it must be actualised by an actual cause, say fire, which scorches something until it is black. This is what 2.a.*i.* in the outline really proves, and point 2.a. with its attendant example is utterly misleading and extraneous to the argument. Some commentators fail to see this point, and treat 2.a. as an essential step in the proof.[76] By producing counter-examples, which is very easy, they believe they have dealt the proof a fatal blow. But this is to treat Aquinas's proof in an unsympathetic manner. The real thrust of the proof is that the actualising of a potential can only be done by some actual thing.[77]

How does he prove this? In the present version, he argues that a change is the actualising of some potential, and this can be done only by something actual. Then in step 2.b. he says that something cannot be potential and actual with respect to the same quality at the same time. This means that if a thing is to change, it requires an actuality to cause that change, and this actuality cannot be this quality in itself, for it cannot both possess and not possess this quality. (Thus, a stone has the potentiality to be in another place, but for this potentiality to be actualised there must be a cause. The cause cannot be the present position of the stone itself, for the stone cannot at the same time both possess and not possess the accident of being in a certain place. It is potentially there, but actually here.) Therefore, anything changing cannot *at the point at which it is changing* cause itself to change. It must be changed by something else. The change in a thing cannot be caused by the quality in a thing that is the point of its change. For then it would both have and not have this quality. And this is what Aquinas is out to show: anything moving from potentiality to actuality is not self-actualising; it must be actualised by something else. Or to put it more simply: anything in a process of change is being changed by something else.

But this leads directly to the third step, that *this something else, if it is in a process of change, is also being changed by something else, and so on.* This immediately follows from the above, for anything changing cannot be self-changed, but must be changed by another.

The fourth step is that *this series of things being changed by something else cannot be endless.* Aquinas argues that unless there is a first cause of motion, there can be no subsequent motion and, hence, no motion. But this is impossible, for premiss 1 states: some things in the world are in a process of change. The support for 4.a. is that the subsequent causes are operative only if there is a first cause; remove the first cause and they cease operating because the intermediate causes have no causal efficacy of their own. Thomas calls this an essentially subordinated series of causes.[78] Cause A does not move cause B, which in turn moves cause C, and so on. Rather cause A moves Z through the intermediate causes B–Y which are 'transparent', as it were, to A. If one removes A, Z will not be moved. The point here is that in an essentially subordinate series, the only cause that is really moving anything is the first cause. The others are like lifeless instruments. The very fact, then, that there is motion implies that the series of movers cannot be infinite.

It is interesting to observe that Aquinas's arguments here have nothing to do with the possibility of the existence of an infinite number of finite things.[79] He himself vacillated on this the question, and it is disputed as to which answer he eventually adopted.[80] His argument in the proof from motion is in no way dependent upon this dispute. Hence, we may conclude the fourth step: this series of things being changed by something else cannot be endless.

The fifth point and conclusion of the proof is that *there must be a first cause of change which is itself unchanging; this we understand to be God.* Aquinas's conclusion that the unmoved first mover is what everybody understands by God is not at all baffling when understood in its historical context. Philosophers of all faiths agreed at least on this point, that God is the one who moves the spheres that cause all sublunary change. Aquinas's conclusion simply reports a fact.[81] And we have also observed that Aquinas has yet to unpack the notion of 'God'. At this point we know very little about 'God' except that He is the unmoved first mover who stands at the peak of an essentially subordinate series of movers. Aquinas has yet to explicate His nature. We may schematise the first way as follows:

1. Things are changing.
2. Everything changing is either self-changed or changed by another.
3. Nothing is self-changed.
   a. Change is actualising some potential.
   b. No potential can actualise itself
      i. To do this it would have to be actual.
      ii. But nothing can be both actual and potential in the same respect.
   c. Therefore, nothing is self-changed.
4. The series of things changed by another cannot be infinite.

a. In an essentially subordinated series, intermediate causes have no causal efficacy of their own.
b. In an infinite series, all the causes are intermediate.
c. Therefore, an infinite series of essentially subordinated causes can have no causal efficacy.
d. But this contradicts (1): Things are changing.
e. Therefore, change is not caused by an infinite series of essentially subordinated causes.

5. Therefore, the series of things changed by another must be finite and terminate in a first unchanging cause of change; everyone understands this to be God.

Now what can be known about the nature of God, the first unchanging cause of change? First, God is not a physical body.[82] In all change involving bodies we find from experience that the body causing the change cannot do so without itself being changed in some respect. Hence, God is not a body, since He is unchanging. Comparison on this brief statement with the *Summa contra gentiles* and the commentary on the *Physics* reveals that Aquinas accepted Aristotle's analysis that in any physical motion the cause of the motion is moved itself.[83] For example, when my hand lifts the pen, my hand, in causing the motion of the pen, is itself moved. When we consider the motion of my hand, we may say that my soul moved my hand without itself moving *per se*, and this is precisely because my soul is not a body. In the same way, God in moving the physical universe must not be a body, otherwise He, too, would be moved and not be the unmoved first mover.

In the proof in the *Summa contra gentiles*, Aquinas claims to have proved the existence of a being which is eternal, one, bodiless, the cause of all change without itself being changed in any way. Interestingly, in the *Summa theologiae* Thomas does not try to prove any more attributes of God from this proof: for all we know, God may be a finite spiritual being. It is to the other proofs that we must turn to learn more of God's nature.

The second way in the *Summa theologiae* is:

> The second way is based on the nature of causation. In the observable world causes are found to be ordered in series; we never observe, nor ever could, something causing itself, for this would mean it preceded itself, and this is not possible. Such a series of causes must however stop somewhere; for in it an earlier member causes an intermediate and the intermediate a last (whether the intermediate be one or many). Now if you eliminate a cause you eliminate its effects, so

> that you cannot have a last cause, nor an intermediate one, unless you have first. Given therefore no stop in the series of causes, and hence no first cause, there would be no intermediate causes either, and no last effect, and this would be an open mistake. One is therefore forced to suppose some first cause, to which everyone gives the name 'God'.[84]

Aquinas names Aristotle as the source of this proof in the version in the *Summa contra gentiles.*[85] Aristotle had analysed the notion of cause into a four-fold typology and argued that an infinite regress of causes was impossible in any of the four.[86] The second way is an argument from efficient causality. Aquinas writes,

> The Philosopher proceeds in a *different* way in 2 *Metaph*, to show that it is impossible to proceed to infinity in efficient causes, and that we must come to one first cause, and this we call God.[87]

His argument may be outlined as follows:

1. We observe in the world efficient causes ordered in a series.
2. Something cannot be self-caused because:
   a. then it would have to precede itself, which is impossible.
3. Such a series cannot be endless because:
   a. in it an earlier cause produces an intermediate one which produces a last one;
   b. and if one eliminates the first cause, there will be no intermediate or last one either,
      i. for if one eliminates a cause, he eliminates its effects.
   c. Thus, in an endless series of causes, one would have no first cause, no intermediate cause, and no last cause, which is absurd.
4. Therefore, there must be a first cause, which everyone calls 'God'.

The first step, that *we observe in the world efficient causes ordered in a series*, involves some difficulties. First, it is not altogether clear what Aquinas means here by efficient cause. Aristotle spoke of efficient causes as moving causes, that is to say, causes which induce change in quantity, quality, and place. On this basis there seems to be little difference between Aquinas's first and second ways; one may suggest that the first way considers change from the standpoint of the changing while the second way approaches it from the standpoint of the changer, but this is a difference of aspect only. Observing that ibn Sīnā draws within the efficient cause a distinction between a *moving* cause and an *agent* cause, Gilson maintains that Aquinas in the second way is contemplating a series of agent causes which produce, not just change, but the very being of their effects.[88] The second way is therefore distinct from the first, since the first way argues from the *change* in things to an unmoved mover while the second argues from the *existence* of things to an uncaused cause. In Gilson's words, 'While the first brings us to God as the source of cosmic motion . . . , the second leads us to Him as the cause of the very existence of things. We knew that God was moving cause. We know now that He is cause of being'.[89] The second way is thus a proof for God as the creative cause of the universe.[90]

While this contention seems to be correct, an important qualification needs to be added. The proof does not concern causes which produce being by conjoining essence and existence in some thing. For one thing we could not observe this type of causal series. Moreover, Aquinas holds that God alone can produce *esse*; He cannot even use the instrumentality of secondary causes in producing the being of things.[91] Therefore, an existential series such as we have in the second way would be impossible, if Aquinas is thinking of causes of *esse*. In what sense, then, are beings the existential cause of other beings? Rosemary Lauer explains that for Aquinas beings other than God cannot cause the act of being itself, but they can cause something to be in a particular way, to be *this* thing, by causing form to structure matter in a specific manner.[92] Natural things can cause matter to acquire certain forms, and the celestial spheres not only cause the form to be received by matter in a certain way, but also cause the form as such. In this sense there is a hierarchical series of causes of existence for any particular being.[93] The second way therefore presupposes the Aristotelian astronomical system; we have noted D'Arcy's contention in this regard. Kenny also interprets the second way in these terms, observing that Aquinas believes that in human procreation the sun and the heavenly bodies constitute a hierarchy of efficient causes that work through men as instrumental causes in the generation of new persons.[94] Accordingly, Kenny flatly rejects the second way as based on an 'archaic fiction'.[95] But the question here is whether there is something which is of value when the proof is divested of its medieval trappings. A sympathetic reformulation of Thomas's second way might suggest, for example, that my existence now is dependent upon the temperature of the earth's atmosphere, which in turn is dependent upon the distance of the earth's orbit from the sun, which is dependent upon the mass of the sun, which is dependent upon the sun's relation to other stars, which are dependent for their existence upon our galaxy, which is dependent for its existence upon surrounding galaxies, and so on and on into the recesses of the universe.[96] Aquinas's argument would contend that we must posit a first efficient cause in this series which is the cause of the present existence of any thing now in existence. The argument would not then be in any sense dependent upon Aristotelian cosmology. But to return to Aquinas, when he states that we observe in the world efficient causes ordered in a series, he is thinking of the system of celestial spheres.

The second step in the outline is that *something cannot be self-caused.* Aquinas argues that this is impossible because for a thing to cause its own existence it would have to exist before itself, which is self-contradictory. The implicit basis of this proof is the actuality/potentiality distinction. One of the corollaries of that distinction is that the potential cannot actualise itself; there must be an actual being to bring the potential to actuality. Thus, a thing that does not have actual existence, but only potentially exists, cannot cause itself to exist. For it would have to be actual to do this, but it is only potential: it has no actual being whatsoever. Thus, nothing can be the cause of its own existence.

Now this seems reasonable enough on a temporal basis, that is to say, on the basis of a regress back to the beginning (if there was one) of the universe; for if originally *nothing* existed, it seems impossible that the world could cause itself to come into being. But the proof is not concerned with a temporal regress; Aquinas is considering a hierarchical series of causes of existence. Therefore, when he says that a thing would have to precede itself to cause itself, he cannot be thinking of chronological precedence, unless he has confounded the argument, but of some sort of metaphysical or logical precedence. But what this means is not altogether clear. It is apparently related to the notion of essence and existence. Aquinas says that the existence of a self-caused being would be caused by its essence, which is impossible:

> . . . it cannot be that existence itself is caused by the form or quiddity as such—caused, I say, as by an efficient cause—for then something would be the cause of itself and something would produce itself in existence, which is impossible.[97]

Thomas thus rejects the notion of a being whose essence involves its existence or of whom it might be said that it is of this being's essence to exist. Such a self-caused being would possess an essence which would exist logically prior to its receiving existence from itself; but this is impossible because essences have no independent status in reality apart from their act of existing. The notion of an essence eternally bestowing existence on itself is absurd because essence and existence are distinct principles, and no essence involves the real act of existing. Aquinas argues,

> . . . properties that belong to a thing over and above its own nature must derive from somewhere, either from that nature itself . . . or from an external cause . . . If therefore the existence of a thing is to be other than its nature, that existence must derive either from the nature or have an external cause. Now it cannot derive merely from the nature, for nothing with derived existence suffices to bring itself into being. It follows then that, if a thing's existence differs from its nature, that existence must be externally caused. But we cannot say this about God, whom we have seen to be the first cause.[98]

Therefore, the first cause will not be a self-caused being, but simply an uncaused being. We shall speak more of this in our discussion of the third way. But since a self-caused being would have to precede itself, that is to say, since no essence can bestow existence upon itself, we must conclude the second step, that something cannot be self-caused.

Aquinas's third step is that *such a series cannot be endless.* His proof is a sort of *reductio ad absurdum* and is a form of the same argument offered in the first way. In any series of causes, there is an earlier, an intermediate, and a last member. If there is no first member in this series, there can be no intermediate or last member either. This is because in an essentially subordinated series the causal efficacy of the subsequent causes is an effect of the first cause. Since if one eliminates a cause one eliminates its effect, then if one removes the first cause one removes its effect, which are the subsequent causes (for a cause without causal efficacy is not a cause). Thus, in an endless series where there is no first cause, there can be no intermediate or last causes either. But this is absurd, for a causal series with no first, intermediate, or last members is precisely no series at all! Hence, the series cannot be endless. It is noteworthy that Aquinas in the second way lumps together, so to speak, all the intermediate causes and considers them as a single whole. Thus, in his commentary on the *Metaphysics*, he writes with regard to Aristotle,

> . . . he argues that it makes no difference . . . whether there is only one intermediate or many, because all of the intermediaries are taken together as one insofar as they have in common the nature of an intermediate. Similarly it makes no difference whether there is a finite

> or infinite multitude of intermediates, because so long as they have the nature of an intermediate they cannot be the first moving cause.[99]

The number of intermediate causes makes no difference; they are still dependent for their causality on a first. Thus, Aquinas adds parenthetically to the version in the *Summa theologiae*: 'whether the intermediate be one or many'.[100] Therefore, such a series cannot be endless.

The final step in the proof is that *there must be a first cause, which everyone calls 'God'*. Here the appellation seems more fitting, for the first cause is the cause of the existence of the whole world. We may schematise Aquinas's argument thus:

1. Things are caused to exist.
2. Everything caused to exist is either self-caused or caused by another.
3. Nothing can be self-caused.
   a. To cause one's existence, one would have to be prior to himself.
      i. No essence involves an act of existing.
      ii. In a self-caused being, the essence would have to involve the act of existing.
   b. But this is self-contradictory and hence impossible.
   c. Therefore, nothing is self-caused.
4. The series of things caused by another cannot be infinite.
   a. In an essentially subordinated series the existence of the subsequent causes depends on a first cause.
   b. In an infinite series, there is no first cause.
   c. Therefore, no subsequent causes exist either.
   d. But this contradicts (1): Things are caused to exist.
   e. Therefore, things are not caused to exist by an infinite series of essentially subordinated things being caused by another.
5. Therefore, the series of things being caused by another must be finite and terminate in a first uncaused cause of all existent things; this everyone calls 'God'.

Now what can be known about the nature of God, the first uncaused cause? First, God cannot contain matter.[101] This is because in any form/matter composite, it is the form that determines how the subject will act; activity flows from the form. Now God is the source of all activity since He is the first efficient cause. Since God is the primary source of all activity, He must be pure form and contain no matter.

Second, God is the same as His essence.[102] Since matter is the principle of individuation of the various forms, in any being lacking matter its form is not individuated. Therefore, the essence of material things includes the entire form/matter composite, but the essence of immaterial beings is of the form alone. Thus, God, being pure form without matter, is His own essence. It is inappropriate to say that a man is identical with 'human-ness', but it is not incorrect to say that an angel is identical with his particular 'angel-ness', or that God is identical with His own godhead or deity.

Thirdly, God's nature is identical with His existence.[103] We have seen that God is the first cause. Now His existence is either (1) derived from His nature or (2) is external to His nature or (3) is His nature. But (1) represents a self-caused being, which we have seen to be impossible, and (2) describes a being whose existence is caused by another, which God is not. Therefore, God's nature is identical with His existence. This is certainly a curious conclusion, one which we shall explore more thoroughly in the third way.

Aquinas goes on to prove further divine attributes with arguments flowing out of the conclusion of the second way, but space does not permit me to survey them here. Aquinas's second way proves very fruitful in disclosing the nature of the first uncaused cause: from this cosmological proof alone Thomas proves that there exists a first uncaused cause of all that exists, which is immaterial, is the same as its essence, is its own existence, is beyond definition by genus and difference, is without accidents, is absolutely simple, does not enter into composition with other things, is perfect, is good, is unlimited, is omnipresent, is unchangeable, is eternal, and is one. If Aquinas's reasoning is valid, most would agree that he is justified in saying, 'and this is what everybody understands by God'.

Aquinas's third cosmological argument is:

> The third way is based on what need not be and on what must be, and runs as follows. Some of the things we come across can be but need not be, for we find them springing up and dying away, thus sometimes in being and sometimes not. Now everything cannot be like this, for a thing that need not be, once was not; and if everything need not be, once upon a time there was nothing. But if that were true there would be nothing even now, because something that does not exist can only be brought into being by something already existing. So that if nothing was in being nothing could be brought into being, and nothing would be in being now, which contradicts observation. Not everything therefore is the sort of thing that need not be; there has got to be something that must be. Now a thing that must be, may or may not owe this necessity to something else. But just as we must stop

> somewhere in a series of causes, so also in the series of things which must be and owe this to other things. One is forced therefore to suppose something which must be, and owes this to no other thing than itself; indeed it itself is the cause that other things must be.[104]

This proof, which at first seemed to me so simple, became as I studied it increasingly difficult because it is riddled with ambiguities and because it is not clear how closely Aquinas sticks to the historical sources from which it is derived. It is obvious that the immediate source of the third way is Maimonides's third proof for God's existence: in structure, argumentation, and phraseology the proofs appear to be nearly identical. A more remote source would be al-Fārābī's argument from contingency. The third way is the only place in which Aquinas expounds this argument. It is commonly thought that a similar version of the same argument is found in the *Summa contra gentiles* in the chapter on proofs for God's eternity.[105] But an examination of this proof reveals that it is nearly identical to ibn Rushd's revision of ibn Sīnā's cosmological argument.[106] If, therefore, Aquinas faithfully adheres to Maimonides's formulation of the proof here, the third way will be entirely distinct from the proof in the earlier *Summa*, just as Maimonides's proof is distinct from ibn Rushd's. The third way may be outlined as follows:

1. We see in the world things that exist but do not *have* to exist, that is to say, their existence is not necessary but merely possible.
   a. For we see them coming into being and going out of being.
2. All things cannot be merely possible things because:
   a. if a thing is merely possible, then at some time it did not exist,
   b. and if all things were merely possible, then at some time all things did not exist: there was nothing.
   c. But if at one time nothing existed, then nothing would exist now
      i. because something that does not exist cannot bring itself into existence.
   d. But this contradicts observation.
   e. Therefore, all things cannot be merely possible things; there must be something that is necessary.
3. A necessary thing may owe the necessity of its existence either to another thing or to itself.
4. The series of necessary things which owe the necessity of their existence to another thing cannot be endless because:
   a. (See the reasoning in the second way concerning things caused by another.)

5. Therefore, there must be an absolutely necessary thing which is necessary of itself and causes the necessity of existence in other necessary things.

The first step of the outline, that *we see in the world things that exist but do not* have *to exist, that is to say, their existence is not necessary but merely possible*, needs clarification. We need to discover exactly what Aquinas means by possible and necessary beings. Here two errors need to be avoided: (1) Aquinas is not speaking about logically possible or necessary beings. He nowhere suggests that some beings are merely possible because their non-existence is logically possible, nor does he say that a necessary being is one whose existence is logically necessary, such that it would be a contradiction to say it does not exist.[107] (2) Aquinas does not define possibility and necessity in terms of the essence/existence distinction. It has been argued that the third way, like the first, really has a 'metaphysical' starting point instead of a merely physical one, that is to say, it considers beings whose essence does not involve their existence. But such an interpretation ignores the second half of the third way as well as the historical ties to earlier Arabic and Jewish versions. It is generally recognised today that the first part of the third way begins by considering possibility and necessity in purely physical terms.[108] In the third way Aquinas does not *define* possible and necessary beings, but he does say that we can be sure a being is possible when we see that it is generated and corrupted. The sign of a possible being is its temporal finitude. Maimonides's proof does not begin with possible beings, but it does begin with beings that have both beginning and end. If Aquinas is following Maimonides closely in this proof, then his possible beings will simply be Maimonides's transitory beings, and a necessary being will be a non-transitory being. Aquinas would not say that a necessary being was eternal, since he did not believe in the eternity of the world. But he would say that a necessary being is a being that is not generated or corrupted, that is, a being which never undergoes substantial change. This would not mean it is eternal, for it could still be created *ex nihilo* or annihilated. In such cases there is no substantial change because there is no enduring substratum. If this interpretation is correct, then Aquinas is arguing that all beings cannot be transitory. There must be non-transitory beings as well. Difficulties arise, however, when we read Aquinas's discussion outside the third way of necessary and possible beings. In his *De potentia* Aquinas inquires as to whether beings are possible or necessary because of some intrinsic element in their nature or because of their relation to a cause.[109] He argues that it is because of their very nature. A possible being is a being that is susceptible to substantial change, while a necessary being is not. Since only material beings are susceptible to substantial change, all possible beings must be material things. But not all material things are possible beings, for material beings whose forms totally exhaust the capacity of their matter to receive new forms are not capable of substantial change; such are the celestial bodies. They have no potency for non-existence and exist forever unless created or annihilated. Only beings that possess matter capable of receiving new forms are possible beings; all other beings are necessary by nature. Thus, for Aquinas a possible being is a being susceptible to substantial change, and a necessary being is a being not so susceptible. This is problematical for the third way, for there we equated possible being with transitory being and necessary with non-transitory. But what about a being which is susceptible to substantial change, but never in fact undergoes such change? Such a being would not be transitory, but it would not *have* to exist either, since it could corrupt. The answer to this problem is that no such being could exist. According to Aristotle, every corruptible being must eventually corrupt.[110] If a being endures forever, it is *ipso facto* an incorruptible being; no merely possible being could endure for infinite time. Therefore, the equation between possible being and transitory being remains correct. I think that in Aquinas's mind 'possible–transitory–susceptible to substantial change' and 'necessary–non-transitory–not susceptible to substantial change' were interchangeable terms. Hence, he probably regarded his possible beings as virtually the same as Maimonides's beings which have beginning and end and considered his proof to be proceeding just as Maimonides's had. Only modern critics who reject the *De caelo* argument would question whether one might have a being susceptible to substantial change but nevertheless lacking a beginning and end.[111] In the third way Aquinas himself implicitly assumes that in demonstrating the existence of a non-transitory being he has proven the existence of a being which *has* to exist because its nature has no potency for substantial change.

The next step is that *all things cannot be merely possible things*. Here the difficulties increase. Step 2.a. states that if a thing is merely possible, then at some time it did not exist. The tense of the Latin verb here is actually to be taken in a timeless sense. Since a possible being is a being which is transitory, then there was a time when it did not yet exist, and there will be a time when it no longer exists; hence, it is true to say that at some time *it is not*. The statement spans the entire life of a possible being, its generation and corruption. The statement is not without controversy, however. Geny has denied its truth because a being could be possible in its nature and yet never happen to corrupt. In other words, to be susceptible to corruption is not necessarily to be transitory. In the face of this difficulty, some expositors such as Chambat and Heris choose to emphasise the other aspect of a possible being, the fact that it is generated.[112] Even if it is not necessary that a possible being must corrupt, it is necessary that it be generated. Hence, it would be true to say that at some time a possible being does not exist. On the other hand, we have seen that writers such as Descoqs, O'Donoghue, and Connolly point out that Aquinas is following Aristotle in *De caelo* 1. 12. 281a28–30, where he declares that the corruptible must at some point corrupt.[113] Aquinas maintains that it is impossible to combine in one being a nature that has both the potential for existing for infinite time and the potential for non-existence. If a thing can exist for infinite time, then it will, since everything has an inclination for existence and will continue to be as long as it can. Thus, if a being has a nature that can exist for infinite time, it will do so necessarily, and it is impossible for it to cease to exist. Natures that have the potency for non-existence are limited in time by their very natures. They have no potency for existence of unlimited duration and must therefore corrupt at some point. Thus, any possible being must be both generated and corrupted, so that at some time it does not exist. A third interpretation, supported by M. F. and Bouyges, is that Aquinas is taking possible beings, not as generable and corruptible beings, but as those that are, in fact, generated and corrupted—and necessary beings as those that are not.[114] Since 'necessary' is defined as everlasting and 'possible' as transitory, it is true by definition that at some time a possible being does not exist.

What may be said about these three interpretations? The first is probably incorrect, as we shall see in our discussion of step 2.b. As for the remaining two, I strongly suspect that we do not have here an either/or situation, but that both views blend together. We have seen that Maimonides set out to prove that it is impossible that all things have beginning and end. Aquinas wants to prove that it is impossible that all things are merely possible. It is a natural inference that the two theologians are talking about the same beings. In this case the point of departure for the third way is not just beings that are susceptible to generation and corruption, but beings that *are* generated and corrupted, that have beginning and end. As Aquinas says, some of the things we come across are merely possible, for we ourselves *see* them springing up and dying away, sometimes in being and sometimes not. Everything cannot be like *this* because every possible being at some time does not exist. As M. F. and Bouyges indicate, the last clause is true by definition:

possible beings are beings which are generated and corrupted and thus are transitory. Since any such being is temporally finite, then at some time it *is not*. This serves to answer Geny's objection, for a possible being *is* a being that we observe to be generated and corrupted. All beings, says Aquinas, cannot be like this. There must exist beings that never suffer substantial change. But here Geny's question might be raised in a new guise: could it not be that these necessary beings are simply beings that just *happen* never to corrupt, but are nevertheless just as susceptible to corruption as the possible beings that do in fact corrupt? In such a case all beings in reality would be equally corruptible, and the fact that some do not corrupt is purely accidental. At this point Aquinas's analysis in terms of the *De caelo* argument would become relevant. He could argue that a being which never undergoes corruption does so, not just accidentally, but only because it is of its very nature insusceptible to substantial change. Given enough time every corruptible being would corrupt because it does not have in its nature the capacity to endure for infinite time. The analysis of the *De potentia* would constitute a further unpacking of the notions of possible and necessary being after it has been proved that they exist. Aquinas may argue in the third way that there must exist in addition to transitory beings one or more non-transitory beings. Then he may analyse the implications of what it means for a being to be transitory and non-transitory; here it is revealed that a transitory being must be a material being susceptible to receiving new forms, while a non-transitory being is a being not even susceptible to substantial change. But this analysis is a second step which backs up the first and takes us beyond the immediate context of the third way. In terms of the proof itself, the analysis need not enter in; Aquinas may simply prove the existence of some non-transitory being(s) and then ask what is the cause of their non-transitory existence, just as Maimonides does. The crucial part of the third way is the second half, as we shall see, so even if Aquinas only concludes to a non-transitory being that is so only in fact, not nature, his argument is unimpaired, for he may still argue in the second half that this non-transitory being must be caused. Be this as it may, the interpretation endorsed by O'Donoghue and Connolly serves to back up, not contradict, the interpretation of M. F. and Bouyges. Aquinas begins with transitory beings and concludes to non-transitory being(s). These in turn reveal themselves under analysis to be being(s) which *cannot* suffer substantial change, not just beings which *do* not suffer substantial change.

Step 2.b. continues, if all things were merely possible, then at some time all things did not exist. This argument has been variously misunderstood.

It has been accused of committing the logical fallacy of making a quantifier shift, that is, reasoning that because all things do not exist at some time, there is some time at which no things exist.[115] Or again, it has been regarded as reasoning by composition, that is, arguing that because all the parts of the world are possible, the whole is possible.[116] But neither of these interpretations seems plausible. The proof is inextricably bound up with *temporal* considerations and attempts to prove that if all beings were possible then there would be a point in time when nothing would exist. Here two interpretations are possible: (1) there was a time before anything was generated, or (2) in an infinite duration of time all possible beings would be corrupted, and nothing would be left. The language of the proof itself could permit either alternative.[117] The first alternative holds that without a necessary being nothing would have come into existence in the first place.[118] Joseph Bobik has argued vigorously for such an interpretation on the basis of the wording of the third way: he contends that the '. . . "quandoque" in St. Thomas' "quod possible est non esse, *quandoque* non est" designates a non-existence which *precedes* the existence of the possible; for this is required by the context . . .'.[119] According to Bobik, the phrase 'once upon a time' cannot refer to a time *after* the existence of the possibles, since the proof concerns actually existing things. The proof seeks to account for currently existing possible beings. It makes no sense to try to account for the existence of past beings that no longer exist. Aquinas is arguing that if all present beings are possible, then there was a time in the past before they were generated.[120] Bobik regards this argument as invalid, for it assumes that all possible beings exist now.

The second interpretation suggests that if all things were merely possible beings, then in an infinite time all the possible beings would have corrupted and ceased to exist.[121] Support for this interpretation is strong. (1) We noted earlier that Aquinas did not believe that the creation of the world in time is demonstrable.[122] Therefore, he assumes the infinite duration of the universe in all his proofs because he held that if one could prove the existence of God on the assumption that the world is everlasting, his argument stands *a fortiori* if the world is temporally finite, and thus his proof is much stronger. The second interpretation seems to accord better with this general position. In effect Aquinas says, 'I grant you infinite time with its infinite *per accidens* regress of generated beings; but at some time they must all corrupt, and nothing will exist unless there are necessary beings as well'.[123] (2) Thomas's model in the third way is Maimonides's proof, and there it is clearly the eventual corruption of all things that is contemplated. According to Gilson,

Aquinas and Maimonides are of one mind on this proof.[124] There are some differences between them at this point, however, most noticeably Aquinas's lack of reference to what is possible of the *whole* class of things. Perhaps one ought not to make too much of this point: the third way is only a proof in outline; or again, Owens notes that in Aquinas's Latin text of Maimonides's proof, this point is easily overlooked: '*possibile autem in genere necessario est*'.[125] On the other hand, it may be that Aquinas saw no need for the emphasis on the whole class, for if matter itself is a possible being, then when it corrupts, everything will cease to exist.[126] The only way to avoid this conclusion would be to say that prior to the existence of matter were immaterial beings who created matter and then passed away. But this is impossible, since, as we have seen, an immaterial being is precisely a necessary being because it cannot suffer substantial change. And if the existence of matter were preceded by nothing, then the point is proved: there was a time when nothing existed. So if everything, including matter, is possible and if every possible must eventually corrupt, then given infinite time everything would have ceased to exist. Thus, no reference to the possibility pertaining to a whole class is necessary. But at any rate, both Maimonides and Aquinas are emphasising that if everything were possible, in infinite time it would all corrupt and nothing would exist now.

As for the first alternative interpretation, O'Donoghue rightly criticises Bobik for failing to reckon with the atemporal character of the Latin verbs as Aquinas employs them; one cannot legitimately infer that only present, actually existing beings are referred to in the proof.[127] In a response to O'Donoghue, Bobik yields the point, but doggedly insists that even if the reference includes past beings, one could never reach a time when absolutely nothing existed.[128] This is because the aspect of the possible operative in the proof is the notion that every possible is generated, and generation is always out of something temporally prior. Thus, there would always be something existent before any generated being. But this is clearly fallacious, for Bobik originally argued that the only aspect of the possible considered in the proof was the possible as generable because the wording of the proof refers only to currently existing beings. But he has now yielded that point to O'Donoghue. Therefore, the proof may include possibles insofar as they are corruptible as well as generable. Thus, Aquinas may argue that if all beings were possible, in infinite time they would all corrupt and nothing would exist. If Aquinas includes matter among the possibles, then its corruption would not necessitate the generation of a new being. There are no good reasons to believe that Aquinas is focusing on the possible as generable;

on the contrary, both his usual procedure and the influence of the Maimonidean formulation on this proof indicate the opposite.

Step 2.c. proceeds, if at one time nothing existed, then nothing would exist now. This is because something that does not exist cannot bring itself into existence. The reader no doubt will recognise the familiar actuality/potentiality distinction. The difference between its use in the second way and its use here is that whereas Aquinas employed it there to prove that a self-caused being could not be logically or metaphysically prior to itself, he utilises it here in the more normal sense to demonstrate that a self-caused being would have to be prior to itself temporally. If nothing existed at any point in time, then nothing would exist now, for a potential cannot actualise itself. Even in the Christian doctrine of *creatio ex nihilo*, it is not said that creation is caused by nothing. The efficient cause of creation is God, who always exists; the universe simply lacks a material cause. But, Aquinas argues, if there is no matter, no God, no *being* of any sort, if there is *absolutely nothing*, how can anything spring out of this abyss? To be self-caused, a being would have to exist to give itself existence, which is absurd. Therefore, if nothing ever existed in the past, nothing exists now.

But this contradicts observation, for we found in step 1 that possible beings do exist. Hence, all things cannot be merely possible beings; there must exist some necessary being or beings. A necessary being is one that is subject to neither generation nor corruption. But what is this necessary being? Like his historical predecessors, Aquinas believed there were many necessary beings.[129] For example, the heavenly bodies are declared to be 'necessary beings', 'unchangeable' and 'incorruptible'.[130] The human soul is likewise incorruptible,[131] as are the angelic beings.[132] Even primary matter could be accorded this status, since it is neither generated nor corrupted.[133] Therefore, even if Aquinas's argument were entirely successful, all he has managed to prove is that the material universe is non-transitory and must exist by necessity of the nature of matter, which cannot be generated or corrupted. This conclusion ought to occasion little joy among theists, for it would be happily embraced by any materialist; indeed, it is strange to see the overwhelming concern of philosophers of religion with the cogency of the first part of the third way to the utter neglect of the second part, which is really the crucial step in proving that God exists. At any rate, the conclusion of the first half of the proof is that some non-transitory being not susceptible to substantial change, that is to say, some necessary being, exists. Hence, all things cannot be merely possible beings.

Step 3 asserts that *a necessary being may owe the necessity of its existence either to another thing or to itself.* This key step in the proof is perhaps the most ambiguous. For what is meant by a cause of necessity? The phraseology is reminiscent of Maimonides's proof, which moves from a being whose existence is necessary on account of some external force to a being whose existence is necessary on its own account. This brought in the essence/existence distinction, for a being necessary on account of another is possible *per se.* One might assume that Aquinas is simply following Maimonides in this step. But this creates certain difficulties: for one thing, Aquinas in *De potentia* specifically rejects ibn Sīnā's understanding of possibility and necessity in terms of the essence/existence distinction in favour of ibn Rushd's view that beings insusceptible to substantial change are absolutely necessary, having no possibility in their natures for non-existence. In the *Summa contra gentiles* proof, he adopts the language of ibn Sīnā (and of Maimonides) in describing a possible being as equally disposed to being and non-being, but he does not understand this in terms of essence and existence and does not apply the distinction to necessary beings as well. Furthermore, Aquinas holds that God alone imparts existence without intermediaries; how then can a chain of causes of existence be constructed as in the third way? It is most interesting that Maimonides's proof has no reference to such a chain of causes of existence; rather he concludes directly from the possible *per se* being to its ground of existence in a being necessary *per se.* If these difficulties indicate a departure from Maimonides's pattern, then the cause of necessity in the third way will be perhaps the sort of cause discussed in the second way, beings that cause the form of the next lowest member in the causal hierarchy.

But are these difficulties so insuperable as to warrant the conclusion that Aquinas has abandoned Maimonides in favour of ibn Rushd? I doubt it. In the first place, what Aquinas rejects in the *De potentia* is calling a being possible because it is composed of essence and existence and therefore requires a cause. But he neither rejects the real distinction nor does he deny the need for an existential cause. In fact he argues against ibn Rushd that the fact that a necessary being has no possibility of non-existence in its nature does not mean that they can exist independently of God or that they cannot be annihilated:

> Nevertheless there is not removed from the nature which has no possibility to non-being, that it has its necessity from another: since whatever perfection it has, it has from another: whence with the action of its cause ceasing, it would cease to exist, not because of an intrinsic

> potency to non-being, but because of the power in God of not giving it being.[134]

Although a necessary being has no potency for non-existence in its nature, that nature itself must still be caused to exist. But this re-introduces the essence/existence distinction. For the nature of a thing (that is, its essence) does not involve its existing; this must be caused by God. Hence, Aquinas says, *it has its necessity from another*, and this consists in God's *giving it being*. This brings us right back to the third way, with its demand for a cause of the necessity of necessary beings. This will accordingly be a cause of their being. What Aquinas objects to in the *De potentia* is calling a being 'possible' because it is composed of essence and existence; but note that he does not do this in the third way, as does Maimonides in his proof. The non-transitory beings concluded to in the first half are still absolutely necessary in their natures, but these natures do not involve the act of existing; hence, they must be caused to exist by a being that conjoins existence with their essence. But what of the infinite regress of causes argument? A reading of his *De ente et essentia* shows that Thomas did not think infinite regress arguments inappropriate in proving a first cause of existence:

> Now whatever pertains to anything is either caused by the principles of its nature . . . , or it stems from some extrinsic principle . . . . But it cannot be that existence itself is caused by the form or quiddity as such—caused, I say, as by an efficient cause—for then something would be the cause of itself and something would produce itself in existence, which is impossible. Therefore everything whose existence is something other than its nature must derive its existence from another. And since everything existing through another is traced back to something existing of itself as a first cause, there must be some thing which is the cause or reason for the existence of all things and which is itself existence pure and simple. Otherwise there would be an infinite regress in causes, since everything which is not existence pure and simple has a cause of its existence, as has been said. It is clear then that an intelligence is form plus existence and that it has existence from the first being which is simply existence. And this is God, the first cause.[135]

In this passage Aquinas considers immaterial necessary beings and contends that they, too, must have a cause of their existence because their essence does not involve the act of existing. And he employs here the infinite regress argument. Therefore, its presence in the third way cannot count against interpreting that proof in terms of the essence/existence distinction. Perhaps this is best explained as a sort of hypothetical concession which Aquinas personally disagrees with but nevertheless includes in the proof because the Arabic philosophers had considered it an option. If this analysis is correct, then Aquinas, in saying that a necessary thing may owe the necessity of its existence either to another thing or to itself, is following Maimonides in demanding an existential cause which conjoins essence and existence in even necessary beings.[136]

The fourth step is that *the series of necessary things which owe the necessity of their existence to another thing cannot be endless.* Aquinas refers us to his arguments in the second way. The reasoning is clearly reminiscent of ibn Sīnā's argument: an essentially subordinated series of causes of existence cannot be infinite because then nothing would exist, which is clearly false.

The conclusion is drawn: *therefore, there must be an absolutely necessary thing which is necessary of itself and causes the necessity of existence in other necessary things.* From the passage in *De ente et essentia* we understand that this being which is necessary of itself will be a being whose essence is its existence, a being which is existence itself, pure and simple.

This deserves comment. Certainly the notion of God as subsistent existence itself is one of the most important features of the Thomistic system. But what can it mean to say that God's essence is existence? Unfortunately, contemporary Thomists are unable to offer us much assistance on this score, for they maintain we *cannot* know what it means to say God's essence is His existence. Gilson explains,

> As Thomas Aquinas understands him, God is the being whose whole nature it is to be . . . an existential act . . . . To say that God 'is this' or that he 'is that', would be to restrict his being to the essences of what 'this' and 'that' are. God 'is' absolutely . . . . God is the being of which it can be said that, what in other beings is their essence, is in it what we call 'to be' . . . .
>
> . . . Since, in God, there is no something to which existence could be attributed, his own *esse* is precisely that which God is. To us, such a being is strictly beyond all possible representation. We can establish *that* God is, we cannot know *what* he is because, in him, there is no what; and since our whole experience is about things that *have* existence, we cannot figure out what it is to be a being whose only essence is 'to be'.[137]

But although we may not be able to comprehend such a being, nevertheless it is the conclusion to which the Five Ways impel us. Gilson states,

> . . . since the Prime Efficient cause does not receive its own existence . . . there is no sense in which it can be said to be distinct from it. If there were such a thing as a pure and absolute 'fire', it would not *have* the nature of fire, it would *be* it. Similarly, God . . . is the very act of what we call 'to be'. . . . Naturally, since we have no experience of this unique being, our mind is unable to conceive it and our language has no fittingly perfect words to express it . . . .
>
> . . . God is the pure act of existing, that is, not some essence or other, such as the One, or the Good, or Thought, to which might be attributed existence in addition . . . ; but Existing itself (*ipsum esse*) in itself and without any addition whatever, since all that could be added to it would limit it in determining it . . . .
>
> Such is the cause of the many deficiencies of the language in which we express him.[138]

There is thus an element of agnosticism in Aquinas's philosophy of God. We are driven by his proofs to assert that God is, but we do not know *what* God is. He has no essence except His act of existing. This is why Thomas employs the *via negativa* in eliminating certain qualities that can not be applied to God. We can schematise the third way as follows:

1. Contingent beings exist.
   a. For we see them coming into and going out of being.
2. All beings cannot be contingent.
   a. If a thing is contingent, then at some point in time it does not exist.
   b. If all beings were contingent, then, given an infinite time, all beings would cease to exist; there would be nothing.
   c. But if nothing existed at any point in time, then nothing would exist now.
      i. Something that does not exist cannot cause itself to exist.
   d. And this contradicts (1): Contingent beings exist.
   e. Therefore, not all beings are contingent; there is something that is necessary (that always exists).
3. A necessary being is either caused to exist by another or is self-existent.

a. A being composed of essence and existence receives its existence from another.
b. A self-existent being is one in which its essence is existence.

4. A series of necessary beings caused to exist by another cannot be infinite.
   a. In an essentially subordinated series of causes of existence, the existence of any member is dependent upon a first cause.
   b. In an infinite series there is no first cause.
   c. Therefore, nothing exists.
   d. But this contradicts (1): Contingent beings exist.
   e. Therefore, the series of necessary beings caused by another cannot be infinite.
5. Therefore, there must be an absolutely necessary being in whom essence and existence are identical and which is the cause of the existence of everything else.

What, then, can be known about this absolutely necessary being? First, He is not a body.[139] In the first existent being, there can be no potentiality whatsoever. For though in generation potentiality precedes actuality, absolutely speaking actual existence is prior to potential existence. Since God is the first existent, He must be fully actual. And since bodies always have the potential to be divided because they are extended, God cannot be a body.

Second, God can contain no matter.[140] God has been shown above to be pure actuality; since matter is pure potentiality, God can contain no matter.

Third, God is His own nature.[141] We discussed the proof of this under the second way. It follows from the absence of matter in God, which can be proved by either the second or third way, as seen above.

Fourth, God is His own existence.[142] If an essence is not itself existence, then it must have the potential to exist. But God has no potentiality, as we have seen; therefore, it must be God's essence to exist. The same thing can be proved in another way, more directly related to the third way. Anything that exists either partakes of existence or is existence. This is the essence/existence distinction once more; in any essence/existence composite, the being partakes of its existence. We have proved God exists. But if He only partakes of existence, He will not be the primary existent, which we have proved Him to be. 'God therefore is not only his own essence, but also his own existence.'[143] This is the conclusion implicit in the third way and unpacked in the *De ente et essentia*.

Once again I do not have space to survey Aquinas's arguments for further divine attributes, but let it be said that the third way provides as fruitful an analysis of God's nature as did the second way. Fifteen divine attributes flow directly out of the reasoning contained in the third way, and Aquinas's arguments for them constitute the second part of this argument for God's existence.

Looking back now on the first three ways, we may wish to ask what is the distinctive contribution that Aquinas has lent to these arguments. Here, if we are to be honest, we must confess that it is small. Sturch's judgment is quite correct:

> . . . Thomas Aquinas . . . is generally regarded as *the* outstanding exponent of the Cosmological Argument. This is, one suspects, due more to his general philosophical importance, and perhaps to the prominent position occupied by the Argument in his 'Summae', than to any particular originality in his presentation of it.[144]

After one has studied the history of the cosmological argument, one realises that Aquinas has said little with regard to it that was not said before him by Aristotle, Fārābī, ibn Sīnā, and Maimonides. The principal contribution of Aquinas comes in his conception of existence as the act of being of a particular essence. Prior to Thomas existence was conceived as an accident added to the essence of a thing, but Aquinas denied the accidentality of existence.[145] This has led some modern Thomists like Gilson and Maritain to see in Aquinas a true 'existentialism' as opposed to the 'essentialism' of his predecessors and successors, who failed to grasp his insight. But if this is Thomas's main contribution to the cosmological argument, it might be questioned whether it was one of which he was fully aware. In his review of Gilson's massive study on John Duns Scotus, George Lindbeck presses this very point:

> Is there adequate justification for using the now familiar 'essentialism versus existentialism motif in any primarily historical study of the middle ages?* After all, the distinction was not part of the self-consciousness of the period. What Gilson considers the great meta-physical conflict of that day was one of which medieval thinkers were themselves largely unaware. Scotus does not consider his differences with St. Thomas as centering around the problem of existence, nor do 14th century thinkers describe him as the exponent of some subtle

* . . . .

kind of 'realism' † (which, while not the same as 'essentialism', is the closest thing to it in medieval vocabulary, and, in the case of Duns Scotus according to Gilson, inextricably involved with it).

† . . . .[146]

So Thomas's most significant contribution to the cosmological argument may be one which he himself did not fully appreciate. Other than this, Aquinas made no original contribution to the cosmological argument itself. And it must be added that if Fazlur Rahman is correct in his contention that ibn Sīnā's doctrine of the accidentality of existence has been misunderstood and that by this ibn Sīnā meant that existence is a 'happening' which instantiates essence, then Aquinas's contribution to the argument recedes still further.[147] But the Five Ways nevertheless remain a model exposition summarising the culmination of hundreds of years of thought on these forms of the cosmological argument.

NOTES

1. The worst offender I have found is Frank B. Dilley, 'Misunderstanding the Cosmological Argument of St. Thomas', *New Scholasticism* 50 (1976): 96–107. The title of Dilley's article might well describe his own exposition of Aquinas's first three ways.
2. For a chronological approach see Jules A. Baisnée, 'St. Thomas Aquinas's Proofs of the Existence of God Presented in their Chronological Order', in *Philosophical Studies in Honor of the Very Reverend Ignatius Smith, O.P.* (Westminster, M. D.: Newman Press, 1952), pp. 29–64.
3. Thomas Aquinas, *Summa theologiae* 1a. 2. 3. Quotations are from Thomas Aquinas, *Summa theologiae*, 60 vols. (London: Eyre & Spottiswoode; New York; McGraw-Hill Book Co. for Blackfriars, 1964).
4. On this point see R. L. Patterson, *The Conception of God in the Philosophy of Aquinas* (London: George Allen & Unwin, 1933), pp. 363–4; Frederick C. Copleston, *A History of Philosophy*, vol. 2: *Mediaeval Philosophy: Augustine to Scoutus* (London: Burns, Oates, and Washbourne, 1950), pp. 342–3; Jacques Maritain, *Approaches to God*, trans. Peter O'Reilly (London: George Allen & Unwin, 1955), p. 55; E. L. Mascall, *The Openness of Being* (London: Darton, Longman, & Todd, 1971), p. 61; William L. Rowe, *The Cosmological Argument* (Princeton, N.J.: Princeton University Press, 1975), pp. 6, 11–12; Édouard Pousset, 'Une relecture du traité de Dieu dans la "Somme théologique" de saint Thomas', *Archives de philosophie* 38 (1975): 559–93.
5. Thomas Aquinas, *Summa contra gentiles* 1. 14.
6. Aquinas, *Summa theologiae* 1a. 3. prol.
7. Ibid., 1a. 2. 3.

8. Ibid., 1a. 2. 2.

9. Ibid.

10. Aquinas, *Summa contra gentiles* 1. 9.

11. Aquinas, *Summa theologiae* 1a. 32. 1.

12. Mascall, *Openness*, p. 61; Cf. E. L. Mascall, *Existence and Analogy* (London: Longmans, Green & Co., 1949), pp. 78–9.

13. Aquinas, *Summa theologiae* 1a. 79. 2, 3; 1a. 84. 6, 7; 1a. 85. 1. See also Jacques Maritain, *An Introduction to Philosophy*, trans. E. I. Watkin (London and New York: Sheed & Ward, 1956), pp. 116–21.

14. Aquinas, *Summa theologiae* 1a. 2. 2.

15. Etienne Gilson, *The Philosophy of St. Thomas Aquinas* [*Le thomisme*], 3rd rev. ed., trans. Edward Bullough (Cambridge: W. Heffer & Sons, 1924), p. 42.

16. Aquinas, *Summa theologiae* 1a. 2. 1.

17. Ibid., 1a. 2. 3.

18. In approximate chronological order: *De veritate* 5. 2; *Summa contra gentiles* 1. 13; *De potentia Dei* 3. 5; *In VIII libros Physicorum Aristotelis* 7, 8; *In XII libros Metaphysicorum Aristotelis* 7; *Compendium theologiae ad Reginaldum* 3 (Gilson, *Philosophy of Aquinas*, pp. 3–5).

19. Aquinas, *Summa contra gentiles* 1. 13.

20. Thomas Aquinas, *Commentary on Aristotle's 'Physics'* 5. 4. 678–81.

21. Ibid., 5. 3. 662; 6. 5. 797.

22. Etienne Gilson, *The Spirit of Mediaeval Philosophy*, trans. A. H. C. Downes (London: Sheed & Ward, 1936), p. 68; Joseph Owens, 'The Conclusion of the *Prima Via*', *Modern Schoolman* 30 (1952): 116–21; Joseph Owens, 'Aquinas and the Five Ways', *Monist* 58 (1974): 21–4. See also Thomas Gilby, Additional Appendices to *Summa Theologiae*, vol. 2: *Existence and Nature of God*, by Aquinas, pp. 191–2.

23. Owens, 'Conclusion', pp. 33–4. Cf. Joseph Owens, 'Aquinas and the Proof from the "Physics"', *Mediaeval Studies* 28 (1966): 134; Joseph Owens, *The Doctrine of Being in the Aristotelian 'Metaphysics'*, 2nd ed. (Toronto, Canada: Pontifical Institute of Mediaeval Studies, 1963), pp. 438–9.

24. Aquinas, *Summa theologiae* 1a. 2. 3.

25. Owens, 'Conclusion', p. 41.

26. Aristotle, *Metaphysica* A. 1. 993b24–26.

27. Owens, 'Conclusion', pp. 44–5.

28. Ibid., p. 53.

29. Ibid., p. 110.

30. Ibid., p. 113.

31. Ibid., p. 115.

32. Ibid., p. 116.

33. Ibid., p. 114

34. Ibid., p. 212.

35. Ibid., pp. 212–13.

36. Stephen L. Weber, 'Concerning the Impossibility of A Posteriori Arguments for the Existence of God', *Journal of Religion* 53 (1973): 83–98. Cf. Stephen L. Weber, 'Proofs for the Existence of God: a Meta-investigation' (Ph.D. dissertation, University of Notre Dame, 1969), pp. 119–38.

37. Weber, 'Impossibility', pp. 88–9. Weber also cites this passage and comments:

'For in Book I of this work it was shown, by means of Aristotle's demonstration, that there is a first efficent cause, which we called God. But an efficient cause brings its effects into being. Therefore God is the cause of being to other things.'* Here again it is St. Thomas's goal to demonstrate that God is the cause of being; that is not, however, the proper conclusion of Aristotle's demonstration . . . .

* *On the Truth of the Catholic Faith*, 2: 36 [*sic*] (Ibid., p. 89).

38. Owens, 'Conclusion', p. 117.
39. Cf. William Bryar, *St. Thomas and the Existence of God: Three Interpretations* (Chicago: Henry Regnery Co., 1951), p. vi.
40. Aquinas, *Summa contra gentiles* 1. 13; Aquinas, *Compendium theologiae* 1. 3; Aquinas, *Summa theologiae* 1a. 2. 3.
41. Bryar, *Thomas*, p. vii.
42. Aquinas, *Summa contra gentiles* 1. 13.
43. See especially the second reason for why the statement, 'everything that causes motion is in motion', is not true accidentally in the second proof in the *Summa contra gentiles*.
44. Aquinas, '*Physics*' 8. 23. 1172.
45. Thomas Aquinas, *On Being and Essence* 4; Aquinas, *Summa contra gentiles* 2. 54. Cf. Etienne Gilson, *Being and Some Philosophers*, 2nd ed. (Toronto, Canada: Pontifical Institute of Mediaeval Studies, 1952), p. 173.
46. Aquinas, '*Physics*' 7. 1. 889.
47. Ibid., 8. 1. 966.
48. Ibid., 8. 1. 967.
49. Owens, 'Conclusion', p. 44.
50. Aquinas, '*Physics*' 8. 1. 970.
51. Thomas Aquinas, *Commentary on the 'Metaphysics' of Aristotle* 12. 5. 2499.
52. Owens, 'Conclusion', p. 109.
53. Ibid.
54. Aquinas, '*Physics*' 8. 9. 1042–49.
55. Ibid., 8. 9. 1044.
56. Ibid., 8. 9. 1046.
57. Aquinas, *Summa contra gentiles* 1. 13.
58. Owens, 'Conclusion', p. 114.
59. Aquinas, *Summa contra gentiles* 1. 13.
60. Frederick C. Copleston, *Aquinas* (Harmondsworth, England: Penguin Books, 1955), p. 116; Aquinas, *Summa theologiae* 1a. prol.
61. Kenny is especially exercised by this point (Anthony Kenny, *The Five Ways: St. Thomas Aquinas' Proofs of God's Existence* [New York: Schocken Books, 1969], pp. 15, 33).
62. Bryar, *Thomas*, p. 199.
63. Aquinas, *Compedium theologiae* 1. 3.
64. Weber's argument against *a posteriori* proofs comes very close to this. He argues that Aquinas wants to prove metaphysical contingency; that is to say, finite things are dependent for their continued existing on a ground of being. But such metaphysical contingency can never be demonstrated from purely physical

contingency (Weber, 'Impossibility', p. 95). From here it is only a short step to arguing that Aquinas has presented an Aristotelian proof, but tries to get more mileage out of it than it can produce.

65. Aquinas, *Summa theologiae* la. 3. 4.

66. Ibid., la. 3. 1.

67. Ibid. In the *Summa contra gentiles* Aquinas argues that because God is immoveable, He is eternal; because He is eternal, He is pure actuality (Aquinas, *Summa contra gentiles* 1. 15, 16). It is clear that even here it is God's eternity, not His being the unmoved first mover that discloses His pure actuality. Aquinas uses a purely physical proof to demonstrate an immoveable being; he then concludes such a being must be eternal; and then he argues that the eternity of this being precludes any potentiality to non-existence. Later he concludes that because God is pure actuality, His essence must be existence (ibid., 1. 22). Therefore, Aquinas's metaphysical conclusions are not directly drawn from the proof itself and, hence, cannot be said to force a metaphysical interpretation of the proof. A purely physical proof will yield eternity of God, from which Aquinas will deduce further attributes. In addition to this, Aquinas also develops a parallel chain of deductions from the first cause argument, concluding that because God is first cause, He is eternal and so forth. And again he concludes directly that because God is first cause and first being, He is pure actuality. It is this latter chain of argument that is preserved in the *Summa theologiae*. Weber in his analysis of the *Summa contra gentiles* 2. 6 has failed to discern the different strands of the argument. His second citation refers to the first cause argument, not the argument from motion. The unmoved mover causes beings only insofar as it is the cause of their generation and corruption through the intermediate motion of the heavenly sphere; this production is referred to in Weber's first citation.

68. Owens, 'Conclusion', p. 121.

69. Kenny, *Five Ways*, p. 11.

70. Owens, 'Five Ways', p. 24.

71. Thomas O'Brien sharply criticises Owens on this point, noting that Aquinas teaches in *Quaestiones quodlibetales* 9. 2. 2 that *esse* is attributed truly and properly solely to a thing, or a substance (Thomas C. O'Brien, *Metaphysics and the Existence of God* [Washington, D.C.: Thomist Press, 1960], p. 256). Cf. Aquinas, *Summa contra gentiles* 2. 57; 3. 65; Aquinas, *Summa theologiae* la. 45. 4; la. 90. 2.

72. Anton C. Pegis, 'St. Thomas and the Coherence of the Aristotelian Theology', *Mediaeval Studies* 35 (1973): 109–13. This article is a searching criticsm of Owens's view that Aquinas believed the prime mover of the *Physics* to be less than God.

73. O'Brien, *Metaphysics*, p. 252. Quinn similarly accuses Gilson of mishandling all of Aquinas's first three ways (John M. Quinn, *The Thomism of Étienne Gilson: A Critical Study* [Villanova, Pa.: 1971], pp. 119–24).

74. Ibid., pp. 249, 253.

75. Cf. Aquinas, *Summa theologiae* la. 4. 2.

76. For example, Kenny, *Five Ways*, pp. 21–2; John Hick, *Arguments for the Existence of God* (New York: Herder & Herder, 1971), pp. 40–1; Rowe, *Argument*, p. 15.

77. 'For that which is a being in potency must always be brought to being in act by an agent, which is being in act' (Aquinas, '*Metaphysics*' 9. 7. 1848; '. . . a

thing is not moved from potency to act except through a being in act . . .' (ibid., 7. 2. 1278).

78. This is contrasted to an accidentally ordered series. The former is hierarchical, the latter linear (Aquinas, *Summa theologiae* la. 7. 4; la. 46. 2; Aquinas, *Summa contra gentiles* 1. 13; Aquinas, '*Physics*' 7. 2. 892). M. C. D'Arcy explains that the essentially subordinated series of causes Aquinas has in mind in the first and second ways is the Aristotelian system of the spheres (M. C. D'Arcy, *Thomas Aquinas* [London: Ernest Benn, 1930], p. 162).

79. See John King-Farlow, 'The First Way in Physical and Moral Space', *Thomist* 39 (1975): 349–74, for this mistaken interpretation.

80. Compare Aquinas's various statements in these works: *Sententiarum* 2. 1. 1. 5; *De veritate* 2. 10; *Summa theologiae* la. 7. 4; *De aeternitate mundi contra murmurantes* 310; *Physicorum* 3. 8; *Metaphysicorum* 11. 10. 2328–2329; *Quaestiones quodlibetales* 12. 2. See also Maritain, *Approaches*, p. 45; Loius De Raeymaeker, *The Philosophy of Being*, trans. Edmund H. Ziegelmeyer (St. Louis, Mo.: 1957), p. 173.

81. Lubor Velecky dryly remarks that Aquinas's assertion is simply a 'sociological-historical comment that in Aquinas's day everybody . . . called the thus opaquely characterized entity by the word "deus"' (Lubor Velecky, 'The Five Ways—Proofs of God's Existence?' *Monist* 58[1974]: 37).

82. Aquinas, *Summa theologiae* la. 3. 1; Aquinas, *Summa contra gentiles* 1. 20

83. Aquinas, *Summa contra gentiles* 1. 13; Aquinas, '*Physics*' 7, 8.

84. Aquinas, *Summa theologiae* la. 2. 3.

85. Aquinas, *Summa contra gentiles* 1. 13.

86. Aristotle, *Metaphysica* B. 2. 994al–15.

87. Aquinas, *Summa contra gentiles* 1. 13.

88. Etienne Gilson, *The Christian Philosophy of St. Thomas Aquinas*, trans. L. K. Shook (New York: Random House, 1956), p. 67.

89. Ibid.; cf. Gilson, *Spirit*, p. 77.

90. Aquinas states, 'We have shown by Aristotle's arguments that there exists a first efficient cause whom we call God. But the efficient cause produces the being of its effects. God, therefore, is the cause of the being of all other things' (Aquinas, *Summa contra gentiles* 2. 6.)

91. Aquinas, *Summa theologiae* la. 45. 5.

92. Rosemary Lauer, 'The Notion of Efficient Cause in the *Secunda Via*', *Thomist* 38 (1974): 757. Cf. Aquinas, *Summa contra gentiles* 2. 21.

93. Lauer, 'Cause', p. 764.

94. Kenny, *Five Ways*, p. 44. A study of Aquinas's historical predecessors makes it abundantly clear that the causal series contemplated in the second way is the Aristotelian system of the spheres, for al-Kindī, al-Fārābī, ibn Sīnā, ibn Rushd, and Maimonides all assigned to the spheres the function of causing things on earth. Cf. Aquinas, *Summa theologiae* la. 46. 2; la. 115. 3, 4.

95. Kenny, *Five Ways*, p. 44.

96. This is suggested, for example, by Luigi Immarrone, 'Il valore metafisico delle cinque vie tomistiche', *Miscellanea Francescana* 68 (1968): 280–1.

97. Aquinas, *On Being and Essence* 4.

98. Aquinas, *Summa theologiae* la. 3. 4.

99. Aquinas, '*Metaphysics*' 2. 3. 303.

100. Aquinas, *Summa theologiae* la. 2. 3.

101. Ibid., la. 3. 2.
102. Ibid., la. 3. 3.
103. Ibid., la. 3. 4.
104. Aquinas, *Summa theologiae* la. 2. 3.
105. Aquinas, *Summa contra gentiles* 1. 15.
106. The *Summa contra gentiles* proof is clearly not patterned on Maimonides's proof, for it lacks the characteristic Maimonidean argument concerning the non-existence of all things. Ibn Sīnā's traces are unmistakable, especially in the demand for a cause which determines whether a merely possible being will acquire existence or not. But the proof is nevertheless not ibn Sīnā's, for ibn Sīnā concluded directly from possible beings to God as the necessary being, whereas Aquinas reaches only non-transitory beings, and then argues thence to God. This is because ibn Sīnā's proof concerns the conjoining of existence and essence in any existent being, which takes him right to God. But Aquinas's proof has nothing to do with that distinction; the causes are simply natural causes of transitory beings. The proof cannot be ibn Sīnā's because his is a one-step argument, whereas Aquinas's has two steps. The peculiar feature of the *Summa contra gentiles* proof is that it employs a double infinite regress argument: first one argues from possible to necessary being, then one argues from caused necessary beings to uncaused necessary being. Now the only place where one encounters such a double infinite regress argument is in ibn Rushd's revision of ibn Sīnā's proof. In fact, when ibn Rushd's revision is compared to the *Summa contra gentiles* proof, they appear to be virtually identical. This dependence on ibn Rushd seems to be confirmed by Aquinas's remarks in *On the Power of God* where he sides with ibn Rushd against ibn Sīnā on the nature of possible and necessary beings. He argues that beings are possible, not because their existence is distinct from their essence, but because they have matter capable of receiving new forms (Thomas Aquinas, *On the Power of God* 5. 3). This is obviously the understanding of possible and necessary found in the *Summa contra gentiles* proof. (Cf. Aquinas, *Summa contra gentiles* 2. 30.) Hence, Aquinas follows ibn Rushd in his revision of ibn Sīnā's argument from possible and necessary being. This also sheds light on two other puzzles: (1) why is the proof included in the chapter on divine eternity instead of existence, and (2) why is the third way included in the section on divine existence in the later *Summa*? The answer to the first may be because ibn Rushd's proof would simply duplicate the second way based on causation which is among the proofs for divine existence. On the other hand, ibn Rushd's proof is well suited to the chapter on divine eternity because to him as a faithful Aristotelian a necessary being was equivalent to an eternal being. The answer to the second question may be that while ibn Rushd's proof would not make a distinctive contribution to the Five Ways, Maimonides's proof would, since it is not the same as ibn Rushd's proof.
107. See Patterson Brown, 'St. Thomas' Doctrine of Necessary Being', *Philosophical Review* 73 (1964): 76–90. The mistake of reading logical necessity into the conclusion of the third way is made by John F. X. Knasas, 'Necessity in the *Tertia Via*', *New Scholasticism* 52 (1978): 373–94.
108. See, for example, Paul Geny, 'A propos des preuves thomistes de l'existence de Dieu', *Revue de philosophie* 31 (1924): 575–601; A.-D. Sertillanges, 'A propos des preuves de Dieu: la troisième "voie" thomiste', *Revue de philosophie* 32 (1925): 24–37; M. F., 'La preuve de l'existence de Dieu par la contingence dans

la "Somme Theologique"', *Revue de philosophie* 32 (1925): 319–30; Pedro Descoqs, 'Les derniers écrits du P. Geny', *Archives de philosophie* 3 (1925): 490–5; A.-D. Sertillanges, 'Le P. Descoqs et la "tertia via"', *Revue thomiste* 9 (1926): 490–502; Lucien Chambat, 'La "tertia via" dans saint Thomas et Aristote', *Revue thomiste* 10 (1927): 334–8; Ch.-V. Heris, 'Comptes-rendus', *Bulletin thomiste* 11 (1928): 317–20; Maurice Bouyges, 'Exegese de la "tertia via" de saint Thomas d'Aquin', *Revue de philosophie* 3 (1932): 113–46; Thomas B. Wright, 'Necessary and Contingent Being in St. Thomas', *New Scholasticism* 25 (1951): 448–50; N. Dermot O'Donoghue, 'An Analysis of the *Tertia Via* of St. Thomas', *Irish Theological Quarterly* 20 (1953): 129–51; Thomas Kevin Connolly, 'The Basis of the Third Proof for the Existence of God', *Thomist* 17 (1954): 281–349; Brown, 'Being', pp. 76–90; Joseph Bobik, 'The First Part of the Third Way', *Philosophical Studies* (Ireland) 17 (1968): 142–60; Joseph Owens, '"Cause of Necessity" in Aquinas' Tertia Via', *Mediaeval Studies* 33 (1971): 21–45; Stanisław Kowalczyk, 'L'argument de contingence formulé par st. Thomas d'Aquin', *Divus Thomas* 75 (1972): 413–30. An admitted *re*-interpretation of possible beings as beings composed of essence and existence is found in Stanisław Ziemiański, 'Proba reinterpretacji "Trzeciej drogi" św. Tomasza z Akwinu', *Studia philosophiae christianae* 13 (1977): 145–61.

109. Aquinas, *On the Power of God* 5. 3.

110. Aristotle, *De caelo* 1. 12. 281a28–30.

111. See Geny, 'Propos', p. 586; Descoqs, 'Derniers', pp. 490–5.

112. Chambat, '"Tertia via"', pp. 335–7; Heris, 'Comptes-rendus', p. 319.

113. Descoqs, 'Derniers', pp. 490–5; O'Donoghue, '*Tertia Via*', pp. 140–3; Connolly, 'Basis', pp. 333–4. Descoqs rejects the argument; O'Donoghue and Connolly consider it sound.

114. M. F., 'Preuve', pp. 321–2; Bouyges, 'Exegese', pp. 132–8.

115. See R. L. Sturch, 'The Cosmological Argument' (Ph.D. thesis, Oxford University, 1970), p. 100.

116. See Rem B. Edwards, 'Composition and the Cosmological Argument', *Mind* 77 (1968): 115–17.

117. Quinn suggests a third alternative: the reason everything would cease to exist is that without a necessary being (= *primum mobile*, the first heavenly sphere), beings subject to generation and corruption could not exist. When the forms cease to exist, matter as pure potency simply disappears. Thus if the first sphere were to cease to exist, everything would instantly vanish (John M. Quinn, 'The Third Way to God: A New Approach', *Thomist* 42 [1978]: 50–68). But Quinn takes no connaissance whatever of Maimonides's proof, where the eventual corruption of all things is contemplated. Thomas's wording does not suggest the instantaneous disappearance of all things. It was a common scholastic principle that if something can possibly happen, then given sufficient time it will (N. L. Rabinovitch, 'The One and the Many: Early Scholastic Reasoning in Philosophy', *Annals of Science* 34 [1977]: 331–44). This presupposition seems to lie behind the third way. It is the second way that envisages the causality of the spheres of which Quinn speaks.

118. Owens, '"Cause"', p. 41.

119. Bobik, 'First Part', p. 147.

120. Ibid., p. 158.

121. Copleston, *Aquinas*, p. 124.

122. See Aquinas, *Summa theologiae* la. 46. 2.

123. There has been some confusion as to whether the third way is inconsistent with Aquinas's position on the possibility of an infinite temporal regress. For example, R. N. Mabey terribly misconstrues the third way by summarising it:

> If something does not always exist, then nothing would exist now.
> Therefore, something always exists. (Not: one and the same thing always exists.)
> If something always exists, then if the number of things that exist (tenseless) is finite, at least one always exists (Rendell N. Mabey, 'Confusion and the Cosmological Argument', *Mind* 80 [1971]: 126).

But what, asks Mabey, if the number is infinite? Since Aquinas admitted the possibility, the third way fails (ibid.) But Aquinas is arguing for the everlasting existence of a *particular* being(s), not just something in general. If such a being does not exist, then eventually there will be nothing, given infinite time. This is not inconsistent with his admission that an infinite temporal regress is possible, for as T. P. M. Solon points out, such a regress is logically possible but not actually necessary. It could become actual only by being caused by a necessary being (T. P. M. Solon, 'The Logic of Aquinas' *Tertia Via*', *Mind* 82 [1973]: 598). But Solon errs when he concludes from this that there must therefore exist a necessary being or otherwise the series would never be actualised, and, hence, nothing would *ever* have existed (ibid.) What Aquinas concludes is that there must exist a non-transitory being(s), or otherwise all the possible beings would have ceased to be, and hence, nothing would exist now. There can only be an infinite temporal regress if something eternal exists. Thus, Aquinas's position on the infinite regress and the third way are in harmony, at least on this score.

124. Gilson, *Philosophy of Aquinas*, pp. 65–6.

125. Owens, '"Cause"', p. 42.

126. This is the position of Sertillanges, 'Descoqs', p. 500.

127. N. D. O'Donoghue, 'In Defence of the Third Way', *Philosophical Studies* (Ireland) 18 (1969): 174–5.

128. Joseph Bobik, 'Further Reflections on the First Part of the Third Way', *Philosophical Studies* (Ireland) 20 (1972): 170.

129. Aquinas, *Summa theologiae* la. 19. 8; la. 22. 4; la. 44. 1; 1a2ae. 93. 4.

130. Ibid., 1a. 10. 5; la. 75. 6; 1a. 115. 6.

131. Ibid., la. 23. 7; 1a. 75. 6.

132. Ibid., 1a. 9. 2; 1a. 10. 5; 1a. 50. 5.

133. Ibid., 1a. 104. 4.

134. Aquinas, *On the Power of God* 5. 3.

135. Aquinas, *On Being and Essence* 4. Gilson has asserted that this passage is not a proof for God (Gilson, *Christian Philosophy of St. Thomas*, p. 82), largely because the real distinction between essence and existence cannot be known prior to the existence of God, in whom they are identical. But this interpretation is surely wrong (see Dennis Bonnette, *Aquinas' Proofs for God's Existence* [The Hague: Martinus Nijhoff, 1973], pp. 57–8). As Beach notes,

> The first two proofs (in the *Sum. Theol.*, I, 3, 4) for the identity of essence and

existence are reared upon their composition in finite beings. Unless we wish to read a vicious circle into Aquinas, the conclusion is unavoidable that he arrives at the essence–existence distinction prior to knowing the nature of God (John D. Beach, 'Another Look at the Thomison of Étienne Gilson', *New Scholasticism* 50 [1976]: 527).

Aquinas employed the same arguments as his Arabic forebears to prove the real distinction. (For a critical study of the development of this doctrine in Aquinas, see M.-D. Roland-Gosselin, *Le 'De ente et essentia' de S. Thomas d'Aquin* [Paris: Vrin, 1926].) For a re-working of the proof for God in *De ente*, see Joseph Bobik, 'A Seventh Way', *New Scholasticism* 50 (1976): 345–52.

136. Cf. Owens, '"Cause"', pp. 30, 43–4. Owens also contends that the third way seeks, in addition to the cause of the existence of necessary beings, a cause of why their natures are necessary, and this cause is the divine will.

137. Etienne Gilson, *History of Christian Philosophy in the Middle Ages* (London: Sheed & Ward, 1955), pp. 370–1.

138. Ibid., pp. 371–2. See also Etienne Gilson, *God and Philosophy* (New Haven, Conn.: Yale University Press, 1946), p. 63; Gilson, *Being*, pp. 3–4, 177, 218, 32; Jacques Maritain, *Existence and the Existent*, trans. Lewis Galantiere and Gerald B. Phelan (New York: Pantheon Books, 1948), pp. 22–34; Owens, 'Conclusion', pp. 118–21.

139. Aquinas, *Summa theologiae* 1a. 3. 1.

140. Ibid., 1a. 3. 2.

141. Ibid., 1a. 3. 3.

142. Ibid., 1a. 3. 4.

143. Ibid.

144. Sturch, 'Argument', p. 135.

145. Copleston, *Aquinas*, p. 107. Cf. Aquinas, '*Metaphysics*' 1. 2. 556, 558.

146. George Lindbeck, 'A Great Scotist Study', *Review of Metaphysics* 7 (1954): 430–1.

147. F. Rahman, 'Essence and Existence in Avicenna', *Mediaeval and Renaissance Studies* 4 (1958): 14–15.

Chapter 6

John Duns Scotus

The cosmological argument of John Duns (1265–1308) of Scotland has been hailed as 'a landmark in the history of the cosmological argument', one that is much more significant than those of his predecessors[1]; indeed, the complexity and length of Scotus's case for the existence of God make Aquinas's proofs look like the summary arguments for theological novices that they purport to be.[2] According to Allan B. Wolter, Scotus devoted more attention to developing a proof for God's existence than any of the other great scholastics.[3] He formulated only one basic argument, which he revised three times during the eight years in which he laboured on it. The proof chosen by Scotus for this intensive study was not the favourite of Aquinas, the proof from motion. According to Harris, Scotus attached 'no weight' to Thomas's first way.[4] F. C. Copleston explains that in Scotus's eyes,

> . . . the conception of God as first Mover was a very inadequate conception, as it does not pass beyond the physical world and attain the transcendent, infinite Being on which all finite beings essentially depend.[5]

Therefore, Scotus bypasses Thomas's *manifestior via* and seeks to develop a metaphysical proof for the existence of an infinite being.[6] In his *Opus oxoniense*, Scotus poses this question: '*whether in the realm of beings something exists which is actually infinite*?'[7] This conception of God as infinite being, states Harris, 'is the fundamental notion of the Scotist natural theology'.[8] For Scotus wants to prove that among beings, an infinite being exists. This implies that we must possess a univocal concept of 'being'.[9] A concept is univocal, according to Scotus, if it has sufficient unity such that to affirm and deny it of a subject results in a contradiction, and such that it may serve as the middle term in a syllogism.[10] Scotus argues that if 'God exists' and 'Creatures exist' do not mean by the word 'exists' the same thing, then it is empty to speak of having proved God's existence. Therefore, we need a univocal concept of being, one that can equally apply to God and creatures. Such a bareboned concept of being is *that which is opposed to nothingness.*[11] In reality, being exists in two modes, according to Scotus: finite and infinite.[12] The univocal conception of being is an abstraction from the actual bifurcated state of reality. God is opposed to nothingness, but in an infinite way. The proper concept of God is not just being, but infinite being, as Wolter states:

> Proper concepts are those which apply exclusively to God, such as 'infinite being', 'highest goodness', and the like. In the first of the two, Scotus emphasises that 'infinite' is not a specific difference or an attribute in any sense of the term. Rather it is an intrinsic mode, expressing something that pertains to the formal character of being as found in God.[13]

Thus, although Scotus insists on a univocal concept of being, he preserves the transcendence of God with regard to the universe by making the being of creatures and of God utterly diverse in reality.[14] The existence of such an infinite being marks the terminus at which Scotus's proof aims. None of his other philosophical doctrines peculiar to himself are presupposed in the proof; indeed, noting that Scotus rewrote a section of the proof lest his theory of univocity pose a stumbling block to some, Wolter remarks that '. . . Scotus tried to free his proof of everything that bordered on the controversial'.[15] His argument for the existence of God may be found in expanded form in his *Opus oxoniense* and in a more concise version in the *De primo principio.* Scotus summarises his argument thus:

> . . . the first article establishes the existence of some being that is simply first by the triple primacy of efficiency, finality and eminence, and is first in such an unqualified sense that it would be impossible for anything to be prior to it. This is to establish the existence of God in so far as the divine properties that have reference to creatures are concerned, or in so far as creatures are dependent upon him.[16]

He then proceeds to prove this being is infinite:

> The second article shows in four ways that this first Being is infinite, first, because it is the first efficient cause; secondly, because as an agent,

it knows all that can be made. . .; thirdly, because it is the last end; and fourthly, because it is most excellent.[17]

The first part of the proof is the cosmological argument proper. It may be outlined in the *Opus oxoniense* as follows:

1. The triple primacy: in the realm of beings something exists which is simply first in the order of efficient causality, final causality, and by reason of pre-eminence because:
   a. The primacy of efficiency:
      i. Among beings which can produce an effect one is simply first.
         a. Some being is produced.
         b. It is produced by itself or nothing or another being.
         c. It cannot be produced by nothing
            (*i*) because nothing causes nothing.
         d. It cannot be produced by itself
            (*i*) because nothing can make itself.
         e. Therefore, it must be produced by another being.
         f. This being is either first or not first.
         g. If it is first, then a first efficient cause exists.
         h. If it is not first, a first efficient cause exists
            (*i*) because we can argue about this being as we did about the one it caused.
            (*ii*) Thus, the series of beings caused by another could go on *ad infinitum.*
            (*iii*) An infinity in an ascending order is impossible.
            (*iv*) Therefore, a first efficient cause must exist.
         i. The objection that an infinite series of causes is possible is not cogent.
            (*i*) Essentially ordered causes differ from accidentally ordered causes in three ways: in essentially ordered causes the second cause depends upon the first precisely in its act of causation, the higher cause is more perfect than the lower cause, and all the causes are simultaneously required to cause the effect, none of which is true of accidentally ordered causes.
            (*ii*) An infinite series of essentially ordered causes is impossible.
               (*a*) First argument:
                  α. Assuming an infinite series of essentially or-

dered causes could exist, the secondary causes depend upon the first.

β. Therefore, the whole infinite series would depend upon a first cause.

γ. This first cause could not be a part of the series
(α) because then it would cause itself.

δ. Therefore, even if there were infinite causes, they would still be dependent upon a first cause outside the series.

(*b*) Second argument:

α. If an infinite number of essentially ordered causes combined to produce an effect, then an infinite number of causes would simultaneously cause the effect.

β. But no one would agree to this.

(*c*) Third argument:

α. To be prior, a thing must be nearer to the beginning.

β. But in an infinite series there is no beginning.

γ. Therefore, nothing could be prior to something else.

(*d*) Fourth argument:

α. In an essentially ordered series, what is infinitely higher is infinitely more perfect.

β. But what is perfect cannot be caused to cause something
(α) because then it would be dependent upon something else for its exercise of causality.
(β) Therefore, it would not be perfect.

(*e*) Fifth argument:

α. A perfect being can exercise causality
(α) because exercising causality implies no imperfection
(β) and what implies no imperfection can be asserted of perfect beings.

β. But if every cause is dependent upon some prior cause, then efficient causality is never found without imperfection.

γ. Thus, it is at least *possible* that a nature exists which causes without imperfection and is simply first.

(*iii*) An infinite series of accidentally ordered causes is impossible unless the essentially ordered series of causes is finite.

(*a*) In an accidentally ordered series, the causes exist successively.

(*b*) But such a series cannot exist without some nature of infinite duration upon which the whole series and every part of it depends

α. because no change in form continues to exist unless something permanent exists which is not part of the succession

(α) because anything in the succession cannot co-exist with the whole series.

β. Therefore, whatever depends upon an accidentally ordered cause depends even more upon an essentially ordered cause.

(*iv*) If an essential order of causes is denied, an infinity is still impossible.

(*a*) Some nature is capable of exercising efficient causality.

α. Because nothing can come from nothing.

(*b*) If it is uncaused, then it is the first efficient cause.

(*c*) If it is caused accidentally, then a first efficient cause must exist

α. because an accidentally ordered series of causes cannot exist without an essentially ordered series of causes (1.a.*i.i.*(*iii*))

j. The objection that this argument does not attain the status of a demonstration because it is based on contingent premisses is not cogent.

(*i*) The argument is based on a contingent but nonetheless manifest proposition

(*a*) because it is obvious that when a change occurs, the end product of the change is produced or effected.

(*b*) Therefore, some nature is produced.

(*c*) Therefore, some efficient cause exists to produce the nature.

(*ii*) The argument can be reformulated such that it is based on necessary premisses, namely, something is able to produce an effect

(*a*) because some nature is able to be produced
α. because something can be changed.

ii. Among beings which can produce an effect the one which is simply first is itself incapable of being caused
a. because it has no efficient cause (1.a.*i.*),
b. and it has no final cause
(*i*) because a final cause only causes metaphorically by moving an efficient cause to produce the effect,
c. and it has no material or formal cause:
(*i*) First reason:
(*a*) if a thing has no extrinsic cause, it does not have an intrinsic cause
α. because an intrinsic cause implies imperfection
(α) because it is part of the thing it causes;
(*b*) thus, an extrinsic cause has priority over the intrinsic cause,
(*c*) and in denying the prior cause, one automatically denies the posterior as well.
(*ii*) Second reason:
(*a*) intrinsic causes are caused by extrinsic causes in either their being, or their composition in things, or both.
(*b*) Thus, without an extrinsic cause, intrinsic causes cannot exist.

iii. Such a being actually exists and some actually existing nature is capable of such causality.
a. A being which is of such a nature that it cannot receive existence from another must exist of itself if it is able to exist.
b. A being first in the order of efficient causality is a being of such a nature.
c. It is possible that this being exists (1.a.*i.i.*(*ii*)(*e*); 1.a.*i.j.*(*ii*)).
d. Therefore, it does exist
(*i*) because unless it *actually* exists, it would not be capable of existing of itself
(*a*) otherwise a non-existent being would cause something to exist,
(*b*) which is impossible,
(*c*) as well as self-contradictory
α. because the first cause would then not be uncaused, but self-caused;

(*ii*) and because it would be unfitting that the universe should lack the highest possible degree of being.

b. The primacy of finality:
  i. Some end is simply ultimate
    a. because of the same reasons as discussed in 1.a.*i.i.*(*ii*).
  ii. The ultimate end cannot be caused in any way
    a. because it cannot be ordained for an end
      (*i*) otherwise it would not be ultimate.
    b. Moreover, it cannot be caused by an efficient cause
      (*i*) because every efficient cause acts for the sake of an end,
      (*ii*) and nothing can be produced without an efficient cause.
      (*iii*) But whatever has no end has no efficient cause.
    c. Moreover, it can have no formal or material cause
      (*i*) because of the same reasons as discussed in 1.a.*ii.c.*
  iii. The being which can be an ultimate end actually exists, and this primacy pertains to some actually existing nature
    a. because of the same reasons as discussed in 1.a.*iii.*

c. The primacy of perfection:
  i. Some nature is first in perfection
    a. because an essential order exists among essences
    b. and in such an order an ultimate nature is to be found
      (*i*) because of the same reasons discussed in 1.a.*i.i.*(*ii*).
  ii. This supreme nature cannot be caused
    a. because it cannot be ordained to an end
      (*i*) for the end surpasses a thing in perfection.
    b. Moreover, it cannot have an efficient cause
      (*i*) because everything produced has an essentially ordered cause,
      (*ii*) and in an essentially ordered series the cause is more perfect than the effect.
  iii. This supreme nature actually exists
    a. because of the same reasons as discussed in 1.a.*iii.*

2. The three primacies are interrelated because:
  a. the first efficient cause is the ultimate end
    i. because the first cause acts for the sake of the first end
      a. because every efficient cause acts for the sake of an end
      b. and every prior cause acts for a prior end;
    ii. the first cause does not act for the sake of anything distinct from itself
      a. because otherwise that thing would be more noble than the efficient cause.

iii. Therefore, the first efficient cause is the ultimate end.

b. And the first efficient cause is the supreme nature

i. because the first efficient cause is more perfect than its effects.

ii. Therefore, it is the supremely perfect nature.

3. The three primacies are united in one nature because:

a. the first efficient cause has necessity of being

i. because it is wholly uncaused;

ii. and nothing can be non-existent unless something positively or privately incompossible with it can exist

a. because no being can be destroyed except by something incompossible with it;

iii. but nothing can be incompossible with a being that is wholly uncaused and exists of itself

a. because what is incompossible can exist by itself or by another.

b. If it can exist by itself, then it will exist by itself;

c. but then two incompossible beings would co-exist, or rather, neither would exist

(*i*) because each would destroy the other.

d. Neither can it exist by another

(*i*) because an effect which is incompossible with some being can destroy that being only if its own existence is more perfect and intense;

(*ii*) but no effect can have existence more perfect than the self-existent being

(*a*) because every effect has a dependent existence, while the self-existent being has independent existence.

b. And two necessary natures cannot exist

i. because if they did, some reality in each would distinguish one from the other.

ii. These real differences are necessary or not.

iii. If they are necessary, then each nature will have two reasons for its necessary existence: the differences and the likenesses they share.

iv. But this is impossible

a. because if one reason were eliminated, the beings would still exist in virtue of the other reason

b. and that means that the beings are necessary in virtue of something that when eliminated leaves them the same as before.

v. If these differences are not necessary, then they are not of the essence of the nature and therefore belong to possible, not necessary being.
vi. But nothing merely possible belongs to what is necessary.

c. And two first efficient causes cannot exist
  i. because two supremely perfect natures cannot exist
    a. because no two occur at the same level.

d. And two ultimate ends cannot exist in the same universe
  i. because if they did, we would have two separate groups of beings, each directed to its ultimate end and unrelated to each other
    a. because what is ordered to one ultimate end cannot be ordered to another
      (*i*) because if it were, one ultimate end could be removed, and nothing would be changed.
  ii. Thus, these two groups would not form one universe.

The arguments are a curious fusion of two types of thought: Aristotelian empiricism and Anselmian *a priorism.* Though influenced by the Thomist–Dominican school, Scotus retained the Augustinian–Franciscan element in his thought as well.[18] The proof itself shows the influence of Henry of Ghent.[19] He had tried to organise the many proofs for the existence of God that had been advanced during the Middle Ages by grouping them into two general categories: the way of causality and the way of eminence. The first set drew its inspiration from the principles of Aristotle, while the second was Augustinian in character and developed out of the school of St. Victor and Anselm. Scotus clearly follows Henry in the triple primacy of his own proof for God's existence.

Let us examine this proof step by step. Scotus begins by positing *the triple primacy: in the realm of beings something exists which is simply first in the order of efficient causality, final causality, and by reason of pre-eminence.* The proof of this step is divided into three parts, but as the outline makes clear, the crux of the argumentation appears in the first section dealing with the primacy of efficiency. Scotus desires to demonstrate that an efficient cause exists which is 'simply first', that is to say, it 'neither can be produced by an efficient cause nor does it exercise its efficient causality in virtue of anything other than itself'.[20] The departure point of the proof is clearly *a posteriori*, for Scotus argues that some being is produced—in other words, we see things in the world that are effects. He employs the by now familiar arguments against anything's being caused by nothing or by itself and concludes that it must be caused by another thing. If this other thing is not the first efficient cause, then we become involved in an infinite regress as we ask for the cause of each cause. But an infinity in an ascending order is impossible, an ascending order being one in which one proceeds from effect to cause in contrast to a descending order in which one moves from cause to effect. Scotus will qualify this assertion, however, for he believed that an ascending order regressing temporally is capable of being infinite, but that an ascending order which is hierarchical in nature cannot be infinite. Because the series is finite, there must be a first efficient cause, since, he adds, causes in a circle are inadmissible. Scotus's proof is thus initially very similar to Aquinas's second way.

But there are two objections to this proof, says Scotus. First, some philosophers argue that an infinite number of ascending causes is possible, as in the series of generations regressing into the past. Therefore, the point must be clarified: Scotus says he is speaking only about causes which are essentially ordered, not causes which are accidentally ordered. In step 1.a.*i.i.*(*i*) are listed the three differences between these types of causal series as Scotus spells them out.[21] The first difference implies that in an essentially ordered series, the intermediate causes have no causal efficacy of their own, but are mere instruments of the prior cause. The second difference reflects the medieval doctrine that essentially ordered causes must differ in nature, the less perfect being caused by the more perfect.[22] The third difference establishes quite clearly the hierarchical nature of the causes, since they all act at the same time.

Scotus is prepared to argue on five counts that an infinite series of essentially ordered causes is impossible. The first argument is very curious, since it seems to assume the existence of the infinite series which Scotus had set out to refute. Although this move is confusing, it does not at all merit the conclusion of William Rowe that Scotus therefore believes that an infinite, essentially ordered causal series is actually possible after all, but that it does not rationally explain *why* these effects exist, that is, does not provide a sufficient reason for these effects.[23] This evinces a complete misunderstanding of the proof, for Scotus proceeds to argue on four other grounds that an essentially ordered series cannot possibly be infinite; besides, Scotus is seeking here a first *efficient cause*, not an ultimate *reason*, and when he does later speak of that which supplies the ultimate sufficient reason for all things, he is talking about the simply first final cause.[24] Rather Scotus assumes here the possibility of an infinite series for the sake of argument ('in essentially ordered causes where *our opponent* assumes an infinity'[25]) in order to demonstrate that even then a first efficient cause would be required. The argument is misplaced, for it does not prove that an infinite series cannot exist; rather it shows that Scotus's proof for a first cause retains its cogency even if an essentially ordered causal series could be infinite. The argument itself is rather obscure and raises the problem of the fallacy of composition. The reasoning seems to be that since every member of the causal series is dependent, then the entire series is itself dependent. But it is very difficult to grasp the relationship of the series to its cause. The cause cannot be related to it as an essential cause would be to an accidental series, for this series is itself essentially ordered. It would thus appear that the infinite, essential order must depend upon an essential cause, but this does not make much sense, since the essential order is endless. Scotus says that the first cause is not part of the series, else it would cause itself; nor can it be the first member in the series, for the series is infinite. It exists in some unexplained fashion 'outside the group' of essential causes and it 'does not pertain to the group that is caused' by it.[26] This is the entire extent of Scotus's explanation of the argument, and it leaves the reader somewhat befuddled by the apparent inconsistency.[27] Scotus's second argument is a *reductio ad absurdum*: if an infinite, essentially ordered causal series could exist, then one would have an infinite number of causes combining simultaneously to cause the effect, which no philosopher would grant. Hence, such a series cannot exist. Again the argument is not clear: Scotus could be arguing, with Aquinas and Aristotle before him, that it is absurd to say a single effect is produced by an infinity of causes, or he could be contending that no actual infinite can exist. We may cautiously regard the second as perhaps more probable, since the *De primo principio* version of the argument seems to imply this ('Furthermore, infinite causes essentially ordered would be simultaneously in act— . . . a consequence no philosopher posits'.[28]), and since his assertion, 'Now no philosopher assumes this',[29] rightly describes the then ubiquitous attitude that an actual infinite magnitude could not exist. But again, Scotus's statement of the argument, all of two sentences long, simply does not permit certainty with regard to interpretation of his meaning. His third argument against an infinite, essentially ordered series is likewise a *reductio ad absurdum*: to be prior, a thing must be nearer the beginning; but since an infinite series has no beginning, nothing in that series could be prior to anything else in the series, which is ridiculous. The argument is based on Aristotle's statement that 'the words "prior" and "posterior" are applied . . . to some things (on the assumption that there is a first, i.e. a beginning, in each class) because they are nearer to some beginning . . .'.[30] The fourth argument is again a *reductio ad absurdum*: if one had an infinite, essentially ordered causal series, then some causes would be infinitely higher in the series than the effect and thus infinitely more perfect; but then they could not be caused to cause, since nothing infinitely perfect could be dependent upon another for its exercise of causality. Hence, there must be an uncaused cause which is simply first. The argument is based on the second difference between essentially ordered and accidentally ordered causes, and it also assumes that in an infinite series there must be a point infinitely removed from the terminus. Scotus's fifth argument foreshadows the thorough overhaul his argument will soon undergo. He simply makes the point that the exercise of causality implies no imperfection in a being. Thus, it is at least possible that some first cause which is perfect exists. Otherwise, causality would always be associated with imperfection. This does not prove that an infinite series of imperfect beings is impossible; it only shows that a perfect first cause is possible. The argument would be worthless if Scotus were to retain the present *a posteriori* character of his proof, but he is about to radically alter that.

Having proved that an infinite, essentially ordered series of causes is impossible, Scotus garnishes his proof with an extra argument: even an infinite, accidentally ordered series of causes is impossible unless a finite, essentially ordered series also exists. Because accidentally ordered causes succeed one another in time, they do not depend on one another for their causal efficacy. But such a series of successive things cannot be infinite 'unless it exists in virtue of some nature of infinite duration from which the whole succession and every part thereof depends'.[31] The reason there must be this ground for the series is that '. . . no change of form is perpetuated save in virtue of something permanent which is not a part of the succession'.[32] Scotus seems to be saying that, in change, there must be something that preserves the change. If all were in flux, no change would endure. This permanent element must be outside the series of successive things because '. . . everything of this succession which is in flux, is of the same nature and no part thereof can be coexistent with the entire series for the simple reason that it would no longer be a part of the latter'.[33] In other words, if the element of permanence were in the series, then it would be subject to succession itself and would come to be and pass away. There must be a permanent ground for the whole series of changing things. Every thing in the series will be essentially dependent upon this ground for its continuing in existence after its accidental cause brings it into being. This means that even the accidentally ordered series of causes cannot exist unless there is an essentially ordered causal series.

It must be said that Scotus has not proved here that this essential order must be finite, as he purports to, but only that it must exist. Its finitude must be demonstrated by the five arguments above.

Scotus then adds his *coup de grace*: if one denies that an essential order exists, an infinity is still impossible. Unfortunately, analysis discloses that Scotus does not really move beyond his second point. He argues that since nothing can come from nothing, there must be a nature that can be an efficient cause. This nature is either caused or uncaused. If it is uncaused, then it is the simply first efficient cause. But if it is caused accidentally, then an essential order of causes has to exist, as demonstrated above. One cannot have an accidental order without an essential order; therefore, the denial of essential causality cannot be maintained. Clearly, the third point is only a restatement of the second.

Thus, Scotus believes that he has decisively refuted the objection that an infinite series of causes is possible. What is of interest is that he has done so without even utilising the argument of Aristotle that intermediate, instrumental causes require the existence of a first or the effect would not be produced. Scotus ignores the argument, perhaps because of its association with the proof from motion, which he disdains, preferring to argue that an infinite regress of essential causes would require a first cause and would be in any case absurd and that a perfect cause that is simply first is possible.

We may wish to ask at this point exactly what Scotus means by efficient causality. It seems clear that he is not speaking of efficient causes of motion or change, for he divorces himself from the physical proof from motion. According to Wolter, Scotus is speaking of efficient causes of existence: 'The efficient cause is defined as one which gives existence to its effect . . .'.[34] This might lead us to think that Scotus is in this proof demonstrating the existence of a first cause in the same way that Fārābī, ibn Sīnā, Maimonides, and Aquinas had before him, that is, by arguing that contingent beings are composed of essence and existence and that their continued existing requires a necessary first cause in which essence and existence are not composed and which conjoins essences with the act of existing. Except for his strange silence in mentioning neither essence nor existence in the proof, this interpretation of efficient causality would accord with the steps of Scotus's proof: the essentially ordered cause and ground of all accidentally ordered causes is the first cause which causes them to continue in existence by conjoining existence to their essences. In fact, this interpretation seems so natural that it is well-nigh impossible to resist. But the major stumbling block to such an interpretation is that

Scotus simply denied the real distinction between essence and existence.[35] In the manner that earned him the title of the Subtle Doctor, Scotus maintained that the distinction between essence and existence was neither real nor purely conceptual, but somewhere in between, a *distinctio formalis a parte rei* or an objective formal distinction. Copleston explains,

> In brief, the doctrine is that there is a distinction which is less than the real distinction and more objective than a virtual distinction. A real distinction obtains between two things which are physically separable, at least by divine power . . . . A purely mental distinction signifies a distinction made by the mind when there is no corresponding objective distinction in the thing itself . . . . A formal distinction obtains when the mind distinguishes in an object two or more *formalitates* which are objectively distinct, but which are inseparable from one another, even by divine power.[36]

We could illustrate each type of distinction as follows: a real distinction would be that between the soul and the body, which though united in man, are separable; a mental distinction would be that between 'man' and 'rational animal'; an objective formal distinction would be that between intelligence and will, for these are not separable, but are, nevertheless, not identical either. Now it must be admitted that Scotus's objective formal distinction differs not at all from Aquinas's real distinction when it comes to the relation of essence to existence.[37] For Thomas did not believe that essence and existence were separable, even by God, so that his essence/existence distinction would not be a 'real' distinction in Scotus's terminology. Scotus's denial of the real distinction would be more directly pertinent to thinkers like Giles of Rome, who held that essence and existence were separable. Aquinas and Scotus would be one in contending that essence and existence are co-created and inseparable elements in existing things and that the distinction between them is not merely mental. But the point is that Scotus *thought* he was rejecting a real distinction and therefore would not employ an argument for the existence of God which was based on a conception he regarded as spurious. The question arises as to whether Scotus might not have tried to found the cosmological argument on the objective formal distinction of essence and existence; but he did not appear to be concerned with the issue. He never mentions it in his proof for God, and he makes nothing out of God's essence involving or being identical with existence.[38] What then is the essentially ordered series of causes of existence, if not the causes of the composition of essence and existence? The answer would probably be the spherical system which is operative in the causal series of Aquinas's second way and ibn Rushd's cosmological argument.

The second objection that might be raised against this proof, Scotus states, is that it does not attain to the level of demonstration because it is based on contingent premisses, that is to say, the premisses assume the actual existence of something that has been caused, and everything caused exists contingently. Therefore, the initial step of the argument is contingent.[39] Now we would not today place such rigorous stringencies upon an argument before it can be called a demonstration, but Scotus considered this objection to be so important that he radically revises the fundamental nature of his proof. He suggests two responses to the objection. First, the argument is based on a contingent proposition, it is true, but this proposition is so manifest that the proof retains its cogency. Thus, Scotus declares that although this proposition is contingent, '. . . it is nevertheless most evident, so that anyone who denies the existence of some being which is not eternal needs senses and punishment . . .'.[40] More specifically he argues from reality of change which we perceive in the world: since we observe that some end result of change is effected, there must be some thing which is an efficient cause of the new nature which is produced. Scotus appears to come very close to sinking back into the proof from motion at this point, but if one remembers that change includes substantial change, then Scotus could still retain the existential causality which he spoke of in dealing with the first objection. At any rate, the *a posteriori* character of the proof is clearly retained. But in his second response to the objection, Scotus performs major surgery on his argument. '. . . the argument can be reformulated in such a way that it proceeds from necessary premises', he declares.[41] Although it is contingent that some caused nature exists, it is necessary that it is *possible* that some caused nature exists:

> . . . although things other than God are actually contingent as regards their actual existence, this is not true with regard to potential existence. Wherefore, those things which are said to be contingent with reference to actual existence are necessary with respect to potential existence. Thus, though 'Man exists' is contingent, 'It is possible for man to exist' is necessary, because it does not include a contradiction as regards existence . . . . Being is divided into what must exist and what can but need not be. And just as necessity is of the very essence . . . of what must be, so possibility is of the very essence of what can but need not be. Therefore, let the former argument be

> couched in terms of possible being and the propositions will become necessary.[42]

This means that Scotus is no longer arguing from the actual existence of beings but merely from the possibility of their existing:

> In this case, the proof . . . proceeds from what the thing is or from its possible existence, but not from its actual existence. The actual existence of this being which up to now we have shown to be merely possible, however, will be established in the third conclusion.[43]

As the outline reveals, the proof is based simply on the possibility of existing things: because something can be changed, some nature is able to be produced. By correlation, because some nature is able to be produced, something is able to produce an effect. This does not mean that something actually exists which can produce an effect; it is simply possible that such a being could exist. Scotus's argument could be pressed if no creatures existed at all: it would still be necessary that it is *possible* for *x* to exist. Many writers, anxious to preserve the *a posteriori* character of the proof, would disagree with this judgement. They emphasise that for Scotus we know that beings are possible only because beings exist; possibility is a modal property of actually existing things.[44] Because they do exist, we know that they have the possibility to exist. Now while this is true, it cannot stay the conclusion that Scotus has converted his proof to an *a priori* argument. For although we may come to know the truth of the first premiss by experience, the truth value of that premiss is in no way dependent upon experience. Wolter admits that 'The factual proposition as such . . . does not enter into the demonstration as a premiss; it is only preliminary to the proof'.[45] As he explains elsewhere, the scholastics held that a necessary proposition might be obtained from a contingent one by an immediate non-syllogistic inference which precedes the demonstration proper.[46] So here Scotus infers from the fact that something exists the fact that it is possible for something to exist. This latter fact possesses a truth value that is wholly *a priori*. Alluntio is mistaken when he says that this premiss is 'founded on and justified by' the facts of experience.[47] Not at all; to use a Kantian turn of phrase, the truth of the premiss may be known upon the occasion of experience, but it is not therefore based on and derived from experience. Julius Weinberg explains,

> . . . such a proposition is necessarily true even though its terms were

> originally obtained from senses capable of error. The senses were only the occasion for the acquisition of these concepts and thus they are not dependent on sensation for the evident truth of some propositions into which they enter.[48]

According to Armand Maurer, this makes the starting point of the argument absolutely necessary: 'Although it is learned through sense experience, in itself it is a truth independent of the actual existence of creatures'.[49] Even if God had not willed to create, says Maurer, it would be eternally true that some being could be produced.[50] This means, as Efrem Bettoni points out, that even if reality were to turn out to be only an illusion and nothing exists, it still remains true that it is possible that something can exist.[51] Therefore, Scotus's argument would retain its cogency wholly apart from the facts of experience which gave rise to the formulation of its first premiss. The upshot of this is, of course, that the argument has now become thoroughly *a priori* in character and can no longer be called a cosmological argument. In fact, Scotus has produced an ontological argument of striking similarity to those of Spinoza and Leibniz. This verdict might be disputed, however, because Scotus is commonly thought to reject *a priori* proofs like the ontological argument in favour of *a posteriori* proofs. But such a statement can be misleading. In the first place, Scotus does not reject the ontological argument out of hand. He initiates his proof for God's existence by stating,

> Although the proposition 'An infinite being exists' can, by the very nature of its terms, be demonstrated by a demonstration of the reasoned fact,* *we* are not able to demonstrate it in this way. Nevertheless, we can demonstrate the proposition by a demonstration of fact beginning with creatures.
>
> * . . . .[52]

Wolter explains that a demonstration of the reasoned fact is equivalent to what we call an *a priori* form of demonstration, while a demonstration of fact is always *a posteriori*.[53] Scotus asserts that an analysis of the terms will disclose the truth of the proposition, but that we cannot carry out such an analysis; this is probably because of our finitude.[54] But we can prove the proposition by beginning with creatures; this statement, we have seen, Scotus later qualifies under the pressure of the second objection such that we would begin with the possibility of creatures.[55] But Scotus is not thereby finished with the ontological argument; he re-introduces it in his discussion of the divine infinity. There he states that the argument if 'touched up' is useful. He writes,

> God is a being conceived without contradiction, who is so great that it would be a contradiction if a greater being could be conceived. That the phrase 'without contradiction' must be added is clear, for anything, the very knowledge or thought of which includes a contradiction, is called 'inconceivable' . . . .
>
> . . . the greatest object conceivable without contradiction can exist in reality . . . .
>
> . . . this being actually exists because the highest conceivable object is not one which is merely in the intellect of the thinker . . . . what exists in reality is conceivably greater than what exists only in the intellect.[56]

In his touching up of Anselm's argument, Scotus clearly anticipates the Leibnizian version of the argument, for the 'touching up' consists in showing that the idea of the most perfect being is non-contradictory.[57] Thus, Scotus did regard the *a priori* argument as having some worth. Why, then did he contend that we can have no demonstration of the reasoned fact of God's existence? Copleston and Gilson agree that the answer is that the argument does not attain the level of demonstration: we cannot prove apodeictically that there is no contradiction in the idea of a most perfect being.[58] Hence, the Anselmian proof is a probability argument only. This is consistent with Scotus's position that a demonstration from the analysis of the terms of the statement, 'An infinite being exists', is possible, but not for *us*. Hence, it is misleading to say that Scotus rejects *a priori* proofs out of hand. But secondly, does this nonetheless imply that Scotus's argument from possible beings is *a posteriori*? I think not. What Scotus is denying is the possibility of a demonstration that deduces the existence of God from the concept of God. We cannot reason that because God is the necessarily existent being, He therefore necessarily exists. But Scotus's cosmological argument, though equally *a priori*, does not proceed along this line. He argues that because it is possible that some caused thing could exist, it is equally possible that some first cause could exist. It is important to realise that the scholastics would have considered this to be an *a posteriori* argument, for living before Kant, they did not conceive of the *a priori* as that which can be known independently of all experience and the *a posteriori* as that which is derived from and based on experience. For them, these terms denoted something altogether different: *a priori* meant proceeding from cause to effect, and *a posteriori* meant reasoning back from effect to the cause. Hence, Scotus's argument, reasoning as it does from the possibility of things' existing to the possibility of God's existing, would be an *a posteriori* argument. In Gilson's words,

> Such demonstrations cannot be made *a priori*, that is to say, starting solely from the definition of God, as Saint Anselm wished . . . . These demonstrations will therefore be *a posteriori*, that is to say, going up from effects to their cause; but the effects from which they start will not be the contingent beings given in sensible experience.[59]

Rather the departure point will be the *possibility* of contingent, or caused beings. Because it is possible that contingent beings could exist, it is possible that a necessary being could exist. Hence, Scotus's argument is *a posteriori* in the scholastic sense, but *a priori* in the Kantian sense.[60] The curious thing about Scotus's revised argument—and Rowe picks this up[61]—is that by formulating the argument in terms of the mere possibility of things existing, Scotus has rendered irrelevant all his detailed analysis of the essentially ordered causal series and so forth. But if the argument is not an *a posteriori* proof, then the question arises as to why we ought to include a chapter on Scotus in this survey. Two reasons might be offered: (1) Scotus, though propounding what amounts to an ontological argument for God's existence, makes so many moves that are typical of the cosmological argument that we would be the poorer were we to pass him by; (2) although he favours the *a priori* form of the argument, Scotus still retains the *a posteriori* form of the proof and insists on its cogency, thus keeping a true cosmological argument along with his ontological proof.

To return to our outline, then, Scotus, having dealt with both objections and having proved that it is possible that there exists a being which is simply first in the realm of efficient causality, now argues that such a being would be wholly uncaused. It could have no efficient cause because it would be first in the order of efficient cause. It can have no final cause because final causes only cause by stimulating efficient causes to action. Therefore, the first efficient cause does not depend for its being on a final cause. Scotus gives two reasons, both of which are rather obscure, for eliminating material and formal causes. First, if a thing lacks an extrinsic cause, it cannot have an intrinsic cause. This is because an extrinsic cause has priority over the intrinsic, since the intrinsic implies imperfection. Therefore, to deny the extrinsic is to deny the intrinsic. Second, intrinsic causes, like matter and form, are caused in their being or composition by extrinsic causes; hence, they could not exist in a being that has no extrinsic cause. These arguments are, of course, archaic and of little more than historical interest, but the thrust of the argumentation is to show that the first efficient cause cannot be part of the material universe.

The next subpoint is that such a being actually exists. This brings into full view the true character of Scotus's proof as an ontological argument. He argues that since the first efficient cause would be a being that could not be caused to exist by some other being, it would have to exist of itself, if it were able to exist. We have seen that the existence of such a being is possible; therefore, it must exist. But why does the mere possibility of such a being necessitate its actual existence? Scotus's compacted argument is difficult to grasp; he appears to argue that unless this being actually exists, then it would not be a being capable of existing of itself. Again, why not? Scotus responds, because otherwise a non-existent being would cause something to exist, which is impossible; moreover, it would then be self-caused, not uncaused. The point of the reasoning appears to be this: such a possible being as the first efficient cause either actually exists or not. If not, then it is possible that it could exist. But if this is a *real* possibility, what could ever bring it about? It could not be caused by another or by itself or by nothing. Therefore, it is not really possible. The only way it could be really possible is if it existed already. Therefore, since a first efficient cause is possible, it must exist.[62] This is clearly an *a priori*, ontological type argument, and it involves no existential premiss whatsoever. But at the same time it must also be remarked that even here Scotus does not forget the *a posteriori* side of the proof. Thus, he states,

> . . . the other proofs of proposition A [step 1.a.*i.i.*(*ii*).] can also be used to establish the existence of this being as proposed by this third conclusion, but in this case they are based on contingent though manifest propositions.[63]

Finally, he adds, rather quaintly, that it is unfitting that the universe should lack the highest degree of being.

Scotus then moves to his second primacy, that of finality. That some end is simply first is established in the same way as the primacy of the first efficient cause. Here it might be wondered what an essential order of final causes would be. Scotus seems to conceive of a final cause as a *being* for which another being exists, not as a *reason* for which something acts. For example, one might say grass exists for the sake of the sheep, and sheep exist for the sake of man, and man exists for the sake of God. Therefore, Scotus is not even here looking for abstract reasons for the being of things; he comes closest here to Leibniz's argument based on the principle of sufficient reason, but Scotus's argument is still not the same as Leibniz's. Scotus may presuppose some form of the principle of sufficient reason, for it is not evident that something has to exist for the sake of another at all; it may simply be there, having only the bare, valueless fact of existence. But he is not seeking the sort of abstract reasons or grounds of intelligibility that Leibniz is.

Next, the ultimate end cannot be caused in any way. It is clear that it cannot have a final cause, for it is the ultimate end for which all things exist. Moreover, it can have no efficient cause because, according to Aristotle, every efficient cause acts for the sake of an end, even if unconsciously. This step represents Scotus's faith in the teleology of nature. Since the ultimate end has no other end for which it exists, it cannot be caused to exist. Finally, Scotus refers to the discussion of efficient causality as to why no material or formal cause of the ultimate end exists. Since the ultimate end has no efficient or extrinsic cause, the intrinsic causes are precluded as well. Thus, it cannot be part of the material universe.

Finally, a being which is the ultimate end actually exists. We are referred to the earlier analysis. Since the ultimate end is uncaused, it must exist of itself, and so forth. It is clear that the key in the second primacy is the demonstration that the ultimate end cannot have an efficient cause, for this enables Scotus to refer everything back to the arguments of the first primacy.

Lastly Scotus turns to the third primacy, that of perfection or pre-eminence. First, some nature is first in perfection. Here no casual series is involved, for just because one being is more perfect than another, it does not follow that the former is the cause of the latter.[64] But an essential order still exists among essences such that the more perfect may be ranged above the less perfect. Now such a gradation cannot be infinite, but must end in a most perfect essence. Scotus refers to the five arguments against the infinite regress. But because this essential order is not a causal one, at least the first, fourth, and fifth arguments cannot be utilised by Scotus in the form in which they stand, for they apply specifically to a causal series.

Second, this supreme nature cannot be caused. It can have no final cause because the end for whose sake a thing is is superior to and more perfect than the effect. This is certainly implied in Scotus's second difference between essentially and accidentally ordered causes. But if the supreme nature does not exist for the sake of an end, it cannot have an efficient cause, since every efficient cause acts for the sake of an end.

Moreover, everything that has an efficient cause is surpassed in perfection by that cause, as was made clear in the second difference between essential and accidental causes, so that if the supreme nature were caused, it would not be supreme in perfection.

Third, this supreme nature actually exists. Because it has no efficient cause, the same analysis applies to it that applied to efficient and final causes.

Having thus investigated the three realms of efficiency, finality, and pre-eminence, Scotus believes he has established the existence of the triple primacy: in the realm of beings something exists which is simply first in the order of efficient causality, final causality, and by reason of pre-eminence.

The next step in the proof is to show that *the three primacies are interrelated*. Scotus will show first that the first efficient cause is the ultimate end and second that the first efficient cause is the supreme nature. The proof of the first is that the first efficient cause must act for the first final cause. As one regresses in each order, he must ultimately come to the first cause and the end for which it acts. Scotus argues that they must be the same nature. Otherewise there would be something more noble than the first efficient cause, which Scotus will not allow. The proof of the second is that since in an essentially ordered series, the first cause will be the most perfect, the first efficient cause of all will be more perfect than all its effects. Again these proofs obviously depend upon medieval conceptions of the 'nobility' of causes, terms in which we do not tend to think today. Scotus's modest conclusion of these identifications is that the three primacies are interrelated.

In step 3 he draws the implicit conclusion: *the three primacies are united in one nature*. As a preliminary point, Scotus wants to show that the first efficient cause has necessity of being. The argument he develops here is very similar to Spinoza's ontological argument. For he argues that no being can prevent the necessary being from existing; therefore, it necessarily exists. Technically, however, Scotus is not here trying to prove something exists; he has already proved the first efficient cause does exist. Now he wants to demonstrate that it exists necessarily. He argues that nothing could prevent the necessary existence of the first cause because if the incompossible being were itself uncaused, then neither could exist, and because if it were a caused being, its dependent, derived existence could never cancel out uncaused, independent existence. Now, he proceeds, two necessary natures cannot exist. His proof seems to assume that the necessity of a nature is caused by the necessity of its attributes. Thus, if one eliminates one attribute, the being is still just as necessary, which Scotus regards as obviously incorrect. The point he seems to be driving at is that a necessary nature must be absolutely simple. Therefore, one could not have two, for there would be no differentiating aspects between the two natures. If one were to say they differed accidentally, Scotus responds that nothing merely possible can belong to a necessary being. Moreover, he argues, two first efficient causes cannot exist because two supreme natures cannot exist. This is because natures are essentially ordered. Scotus has shown that the first efficient cause is the supreme nature; therefore, two first causes cannot exist. Furthermore, two ultimate ends cannot exist in the same universe. For this duality would produce two separate orders of reality, wholly unrelated to each other. The implication seems to be that since two universes is a contradictory notion, there must be only one ultimate end, and the identity of this with the first efficient cause has already been demonstrated. Therefore, the three primacies are united in one nature. Now it must be noted that Scotus does not believe he has proved that only one being possesses this nature; he has shown the triple primacy exists in one nature, but he has not proved this nature exists in one being. His comment in the *De primo principio* makes this clear:

> . . . some one nature is simply first. However, I say one *nature* for this reason, because . . . the three primacies will be shown, not about a unique singular or one in number, but about a unique quiddity or nature. There will, however, be mention of numerical unity later.[65]

Hence, at this juncture Scotus believes he has proven the actual existence of an incorporeal, necessarily existing nature that is the first efficient cause of all existence, the ultimate end for the existence of all things, and the most perfect of all beings.

From what we have said in this analysis it is apparent that Scotus has really two distinct proofs for God's existence, one *a priori* and ontological, one *a posteriori* and cosmological. Though Scotus himself undoubtedly regarded the proof from the possibility of beings as more certain and important, our interest in this study is only with the argument from actual existence. Accordingly, we schematise it as follows:

1. The triple primacy: in the realm of beings there exist a first efficient cause, an ultimate end, and a most perfect being.
    a. There exists a first efficient cause.
        i. Caused beings exist.
            a. Beings come into existence.

b. Change exists.

ii. These beings are either caused by nothing, caused by themselves, or caused by another.

iii. They cannot be caused by nothing.

a. Nothing cannot cause anything.

iv. They cannot be caused by themselves.

a. A thing cannot cause itself to exist.

v. Therefore, they are caused by another.

vi. This cause is either first or not.

vii. If it is first, a first efficient cause exists.

viii. If it is not first, a first efficient cause exists.

a. This cause is caused by another, which is either first or not, and so on.

b. An essentially ordered causal series cannot be infinite.

(*i*) If it were infinite, it would still depend on a first cause outside it.

(*ii*) It is impossible to have an infinite number of simultaneous causes acting to produce an effect.

(*iii*) In an infinite series, nothing could be prior to anything else.

(*iv*) It is impossible to have infinitely higher and perfect beings being caused to cause something.

c. An essentially ordered causal series exists.

(*i*) A successive, accidentally ordered causal series cannot exist without a nature of eternal duration upon which the whole series and every part of it depends.

(*a*) Change cannot be perpetuated unless something permanent exists outside the succession.

(*ii*) Therefore, whatever has an accidentally ordered cause also has an essentially ordered cause.

d. This finite, essentially ordered causal series cannot be circular.

(*i*) A being causally prior to a cause is also causally prior to the cause's effect.

(*ii*) Therefore, a cause cannot be the effect of its own effect.

e. Therefore, the series must terminate in a first efficient cause.

ix. This first efficient cause is wholly uncaused.

a. It has neither efficient, final, material, nor formal causes.

b. There exists an ultimate end.
   i. Anything caused is caused for the sake of some end.
   ii. An ultimate end must exist (1.a.*viii.*).
   iii. This ultimate end is wholly uncaused.
      a. It has neither efficient, final, material, nor formal causes.
c. There exists a most perfect being.
   i. An essential order exists among natures.
   ii. A most perfect nature must exist (1.a.*viii.*).
   iii. This ultimate nature is wholly uncaused.
      a. It has neither efficient, final, material, nor formal causes.

2. These three primacies are interrelated.
   a. The first efficient cause is the ultimate end.
      i. The first efficient cause acts for the ultimate end.
      ii. The first efficient cause does not act for anything other than itself.
      iii. Therefore, the first efficient cause is the ultimate end.
   b. The first efficient cause is the most perfect nature.
      i. The first efficient cause is more perfect than all its effects.
      ii. Therefore, it is the most perfect nature.
3. These three primacies are united in one nature.
   a. Whatever has no efficient cause has necessary existence.
      i. Nothing could force it to not exist.
         a. If an uncaused incompossible being exists, it could not force it to not exist.
            (*i*) Both or neither would exist.
         b. If a caused incompossible being exists, it could not force it to not exist.
            (*i*) No caused, dependent existent could supplant an uncaused, independent existent.
   b. Necessary existence belongs to one nature only.
      i. If two necessary natures existed, they could not be distinguished from each other.
      ii. Two necessary natures could not both be perfect.
      iii. Two necessary natures could not exist in the same universe.
   c. Each primacy has no efficient cause.
   d. Therefore, each primacy exists in the one necessary nature.
4. Therefore, there exists an incorporeal, necessary nature which is the first efficient cause of, the ultimate end of, and the most perfect being of all that exists.

At this point, Scotus has not yet concluded that this nature is God.

Hence, in the *De primo principio*, he launches into an elaborate discussion of the simplicity, infinity, and intellectuality of the first being. His discussion may be summarised and distilled into eleven propositions. First, *the First Nature in itself is simple.*[66] This follows as a corollary of what has been said, for the first nature is not composed of matter and form, nor is it in a genus differentiated by some specific attribute.

Second, *whatever is intrinsic to the Highest Nature is such in the highest degree.*[67] Any quality possessed by this nature simply is the nature, since it is simple. Since the nature is of the highest degree, so is anything intrinsic to it.

Third, *every pure perfection is predicated of the Highest Nature as necessarily existing there in the highest degree.*[68] A pure perfection is that which is unqualifiedly better than anything incompatible with it. These must exist necessarily in the first nature because they are compatible with it if they are compatible with any being. Since the first nature is simple, they must exist in it necessarily, not accidentally.

Fourth, *the First Efficient Cause is intelligent and endowed with will.*[69] Scotus again has reference to Aristotle's teleological analysis of causation. Things which move towards an end naturally do so only in virtue of something that does so by intention. The first efficient cause must, as the source of both kinds of motion—natural and intentional—be intelligent and volitional. Scotus buttresses his point by arguing that evil would be impossible in the world if everything flowed naturally and necessarily from the first cause, which is perfect. That means the first cause must act by will, not by necessity of nature, or otherwise freedom of the will would be denied to man.

Fifth, *the First Principle causes contingently whatever It causes.*[70] If it did not cause freely, then everything would be determined. Because man acts freely, so must the first cause.

Sixth, *for the First Nature to love Itself is identical with the First Nature.*[71] Scotus argues that since the first cause loves the ultimate end and is moved by it, and since such an act is wholly uncaused, then this act will be necessary of itself. Since whatever is uncaused and necessary of itself belongs to the necessary nature, this act is identical with that nature. This implies, Scotus notes, that the will and intellect of the first being are identical with its nature.

Seventh, *no act of understanding can be an accident of the First Nature.*[72] Before something can be caused, it must be known and willed by its cause. Thus, the first cause must know all its effects in order to cause them. Since causality is of its very nature, understanding, which is presupposed by causality, must likewise be of its nature. Hence, no act of understanding can be accidental. Scotus multiplies his arguments here to underline the same point.

Eighth, *the intellect of the First Principle actually understands every intelligible always and necessarily and distinctly, prior to its existence.*[73] Every act of the intellect of the first principle is identical with its nature; thus, it must know every intelligible. Scotus at this point begins to call the first nature God. God, he says, must know every intelligible because, as first cause, He must have a knowledge of all producible things.

Ninth, *God is infinite and incomprehensible by the finite.*[74] Scotus employs several arguments to prove this conclusion, which is so central to his conception of God. First, because God knows all intelligibles, and the intelligibles are infinite, God's intellect must be equally infinite. Therefore, His nature, one with His intellect, must be infinite. Second, the divine intellect knows objects without the necessity of those objects' existing; it knows them by the contemplation of its own nature. It can produce the effect (the knowledge of objects) without the immediate cause (the objects themselves). The immediate cause would add nothing should it exist. But any finite cause is perfected in its causality by the addition of a secondary cause. Since this is not the case with the divine intellect, it must be infinite. Third, in finite beings the act of understanding is an accident because it is a quality. No finite act of understanding can be a substance. But God's act of understanding is His very substance, as we have seen; therefore, He must be infinite. Fourth, every finite substance may be classed according to some genus. But the first nature does not belong to a genus. Therefore, it must be infinite. Fifth, there are several ways of formulating a probabilistic argument from eminence. For example, it is incompatible with the most eminent that there should be something more perfect. But there is no incompatibility with the finite that the infinite should exist. Therefore, infinite being exists. It is at this point that the touched up Anselmian ontological argument is introduced as a persuasive proof. Sixth, the human will seems to be inclined toward the infinite good as its ultimate end; therefore, the infinite ought to exist. Seventh, the first cause has the power to produce an infinite number of beings, even if not simultaneously; therefore, it is infinite.

Tenth, *from infinity there follows every kind of simplicity.*[75] Any composition in an infinite being would involve the absurdities attendant on actually existing infinite magnitudes. Scotus underlines the point with several other arguments showing the impossibility of accidents in the divine nature.

Eleventh, *there is one God.*[76] Only now does Scotus attempt to prove that the one nature embracing the triple primacy is found in one being.

He offers five arguments. First, an infinite intellect is only one in number. For if two infinite intellects could exist, they would be lacking in perfection because they would know each other in virtue of each other, not in virtue of their own nature. Second, an infinite will is only one in number. An infinite will loves the supremely lovable. But if two such wills existed, each would love itself supremely rather than the other, which is contradictory, since both are supreme. Third, an infinite power is only one in number. Two infinite powers would imply two essential orders of causation, which is impossible in the same universe. Fourth, a necessary being is only one in number. If necessary being could be more than one, there would be an infinite number because if it is possible it must exist. Fifth, an infinite goodness is only one. The will is rightly satisfied with one infinite good. If there were more than one, it would wish that both exist and, thus, not be satisfied with the infinite good. Through these five arguments, Scotus essays to prove that there is but one God.

In conclusion it is clear that Scotus's cosmological argument for an infinite being inhabits the borderland between the cosmological and ontological arguments. His lengthy and painstaking development of the case for the existence of God is a valuable resource for students of both types of argument and serves to remind us that in practice these arguments are often so blended together that it is difficult to separate one from the other.

NOTES

1. R. L. Sturch, 'The Cosmological Argument' (Ph.D. thesis, Oxford University, 1970), p. 145.
2. See C. R. S. Harris, *Duns Scotus*, 2 vols. (Oxford: Clarendon Press, 1927), 1: 267.
3. Allan B. Wolter, 'Duns Scotus and the Existence and Nature of God', *Proceedings of the American Catholic Philosophical Association* 28 (1954): 94–5. For a history of the development of Scotus's proof, see Camille Bérubé, 'Pour une histoire des preuves de l'existence de Dieu chez Duns Scot', in *Deus et Homo ad Mentum I. Duns Scoti: Acta Tertii Congressus Internationalis Vindobonac* 28 *Sept.–2 Oct.* 1970 (Rome: Societas Internationalis Scotistica, 1972).
4. Harris, *Scotus*, 2: 165.
5. Frederick Copleston, *A History of Philosophy*, vol. 2: *Mediaeval Philosophy: Augustine to Scotus* (London: Burns Oates & Washbourne, 1950), p. 483. Cf. pp. 520–1.
6. See Allan Bernard Wolter, *The Transcendentals and their Function in the Metaphysics of Duns Scotus* (Washington, D.C.: Catholic University of America Press, 1946), pp. 130–1; Roy Effler, 'Duns Scotus and the Physical Approach to God', in *Studies in Philosophy and the History of Philosophy*, vol. 3: *John Duns*

Scotus, 1265–1965, ed. John K. Ryan and Bernardine M. Bonansea (Washington, D.C.: Catholic University of America Press, 1965), pp. 171–90.

7. John Duns Scotus, *Opus oxoniense*, I, dist. II, q.i., in *Philosophical Writings*, ed. and trans. Allan Wolter (London: Nelson, 1962), p. 35.

8. Harris, *Scotus*, 2: 176. Cf. Joseph Owens, 'Up to What Point is God Included in the Metaphysics of Duns Scotus?', *Mediaeval Studies* 10 (1948): 163–77.

9. See F. C. Copleston, *A History of Medieval Philosophy* (London: Methuen & Co., 1972), p. 219.

10. See Copleston, *Augustine to Scotus*, pp. 502–3.

11. See ibid., p. 503.

12. See Etienne Gilson, *History of Christian Philosophy in the Middle Ages* (London: Sheed & Ward, 1955), pp. 456–7.

13. Allan Wolter, 'Duns Scotus on the Nature of Man's Knowledge of God', *Review of Metaphysics* 1 (1947): 7.

14. See Owens, 'Metaphysics', pp. 172–3.

15. Wolter, 'Existence and Nature', p. 120.

16. Scotus, *Opus*, p. 75.

17. Ibid., pp. 75–6.

18. Harris, *Scotus*, 1: 271. For an analysis of Bonaventure's influence, see Wolter, *Transcendentals*, pp. 132–6.

19. *Encyclopedia of Philosophy*, s.v. 'Duns Scotus, John', by Allan B. Wolter.

20. Scotus, *Opus*, p. 39.

21. Ibid., p. 41.

22. See Wolter, 'Existence and Nature', pp. 106–7.

23. William L. Rowe, *The Cosmological Argument* (Princeton, N.J.: Princeton University Press, 1975), p. 49–50.

24. Rowe neglects entirely the second and third portions of Scotus's triple primacy (Rowe, *Argument*, p. 51). This probably contributes to his misunderstanding.

25. Scotus, *Opus*, p. 41 [Italics mine].

26. Ibid., p. 42. The picture one gets of this scheme is that of an infinite, horizontal, accidentally ordered series of causes, each dependent upon an infinite, vertical, essentially ordered series of causes, each of which depends horizontally upon God, who exists outside the series. But this treats the essential series like an accidental one, and fails to reckon with the fact that, given a prior essential cause, no further cause is necessary for the production of a thing.

27. Wolter explains the argument as being a demonstration of the absurdity of an infinite essential series:

> The series is both caused and uncaused; caused inasmuch as the causality of every cause within the series and consequently the causality of the series as a whole is dependent on something prior. Still the series as a whole must be uncaused for nothing is its own cause. Yet the very nature of essentially ordered series implies that it cannot be dependent on something beyond the series, because that on which it depends becomes a part of the series in virtue of this dependence. Hence the series as a whole is always dependent on something prior; yet since nothing is prior to the series as a whole, it depends on nothing apart from itself (Wolter, 'Existence and Nature', p. 107).

Although this interpretation irons out the inconsistencies in Scotus's argument, it is certainly not what he himself maintains in either the *Opus oxiniense* or the *De primo principio*.

28. Scotus, *De primo principio* 3. 2. Our interpretation is confirmed by Étienne Gilson, 'L'existence de Dieu selon Duns Scot', *Mediaeval Studies* 11 (1949): 34. The contents of this article are duplicated in Étienne Gilson, *Jean Duns Scot* (Paris: Librairie Philosophique J. Vrin, 1952), pp. 116–77.

29. Scotus, *Opus*, p. 42.

30. Aristotle, *Metaphysica* Δ. 11. 1018b9–11. But Scotus ignores Aristotle's further comment that in other classes of things (such as past events), priority is determined by reference to the terminus in the present (ibid. Δ. 11. 1018b5).

31. Scotus, *Opus*, p. 43.

32. Ibid.

33. Ibid.

34. Wolter, *Transcendentals*, pp. 143–4.

35. Ibid., pp. 21–4. Wolter cites Scotus's emphatic statement that the real distinction between essence and existence is a fiction of which he knows nothing (ibid., p. 66).

36. Copleston, *History*, pp. 508–9.

37. See Allan B. Wolter, 'The Formal Distinction', in *Scotus*, ed. Ryan and Bonansea, pp. 45–6. See also A. J. O'Brien, 'Scotus on Essence and Existence', *New Scholasticism* 38 (1964): 61–77.

38. As M. J. Grajewski points out, although Scotus did hold that God is the only being in whom essence and existence are identical, the major application of the formal distinction in matters of theodicy was not to the problem of proving divine existence, but of reconciling the simplicity of God's essence with the multiplicity of persons within the Trinity and the plurality of divine attributes (Maurice J. Grajewski, *The Formal Distinction of Duns Scotus* [Washington, D.C.: Catholic University of America Press, 1944], pp. 180–97). See also Béraud de Saint-Maurice, *John Duns Scotus: a Teacher for our Times*, trans. Columban Duffy (St. Bonaventure, N.Y.: Franciscan Institute, 1965), pp. 188–200.

39. Scotus, *Opus*, p. 39. The scholastics, following Aristotle, claimed that the conclusion of a syllogism could be no stronger than its weakest premiss, and, hence, all premisses of a demonstrative syllogism must be necessary (Allan B. Wolter, Introduction to *A Treatise on God as First Principle*, by John Duns Scotus, trans. Allan B. Wolter [Chicago: Franciscan Herald Press; Forum Books, 1966], p. xvii; cf. Wolter, 'Nature and Existence', pp. 101–5).

40. John Duns Scotus, *Lectures on Book I of 'The Sentences'*, in *Treatise*, p. 175.

41. Scotus, *Opus*, p. 44.

42. Scotus, *Lectures*, p. 175.

43. Scotus, *Opus*, pp. 44–5. Gilson points out that the point of departure for Scotus's proof is 'some modality of being considered as being, not the contingent existence of some existent' (Gilson, *History*, p. 457).

44. For example, Harris, *Scotus*, 2: 163; Gilson, 'Scot', pp. 38–9; Wolter, Existence and Nature', p. 105; Felix Alluntio, 'Demonstrability and Demonstration of the Existence of God', in *Scotus*, ed. Ryan and Bonansea, pp. 133–4; Copleston, *Medieval Philosophy*, p. 220.

45. Wolter, 'Existence and Nature', p. 105.

46. Wolter, Introduction, p. xvii.

47. Alluntio, 'Demonstrability', p. 134.

48. Julius R. Weinberg, *A Short History of Medieval Philosophy* (Princeton, N.J.: Princeton University Press, 1964), p. 220.

49. Etienne Gilson, gen. ed., *A History of Philosophy*, 4 vols. (New York: Random House, 1962), vol. 2: *Medieval Philosophy*, by Armand A. Maurer, p. 223.

50. Ibid.

51. Efrem Bettoni, *Duns Scotus: The Basic Principles of His Philosophy*, trans. and ed. Bernardine Bonansea (Washington, D.C.: Catholic University of America Press, 1961), pp. 137–8.

52. Scotus, *Opus*, pp. 36–7.

53. Ibid., p. 169.

54. See Harris, *Scotus*, 2: 161–2; Gilson, 'Scot', pp. 27–8.

55. Scotus, *Opus*, p. 73.

56. Ibid., p. 74.

57. Copleston, *History*, p. 526.

58. Ibid., pp. 526–7; Gilson, 'Scot', pp. 28–9, 56.

59. Gilson, *History*, p. 457.

60. This needs to be borne in mind when one confronts statements like that of Gilson: 'One cannot maintain that Duns Scot proceeds *a priori* in any moment of the proof' (Gilson, 'Scot', p. 38). For this is so only in the medieval sense; it remains true, admits Gilson, that for Scotus '. . . existence is concluded from an idea' (ibid., p. 39). Although Gilson adds quickly that the idea has 'a real content borrowed from experience', this cannot change the fact that the truth value of Scotus's first premiss is determined entirely *a priori* (ibid.).

61. Rowe, *Argument*, pp. 50–1.

62. On this argument see Harris, *Scotus*, 2: 164; Gilson, 'Scot', p. 39; Bettoni, *Scotus*, p. 139; Wolter, Introduction, p. xxi.

63. Scotus, *Opus*, p. 46.

64. Ibid., p. 38.

65. Scotus, *De primo principio* 3. intro.

66. Ibid., 4. 1.

67. Ibid., 4. 2.

68. Ibid., 4. 3.

69. Ibid., 4. 4.

70. Ibid., 4. 5.

71. Ibid., 4. 6.

72. Ibid., 4. 7.

73. Ibid., 4. 8.

74. Ibid., 4. 9.

75. Ibid., 4. 10.

76. Ibid., 4. 11. It is interesting to observe that his first two arguments would be difficult to reconcile with Trinitarian theology.

Chapter 7

Benedict de Spinoza

In its long and variegated history, the cosmological argument probably receives no more unusual a twist than that given it by Benedict de Spinoza (1632–1677). Although his version of the argument itself is not so noteworthy and is completely overshadowed by his use of the ontological argument, it is Spinoza's *conclusion* to the cosmological argument that is significant and merits its inclusion in our historical survey. For it raises very important questions about the nature of the necessary being to which the argument concludes.

Fortunately, Spinoza himself lays out for us all of the definitions of terms that are requisite for an understanding of his proof for the existence of God. First, by *cause of itself*, Spinoza means 'that, whose essence involves existence; or that, whose nature cannot be conceived unless existing'.[1] This definition makes it clear that by 'self-caused' Spinoza does not understand the temporal act of a thing's bringing itself out of non-existence into existence. Rather, this describes a thing which exists necessarily; it is of its essence to exist. Note that he does not say, with the scholastics, that its essence *is* its existence. He speaks of a thing which has an essence that cannot be conceived unless it is conceived as existing. Aquinas argued against the possibility of such a self-caused being, but Spinoza affirms it. But furthermore, Spinoza does not mean the same by 'cause' as did Aquinas; for Aquinas the term in the cosmological proof meant 'efficient cause', while Spinoza employs the word more in the sense of 'reason'. Stuart Hampshire explains,

> The word 'cause,' as it is generally used in rationalist philosophies and throughout Spinoza's writing, must be divested of many of its present associations . . . . What is common to Spinoza's use and to our contemporary use of the word is simply that a cause is to be taken as anything which *explains* the existence or qualities of the effect . . . . To Spinoza . . . to 'explain' means to show that one true proposition is the logically necessary consequence of some other; explanation

essentially involves exhibiting necessary connexions, and 'necessary connexion' in this context means a strictly logical connexion to be discovered by logical analysis of the ideas involved.[2]

For example, Spinoza states that things are caused by God 'in the same way as it follows from the nature of a triangle . . . that its three angles are equal to two right angles'.[3] Thus, Spinoza perceives causality as any relation involving ground and consequent.[4] When Spinoza speaks of a thing that is the cause of itself, therefore, he means a being that is self-explained, that is its own reason for existing.[5] This led Frederick Pollock to comment, 'Spinoza takes the current phrase *causa sui*, and defines it in a way which leaves causation wholly out of account'.[6] Such a judgement is probably too strong, for Spinoza may have regarded God's existence as actually caused by his essence; but it is equally true that God is also self-caused in that his essence is the logical basis or reason for his existence.

A second key definition is that of *substance*: 'that which is in itself and is conceived through itself; in other words, that, the conception of which does not need the conception of another thing from which it must be formed'.[7] It is important at once to distinguish this from the definition employed by scholastics. For Aquinas, substance is in itself in the sense that it is not an accident modifying some thing, but he did not regard it as conceived through itself—this additional phrase serves to distinguish Spinoza's definition from that of the scholastics and also of Descartes.[8] Spinoza regarded as axiomatic the truth that 'The knowledge (cognitio) of an effect depends upon and involves the knowledge of the cause'.[9] Hence, in defining substance as that which does not require the conception of anything else in order to be conceived, he implicitly asserts that substance is not an effect, that is to say, it has no external cause. The concept of a substance is, as Curley observes, 'the concept of a being independent of all causes'.[10] Remembering the way in which Spinoza employs the term 'cause', we may say that for him substance must be conceived 'as existing without any external reason for its existence'[11]—that is, it is explained by reference only to itself. Thus, in stating that substance is that which is conceived through itself, Spinoza completely cuts himself away from any scholastic bonds. Seen in this light, even his definition of substance as that which is in itself takes on new meaning; for to be in itself, according to Spinoza, is to exist *a se*, to be a necessary being, a designation which no scholastic would ever dream of ascribing to substance.

A third important definition is that of *God*: 'Being absolutely infinite, that is to say, substance consisting of infinite attributes, each one of which expresses eternal and infinite essence'.[12] An understanding of this definition requires a definition of what Spinoza means by 'attribute'. He writes, 'By attribute I understand that which the intellect perceives of substance, as if constituting its essence'.[13] Substance is knowable by us only through the attributes which we perceive in it. God is declared to be a substance of infinite attributes. He must, therefore, be *absolutely* infinite because he is not simply infinite in one way (say, infinite thought in a finite body), but infinite in all respects.[14] God, then, is an absolutely infinite substance.

It must be remarked that any examination of these three major definitions reveal that they all come to the same thing. As James Martineau points out, 'That primary entity he defines three times over under different names . . .'.[15] To be self-caused is to be substance and to be substance is to be God. But to say this is simply to affirm that Spinoza's is a rationalistic system; the conclusion *must* be there, hidden in the definitions and axioms, waiting to be unpacked. But it is still worth noticing at this point that these three definitions all point toward the same referent.

At this point we may proceed directly to Spinoza's cosmological argument for the existence of God. It lies almost ignominiously sandwiched between two versions of the more celebrated ontological argument; it is the third proof employed by Spinoza. There exists some dispute as to the exact nature of this argument. On the one hand, some contend that this is but another version of the ontological argument and is not *a posteriori* at all. The great Spinoza scholar Martial Gueroult regarded the third proof as *a posteriori* 'in appearance only'; once it is seen that substance exists necessarily through itself and that God is substance, one sees that God exists necessarily without reference to my existence.[16] The *a posteriori* character of the proof is 'illusory', an 'artifice' used by Spinoza to make the *a prlori* proof easier to grasp; there is 'no true *a posteriori*' by Spinoza.[17] R. L. Sturch in his study of the cosmological argument similarly asserts, 'This argument is no more cosmological than the last . . . , and Spinoza does in fact go on to rephrase it without even . . . reference to finite beings'.[18] But on the other hand, some writers believe *all* the proofs offered by Spinoza are really *a posteriori*. For example, Joachim insists,

> There is a common thought running through all the four proofs, and it is simply this: —'If anything in any sense is, then God is and is of necessity . . .'.
>
> Except in the third proof, Spinoza has not expressly supplied the

> minor premiss for this reasoning, and hence he has been misunderstood. The first proof . . . says simply 'God is Substance and therefore . . . he must exist': but the cogency of the argument depends upon the unexpressed postulate 'something . . . does exist'. But this is a postulate . . . which assuredly did not require explicit statement. For deny that anything in any sense is, and in your denial you assert at least your own existence.[19]

In effect Joachim is arguing that Spinoza's ontological argument presupposes the cosmological. More recently, James Humber has defended a similar position.[20] He argues that the four proofs are really one extended argument and that they are all empirically based. They all assume the existence of substance. Even proposition VII in the *Ethics* assumes that substance already exists; it merely proves it is of the *nature* of substance to exist. Humber believes that Spinoza justifies the existence of substance empirically, namely by perception. The proofs for God are attempts to show that God belongs to the category of substance and thus exists by nature.

Neither of these interpretations of Spinoza appears to be correct. On the one hand, the third proof is definitely *a posteriori* in nature, involving an existential premiss, as we shall see. That Spinoza restates it without this premiss does not mean the third proof is itself *a priori*, but only that Spinoza believed it could be stated both ways with equal validity. Commenting that the *a posteriori* version is *supposed* to be more easily accessible than the *a priori*, André Doz insists, '. . . the proof is authentically *a posteriori*, as Spinoza intended it to be'.[21] On the other hand, it contradicts Spinoza's plain language to contend that all the proofs are *a posteriori*. While Humber's discussion contains some valuable insights, his belief that Spinoza means to justify the existence of substance empirically is just not convicing. (1) Spinoza nowhere prior to proposition VII attempts to prove that substance exists. Humber's citations, which themselves do not clearly support his point, are drawn from a later portion of the *Ethics*. Spinoza's references to substance in propositions IV and VI do not assume its real existence, but simply assert that by definition anything, if it exists, will be either substance or mode. (2) Spinoza makes it quite clear that proposition VII does prove the existence of substance (even if that is not its primary intent), and this *a priori*, from the mere concept of substance:

> But if men would attend to the nature of substance, they could not entertain a single doubt of the truth of Proposition 7; indeed this

> proposition would be considered by all to be axiomatic . . . . For by 'substance' would be understood that which is in itself and is conceived through itself . . . . If any one, therefore, were to say that he possessed a clear and distinct, that is to say, a true idea of substance, and that he nevertheless doubted whether such a substance exists, he would forsooth be in the same position as if he were to say that he had a true idea and nevertheless doubted whether or not it was false . . . . It is therefore necessary to admit that the existence of substance, like its essence, is an eternal truth.[22]

As Spinoza later adds, since '. . . it pertains to the nature of substance to exist . . . , its definition must involve necessary existence, and consequently from its definition alone its existence must be concluded'.[23] This means, of course, that when Spinoza proves that God, or a substance of inifinite attributes, must exist because his very concept involves existence, the proof is strictly *a priori.* There is no hidden existential premiss, as Joachim assumes. Spinoza himself says as much. Thus, in the 'Short Treatise' he presents an ontological argument very similar to the one found in the *Ethics* and calls it an '*a priori*' proof; he also adds an '*a posteriori*' proof from our idea of God.[24] And in the *Ethics* he comments after the third proof,

> In this last demonstration I wished to prove the existence of God *a posteriori*, in order that the demonstration might be the more easily understood, and not because the existence of God does not follow *a priori* from the same grounds.[25]

The truth of the matter, then, seems to be that Spinoza believed the existence of God can be proved both *a priori* and *a posteriori.* We shall, of course, examine only the latter.

One other general point ought to be made about the nature of Spinoza's cosmological argument. He is often represented as arguing that finite beings are contingent, that is, dependent upon another for their existence, and that there must, therefore, exist a necessary being as their ground of existence. Joachim presents the proofs in this light.[26] Wild describes Spinoza's arguments in such a way as to make it virtually impossible to distinguish them from Thomas Aquinas's second way.[27] Support for such an interpretation comes from one of Spinoza's letters to Meyer in which he writes,

> . . . I should like it to be noted in passing that the more recent

Peripatetics . . . misunderstood the argument of the Ancients by which they strove to prove the existence of God. For, as I find it in the works of a certain Jew, named Rab Chasdai, it reads as follows. If there is an infinite regression of causes, then all things which exist will be things that have been caused. But it cannot pertain to anything that has been caused that it should necessarily exist in virtue of its own nature. Therefore there is in Nature nothing to whose essence it pertains that it should exist necessarily. But this is absurd: and therefore also that. Therefore the force of the argument lies not in the idea that it is impossible for the Infinite actually to exist, or that a regression of causes to infinity is impossible, but only in the impossibility of supposing that things which do not exist necessarily in virtue of their own nature, are not determined to existence by something which does exist necessarily in virtue of its own nature, and which is a Cause, not an Effect.[28]

Two things may be said about this. (1) The immediate topic of discussion here is not God's existence, but the nature of the infinite, about which Meyer had previously written to Spinoza. Spinoza is not arguing here that God exists, but that the argument that there must be a first cause is not based upon the impossibility of an actually existing infinite multitude, but upon the lack of a ground for the infinite series. (2) Spinoza, to my knowledge, never employs such an argument to prove God's existence. Given his metaphysical system, perhaps he should have done so. But the fact is he did not, as will become plainly evident when we examine his cosmological argument. Gueroult correctly distinguishes Spinoza's proof from the classic cosmological argument in that it lacks any reference to an infinite regress and has nothing to do with a cause/effect relationship.[29] His conclusion is fully justified: 'There is nothing there that resembles the classic proof *a contingentia mundi*, or the Cartesian proof'.[30]

This is Spinoza's argument:

Inability to exist is impotence, and, on the other hand, ability to exist is power, as is self-evident. If, therefore, there is nothing which necessarily exists excepting things finite, it follows that things finite are more powerful than the absolutely infinite Being, and this (as is self-evident) is absurd; therefore either nothing exists or Being absolutely infinite also necesarily exists. But we ourselves exist, either in ourselves or in something else which necessarily exists (Ax. 1 and Prop. 7).

> Therefore the Being absolutely infinite, that is to say (Def. 6), God, necessarily exists.—Q.E.D.[31]

Wolfson asserts that this proof is based on the second proof of Descartes's third meditation.[32] But while it is true that Spinoza evolved his proofs of God's existence from the Cartesian versions of the arguments, nevertheless to try to assimilate Spinoza's argument to Descartes's can only lead to misunderstanding. This is exactly what happens to Wolfson; he expresses the essence of the proof as being that God must exist or otherwise the idea of our existence would be more powerful than the idea of God's existence.[33] But this denudes the proof of its *a posteriori* character and, in effect, turns it into an ontological argument. In contrast to Descartes, Spinoza reasons not from the *idea* of finite existence, but from the *fact* of finite existence and the actual power required for the ability to exist. As Hubbeling points out, although Spinoza does have a Cartesian proof from our idea of God in the 'Treatise' as well as in his *Renati Des Cartes principiorum philosophiae* (1, prop. 6), this proof is dropped in the *Ethics.*[34] The third proof in the *Ethics* is based, according to Hubbeling, on the third argument of the *principiorum philosophiae*, which is Spinoza's reformulation of Descartes's third proof for God's existence.[35] Although Descartes's version centres around our idea of God, Spinoza's reformulation revolves more around the notion of power to exist: since we cannot preserve ourselves in existence, there must be a necessary being that preserves us. In the final version in the *Ethics*, the *idea* we have of God plays no role; the thrust of the argument is:

> Potentia is realization of being. If we are said to exist and God's existence is denied, then we should have more power (*potentia*) than God or in other words finite beings would have more *potentia* than the infinite being. This is absurd.[36]

To attempt, therefore, to reduce the argument to the Cartesian proof falsifies the true nature of the argument.

Before we can outline the argument, we must come to terms with the contention of Gueroult that what we have here is not one proof, but really an amalgamation of two proofs.[37] The first proof, which goes up to the disjunction 'either nothing exists or Being absolutely infinite also necessarily exists', is designed to prove that we 'must *necessarily affirm that God exists*', while the second, which begins with 'But we ourselves exist', intends to show that '. . . *God exists necessarily through himself*'.[38]

In the first proof the necessity concerns the manner of the affirmation (we must necessarily affirm) while in the second the necessity concerns the manner of God's being (God exists necessarily). The first proof implicitly assumes that we exist; indeed, we *must* exist (= necessarily exist) because we cannot deny the fact: '. . . as it is *impossible* that I think without existing, it is *necessary*, since I think, that in fact I actually exist'.[39] Because I exist, God must also exist. But the first proof does not tell us if God's existence is necessary existence in himself. The second proof remedies this defect and in fact stands alone, complete in itself.[40] It presupposes the substance/mode distinction. Being finite, I am a mode. But since mode is a feature of substance, because I exist substance must also exist. Substance exists necessarily in itself; therefore, God as absolutely infinite substance exists necessarily in himself.[41] Gueroult grants that the two proofs are not accurately formulated by Spinoza; the amalgamation of the two creates some confusion. After the disjunction we expect 'Now we exist; therefore, it is necessary that a being absolutely infinite exists', and to pass to the second proof we expect '*Immo*', 'Moreover'.[42] But Spinoza neglects to express these. André Doz has raised six problems with Gueroult's reconstruction:[43] (1) The expression 'necessarily exists' is identical in both halves of the proof, but Geuroult would have us understand the first use in a way utterly different from the second, a way not often used by Spinoza except in clear contexts. (2) The argument would be singularly defectively formulated, for the conclusion to the first proof would be lacking and the 'But' at the start of the second would serve no purpose. Only by adding phrases can Gueroult's interpretation be made to make sense. To say in the first proof 'I necessarily exist' presupposes the 'But we exist' of the second proof. (3) Gueroult's interpretation results in the improbable situation that the first half of the argument is totally unnecessary, since the second part does everything it does and more. Spinoza is not likely to be referring to the insignificant first proof alone when he subsequently says that he has used the principle 'Inability to exist is impotence, etc.' to prove God's existence *a posteriori* and that he will proceed to do it *a priori*. (4) In the proof itself Spinoza in no way implies 'I am a mode'. Rather he leaves it open whether we exist in ourselves or in something else. (5) The second half of the proof does not stand alone. If God's existence is already taken to be proved by the time we arrive at the argument, the 'But we exist' is perfectly useless. If God's existence is not yet taken to be proved, then the argument is insufficient to prove that this substance is infinite. One cannot appeal to the fact that if there is a substance, it must be God, for one would have to know already that God exists and that outside him there can be no substance, which Spinoza is to prove later. (6) The first half of the proof would not be sufficient even to prove God exists. For suppose finite beings existed and God did not exist. In that case finite beings are able to and do exist, but are still able to not-exist; while God is able to and does not-exist, but is still able to exist. Hence, God and finite beings would be on an exact par, each possessing the same impotency and the same power, and it would not be true that finite things are more powerful than absolutely infinite being. Although Doz's sixth objection certainly seems to be faulty, his first five are compelling.[44] Accordingly, Doz prefers to speak of one proof in two stages: (1) If something exists necessarily, God exists necessarily. (2) Now something exists necessarily; therefore God exists necessarily.[45] If we follow Spinoza's own formulation, however, it yields the following outline:

1. Inability to exist is impotence, while ability to exist is power.
   a. This is self-evident.
2. If only finite beings exist, then finite beings are more powerful than absolutely infinite being.
3. But this is absurd.
   a. This is self-evident.
4. Therefore, either nothing exists or being absolutely infinite necessarily exists.
5. But we ourselves exist.
6. Therefore, being absolutely infinite, or God, necessarily exists.

Spinoza's principle, *Inability to exist is impotence, while ability to exist is power*, is taken as self-evident. Accordingly, he should perhaps have included it among his axioms. As we have seen, Spinoza is not here referring to the possible or contingent beings of the classical cosmological argument, beings which may or may not exist. Rather he is asserting that to be unable to exist is to be weaker than to be able to exist. Consequently, something that exists has more *potentia* than something that does not.

If only finite beings exist, then finite beings are more powerful than absolutely infinite being. This follows logically: an existent man has more *potentia* than a non-existent God. I do not think Spinoza means to say here, *if only finite beings exist necessarily, then finite beings are more powerful than absolutely infinite being.* Doz's interpretation of the argument (if something exists necessarily, God exists necessarily, etc.) would imply this. But in this case, (1) Spinoza would not have justified including the word 'necessarily' in the premiss's ground, since the consequent follows without it. (2) Step 4 should then read 'either nothing exists necessarily, etc.' and step 5 should read 'But we ourselves exist necessarily'. These additions might be taken to be implied, since for Spinoza anything that exists does so necessarily either in itself or through another.[46] But then the original principle would mean 'Ability to exist necessarily is power; inability to exist necessarily is impotence', which does not seem to be what was intended. Worse than that, by taking 'necessarily' as implied in steps 4 and 5, one reduces the notion of necessary existence to mere existence, such that the existence of God concluded to in step 6 is no more necessary than that of finite beings. Spinoza would not have proved God exists in himself. He would still have to argue: 'To exist in oneself is power; to exist in another is impotence. Either nothing exists through another or God exists in himself; something exists through another; therefore God exists in himself'. But this is virtually the same as Gueroult's already rejected interpretation. Not only would it involve proving that I am a mode, but it would also draw in the infinite regress question and turn the proof into a contingency argument. Therefore, I do not think that Spinoza meant to imply but did not say 'necessarily' in steps 4 and 5. He wants to prove a necessity of existence for God that is not true of finite beings. Hence, I think his dilemma ought to be paraphrased: if only finite beings exist, then finite beings are more powerful than absolutely infinite being.

But this is absurd; it is self-evident that finite beings cannot exceed infinite being in power. *Therefore, either nothing exists or being absolutely infinite necessarily exists.* If nothing exists, then finite beings are not more powerful than infinite being. Spinoza's thought may be that if nothing exists, then neither disjunct has more power than the other. But even at that, it still seems absurd that infinite being should not have more power than finite being. Perhaps he means that if nothing at all exists, then no meaningful comparisons of power can be drawn. But then, could one not say that the comparison between finite beings and a non-existent infinite being in step 2 is equally specious? Or perhaps he has in mind that only a logically impossible essence could prevent an infinite being from existing; therefore, if finite beings also do not exist, they must be equally logically impossible. But there is no reason to believe that Spinoza would think the existence of finite beings could be logically impossible or that logical possibility is operative in this argument. What I mean to say is that it is difficult to see how a state of nothingness can be a 'neutral ground' on Spinoza's principles, and, hence, the dilemma does not appear to be genuine. Assuming, however, that it is, Spinoza argues that if anything at all exists, then a necessary being exists. As Gueroult points out, the argument here is not *a posteriori* in the medieval sense of reasoning from effect to cause as in the contingency proof; rather the argument is *a fortiori.*[47] One sees what the finite is capable of and concludes immediately to an at least equal capability in the infinite. If finite being can exist, then infinite being can exist. Spinoza takes for granted, I think, that the existence of an infinite being would be necessary existence, since existence would be part of the essence of an absolutely infinite being. Therefore, either nothing exists or being absolutely infinite necessarily exists.

But we ourselves exist. No doubt the Cartesian *cogito* lies behind this step. The existence of something is undeniable because we affirm our existence in the very act of denying it. Spinoza leaves it undecided whether we exist as a substance or as a mode of some substance, which exists necessarily in itself.

Therefore, being absolutely infinite, or God, necessarily exists. Because finite being exists, *a fortiori* God exists as a necessary, absolutely infinite being. We may schematise Spinoza's cosmological argument:

1. Either a necessary, absolutely infinite Being exists or does not exist.
2. If a necessary, absolutely infinite Being does not exist, nothing exists.
   a. If a necessary, absolutely infinite Being does not exist, either nothing exists or only finite being exists.
   b. But it is impossible for only finite being to exist.
      i. Ability to exist is power; inability to exist is impotence.
      ii. If only finite being exists, then finite being would be more powerful than necessary, absolutely infinite Being.
      iii. And this is absurd.
   c. Therefore, if there is no necessary, absolutely infinite Being, nothing exists.
3. But something exists, namely ourselves.
4. Therefore, a necessary, absolutely infinite Being exists.

As remarked earlier, what makes Spinoza's thought so interesting is his exposition of the nature of the necessary, absolutely infinite Being to which he has concluded.

First, he tells us, '*Besides God, no substance can be nor can be conceived*'.[48] In other words, God is the only being which is in itself and conceived through itself; Spinoza here makes explicit the identity of substance and God. He argues that since God, by definition, is a being possessing infinite attributes, if there were any other substance in existence, then it would share a common attribute with God. But this, says Spinoza, is absurd. For two substances having the same attribute are the same substance.[49] The reason for this appears to be found in Spinoza's principle of individuation.[50] The only way substances could be individuated would be by their attributes or by their modes, a mode being defined as 'the affections of substance, or that which is in another thing through which also it is conceived'.[51] Mere modes of substances, however, can never serve to individuate them, for the substances as substance are identical; only their modes differ.[52] Spinoza says we may, so to speak, put the modes on one side and the substances on the other; looking then at the substances as they truly are in themselves, we can see they are identical. Hence, if two substances are to differ, they must differ in their attributes; they must differ essentially. But since God possesses all attributes, any attributes possessed by another substance comprise part of the essence of God. Thus, the substance is really part of God. Spinoza would probably call it a mode of God since it would have no independent being of its own. Spinoza adds that we cannot even *conceive* of another substance besides God, for we would conceive of it as existing, and this, too, is part of God's essence.[53] Therefore, God is the only substance, the only Being in itself and conceived through itself.

This leads inevitably on to Spinoza's second point: '*Whatever is, is in God, and nothing can either be or be conceived without God*'.[54] Spinoza does not mean to assert here God's omnipresence; rather he means that whatever is is God. This follows from Spinoza's definition of the categories of reality. Everything is either a substance or a mode of a substance. Since, therefore, God is the only substance and modes are mere modifications of substance, then all that is is simply God and his various modes. Thus, for Spinoza, 'God' is identical with 'Nature', and, indeed, it is this latter term which he employs for God in his earlier 'Short Treatise'.[55] '. . . Nature, which results from no causes', he informs us, '. . . must necessarily be a perfect being to which existence belongs'.[56] In the *Ethics*, too, he employs his famous phrase 'God or Nature', a phrase that poignantly expresses the entire orientation of Spinoza's thought.[57] Spinoza, then, is a pantheist. The necessary, absolutely infinite Being to which he argues is the universe itself, plain and simple. Wild comments,

> Only then do we seem to have a reality truly self-dependent. Anything we could fasten upon, short of the whole of things, would turn out to be intertwined with other things themselves interconnected with others until we should have the whole again. Now as Spinoza pointed out, this vast totality of things *must* exist because it is by definition all inclusive. There is nothing else for it to be dependent upon. Therefore

> it must be its own reason for existing,—its own 'cause'. As Spinoza says . . . 'its essence necessarily involves existence'.[58]

Thus, the universe itself is the only substance; Joachim states: 'Reality, God, Nature, the Most Perfect Being—however we name it—this alone is self-dependent and self-contained'.[59]

Spinoza argues that the two major orders of reality—thought and extension—are actually characteristics of God. 'It follows . . . that the thing extended (*rem extensam*) and the thing thinking (*rem cogitantem*) are either attributes of God or . . . affections of the attributes of God.'[60] He notes that many would object to saying that extension is an attribute of God, but he is ready with a defence.[61] All arguments against God's being extended, he observes, rest solely on the assumption that bodily substance consists of parts, an assumption which Spinoza labels 'absurd'.[62] He is here thinking of his analysis of substance. For substance is in itself (1) necessarily infinite, (2) the cause of itself, (3) individuated by its attributes, and (4) incapable of being produced. With regard to the first, Spinoza states that substance exists either as a finite substance or as an infinite substance.[63] But the first alternative is impossible. A thing is finite if it is limited by another thing of the same nature.[64] For example, a finite extended thing is limited by another extended thing and a finite thought by another thought, but an extended thing does not render a thought finite nor vice versa. Thus, one might have infinite extension and infinite thought, but one could not have two extended things or two thoughts both of which were infinite. But substance cannot be limited by something of the same nature because, as we have seen, there cannot be two substances of one nature, for there would be no principle of individuation between the two. Since the only way substances could differ would be by their natures, each substance is necessarily infinite. Secondly, substance is the cause of itself.[65] This follows from the same principle of individuation. For if substances could be two only by differing in nature, then they can have nothing in common. And this means one cannot be the cause of the other, because a cause and its effect always have something in common.[66] This is so because, since the substances have nothing in common, the conception of one does not necessitate the conception of the other, while the conception of an effect always, according to Spinoza's axioms, involves the conception of the cause. If, then, substances cannot be caused, they must be the cause of themselves. This can be shown more easily, adds Spinoza, by realising that if substance were caused, then its conception would involve the conception of something else, and this contradicts the definition of substance as that which is conceived through itself.[67] Third, substance is individuated through its attributes.[68] This we have already seen, for attributes must individuate substances if they are to differ, since mere modes cannot perform this function. Fourth, substance is incapable of being produced.[69] This follows from point 2. Because substances cannot be caused, they cannot be produced in being.

With this analysis in hand, Spinoza is prepared to argue that substance cannot be divided.[70] If substance could be divided, then its parts would either retain the nature of substance or they would not. If they did retain it, then it follows that each part would be infinite, would be the cause of itself, and would consist of an attribute which individuated it from every other part with the result that from the one overall substance, many substances were produced, all of which is contradictory to the nature of substance and therefore absurd.[71] Moreover, since the parts would be substances, they would have nothing in common with the whole, and the whole, since it is a substance, could exist and be conceived without its parts, which is also absurd. On the other hand, if the parts did not retain the nature of substance, then when the whole was divided up into its parts, the substance would perish. But this cannot be, asserts Spinoza, because substance, now identified with the cause of itself, is that whose essence involves existence. Therefore, it cannot cease to exist. Hence, it is absurd to suppose that substance can be divided up into parts not retaining the nature of substance. As both alternatives, then, lead to self-contradictory conclusions, it must be that substance is indivisible.[72]

The import of all this is '. . . that no substance, and consequently no bodily substance in so far as it is substance, is divisible'.[73] This is made even clearer when one reflects on the fact that a part of a substance would be a finite substance, which is a contradiction in terms. Now Spinoza has shown that God is the only substance; therefore, extension must be one of his attributes. God as substance is not made up of finite parts—he is infinite, one, and indivisible.[74] But what of the parts we perceive in the world? Elsewhere Spinoza replies, '. . ."part" and "whole" are not true or real entities, but only "things of reason", and consequently there are in Nature . . . neither whole nor parts'.[75] The universe as substance is one; the 'parts' we perceive do not divide its substance. As Spinoza says,

> . . . matter is everywhere the same, and . . . except in so far as we regard it as affected in different ways, parts are not distinguished in it; that is to say, they are distinguished with regard to mode, but not with regard to reality . . . . I do not know why matter should be unworthy

of the divine nature, since . . . outside God no substance can exist . . . . All things, I say, are in God . . . .[76]

A third thing that can be known about God's nature is that God is eternal.[77] For God is substance, and it is of the nature of substance to exist. And by definition whatever exists by its essence is eternal; Spinoza says, 'It cannot therefore be explained by duration or time, even if the duration be conceived without beginning or end'.[78] By this Spinoza apparently means to assert that the universe itself is outside of the temporal process, though presumably its modes take part in that process.

Fourth, the essence and existence of God are the same thing.[79] Since God and his attributes are eternal, his attributes express his existence. Since these same attributes express his essence, it follows that his essence and existence are identical. Now although the terminology is the same, Spinoza obviously does not mean the same thing as Thomas Aquinas in identifying God's essence with his existence. For Aquinas, existence is an act; it is existing. But Spinoza conceives existence as a sort of property, itself an essence. For example, in the 'Short Treatise' he makes the statement: 'the existence of God is essence; Therefore . . . [God exists]'.[80] This is certainly not Aquinas's way of speaking. For though Aquinas would say God's essence is his existence, he would not say God's existence is essence. For Aquinas the act of existing is primary, and God's essence reduces to it; but for Spinoza essence is primary, and God's existence reduces to (and is deduced from) it. This serves to distinguish Spinoza from the scholastics, with whose language his own is so similar.

Fifth, and, for our study, last, Spinoza maintains that '*In nature there is nothing contingent, but all things are determined from the necessity of the divine nature to exist and act in a certain manner*'.[81] In the universe, everything follows according to an inexorable determinism. Whatever is is God, as we have seen. All the modes of God flow from his substance necessarily and not contingently. For God possesses infinite attributes each of which expresses his essence in its own way. Thus, from God's nature 'infinite numbers of things in infinite ways' must necessarily follow.[82] God is the cause of the existence and essence of all things, for only he is conceived through himself.[83] He is also the cause of every action of all things.[84] For anything determined to action has been so determined by some thing, and God is the cause of that thing, both of its essence and existence. 'Wherefore all things are determined from a necessity of the divine nature, not only to exist, but to exist and act in a certain manner, and there is nothing contingent.—Q.E.D.'[85] For

Spinoza, then, all things that do happen *must* happen; the causal network of causes and effects unfolds with absolute necessity.

Now this is certainly not the theistic conception of God to which the cosmological argument normally purports to lead us. For the conclusion adduced by Spinoza is the necessary existence of the universe itself, a Being absolutely infinite and unique, existing eternally and changelessly in an infinite variety of modes, which flow from its nature in complete necessity. Spinoza specifically states that traditional theistic attributes,

> such as *omniscient*, *merciful*, *wise* and so forth, which things, since they are only certain modes of the thinking things, and can by no means be, or be understood without the substances whose modes they are, can, consequently, not be attributed to him, who *is a Being subsisting without the aid of anything*, and solely *through himself*.[86]

Nor can God be called the highest Good; this misconception results from the theologians' desire to absolve God from man's sin and evil. But this cannot be the case, explains Spinoza, for God is the cause of all things.[87] Accordingly, good, evil, and sin are 'only modes of thought', not anything that has reality; 'For all things and works which are in Nature are perfect'.[88] And although Spinoza posits thought as one of the two attributes of God known to us, the other being extension, this should not be taken to mean that God has a mind or is a bi-polar entity analogous to the soul/body composite. The only mind in the universe is our minds, which 'all taken together form the eternal and infinite intellect of God'.[89] But, as is evident from above, even this collection of minds is only a mode, the universe itself does not *think*. As Spinoza says, our intellects are part of the *natura naturata* (all the modes of God) not part of the *natura naturans* (reality in itself and conceived through itself).[90] Intellect and will predicated of God bears no relation to the meaning generally associated with those terms:

> Moreover—to say a word, too, here about the intellect and will which we commonly attribute to God—if intellect and will pertain to His eternal essence, these attributes cannot be understood in the sense in which men generally use them, for the intellect and will which could constitute His essence would have to differ entirely from our intellect and will, and could resemble ours in nothing except in name. There could be no further likeness than that between the celestial constellation of the Dog and the animal which barks.[91]

For Spinoza, then, God is not personal, except insofar as persons are modes of God. God himself is simply substance, that is to say, the self-existent being of which everything is but a mode or attribute.

Therefore, Spinoza's cosmological argument is of tremendous significance because his God is so antithetical to the traditional God of theism.[92] His argument raises the vital question as to whether the absolutely necessary being posited by the cosmological argument may be nothing more than the universe itself.

NOTES

1. Benedict de Spinoza, *Ethic* I. Def. I. Quotations from *Spinoza Selections*, ed. John Wild, The Modern Student's Library (London: Charles Scribner's Sons, 1930), p. 94.

2. Stuart Hampshire, *Spinoza* (Harmondsworth, England: Penguin Books, 1951), p. 35.

3. Spinoza, *Ethic* I. Prop. XVII, Schol. *Selections*, p. 115.

4. Harold H. Joachim, *A Study of the 'Ethics' of Spinoza* (Oxford: Clarendon Press, 1901), p. 12.

5. J. N. Chubb, 'Spinoza's Arguments for the Existence of God', *Indian Journal of Theology* 17 (1968): 119–20. But see Harvey B. Natanson, 'Spinoza's God: Some Special Aspects', *Man and World* 3 (1970): 210–12. Natanson takes *causa sui* as meaning the efficient cause of self-existence. Whereas all other beings are caused to exist by eternal factors, only God is caused to exist by internal factors, i.e. his own essence.

6. Frederick Pollock, *Spinoza: His Life and Philosophy*, 2nd ed. (London: Duckworth, 1899), p. 149.

7. Spinoza, *Ethic* I. Def. III. *Selections*, p. 94.

8. Cf. John Wild's comment in Spinoza, *Ethic*, p. 94, and E. M. Curley, *Spinoza's Metaphysics: An Essay in Interpretation* (Cambridge, Mass.: Harvard University Press, 1969), p. 15.

9. Spinoza, *Ethic* I. Axiom IV. *Selections*, p. 95. Thus, according to Jarrett, in Spinoza's system to be conceived through something is to be explained in terms of it and is equivalent to being caused by it (Charles E. Jarrett, 'The Concepts of Substance and Mode in Spinoza', *Philosophia* 7 [1977]: 83–105).

10. Curley, *Metaphysics*, p. 39.

11. Pollock, *Spinoza*, p. 151.

12. Spinoza, *Ethic* I. Def. VI. *Selections*, p. 94.

13. Ibid., I. Def. IV. *Selections*, p. 94. Whether the attributes are aspectival only or really distinct in substance and whether this destroys Spinoza's monism is one of the most disputed topics of Spinoza scholarship. Cf. Harry Austryn Wolfson, *The Philosophy of Spinoza*, 2 vols. (Cambridge, Mass.: Harvard University Press, 1934), 1: 146–57; Curley, *Metaphysics*, pp. 16–17; H. F. Hallett, *Benedict de Spinoza: The Elements of his Philosophy* (London: Athlone Press, 1957), pp. 9–53; Martial Gueroult, *Spinoza I: Dieu* (Hildesheim: Georg Olms, 1968), pp. 47–56;

Alan Donagan, 'Essence and the Distinction of Attributes in Spinoza's Metaphysics', in *Spinoza: A Collection of Critical Essays*, ed. Marjorie Grene, Modern Studies in Philosophy (Garden City, N.Y.: Doubleday; Anchor Books, 1973), pp. 164–81; Claude Troisfontaines, 'Dieu dans le premier livre de l'Éthique', *Revue philosophique de Louvain* 72 (1974): 467–81; Thomas Carson Mark, 'The Spinozistic Attributes', *Philosophia* 7 (1977): 55–82.

14. Spinoza, *Ethic* I. Def. VI. Expl. *Selections*, p. 95.

15. James Martineau, *A Study of Spinoza*, 3rd ed. (London: Macmillan, 1895), p. 173.

16. Gueroult, *Spinoza*, pp. 195, 197.

17. Ibid., p. 198.

18. R. L. Sturch, 'The Cosmological Argument' (Ph.D. thesis, Oxford University, 1970), p. 181.

19. Joachim, *Study*, pp. 51–3. Joachim's view is upheld by Lee C. Rice 'Methodology and Modality in the First Part of Spinoza's *Ethics*', in *Spinoza on Knowing, Being and Freedom*, ed. J. G. Van Der Bend (Netherlands: Van Gorcum & Co., 1974), p. 152. 'The proofs in the *Ethics* depend simply upon the existence of something as their point of departure' (ibid.).

20. James M. Humber, 'Spinoza's Proof of God's Necessary Existence', *Modern Schoolman* 49 (1972): 221–33.

21. André Doz, 'Remarques sur les onze premières propositions de l'*Éthique* de Spinoza', *Revue de métaphysique et de morale* 81 (1976): 260.

22. Spinoza, *Ethic* I. Prop. VII. Schol. 2. *Selections*, p. 100.

23. Ibid. *Selections*, p. 101.

24. Benedict de Spinoza, 'Short Treatise on God, Man, and His Well-Being', in *Selections*, ed. Wild, pp. 45–6. It may seem odd to call a proof for God from our idea of God *a posteriori*. But Spinoza calls an argument *a posteriori* 'when it proceeds from consequences to conditions, or from effects to causes'; an *a priori* argument 'proceeds from the character of a thing to its implications, from conditions to consequences, or from causes to effects' (A. Wolf, Commentary to *Short Treatise on God, Man, & His Well-being*, by Benedict de Spinoza, trans. and ed. A. Wolf [London: Adam and Charles Black, 1910], p. 167). Spinoza is using these terms in their medieval sense; hence, it is possible that Spinoza could call an argument *a posteriori* which we would today label *a priori*. This would lend credence to Sturch's contention that all the proofs for God are *a priori*; but, as we shall see, this contention is nonetheless incorrect because the third proof involves an existential premiss. According to Wolfson, this third proof is 'an *a posteriori*, cosmological argument, pure and simple . . .', even though, in the fourth proof, Spinoza converts it into an ontological form (Wolfson, *Spinoza*, 1: 205, 213).

25. Spinoza, *Ethic* I. Prop. XI. Schol. *Selections*, pp. 104–5.

26. Joachim, *Study*, pp. 50–5.

27. John Wild, Introduction to *Selections*, ed. Wild, p. xxvii.

28. Benedict de Spinoza to Ludovicus Meyer [Letter XII], in *Selections*, ed. Wild, pp. 416–17.

29. Gueroult, *Spinoza*, pp. 195–7. Gueroult's other two grounds of dissimilarity can, however, be sustained, as we shall see.

30. Ibid., p. 194.

31. Spinoza, *Ethic* I. Prop. XI. Another Proof. *Selections*, p. 104.

32. Wolfson, *Spinoza*, p. 201.

33. Ibid., pp. 205–6.

34. H. G. Hubbeling, *Spinoza's Methodology* (Groningen, Netherlands: Van Gorcum & Comp., 1964), pp. 87–90.

35. Ibid., pp. 90–92, 98.

36. Ibid., p. 98. Cf. Rice, 'Methodology', p. 148.

37. Gueroult, *Spinoza*, pp. 193–5.

38. Ibid., p. 193.

39. Ibid.

40. Ibid., p. 194.

41. Ibid., p. 196.

42. Ibid., p. 195.

43. Doz, 'Remarques', pp. 247–51.

44. Against Doz's sixth point it might be urged: (1) Spinoza does not say that ability to not exist is impotence, but rather inability to exist is impotence. Ability to exist and inability to exist are, hence, incompatible properties. Thus, if only finite beings existed, they would have ability to exist; they would not have inability to exist. God would have inability to exist, but not ability to exist. They would therefore be more powerful than him. (2) Even on Doz's phrasing of the principle, it is not clear that Spinoza would say that existent finite beings have the ability to not-exist or that a non-existent God would have ability to exist. In his proof he speaks of finite beings' existing *necessarily*, i.e. if they exist they do not have the ability to not-exist. Similarly, Spinoza would say that if God does not exist, then he has no ability to exist, since only if his existence were logically impossible could he not exist. (3) Even apart from this, Spinoza's argument would still work even if finite beings had the *same* power as absolutely infinite being, since this, too, is absurd. (4) Even if Doz is correct, it provides no grounds for regarding the two proofs as one, since Doz's objection would apply with equal force to the whole.

45. Doz, 'Remarques', p. 252.

46. Ibid., pp. 253–4.

47. Gueroult, *Spinoza*, p. 194.

48. Spinoza, *Ethic* I. Prop. XIV. *Selections*, p. 107.

49. Ibid. I. Prop. V. *Selections*, p. 97.

50. Ibid. I. Prop. IV. *Selections*, p. 96.

51. Ibid. I. Def. V. *Selections*, p. 94. For Spinoza a mode is a way in which substance exists; it is a state of being. A mode has no independent existence of its own, and it can only exist insofar as it is a modification of substance. It cannot, therefore, be conceived through itself but only through the substance which it modifies. For a detailed discussion of modes, see Hallett, *Spinoza*, pp. 31–43.

52. Spinoza, *Ethic* I. Prop. V. Demonstr. *Selections*, p. 97.

53. Ibid. I. Prop. XIV. Demonstr. *Selections*, p. 107.

54. Ibid. I. Prop. XV. *Selections*, p. 108.

55. Spinoza, 'Short Treatise', pp. 54–9. But cf. Natanson, who argues vigorously that God is not to be equated with the whole of Nature in Spinoza's philosophy (Natanson, 'Aspects', pp. 215–19). Also cf. Hubbeling, *Methodology*, pp. 56–7; Leon Roth, *Spinoza* (London: Ernest Benn, 1929), p. 59.

56. Spinoza, 'Short Treatise', p. 56.

57. Spinoza, *Ethic* IV. Preface. *Selections*, p. 284. He refers to 'that eternal and infinite Being whom we call God or Nature' (ibid.). On Spinoza's metaphysical

pantheism, which this phrase describes, see James Collins, *A History of Modern European Philosophy* (Milwaukee: Bruce Publishing Co., 1954), pp. 223–4. Although Jarrett wants to deny that for Spinoza, God is the totality of all things, I do not see the incompatibility of saying God or substance is, as Jarrett prefers, matter plus 'mental stuff' and saying God is the totality of all things. In no way for Spinoza is God the soul of the universe. Spinoza was no process theologian; the universe as a whole simply is God for him (Jarrett, 'Concepts', pp. 101–02).

58. Wild, Introduction, pp. xxvii–xxviii. Or as Roth puts it, 'God is not a spirit omnipresent in the universe. He *is* the universe' (Roth, *Spinoza*, p. 60).
59. Joachim, *Study*, p. 8.
60. Spinoza, *Ethic* I. Prop. XIV. Corol. 2. *Selections*, p. 108.
61. Ibid. I. Prop. XV. Schol. *Selections*, p. 109.
62. Ibid. *Selections*, p. 110.
63. Ibid. I. Prop. VIII. Demonstr. *Selections*, p. 98.
64. Ibid. I. Def. II. *Selections*, p. 94.
65. Ibid. I. Prop. VI. Demonstr. *Selections*, p. 97.
66. Ibid. I. Prop. III. *Selections*, p. 96.
67. Ibid. I. Prop. VI. Another Demonstr. *Selections*, p. 98.
68. Ibid. I. Prop. V. Demonstr. *Selections*, p. 97.
69. Ibid. I. Prop. VI. *Selections*, pp. 97–98.
70. Ibid. I. Prop. XIII. *Selections*, pp. 106–7.
71. Ibid. I. Prop. XII. Demonstr. *Selections*, p. 106.
72. Ibid.
73. Ibid. I. Prop. VIII. Corol. *Selections*, p. 107.
74. Ibid. I. Prop. XV. Schol. *Selections*, p. 112.
75. Spinoza, 'Short Treatise', p. 56.

> 'Things of reason' = mere modes of thought. In the *Cog. Metaph.* (I. i. and iii.). Spinoza distinguishes as follows between a real thing (*ens reale*), a chimera, a thing of reason (*ens rationis*), and a fiction (*ens fictum*): A *chimera* is only a verbal expression denoting something which can neither be nor be conceived, because it involves a self-contradiction (*e.g.*, a square circle); a *thing of reason* (or a merely logical entity) is a mode of thought which does not exist outside the thinking mind, though it may be an important means of representing extra-mental realities (*e.g.*, genera and species, time, number, and measure); a *fiction* is a 'thing of reason'. . . and has no corresponding reality outside the mind; but not all 'things of reason' are fictions, only those which involve arbitrary or accidental imaginary combinations (Wolf, Commentary, pp. 178–9).

76. Spinoza, *Ethic* I. Prop. XV. Schol. *Selections*, p. 112.
77. Ibid. I. Prop. XIX. *Selections*, p. 118.
78. Ibid. I. Def. VIII. Explan. *Selections*, p. 95.
79. Ibid. I. Prop. XX. *Selections*, p. 118.
80. Spinoza, 'Short Treatise', p. 45.
81. Spinoza, *Ethic* I. Prop. XXIX. *Selections*, p. 125.
82. Ibid. I. Prop. XVI. *Selections*, p. 113.
83. Ibid. I. Prop. XXV. *Selections*, p. 122. For Spinoza, God is the 'immanent' not the 'transitive' cause of all things (ibid. I. Prop. XVIII. *Selections*, p. 117). He means that God is not outside the universe acting upon it, but that God is the

universe, and all its causal connections are from itself, just as the geometric properties of a triangle are immanently caused by the nature of the triangle itself.

84. Ibid. I. Prop. XXVI. *Selections*, p. 123.
85. Ibid. I. Prop. XXIX. Demonstr. *Selections*, p. 126.
86. Spinoza, 'Short Treatise', p. 78.
87. Ibid., pp. 78–9.
88. Ibid., p. 76.
89. Spinoza, *Ethic* V. Prop. XL. Schol. *Selections*, p. 397.
90. Ibid. I. Prop. XXIX. Schol. *Selections*, pp. 126–7. It is important not to read Kant's phenomena /noumena distinction back into Spinoza under the guise of the mode/substance distinction. Substance is not some unknowable thing-in-itself, and its modes are not equivalent to Kant's phenomena. Rather modes *are* substance in its various manifestations, and we know substance through its modes.
91. Ibid. I. Prop. XVII. Schol. *Selections*, p. 116.
92. One cannot help but wonder why Spinoza continually employs such theistic language as he does, for he speaks of creation, providence, free causality, and so forth, but in a manner utterly contrary to their normal meaning. As Misrahi observes, 'Spinoza certainly preserves the traditional terms: morality, salvation, creation, but for him they have an *entirely different meaning*. Creation in particular (as in the *Ethics*) is nothing other than the actual power, that is, the actual activity of God in nature, that is, of nature in nature itself' (Robert Misrahi, 'Spinoza face au christianisme', *Revue philosophique de la France et de l'Étranger* 167 [1977]: 247). Martineau comments,

> 'Nature', emptied of its living moment, was reduced to mechanical necessity; and 'God', at first endowed with 'goodness and simplicity of will', and 'absolute liberty of will',* surrendered such mental qualities either altogether or to finite beings, and lapsed into the underlying condition of all things. As this surrender cancels from the Divine name the characteristic significance of Theism, Ueberweg naively protests against the retention of the word 'God' to denote anything so heterogeneous as 'Substance', and complains of such 'perversion of religious terms as misleading and repulsive', † Till it is found out, it is misleading; and when it is found out, it is repulsive; but in the meanwhile it gains a hearing for Spinoza which would else be denied him by public law and private feeling.
>
> * Suppl. pp. 19, 21, 23. Cogit. Metaph. I. c. ii. 3.
> Cf. Eth. I. xxxii. Cor. 1. . . . .
>
> † Geschichte der Philosophie, iii. S. 6, ap. Busolt, p. 120 (Martineau, *Study*, pp. 171–2).

But in reading Spinoza's works, it seems difficult to believe Spinoza was such a pragmatist. It seems more likely that he really thought of himself as a religious philosopher, though not, of course, in the traditional sense. For an interesting analysis of Spinoza's personal religious beliefs, consult Hubbeling, *Methodology*, pp. 58–68. On Spinoza's attractiveness for a modern atheist, see Wallace Matson, 'Step towards Spinozism', *Revue internationale de philosophie* 31 (1977): 69–83.

Chapter 8

G. W. F. Leibniz

Gottfried Wilhelm Freiherr von Leibniz (1646–1716) is without a doubt one of the most important figures in the history of philosophical theism. His entire philosophical system might be termed a theodicy; in fact, the only book he ever wrote and published bears that title.[1] All of Leibniz's philosophical powers are brought to bear in support of the existence of the traditional theistic God, so much so that some have thought it incredible that such an innovative thinker as Leibniz should culminate and even centre his system in such a conservative, orthodox theology.[2] But this he did, and he was eager to prove God's existence by all means available, utilising the ontological argument, the cosmological argument, a special form of the teleological argument dependent upon his monadology, and the argument from eternal truths.[3] He remarked, 'I believe also that nearly all the means which have been employed to prove the existence of God are good and might be of service, if we perfect them . . .'.[4] Leibniz's attempt to perfect the ontological argument by supplying a missing premiss is well-known; however, the centre of our attention shall be directed toward the contributions he made in formulating the cosmological argument. These are substantial; it is his version of the argument that was employed by Christian Wolff and subsequently attacked by Immanuel Kant and that is the basic form of the argument discussed today. Fortunately, in terms of presuppositions, Leibniz's version of the proof is largely independent of his monadological system, and we can therefore forgo a discussion of his general metaphysical *Weltanschauung*. But there are some underlying principles, an understanding of which is critical if we are to fully appreciate the thrust of his proof.

Presupposed in Leibniz's cosmological argument are two principles: *the law of contradiction* and *the principle of sufficient reason*. These indeed form the basis of all reasoning; he writes,

Our reasonings are founded on *two great principles*, *that of contradiction*, in virtue of which we judge that to be *false* which involves contradiction, and that *true*, which is opposed or contradictory to the false.

And *that of sufficient reason*, in virtue of which we hold that no fact can be real or existent, no statement true, unless there be a sufficient reason why it is so and not otherwise, although most often these reasons cannot be known to us.[5]

Leibniz's views on the law of contradiction need not cause us much difficulty. His formulation of the law is typical; sometimes he expresses it in a sentence and sometimes symbolically.[6] He regarded the law as synonymous with the law of identity; writing to Clarke, he calls it '*the principle of contradiction or identity*'.[7] Elsewhere, he asserts, 'The first of the truths of reason is . . . the principle of *contradiction* or, what amounts to the same thing, of *identity*'.[8] The law of contradiction or identity is absolutely fundamental to thought and is therefore the first principle of reason. He writes,

> My view, then, is that nothing should be taken as first principles but experiences and the axiom of identity or (what is the same thing) contradiction, which is primitive, since otherwise there would be no difference between truth and falsehood; and all investigation would cease at once, if to say yes or no were a matter of indifference. We cannot, then, prevent ourselves from assuming this principle as soon as we wish to reason. All other truths are demonstrable . . . .[9]

The law of contradiction cannot be denied if we are to reason. The reference to experience here apparently refers to immediate, undeniable experiences, such as the awareness of one's own existence:

> We can always say that this proposition *I exist*, is of the highest evidence, being a proposition which cannot be proved by any other, or rather an *immediate truth*. And to say *I think*, *therefore I am*, is not properly to prove existence by thought, since to think and to be thinking is the same thing; and to say, I am thinking, is already to say, *I am* . . . . it is a proposition of fact based upon immediate experience . . . . it is a primitive truth . . . .[10]

One's existence is not a deduction, but is an undeniable datum of experience. In that 'I exist' is a primitive truth, it shares the status of being a first principle with the law of contradiction. In all our argumentation, therefore, we must employ the first of the two great principles, the law of contradiction.

The second great principle, that of sufficient reason, is more difficult to understand, as to both its formulation and basis. Leibniz may be credited as being the originator of the principle; though Spinoza employed it, it was Leibniz who distilled the principle and gave it proper expression.[11] But the principle is variously stated, and the different formulas are not always clearly identical in meaning. It would be helpful, therefore, to set out in chronological sequence some of the characteristic definitions of the principle of sufficient reason:

> . . . the determination of the resultant *conatus* of two forces (equal but acting in different directions) depends on a principle of higher rank: *Nothing happens without a reason.*[12]
>
> There are two first principles of all reasonings, the principle of contradiction . . . and a principle that a reason must be given, *i.e.*, that every true proposition which is not known *per se*, has an a *priori* proof, or that a reason can be given for every truth, or, as is commonly said, that nothing happens without a cause.[13]
>
> . . . it is one of the greatest principles of good sense that nothing ever occurs without cause or determining reason.[14]
>
> . . . the other principle is that of *determinate reason*: it states that nothing ever comes to pass without there being a cause or at least a reason determining it, that is, something to give an *a priori* reason why it is existent rather than non-existent, and in this wise rather than in any other. This great principle holds for all events, and a contrary instance will never be supplied . . . .[15]
>
> . . . the great principle . . . which teaches that *nothing happens without a sufficient reason*; that is to say, that nothing happens without its being possible for him who should sufficiently understand things, to give a reason sufficient to determine why it is so and not otherwise.[16]
>
> And *that of sufficient reason*, in virtue of which we hold that no fact can be real or existent, no statement true, unless there be a sufficient reason why it is so and not otherwise, although most often these reasons cannot be known to us . . . .[17]
>
> . . . *the principle of a sufficient reason, viz:* that nothing happens without a *reason* why it should be *so*, rather than *otherwise.*[18]

> . . . 'tis very strange to charge me with advancing my principle of *the want of a sufficient reason*, without any proof drawn either from the nature of things, or from the divine perfections. For the *nature of things* requires, that every event should have beforehand its proper conditions, requisites, and dispositions, the existence whereof makes the sufficient reason of such an event.[19]

> The principle in question, is the principle of the *want of a sufficient reason*; in order to any thing's existing, in order to any event's happening, in order to any truth's taking place.[20]

It seems reasonable that the most weight be given to definitions contained in works prepared for publication, such as the *Theodicy*, the 'Monadology', and the correspondence with Clarke. Fortunately, these are also the latest works Leibniz authored, his correspondence with Clarke actually being cut short by his death; thus, these passages embody his most mature thought. On the basis of the above passages, Louis Couturat contends that the principle in question evolved from the principle of 'giving the reason' to the principle of 'determining reason' to the principle of 'sufficient reason'.[21]

Now it seems clear that 'reason' often means for Leibniz 'cause', and in this case the principle of sufficient reason would simply be the principle of causality. Even in his last letter to Clarke, Leibniz seems to be using 'reason' in this way: when he says every event has beforehand its proper conditions, requisites, and dispositions whose existence constitutes the sufficient reason of the event, it sounds very much like he is saying every event has necessary and sufficient conditions or, more simply, every event has a cause. This use of 'reason' as synonymous with 'cause' is particularly clear in the example used to illustrate the principle in the second letter to Clarke:

> . . . Archimedes . . . was obliged to make use of a particular case of the great principle of a *sufficient reason*. He takes it for granted, that if there be a *balance*, in which everything is alike on both sides, and if equal weights are hung on each end of that balance, the whole will be at rest. 'Tis because no *reason* can be given, why one side should weigh down, rather than the other.[22]

Certainly the 'reason' for a drop on one side of the balance will be a cause which makes it descend. An efficient cause is thus a particular type of sufficient reason. What this means, as Gottfried Martin points out, is that the principle of causality is 'a special case of the universal principle of sufficient reason'.[23] Leroy Loemker states that the principle of mechanical or efficient causality is simply the general principle of sufficient reason applied temporally, and this seems to be a reasonable interpretation of Leibniz.[24] When we ask for the sufficient reason for a thing or an event in a temporal sense, we are asking for its antecedent and contemporaneous necessary and sufficient conditions. In giving this sort of sufficient reason, we are designating the cause.

But Leibniz also uses 'reason' in a second sense; a sufficient reason may be a *purpose* rather than an efficient cause. Hence, he observes, '. . . cause indeed is often called reason, and particularly final cause'.[25] The question 'Why?' may be answered by giving final causes as well as efficient causes. For example, when asked, 'Why is the kettle boiling?', I might respond by describing the action of the heat from the fire in causing the water molecules to vibrate faster and faster until they escape in the form of steam—or I might respond that the kettle is boiling because my wife is preparing me a cup of tea. Both provide a sufficient *reason*: one in terms of efficient causality, the other in terms of final causality. It is with this distinction in mind that Leibniz asserts that '. . . nothing ever comes to pass without there being a cause or at least a reason determining it . . .'.[26] 'Reason' in this case would appear to involve the notion of purpose.

But 'reason' is also used by Leibniz in an even wider sense. For Leibniz in his last letter to Clarke spells out three applications of the principle of sufficient reason: (1) the existence of any being has a sufficient reason, (2) the occurrence of any event has a sufficient reason, and (3) the 'taking place' of any truth requires a sufficient reason. Now while the first two might be interpreted simply in terms of efficient and final causes, it certainly does not make much sense to speak of a truth's being caused. Leibniz is here referring to his well-known doctrine that the predicate of every true affirmative statement is contained in the subject. He writes,

> In demonstration I use two principles, of which one is that what implies a contradiction is false, the other is that a reason can be given for every truth (which is not identical or immediate), that is, that the notion of the predicate is always expressly or implicitly contained in the notion of its subject, and that this holds good no less in extrinsic than in intrinsic denominations, no less in contingent than in necessary truths . . . .[27]

Leibniz is saying that any true proposition must have a reason for being true, and this reason is that the predicate is contained in the subject. To use his own example, when we say 'Caesar crossed the Rubicon', the concept of crossing the Rubicon is actually part of the concept of Caesar, is part of what we mean by 'Caesar'.[28] This is *why* true propositions are true: because the predicate is simply an 'unpacking' of what is already implicit in the subject. Now this does not mean that anyone can always so analyse a subject, say Caesar, to determine which predicates are contained therein. Only God in his omniscience can comprehend all the predicates of a subject:

> In contingent truths, however, though the predicate inheres in the subject, we can never demonstrate this, nor can the proposition ever be reduced to an equation or an identity, but the analysis proceeds to infinity, only God being able to see, not the end of the analysis indeed, since there is no end,* but the nexus of terms, or the inclusion of the predicate in the subject, since he sees everything which is in the series.
>
> * Reading *sed* for *sic* . . . .[29]

We are led, then, to a third meaning of the word 'reason'; in addition to efficient and final cause, it also means, when applied to truths, a rational basis. When we ask for the sufficient reason of a truth, we are asking for the rationally intelligible basis of that truth, and the answer is that the basis of the truth is the predicate's being contained in the subject. Leibniz has this in mind when he defines 'reason':

> The *reason* is the known truth whose connection with another less known makes us give our assert to the latter. But in particular and pre-eminently we call it reason, if it is the cause not only of our judgement, but also of the truth itself, which we also call *reason apriori*, and the *cause* in things corresponds to the *reason* in truths.[30]

There is thus an analogous usage of 'reason' and 'cause', and the principle of sufficient reason covers both.

Now it remains to be seen which sense Leibniz has in mind when he asks for the sufficient reason of the world, why there is something rather than nothing; but it is true that, in general, the reason for a thing's existing, an event's happening, or a truth's taking place can be given in terms of an efficient cause, a final cause, or a rational basis. Accordingly, the principle could be variously formulated: every event has a cause; everything has a purpose; everything has a rational basis. In fact, there seems to be an ascending order here. In order to fully explain something, to give its sufficient reason, it is not enough to give its efficient causes; nor is explanation truly complete by giving final as well as efficient causes. Only when a ground of intelligibility is given can a thing be said to have been thoroughly explained.

When we ask for the basis of the principle of sufficient reason, we find that Leibniz does not clearly spell out a defence of the principle; but in his last letter to Clarke he indicates two lines of defence: an *a priori* and an *a posteriori* justification.[31] For Leibniz it seemed astounding that anyone would ask for proof of this principle. Nevertheless, he suggests that the principle can be demonstrated both *a priori* and *a posteriori*. With regard to the first, he says the principle is required by the nature of things; it is an essential principle of reason, the denial of which leads to an indefensible position and the overthrow of the most important part of philosophy; it is justified *a priori*, by bare reason; to deny it is comparable to denying the law of contradiction and reduces one to absurdity. Now there appear to be two *a priori* demonstrations here: (1) the nature of things requires the principle, and (2) the principle cannot be consistently denied. Turning to the first, we may ask what Leibniz means by the phrase 'the nature of things'. For Leibniz the phrase seems to mean 'reality in itself', and he is stating that reality in itself requires this principle. Epistemologically, this implies that this principle is an innate principle, as the discussion in the *New Essays* makes evident:

> *Ph*. If the mind acquiesces so promptly in certain truths, cannot that acquiescence come from the consideration itself of the nature of things, which does not allow it to judge of them otherwise, rather than from the consideration that these propositions are engraved by nature in the mind?
>
> *Th*. Both are true. The nature of things and the nature of mind agree . . . . But what is called *natural light* supposes a distinct knowledge, and very often the consideration of the nature of things is nothing else than the knowledge of the nature of our mind, and of these innate ideas which we have no need to seek outside. Thus I call innate the truths which need only this consideration for their verification.[32]

Now the immediate object of the discussion are truths such as the law of contradiction;[33] accordingly, Leibniz is ascribing to the principle of sufficient reason the same sort of innate status. The truth of the principle, then, does not depend on experience. But we have seen that Leibniz in that same work states that only the law of contradiction and immediate experiences have the privileged status of being absolutely primitive; 'All other truths are demonstrable . . .'.[34] How then is the principle of sufficient reason to be demonstrated? In one early work, he appears to deduce it from the nature of truth itself: he argues that one cannot proceed to infinity in proofs, but must stop at some first unproved assumption; he takes this to be the law of contradiction. All identity statements are true as a result. But all other statements may be proved *a priori* as well because in every true proposition, there must be a connection between the predicate and the subject; the predicate of every true statement is contained in the subject. An omniscient mind could analyse the subject and deduce the predicate to form a true proposition.

> It is certain, therefore, that all truths, even highly contingent ones, have a proof *a priori* or some reason why they are rather than are not. And this is what is commonly asserted: that nothing happens without a cause, or there is nothing without a reason.[35]

This axiom, that '*there is nothing without a reason*', is foundational for a large part of metaphysics, physics, and moral science; without it one could not reason causally nor draw any conclusions in civil matters—the story of Archimedes and his balance is employed as an illustration of the application of the principle.[36] The *a priori* basis of the principle of sufficient reason would seem to be the principle that every predicate of a true statement is contained in the subject. Indeed, Leibniz sometimes speaks in his early works as though the principle of predicate in subject *is* the principle of sufficient reason. Writing to Arnault, he says,

> For there must always be some foundation for the connection between the terms of a proposition, and this must be found in their concepts. This is my great principle, with which I believe all philosophers should agree, and one of whose corollaries is the commonly held axiom that nothing happens without a reason, which can always be given, why the thing has happened as it did rather than in another way . . . .[37]

This makes it sound as though what we have called the principle of sufficient reason is but a corollary of a deeper principle. In fact, the relationship of the principle of sufficient reason to the principle of predicate in subject is a matter of some debate.

Couturat has contended that the principle of sufficient reason is most accurately stated as simply, 'all truths are analytic' and is the converse of the principle of contradiction, which states, 'all analytic propositions are true'.[38] Leibniz in his early works seems to suggest this; for example, he states,

> The predicate or consequent therefore always inheres in the subject or antecedent .... In identities this connection and the inclusion of the predicate in the subject are explicit; in all other propositions they are implied and must be revealed through the analysis of the concepts, which constitutes a demonstration a priori.
>
> This is true, moreover, in every affirmative truth, universal or singular, necessary or contingent, whether its terms are intrinsic or extrinsic denominations ....
>
> These matters ... give rise to the accepted axiom that *there is nothing without a reason, or no effect without a cause.*[39]

According to Couturat, this 'formulates precisely' the principle of sufficient reason; he comments,

> In its exact sense this principle means that in every true proposition the predicate is contained in the subject; therefore that every truth can be demonstrated *a priori* by the simple analysis of its terms. In a word, that *every truth is analytic.*[40]

Rescher faithfully follows Couturat in his exposition of the principles of contradiction and sufficient reason.[41]

On the other hand, G. H. R. Parkinson disputes Couturat's reduction of the principle of sufficient reason to 'every true proposition is analytic'.[42] Parkinson argues that the principle of sufficient reason follows from Leibniz's definition of truth. According to Leibniz, a true proposition is one which is or is reducible to an identical proposition and conversely. The principle of sufficient reason states that every true proposition can be proved.[43] On Parkinson's view, the principle of sufficient reason follows logically from, but is not reducible to, the assertion that all truths are analytic. E. M. Curley takes the argument against Couturat's position one step further. He contends that for Leibniz existential propositions are an exception to the principle that all truths are analytic.[44] He cites several texts to prove that while it is true that Leibniz regarded existence as a predicate, only the concept of God involves existence as part of that notion. Hence, the only existential proposition in which the predicate is part of the subject is 'God exists'; this, indeed, forms the basis of Leibniz's ontological argument. Thus, Curley states, 'True existential propositions are an exception to the general run of true propositions, in that all but one of them are strictly synthetic'.[45] But if this is so, then Couturat is incorrect in contending that the principle of sufficient reason states that all truths are analytic. Curely argues that this statement of the principle does not reflect Leibniz's mature view:

> From what has been said now, I think it is clear that we cannot accept these formulations of the principle as reflecting Leibniz's most accurate statment of his views. 'I cannot always explain myself fully,' writes Leibniz, '. . . but I always try to speak accurately. I begin as a philosopher, but I end as a theologian. One of my great principles is that nothing happens without reason. That is a principle of philsophy. Nevertheless, at bottom it is nothing but an affirmation of the divine wisdom, though I do not speak of this at first.'*
>
> * Eduard Bodeman, *Die Leibniz-Handschriften der königlichen öffentlichen Bibliothek zu Hannover*, Hildesheim, Georg Olms, 1966, p. 58 . . . .[46]

Accordingly, Curley maintains that the principle of sufficient reason means that there must be in some sense be a final cause (in addition to efficient cause) for everything that is. Martin adopts a similar view, and he speaks of the different *functions* of the principle of sufficient reason, now in physics, now in mathematics, which require different formulations of the one principle.[47]

Because Leibniz did not intend much of what he wrote to be published, it is difficult to be dogmatic about the relationship between the principle of predicate in subject and the principle of sufficient reason. Certainly it is difficult to believe they are *identical*; nevertheless, the early Leibniz clearly saw a connection between them. Unfortunately, in his later works he does not go beyond the usual familiar statement of the principle of sufficient reason—could his doctrine of predicate in subject have been what he was referring to when he wrote to Clarke in defence of his principle that '. . . I might say something more upon it; but perhaps it would be too abstruse for this present dispute'?[48] We do not know. But this uncertainty seems to be one of the invitable consequences of a philosopher who did not compose a *magnum opus*, but left behind thousands of sheets of assorted letters, papers, notes, and fragments. But at any rate, Leibniz certainly regarded the principle of sufficient reason as an innate truth and capable of demonstration *a priori*.

A second *a priori* justification hinted at by Leibniz is that the principle, like the law of contradiction, cannot be consistently denied. The law of contradiction cannot be denied, for otherewise there would be no difference between truth and falsehood; 'We cannot, then, prevent ourselves from assuming this principle as soon as we wish to reason'.[49] Now we have seen that Leibniz in writing to Clarke asserts that a denial of the principle of sufficient reason, like the denial of the law of contradiction, reduces one to absurdity. Now the question is, why does the denial of the principle, *nothing is without a sufficient reason*, lead one to absurdity? If the proof is analogous to that for the law of contradiction, then in denying the principle one must somehow affirm the principle. Perhaps Leibniz would say that the very denial of the principle presupposes the principle. Either my denial has a sufficient reason for its truth or not: if not, then it is groundless and can be disregarded; if it does have a sufficient reason, then it is false, for it purports to deny the principle. Or perhaps Leibniz would return to the principle of predicate in subject: in any true statement the predicate is contained in the subject, and, hence, even the denial of the principle of sufficient reason must have its predicate contained in its subject, if it is to be a true statement. And this is self-defeating because the principle of predicate in subject *is* the principle of sufficient reason, in at least one of its forms. Thus, to deny the principle presupposes the principle. This is, of course, speculative, and Leibniz does not make explicit his defence of the principle. But he does say it can be proved *a priori*, and these two methods of argument seem to be alluded to in Leibniz's correspondence with his English rival.

But in addition to *a priori* demonstration, the principle can also be proved *a posteriori*. Leibniz argues that everyone employs the principle; its neglect leads to fantasies. An exception to the principle has never been found; it is repeatedly verified. Again, there appear to be two arguments operating here. First, the principle is pragmatically justified. We simply cannot get along without it: we implicitly affirm its truth every day; if we deny its truth, we are led into delusions. The principle is simply necessary to life and learning, and it would be foolishness indeed to abandon it. As Leibniz elsewhere asserts,

> This axiom, however, *that there is nothing without a reason*, must be considered one of the greatest and most fruitful of all human knowledge, for upon it is built a great part of metaphysics, physics, and moral science; without it, indeed, the existence of God cannot be proved from his creatures, nor can an argument be carried from causes to effects or from effects to causes, nor any conclusions be drawn in

> civil matters. So true is this that whatever is not of mathematical necessity . . . must be sought here entirely.[50]

In sum, *all* our inductive reasoning presupposes the validity of this principle.

Secondly, the principle of sufficient reason has never been falsified and is repeatedly verified. Leibniz notes that an exception to the principle has never been found; hence, it has never been (nor will it ever be) falsified by finding something without a sufficient reason. And it is on every occasion corroborated: it is verified again and again. Thus, it has the strongest *a posteriori* proof available. By these two methods, the principle of sufficient reason is established with the strongest empirical justification possible.

With these *a priori* and *a posteriori* arguments Leibniz believes to have established the truth of his great principle beyond question. The principle of sufficient reason together with the law of contradiction govern all reasoning:

> The great foundation of *mathematics*, is *the principle of contradiction or identity*, that is, that a proposition cannot be *true and false* at the same time; and that therefore *A* is *A*, and cannot be *not A*. This single principle is sufficient to demonstrate every part of arithmetic and geometry, that is, all *mathematical* principles. But in order to proceed from *mathematics* to *natural philosophy*, another principle is requisite . . .: I mean, *the principle of a sufficient reason*, *viz*: that nothing happens without a *reason* why it should be *so*, rather than *otherwise*.[51]

A fundamental understanding of these principles is essential, therefore, to Leibniz's cosmological proof for the existence of God, to which we now turn.

Leibniz's arguments for the existence of God are brief, and it may be worthwhile to compare them. In an early work, "On the Ultimate Origin of Things', [1697] he argues thus:

> In addition to the world or aggregate of finite things, there is some unity which dominates, not only like the soul in me, or rather like the Ego itself in my body, but in a much higher sense. For the unity dominating the universe . . . creates and fashions it, is superior to the world, and, so to speak, extramundane, and is thus the ultimate reason of things. For the sufficient reason of existence cannot be found either in any particular thing or in the whole aggregate or series. Suppose a

book on the elements of geometry to have been eternal and that others had been successively copied from it, it is evident that, although we might account for the present book by the book which was its model, we could nevertheless never, by assuming any number of books whatever, reach a perfect reason for them; for we may always wonder why such books exist at all and why they are thus written. What is true of books is also true of the different states of the world, for in spite of certain laws of change a succeeding state is in a certain way only a copy of the preceding, and to whatever anterior state you may go back you will never find there a complete reason why there is any world at all . . . . And even if you imagine the world eternal, nevertheless since you posit nothing but a succession of states, and as you find a sufficient reason for them in none of them whatsoever, and as any number of them whatever does not aid you in giving a reason for them, it is evident that the reason must be sought elsewhere . . . . From which it follows that even by supposing the eternity of the world, an ultimate extramundane reason of things, or God, cannot be escaped.[52]

Several points of this proof are noteworthy: (1) 'Reason' is not used in the sense of efficient cause in this proof. Leibniz is willing to grant that temporally considered the world is caused by its prior states. But he is demanding in addition either a final cause for the world or else its rational basis of intelligibility. This is evident when he remarks, 'For in eternal things even where there is no cause there must be a reason . . .'.[53] (2) Leibniz also grants the eternity of the world for the sake of argument. His proof has no relation to a temporal infinite regress. (3) Leibniz asks for the reason for the world considered as a whole. He wants to explain 'the very fact that something exists rather than nothing'.[54] (4) For Leibniz God is thus the ultimate reason for all things. This will bear greater examination later.

Second, we may consider the version found in the *Theodicy* [1710]:

God is the first reason for things: for such things as are bounded, as all that which we see and experience, are contingent and have nothing in them to render their existence necessary, it being plain that time, space and matter, united and uniform in themselves and indifferent to everything, might have received entirely other motions and shapes, and in another order. Therefore, one must seek the reason for the existence of the world, which is the whole assemblage of *contingent* things, and seek it in the substance which carries with it the reason for its existence, and which in consequence is *necessary* and eternal.[55]

It may be noted (1) This proof argues that contingent things need an explanation for their existence because, as contingents, they might not have existed at all. Leibniz does *not* argue that they are contingent because their non-existence is logically conceivable. (2) The reason sought here could be either an efficient cause or a final cause or a rational basis of intelligibility for contingent things. (3) God is a necessary being, that is to say, He cannot not-exist. Again, Leibniz does *not* define necessity here as logical necessity.

A third version of the proof is found in 'The Principles of Nature and of Grace, Based on Reason', [1714]:

> . . . *nothing happens without a sufficient reason* . . . . This principle laid down, the first question which should rightly be asked, will be *Why is there something rather than nothing*? For nothing is simpler and easier than something . . . .
>
> Now this sufficient reason for the existence of the universe cannot be found *in the series of contingent things*, that is, of bodies and of their representations in souls; for matter being indifferent in itself to motion and to rest, and to this or another motion, we cannot find the reason of motion in it, and still less of a certain motion. And although the present motion which is in matter, comes from the preceding motion, and that from still another preceding, yet in this way we make no progress, go as far as we may; for the same question always remains. Thus it must be that the sufficient reason, which has no need of another reason, be outside this series of contingent things and be found in a substance which is its cause, or which is a necessary being, carrying the reason of its existence within itself; otherwise we should still not have a sufficient reason in which we could rest. And this final reason of things is called *God*.[56]

Now what points of difference are there between this proof and the preceding? (1) Its point of departure is local motion; this is evident from the phrase 'matter being indifferent in itself to motion and to rest'.[57] (2) The proof appears to ask for a final cause, although one cannot rule out the rational basis of intelligibility either. Leibniz defines the principle of sufficient reason in such a way as to suggest a search for a final cause: '. . . nothing happens without its being possible for him who should sufficiently understand things, to give a reason sufficient to determine why it is so and not otherwise'.[58] Thus, he is asking, why, to what purpose, is there something rather than nothing? However, the conclusion of the argument should then have been, not that the final reason of things is God, but that the final reason of things is the will of God. This could simply be imprecision on Leibniz's part, for a sentence earlier he said that the sufficient reason of all things must be (a) outside the series of contingent things and (b) *in* a substance or being which causes contingent things, which is true of God's will. Or it may be that Leibniz is not seeking just a final cause, but a rational basis of intelligibility for the motion in the world, and this basis is God himself. (3) The argument begins with motion, but shifts mid-course to a reason for existence. God is the reason for not only the motion of the world, but for its existence as well. The example of motion seems to be a digression from the more fundamental question of why something exists rather than nothing.

Finally, a fourth version of the proof is to be found in the 'Monadology' [1714]:

> . . . there must . . . be a *sufficient reason* for *contingent truths*, or those *of fact*—that is, for the sequence of things diffused through the universe of created objects—where the resolution into particular reasons might run into a detail without limits, on account of the immense variety of the things in nature and the division of bodies *ad infinitum*. There is an infinity of figures and of movements, present and past, which enter into the efficient cause of my present writing, and there is an infinity of slight inclinations and dispositions, past and present, of my soul, which enter into the final cause.
>
> And as all this *detail* only involves other contingents, anterior and more detailed, each one of which needs a like analysis for its explanation, we make no advance: the sufficient or final reason must be outside of the sequence or *series* of this detail of contingencies, however infinite it may be.
>
> And thus it is that the final reason of things must be found in a necessary substance, in which the detail of changes exists only eminently, as in their source; and this is what we call God.[59]

It should be noted: (1) In this proof Leibniz appears to be arguing that the existence of the world must have a rational basis. This seems to be so because (a) he is asking for a reason for contingent *truths*, truths about things in the world, such as 'I exist'. For Leibniz, all truths are either truths of reason or truths of fact; the former are logically necessary while the latter are not.[60] The truth of the former is grounded in the law of contradiction; but, Leibniz argues, there must also be a basis for truths of fact—there must be a rational basis for every truth's taking place. Thus, he is arguing for God as the ultimate basis for the intelligibility of the world. This also seems to be so because (b) Leibniz specifically states that efficient and final causes can go to infinity without ever providing a sufficient reason for the world of contingent things. (2) In this version as in the preceding God is called necessary. By this Leibniz means here *actually* necessary, that is, not dependent on extrinsic determinations. In his proofs for the existence of God, Leibniz does not define contingency and necessity in terms of logical considerations. This comes later as an unpacking of what these terms mean. His argument does not depend on the notion of God as a being whose non-existence involves a contradiction. Leibniz describes God as a metaphysically necessary being.[61] Now a metaphysically necessary being, says Leibniz, is one 'whose essence is existence'.[62] But it is important to realise that for Leibniz the distinction between essence and existence was merely conceptual, as Lovejoy explains,

> Most non-materialistic philosophers of the seventeenth and eighteenth centuries still habitually thought in terms of two realms of being. The world of essences, 'natures', or Platonic Ideas, was to them as indubitably and objectively there to be reckoned with as the world of individual, temporal existents, physical or spiritual. The former, indeed, though it did not 'exist', was the more fundamental and solid reality of the two . . . . It is true that conceptualism rather than straight Platonic realism was the commonly accepted doctrine about the status of the Ideas; Leibniz himself, for example, held that the realm of essences would have no being at all, if it were not eternally contemplated by the mind of God.[63]

Leibniz was thus a nominalist, holding that essences exist only in the mind, whether ours or God's. Therefore, when Leibniz says God's essence is existence, he means that the definition of 'God' entails the predicate 'existence'. Metaphysical necessity is now seen, therefore, to be synonymous with logical or mathematical necessity.[64] When something is metaphysically necessary, its opposite involves a contradiction or logical absurdity.[65] Hence, Leibniz argues that to say that God's 'essence comprises existence' is simply to say that He must exist if He is possible; this is, of course, Leibniz's famous ontological argument.[66] But, as we have seen, his cosmological argument does not depend upon such an understanding of 'metaphysically necessary'. This involves a later analysis of what this phrase implies. Now Leibniz does not usually say that God's essence *is* existence, but rather that His essence 'involves' existence, or God 'embraces the perfection called *existence*', or God is a being which 'exists by its essence'.[67] It would seem, then, that Leibniz did not equate God's essence and existence; rather the latter is included in and depends on the former; as he wrote in his critique of Spinoza: '. . . the essence of God involves existence, although it may not be admitted that they are one and the same'.[68] Hence, Leibniz is arguing for the existence of a being whose essence necessarily involves its actual existence, although this reasoning is not explicity found in the cosmological argument itself.

Now it seems clear that these arguments are not separate, distinct proofs, but merely versions of the same proof. But it is not so clear what Leibniz is seeking in his proof: a final cause or a basis of intelligibility for the world? Loemker contends that Leibniz is seeking a final cause of the world and this is God's will:

> Causal explanations within nature never escape contingency and therefore still leave unanswered the question, 'Why this world rather than another?' . . . To answer this question is to be driven beyond 'thisness' to the will of God as an explanation, since this question necessarily involves a principle of selection.[69]

But, fact, this seems to be a misconstruction of Leibniz's argument: Leibniz is not initially inquiring, 'Why *this* world rather than *another*?' but 'Why *the* world rather than *nothing*?' It is not the 'thisness' of the world that here bewilders him, but why there is *any* world at all. It is not a final cause that is sought, but a rational basis of intelligibility for the world. Lovejoy explains,

> The motive which can be shown to have begotten his [Leibniz's] faith in the principle of sufficient reason, as a cosmological generalization, was not chiefly a desire to find what is commonly meant by teleology in nature . . . . Leibniz was less concerned . . . to maintain that the reason for a thing is a 'good', in the common sense of conduciveness to the subjective satisfaction of God or man or animal, than to maintain that the thing at all events has *some* reason, that it is *logically* grounded in something else which is logically ultimate.[70]

Now this is not to say that Leibniz was unconcerned with the 'thisness' of this world. On the contrary, his next step was to account for the particularly of this world; the essences of all possible beings have an exigency or claim to existence and will, in fact, exist unless precluded by the existence of something else with which it would be incompatible.[71]

But of all the sets of 'compossible' beings, there must be a sufficient reason why this set exists and the others do not. This does, as Loemker states, demand a principle of selection by which God permits some things to be and not others. The sufficient reason for *this* world is God's will, and God's will follows the principle of the best, by which He allows that to exist which will produce the best over-all world.[72] That is why this world is the best possible world. But this is a second step, as we said; the first metaphysical question is, why is there something rather than nothing? As A. T. Tymieniecka observes, the underlying point at issue here is '*whether the universe is rational or not*'.[73] This seems to be the thrust of Leibniz's argument: there must be a reason, a ground of intelligibility or rationality for everything, including the world. We may schematise Leibniz's argument in this way:

1. Something exists.
2. There must be a sufficient reason or rational basis for why something exists rather than nothing.
3. This sufficient reason cannot be found in any single thing or in the whole aggregate of things or in the efficient causes for all things.
   a. Things in the world are contingent, that is, determined in their being by other things such that if matter and motion were changed, they would not exist.
   b. The world is simply the conglomeration of such things and is thus itself contingent.
   c. The efficient causes of all things are simply prior states of the world, and these successive states do not explain why there are any states, any world, at all.
4. Therefore, there must exist outside the world and the states of the world a sufficient reason for the existence of the world.
5. This sufficient reason will be a metaphysically necessary being, that is, a being whose sufficient reason for existence is self-contained.

What can be known about God, the ultimate reason for all things?

First, God must possess all perfections. Leibniz argues that in order to cause perfections in creatures, God must possess them Himself:

> This primitive simple substance must contain in itself eminently the perfections contained in the derivative substances which are its effects; thus it will have perfect power, knowledge and will: that is, it will have supreme omnipotence, omniscience and goodness.[74]

Elsewhere Leibniz takes a different tack, arguing that absolute perfection is a consequence of God's plenitude of being.[75] Since God is dependent upon nothing extrinsic for His existence, He has all the fullness of reality in Himself, and this is what perfection means—'the magnitude of positive reality', which in God is infinite.[76] Leibniz also argues for specific attributes of God based on the particularity of this world:

> . . . this cause must be intelligent: for this existing world being contingent and an infinity of other worlds being equally possible, and holding, so to say, equal claim to existence with it, the cause of the world must needs have had regard or reference to all these possible in order to fix upon one of them . . . . to fix upon one of them can be nothing other than the act of the *will* which chooses. It is the *power* of this substance that renders its will efficacious. Power relates to *being*, . . . understanding to *truth*, and will to *good*. And this intelligent cause ought to be infinite in all ways, and absolutely perfect in *power*, in *wisdom* and goodness, since it relates to all that which is possible.[77]

As the creator of this world out of the infinity of possible worlds, God must be perfect in all the ways necessary to actualise this world's possibility.

Secondly, there can only be one God. This is the necessary implication of Leibniz's quest for an ultimate, sufficient reason for all there is:

> . . . the final reason of things must be found in a necessary substance . . .; and this is what we call God.
>
> Now this substance, being a sufficient reason of all this detail, which also is linked together throughout, *there is but one God, and this God is sufficient.*[78]

His phrase about the world's being linked together indicates a second argument for one God from the unity of the world; as he writes in the *Theodicy*, '. . . since all is connected together, there is no ground for admitting more than *one*'.[79] Hence, God is the single being who is the sufficient reason for the existence of all else.

Now this leads at once to a very interesting question for Leibniz: if everything has a sufficient reason, then what is God's sufficient reason? Leibniz sometimes speaks as though God has no sufficient reason; other times he states that God somehow is His own sufficient reason:

> . . . something which is absolute or metaphysical necessity, the reason for which cannot be given.[80]

> . . . one must seek the reason for the existence of the world . . . in the substance which carries with it the reason for its existence, and which in consequence is *necessary* and eternal.[81]

> . . . a substance . . . which is a necessary being, carrying the reason of its existence within itself . . . .[82]

> . . . contingent beings . . . can only have their final or sufficient reason in a necessary being who has the reason of his existence in himself.[83]

One of the things that so scandalised Samuel Clarke was Leibniz's unwavering insistence that the principle of sufficient reason allows no exceptions, not even in the divine being. Thus, even God must have a reason for doing what He chooses to do.[84] Presumably, then, Leibniz would also say that God needs a sufficient reason why He exists, that is to say, that there must be rational basis that makes it intelligible why there is a God. But Leibniz would also say that God is a self-explanatory being; He is His own rational basis. His existence is explained by reference to Himself. Thus, the whole realm of contingent beings are rationally based in and explained by a necessary being, who is His own rational basis and is self-explained.

Finally, it might be instructive to draw some comparisons between Leibniz's cosmological argument and Thomas Aquinas's third way.[85] (1) Aquinas's argument involves efficient causality, while Leibniz's does not. It will be remembered that Aquinas is searching for the efficient cause of the present act of existing in contingent beings. Leibniz, on the other hand, is searching for the ultimate explanation or rational basis of why there are contingent beings. Leibniz's God is, of course, the efficient cause of the world, but his proof for God's existence does not proceed along the chain of efficient causes to a first cause, but seeks a reason for the whole world. (2) Aquinas's proof involves an argument against an infinite regress, while Leibniz's does not. Aquinas reaches the absolutely necessary being by ascending a series of essentially subordinated agents, a series which, he argues, cannot be endless. Leibniz's proof involves no regress argument at all; he, like Aquinas, grants the temporal infinite regress, but he does not argue against a hierarchical series of sufficient reasons. Rather, asking why there is something rather than nothing, he proceeds immediately and without intermediaries to an ultimate reason for the whole world and its prior states. (3) Aquinas's argument presupposes the real distinction between essence and existence, while Leibniz's does not. For Thomas there must be an absolutely necessary being who continually sustains the act of every essence's existing. But Leibniz holds to a conceptual distinction only; hence, the metaphysically necessary being does not conjoin essence and existence in things, but furnishes the reason why beings which could just as easily not have existed do, in fact, exist.

Therefore, it seems clear that in Aquinas and Leibniz, we have two distinct types of cosmological argument. It is really quite amazing that the two should ever be confused, but, in fact, they are.[86] Any grouping of the respective proofs of each thinker under a common head as though they are the same will only distort an accurate understanding of both of them.

NOTES

1. G. W. Leibniz, *Theodicy: Essays on the Goodness of God, the Freedom of Man, and the Origin of Evil*, trans. E. M. Huggard (London: Routledge & Kegan Paul, 1951). Most of Leibniz's philosophy must be garnered from short essays, letters, and notes never intended for publication. Two important collections of these documents in the original languages are Gottfried Wilhelm Leibniz, *Sämtliche Schriften und Briefen* (Darmstadt, Deutschland: Otto Reichel, 1923) and Gottfried Wilhelm Leibniz, *Die philosophischen Schriften von Gottfried Wilhelm Leibniz*, ed. C. I. Gerhardt (Berlin: Wiedmannsche Buchhandlung, 1875).

2. For example, Bertrand Russell, *A History of Western Philosophy* (New York: Simon & Schuster, 1945), pp. 581–96.

3. These four are discussed in Bertrand Russell, *A Critical Exposition of the Philosophy of Leibniz* (Cambridge: Cambridge University Press, 1900), pp. 172–85. Nicholas Rescher suggests the presence of a fifth argument, a modal proof (Nicholas Rescher, *The Philosophy of Leibniz* [Englewood Cliffs, N.J.: Prentice-Hall, 1967], pp. 66–70). But this proof, which is found in Leibniz's letter to the editor of the *Journal de Trevoux*, is clearly a cosmological argument, since it involves an existential premiss. The proof may be schematised:

1. If necessary being is possible, it exists.
   a. Necessary being is being whose essence involves existence.
   b. The essence of a being determines the possibility of that being.
   c. Therefore, if the essence of necessary being is a possible essence, it necessarily involves existence.
2. If necessary being is not possible, nothing exists.
   a. Things that receive existence from another ultimately depend on a being that is self-existent.
   b. Therefore, if there is no self-existent being, there are no other beings as well.

3. But something exists.
4. Therefore, necessary being is possible.
5. Therefore, necessary being exists.

That this argument is not a separate type is evident from reflection on step 2.a. For the only way Leibniz could support it is by his usual cosmological argument: 2.a. is true because things must have a sufficient reason for their existence, and this can only be found in a necessary being. But in this case the rest of the argument becomes superfluous. For given premiss 3, what follows is not the *possibility* of the necessary being, but the actual existence of the necessary being.

4. Gottfried Wilhelm Leibnitz, *New Essays on the Understanding, by the Author of the System of Pre-established Harmony*, trans. Alfred G. Langley (New York: Macmillan, 1896), p. 505.

5. G. W. Leibniz, 'The Monadology', in *Leibniz Selections*, ed. Philip P. Wiener, The Modern Student's Library (New York: Charles Scribner's Sons, 1951), p. 539. (I have omitted in all quotations Leibniz's footnotes as well as the paragraph numbers.) Cf. his statement in the *Theodicy*:

> . . . there are two great principles of our arguments. The one is the principle of *contradiction*, stating that of two contradictory propositions the one is true, the other false; the other principle is that of the *determinate reason*: it states that nothing ever comes to pass without there being a cause or at least a reason determining it . . . (Leibniz, *Theodicy*, p. 147).

6. For an example of both, see G. W. Leibniz, 'Mr. Leibniz's Second Paper: Being an Answer to Dr. Clarke's First Reply', in *Philosophical Works of Leibniz*, ed. George Martin Duncan (New Haven, Conn.: Tuttle, Morehouse & Taylor, 1890), p. 239. Here Leibniz states the principle: 'a proposition cannot be *true and false* at the same time', and he expresses it: '*A* is *A*, and cannot be *not A*' (ibid.).

7. Ibid.

8. G. W. Leibniz, 'Animadversions on Descartes' *Principles of Philosophy*', in *Works*, ed. Duncan, p. 48.

9. Leibnitz, *New Essays*, pp. 13–14.

10. Ibid., p. 469.

11. Spinoza had written, 'For the existence or non-existence of everything, there must be a reason or cause' (Benedict Spinoza, *Ethic*, in *Spinoza Selections*, ed. John Wild, The Modern Student's Library [London: Charles Scribner's Sons, 1930], p. 103). Leibniz had commented with regard to this, 'This is rightly observed, and agrees with what I am wont to say, that nothing exists unless a sufficient reason of its existence can be given, which is easily shown not to lie in the series of causes' (G. W. Leibniz, '*Communicata ex literis* D. Schull(eri)', in *philosophische Schriften*, 4: 138).

12. G. W. Leibniz, *Theoria motus abstracti* (sec. 23–4), 1671, in *Selections*, ed. Wiener, p. 93.

13. G. W. Leibniz, '*Specimen Invontorum de admirandis naturae Generalis arcanis*', in *philosophische Schriften*, 7: 309. This is included in *Selections*, ed. Wiener, p. 94.

14. G. W. Leibniz, 'Letter to M. Coste on Necessity and Contingency. 1701.', in *Works*, ed. Duncan, p. 172.

15. Leibniz, *Theodicy*, [1710], p. 147.

16. G. W. Leibniz, 'The Principles of Nature and of Grace, Based on Reason' [1714], in *Selections*, ed. Wiener, p. 527.

17. Leibniz, 'Monadology' [1714], p. 539.

18. Leibniz, 'Second Paper' [1715], p. 239.

19. G. W. Leibniz, 'Mr. Leibniz's Fifth Paper: Being an Answer to Dr. Clarke's Fourth Reply' [1715], in *Works*, ed. Duncan, p. 258.

20. Ibid., p. 285.

21. Louis Couturat, 'On Leibniz's Metaphysics', in *Leibniz*, ed. Harry G. Frankfurt, Modern Studies in Philosophy (Garden City, N.Y.: Doubleday; Anchor Books, 1972), p. 21.

22. Leibniz, 'Second Paper', p. 239. The similarity between this use of the principle of sufficient reason and the principle of determination of the Arabic *mutakallimūn* is startling: both speak of the need for a determinant, both demand a cause why something should be existent or non-existent, and both employ the illustration of the balance. Nevertheless, the *mutakallimūn* did not employ the principle as broadly as Leibniz, restricting it to the realm of causality alone.

23. Gottfried Martin, *Leibniz: Logic and Metaphysics*, trans. K. J. Northcott and P. G. Lucas (Manchester: Manchester University Press, 1964), p. 9.

24. Leroy E. Loemker, Introduction to *Philosophical Papers and Letters*, 2nd ed., by Gottfried Wilhelm Leibniz, ed. Leroy E. Loemker (Dordrecht, Holland: D. Reidel, 1969), p. 26.

25. Leibniz, *New Essays*, p. 556.

26. Leibniz, 'Letter to M. Coste', p. 172.

27. G. W. Leibniz, '*Vorarbeiten zur allgemeinen Charakteristik*', in *philosophische Schriften*, 7: 199. This is included in *Selections*, ed. Wiener, p. 94. Cf. '. . . in every true affirmative proposition, whether necessary or contingent, universal or particular, the notion of the predicate is in some way included in that of the subject' (G. W. Leibniz to Antoine Arnauld, 14 July 1686, in *Papers and Letters*, ed. Loemker, p. 337).

28. G. W. Leibniz, *Meditationes de Cognitione, Veritate et Ideis*', in *Schriften*, 4: 438. This is included in *Selections*, ed. Wiener, p. 94.

29. G. W. Leibniz, 'On Freedom', in *Papers and Letters*, ed. Loemker, pp. 265–6.

30. Leibniz, *New Essays*, pp. 555–6.

31. Leibniz, 'Fifth Paper', pp. 258, 285–6.

32. Leibnitz, *New Essays*, p. 74.

33. Ibid., p. 72.

34. Ibid., p. 14.

35. Leibniz, 'On the General Characteristic', in *Papers and Letters*, ed. Loemker, pp. 226–7.

36. Ibid., p. 227.

37. Leibniz to Arnault, in *Papers and Letters*, ed. Loemker, p. 337.

38. Louis Couturat, *La Logique de Leibniz* (Paris: Ancienne Librairie Germer Baillière & Cie., 1901), pp. 214–16.

39. G. W. Leibniz, 'First Truths', in *Papers and Letters*, ed. Loemker, p. 268.

40. Couturat, 'Metaphysics', p. 20. Elsewhere he asserts, 'It is in this that properly consists the *principle of reason*, for it signifies nothing more than . . . that one must be able to "give a reason" to all truth, even contingent

truth, that is to say, to prove it by simple analysis of its terms. Such is the exact logical sense of this famous principle, whose normal statement: "nothing is or is done without a reason" is only a common formula borrowed from common sense' (Couturat, *Logique*, p. 214).

41. Rescher, *Leibniz*, pp. 25–7.

42. G. H. R. Parkinson, *Logic and Reality in Leibniz's Metaphysics* (Oxford: Clarendon Press, 1965), pp. 67–8.

43. Ibid., pp. 184–5.

44. E. M. Curley, 'The Root of Contingency', in *Leibniz*, ed. Frankfurt, pp. 83–96.

45. Ibid., p. 90.

46. Ibid., p. 96.

47. Martin, *Leibniz*, pp. 8–11, 15–16.

48. Leibniz, 'Fifth Paper', p. 286.

49. Leibnitz, *New Essays*, p. 14.

50. Leibniz, 'Characteristic', p. 227.

51. Leibniz, 'Second Paper', p. 239.

52. G. W. Leibniz, 'On the Ultimate Origin of Things', in *Selections*, ed. Wiener, pp. 345–6.

53. Ibid., p. 346.

54. Ibid., p. 347.

55. Leibniz, *Theodicy*, p. 127.

56. Leibniz, 'Principles', pp: 527–8.

57. Ibid., p. 527.

58. Ibid.

59. Leibniz, 'Monadology', p. 540.

60. Ibid., p. 539. Truths of reason are tautologous propositions; truths of fact appear to be synthetic (only *appear to be* because the principle of predicate in subject would reduce them to tautologies) propositions.

61. Leibniz, 'Origin', p. 346.

62. Ibid.

63. Arthur O. Lovejoy, *The Great Chain of Being: A Study of the History of an Idea* (New York: Harper & Row, 1936; Harper Torchbooks, 1960), p. 147.

64. Leibniz, 'Fifth Paper', p. 155.

65. Leibniz, 'Origin', p. 349.

66. G. W. Leibniz, 'Extract from a letter to —', 1700, in *Works*, ed. Duncan, p. 135; G. W. Leibniz, 'Extract from a letter to the editor of the *Journal de Trevoux*', 1701, in *Works*, ed. Duncan, p. 137.

67. Leibniz, 'Monadology', p. 541; Leibniz, 'Letter to —', p. 135; Leibniz, 'Letter to editor', p. 137.

68. G. W. Leibniz, 'Notes on Spinoza's *Ethics*', in *Works*, Duncan, p. 20.

69. Loemker, Introduction, p. 50.

70. Lovejoy, *Chain*, p. 146.

71. Leibniz, 'Origin', p. 347.

72. Leibniz, 'Fifth Paper', pp. 255–6.

73. Anna Teresa Tymieniecka, *Leibniz' Cosmological Synthesis* (Netherlands: Van Gorcum, 1964), p. 14. Cf. Herbert Wildon Carr, *Leibniz* (New York: Dover Publications, 1960), pp. 119, 121; Ruth Lydia Saw, *Leibniz* (Harmondsworth, England: Penguin Books; Pelican Books, 1954), p. 74.

74. Leibniz, 'Principles', p. 528.
75. Leibniz, 'Monadology', pp. 540–1.
76. Ibid., p. 541.
77. Leibniz, *Theodicy*, pp. 127–8.
78. Leibniz, 'Monadology', p. 540. For an analysis of this last phrase, see David Blumenfield, 'Leibniz's Proof of the Uniqueness of God', *Studia Leibnitiana* 6 (1974): 262–71.
79. Leibniz, *Theodicy*, p. 128.
80. Leibniz, 'Origin', p. 346.
81. Leibniz, *Theodicy*, p. 127.
82. Leibniz, 'Principles', p. 528.
83. Leibniz, 'Monadology', p. 542.
84. Leibniz, 'Fifth Paper', pp. 254–5.
85. This is also done by J. Jalabert, *Le Dieu de Leibniz* (Paris: Presses Universitaires de France, 1960), p. 111. Unfortunately Jalabert fails to discern the most important contrasts.
86. For example, Patterson asserts that the cosmological argument attacked by Kant is the proof that Leibniz called the argument from contingent things and 'is identical with the third proof of St. Thomas' (R. L. Patterson, *The Conception of God in the Philosophy of Aquinas* [London: George Allen & Unwin, 1933], p. 94). That this statement could appear in a doctoral thesis on Aquinas's concept of God shows how greatly misunderstood are the arguments of both Aquinas and Leibniz.

Chapter 9

A Typology of Cosmological Arguments

The critical attacks of Hume and Kant mark a watershed in the history of the cosmological argument. Leibniz and Wolff were probably the last significant philosophers who felt it sufficient simply to present the argument in a brief form, confident that it needed no further underpinning. Hume and Kant ushered in what might be called the modern era of the cosmological argument; things could never be quite the same after their sceptical critique: Arthur Schopenhauer noted that Kant had dealt a 'death blow' to the cosmological argument and that by the time of his own writing, theistic proofs had 'lost all credit'.[1] Modern defenders of the argument have felt obliged to expound the proof at greater length, defending it against the combined criticisms of the two English and German philosophers. It seems natural, then, to halt at this juncture and survey the ground over which we have travelled without moving into contemporary discussions of the cosmological argument. I propose in this brief chapter to develop a typology of cosmological arguments which, I hope, may serve contemporary philosophers as a guide in discussion of the argument.

In developing a typology we need some common criterion by which all or most of the arguments can be categorised. Otherwise we would have an unmanageable plethora of different arguments from motion, contingency, causality, and so forth. During the historical survey of the argument, my attention was drawn to one very important feature of the cosmological proof: the role of the infinite regress in the argument. If we use this feature as our criterion we can categorise the arguments into three types: (1) those that maintain the impossibility of an infinite temporal regress, (2) those that maintain the impossibility of an infinite essentially ordered regress, and (3) those that have no reference to an infinite regress at all. The first type embraces the *kalām* proofs for the beginning of world and the existence of a Creator. The second type enfolds all the proofs in Aquinas's first three ways: proofs from motion, causality, and possible and necessary being which respectively conclude to a prime mover, first cause, and absolutely necessary being. The third type is Leibniz's (and Spinoza's) version of the proof, for his argument contains no reference to the impossibility of any sort of infinite regress, but directly seeks a sufficient reason for all things.

Interestingly, there is an even more basic criterion by which the arguments may be categorised which yields precisely the same typology: the basic principle on which they operate and by which the existence of God is inferred. Such a criterion produces three types: (1) arguments based on the principle of determination, (2) arguments based on the principle of causality, and (3) arguments based on the principle of sufficient reason. The first type is again the *kalām* arguments, the second the Thomist arguments, and the third the Leibnizian argument. Since both criteria yield the same categorisation, this threefold typology seems well-suited to guide critical discussions of the argument.[2]

It is important to understand clearly the distinction of the types. Failure to appreciate their demarcation not only leads to an incorrect understanding of the historical versions, but also conceals the crucial fact that one type may be impervious to a criticism that is fatal to another. All too many modern discussions on the cosmological argument proceed on the basis of some blurry amalgamation of different types of the argument. Undoubtedly, the most obvious example of this is the mutual assimilation of the Thomist and Leibnizian proofs. William L. Rowe is only continuing a long tradition of post-Leibnizian philosophy when he writes,

> The proponents of the Cosmological Argument insist that the fundamental principles appealed to in the argument are necessary truths, known either directly or by deduction from other *a priori* principles that are known directly . . . . Such a principle . . . is the Principle of Sufficient Reason, the pivot on which the cosmological argument turns . . . .
>
> . . . There are a number of versions or forms of the Cosmological Argument. Apart from the versions in Plato or Aristotle, which represent the early beginnings of the argument, the most forceful and, historically, the most significant versions of the argument appeared in the writings of Aquinas and Duns Scotus in the thirteenth century and in the writings of Leibniz and Samuel Clarke in the eighteenth century . . . .
>
> . . . Criticisms that may be definitive against one version of the

> argument may turn out to be utterly irrelevant to some other important version. On the other hand, . . . all versions of the argument rely on some form of the Principle of Sufficient Reason.[3]

It is not difficult to find specific examples of this error. Howard Congdon presents Plato and Aristotle's proofs from motion as based on the principle of sufficient reason.[4] John Randall characterises Aristotle's prime mover as 'a logical explanation, not a physical cause, a natural law, not a force . . . . It is an *archē*, a principle of intelligibility, a "reason why" '.[5] Fazlur Rahman asserts that ibn Sīnā's cosmological argument is based, not on the principle of causality, but on the principle of sufficient reason.[6] Etienne Gilson writes that Aquinas's proofs seek a sufficient reason to explain an observed effect, a reason without which the effect is unintelligible.[7] Similarly, R. Garrigou-Lagrange's exposition of Thomas's first three ways is infected throughout by the Leibnizian principle of sufficient reason.[8] Efrem Bettoni observes that Scotus, as well as Aquinas, is seeking a being that has in itself the sufficient reason for its existence and operations.[9] G. H. R. Parkinson confuses the Leibnizian argument with the Thomist when he contends that Leibniz fails to refute an infinite regress, since each question 'why?' is answered in a prior being.[10]

It might be said that Rowe's conclusion is nevertheless true in that the principle of causality is a specific form of the principle of sufficient reason.[11] Leibniz certainly thought this was so, and in this sense Rowe's conclusion would be correct, but highly misleading. For it gives the impression that the Thomist and Leibnizian proofs are of the same type, and, indeed, most modern authors do confuse the two. This is plainly evident in their exposition of the argument against an infinite regress. For while the defenders of the Thomist argument clearly maintained that an essentially ordered infinite regress of causes simply cannot exist, modern writers looking through Leibnizian spectacles read them to mean, not that such a series cannot exist, but that if it did exist it would yield no ultimate explanation of the effect. We need not look far for examples. Congdon states that Aristotle argues against an infinite regress of *explanations.*[12] E. L. Mascall interprets Aquinas as saying, not that we *cannot* proceed to infinity, but that if we do we come no nearer to the solution to the problem, to the sufficient reason for the effect.[13] Blair asserts that for Aquinas it is a matter of indifference whether there be an infinite number of 'moved movers'; he argued that the only way of accounting for such a collection is by something *outside* the series.[14] Bettoni interprets Scotus's argument against an infinite regress as holding that the search for the reason for all beings' possibility of existence cannot go on forever, '. . . or else we would have to renounce finding the reason for the effectibility that was our starting point'.[15] Similarly, Rowe states that Scotus and Aquinas reject an infinite regress because it does not ultimately explain anything.[16] These interpretations are certainly incorrect. Defenders of the argument from Plato and Aristotle to Scotus agree that an essentially ordered, infinite causal regress cannot exist, not just that it cannot explain anything. This latter interpretation arises from reading the principle of sufficient reason back into these pre-Leibnizian thinkers so that their quest for causes becomes a quest for reasons. In each case such a transformation is illicit. Joseph Owens is at pains to emphasise that Aristotle begins with sensible things, asks for causes, and proceeds to an ultimate cause of the world; he is not seeking abstract reasons, but physical causes.[17] Julius Weinberg explains that in Aquinas's first way, Thomas argues that an infinite regress of causes is impossible because '. . . no actual motion would ever occur. Now we already know that this is not the case . . . hence, after a finite number of regressive steps from any actual motion, we must assume an unmoved mover'.[18] The point in all three ways is not that the effect would exist unexplained, but that it would not exist at all. The same is true for Scotus; he does not argue that an infinite regress fails to yield a sufficient reason for the effect, but in Felix Alluntio's words, '. . . he simply says that an infinite regress is impossible for essentially ordered causes'.[19] Modern authors who read Leibniz back into these thinkers inevitably interpret these proofs as a search for an ultimate explanation instead of a cause.[20]

Oddly enough, Thomists are themselves partly to blame for this misinterpretation of their proof. For as John Gurr shows in his careful study of the principle of sufficient reason in scholastic systems from 1750 to 1900, Catholic scholastic manuals gradually assimilated the Leibnizian–Wolffian emphasis on sufficient reason so that the Thomist and Leibnizian arguments became blended together.[21] As a result, modern Thomists—and Gurr specifically names Garrigou-Lagrange—read the principle of sufficient reason back into Aquinas and Aristotle.[22] Dennis Bonnette also discerns the shift among modern Thomists such as Gilson and Garrigou-Lagrange from Aquinas's reasoning to Leibniz's; but he casually remarks that in their use of the principle of sufficient reason they are just trying to say the same thing in a more contemporary way in order to appeal to 'modern mentality'.[23] Such an attempt is extremely misleading and counterproductive. For it gives the impression that by denying the principle of sufficient reason one has thereby undercut all versions of the cosmological argument.[24] But this is not true. For one might argue with Antony Flew that the principle of sufficient reason is false because one must ultimately reach an explanatory ultimate for which no reason can be given.[25] But even if this were successful against the Leibnizian proof, it does not touch the Thomist proof, for it concerns causes, not reasons, and it does not depend on everything's having a cause, but specifically aims at reaching an uncaused cause. Moreover, while one may toss off the principle of sufficient reason as false, it is not so easy to deny honestly the principle of causality. Likewise, only by carefully distinguishing between the two principles can one avoid the allegation that the argument posits a self-caused being, a notion caricatured by Schopenhauer as being like Baron Munchhausen pulling himself and his steed out of the water by his pigtails.[26] For the Leibnizian argument concludes to a being which is self-explained in that its existence is intrinsically intelligible, and the Thomist argument posits a being which is uncaused.[27] Only by confusing the two types of argument and combining the notions of 'self-explained' and 'uncaused' does one wind up with a being that is self-caused in the Baron Munchhausen sense.[28] Though they thus have ample reason for carefully delineating the Thomist and Leibnizian proofs, modern Thomists fairly fling themselves onto the funeral pyre by framing their arguments in terms of the principle of sufficient reason. Therefore, it is best in my opinion to keep the principle of causality distinct from the principle of sufficient reason and recognise that in the Thomist and Leibnizian proofs we have two distinct types of cosmological argument.

It is also important to keep the *kalām* proof distinct from the above two, although it suffers more from being ignored than being misconstrued. Occasionally one reads statements to the effect that an infinite temporal regress of events is not self-explanatory and therefore needs a cause.[29] But this is clearly not the *kalām* argument, but a Leibnizian–Thomist hybrid, seeking an essential cause of a non-self-explanatory, infinite temporal regress. I have already argued that the principle of determination is not the same as the principle of sufficient reason. Perhaps a greater temptation would be to regard the *kalām* proof as based, along with the Thomist argument, on the principle of causality. But this is inadequate, for the cause of the world to which the *kalām* argument concludes is not just a mechanically operating set of necessary and sufficient conditions, but a personal agent who chooses by an act of the will which of two alternative options—universe or no universe—will be realised. As A. J. Wensinck emphasises,

> If the world was produced, that signifies therefore that it did not exist at some time and that it came to be afterwards. It is not permitted, therefore, to conceive of the production of the world by God as the production of the effect by the cause: God is not cause, but Creator.[30]

The principle of determination is not, therefore, reducible to the principle of causality *simpliciter*. Such a reduction would rob the *kalām* argument of one of its most interesting and distinctive features: the necessity of a personal agent who freely chooses between equally possible and competing alternatives. The *kalām* argument is thus, along with the Leibnizian and Thomist proofs, a distinct type of cosmological argument.

Although this is a historical survey and not a critical work, it might be appropriate to conclude our study with an outline of what I perceive to be the major philosophical issues raised by each argument type. Turning first to the Leibnizian argument, I think that two problems are of overriding concern: (1) the status of the principle of sufficient reason and (2) the nature of the necessary being at the argument's conclusion.

(1) With regard to the first problem, it must be determined whether such a principle can be successfully formulated and defended. Leibniz suggested several formulations and offered *a priori* and *a posteriori* defences of the principles, and these need to be weighed. Opponents of the Leibnizian cosmological argument have usually lodged two objections against the principle: (a) the principle is false when applied to the universe and (b) the principle cannot be legitimately applied to the universe. The first objection asserts that there is no sufficient reason for the universe, that it is simply unintelligible.[31] This perspective raises serious existential questions, since it implies that man and the universe are ultimately meaningless. If we are reluctant to fly in the face of basic human intuitions that life and the universe are valuable and meaningful, then this viewpoint could only be embraced on the basis of convincing proof that the universe is ultimately unintelligible and so constitutes an exception to a principle otherwise always accepted. The second objection holds that the principle cannot be applied to the universe, so that the universe cannot be said to be unintelligible.[32] By the nature of explanation itself, one must reach an explanatory ultimate which remains unexplained. Facts about God are just as brute as facts about the universe, and neither can be said to be more intelligible than the other. The objection hinges on the assumption that *something cannot be self-explained*. Since most critics overlook this presupposition, more work

needs to be done on the nature of explanation itself, whether an explanation must always be in terms of something else or whether an explanatory ultimate could be explained in terms of itself and its own intrinsic intelligibility.

(2) The second major problem raised by the Leibnizian argument is the nature of the necessary being concluded to. Leibniz regarded the necessary being as self-explanatory because it was logically necessary. Although some philosophers still want to defend the notion of a logically necessary being, most prefer to speak of a factually necessary being.[33] But the problem with this notion is that the universe itself could be such a necessary being.[34] Matter and energy could exist eternally and indestructibly in a temporally infinite regress of various configurations. Although Spinoza embraced this conclusion willingly, most theists would recoil at the prospect. Accordingly, the defender of the Leibnizian argument needs to show why the universe is not the necessary being. He might attempt to do this by means of a teleological argument, maintaining that the presence of order and especially of mind in the universe cannot be satisfactorily accounted for unless the necessary being were also Mind. Or he might argue that an ultimate Mind is a more intelligible explanation of the universe than matter and energy alone. At any rate, there is considerable room for interesting and fruitful work on this problem.

With regard to the Thomist cosmological argument, there are, I think, two paramount issues: (1) the status of the essence/existence distinction and (2) the cogency of the infinite regress argument. (1) The real distinction between essence and existence lies at the heart of the Thomist proof.[35] The proof's proponent wants to prove that because all finite beings are composed of essence and existence, there must be a ground of being in whom essence and existence are identical. In order to do this, he must first show (a) that things have essences and (b) that these essences are metaphysically distinct from the act of existing. The first subpoint raises the issue of essentialism, for although this is often in other contexts used as a derogatory term by Thomists who prefer to characterise their philosophy as a true existentialism, it remains nevertheless the case that Thomism is a form of essentialism, since it holds that things actually do have essences. There is considerable debate today over essentialism, which is defended vigorously by an articulate minority of philosophers, but defenders of the Thomist cosmological argument do not appear by and large to have profited much from this debate. There is a great deal to be done here, for it needs to be determined (i) whether a form of essentialism can be successfully formulated and defended and (ii) whether such a form would be amenable to a cosmological proof from the composition of essence and existence in things. So there is also room for further philosophical exploration here. As to the second subpoint, the proof's defender needs to show, not only that there are essences, but that these essences are metaphysical components of finite things and not mere mental abstractions. In other words, is the distinction between essence and existence a logical or conceptual one alone, or is there really an act of existing conjoined to an essence in finite things? Thomists too often assume that a real distinction can be proved by the fact of change and dependence in finite beings, arguing that such beings cannot be necessary. But this only shows them to be naturally contingent, not metaphysically contingent. The notion that natural contingency implies metaphysical contingency is an erroneous assumption that arises from confusing the Aristotelian act/potency distinction with the Thomist act/potency distinction. Factors such as change could be taken to imply that a thing is composed of actuality and potentiality in the physical Aristotelian sense, but they do not imply a composition in the more metaphysical Thomist sense of essence and existence. The proof's proponents need to be more careful in avoiding this confusion and must give more attention to a defence of the real distinction if the proof is to be successful. In all fairness, however, it must be said that modern critics of the Thomist version of the cosmological argument have utterly failed to understand it or to appreciate the centrality of the real distinction to the proof's cogency. (2) The second major issue raised by the Thomist version is the possibility of an infinite regress of causes.[36] The principal argument used to eliminate such a regress is that in essentially ordered infinite regress of causes, only instrumental causes would exist, and, hence, there would be no intrinsic causality in the series to produce the observed effect. The defender of this argument faces, however, this dilemma: if an instrumental cause is defined as a cause lacking intrinsic causal efficacy, one cannot preclude an infinite regress of instrumental causes each receiving its causal efficacy extrinsically from its predecessor; but if an instrumental cause is defined as a cause depending ultimately upon a first cause, then it cannot be shown that the causes in an infinite regress are truly instrumental. Even should this dilemma be irresolvable, however, it could still be the case that an infinite regress of essentially ordered causes is intuitively implausible: it would mean, for example, that a watch could run without a spring if it had an infinite number of gears or that a train could move without an engine simply by having an infinite number of box cars. Therefore, I do not think the problem of the possibility of an infinite regress is at all a closed and settled question.

Finally, the *kalām* cosmological argument raises the question of whether the temporal regress of events can be infinite. Basically two problems arise here: (1) whether an actual infinite can exist in reality and (2) whether an actual infinite can be formed by successive addition.

(1) The first problem concerns all the paradoxes which arise if we assume that an actual infinite can exist in the real world.[37] It is often assumed that these paradoxes were resolved by Georg Cantor's founding of infinite set theory and trans-finite arithmetic. But this assumption could well be hasty, for Cantor's theories concern the conceptual realm only, not the world of things. It might be that Cantor's theories, given certain axioms and conventions, comprise a logically consistent mathematical system that has nothing to do with reality.[38] In other words, the existence of an actual infinite could be logically possible, but really impossible. For example, that 'the whole is not greater than its part' is *logically* possible, but can we be so confident that it is *really* possible, in view of the counter-intuitive situations it would entail? If the *kalām* argument's proponent frames the proof in terms of real and not simply logical possibility, then it is insufficient to point to conceptual entities such as the set of all natural numbers {1, 2, 3, . . .} as decisive proof that an actual infinite can in fact exist. A great deal of work remains to be done on the problem of the existence of an actual infinite and its relation to Cantor's discoveries. And one might remark in passing that Cantor's theories are by no means universally accepted by mathematicians, since the small, but brilliant school of intuitionists rejects even the conceptual existence of the actual infinite.

(2) The second problem concerns, not the existence of an actual infinite, but rather its formation.[39] Cantor's system is doubly irrelevant to this issue, for the argument does not deny that an actual infinite can exist. Critics sometimes assert that an actual infinite cannot be formed by successive addition *in a finite time*, but if the universe is eternal, then such a formation is possible. That this criticism misses the mark may be seen by the fact that the argument may be applied to time itself. The past cannot be actually infinite, one might argue, because an infinite number of equal time segments, say, hours, could not successively elapse. It would be foolish to say that they could elapse *given infinite time*, for the argument is precisely about time itself, and the objector fallaciously posits a time 'above' time. Another perhaps more common error is to regard the past as a potential infinite beginning in the present and

regressing backwards in time. But this confuses the mental regress of events with the real progressive instantiation of events. For the past to be a potential infinite it would have to be finite, but growing in a 'backwards' direction. It is thus very difficult to see how the series of past events can be both progressively formed *and* actually infinite. Once again, I can only conclude that the issue is still in dispute and merits further research.

Through this brief overview of some of the issues involved in the critical discussion of the cosmological argument, I hope that it has become obvious that the proof in its various forms is still bristling with interesting philosophical conundrums. And I trust that the foregoing expositions of the historical versions of the argument will prove helpful both in understanding the argument itself and in informing critical analyses of the problems involved. The book has not been shut on the cosmological argument for the existence of God, and it deserves full and critical attention on the part of philosophical theism.

NOTES

1. Arthur Schopenhauer, 'On the Fourfold Root of the Principle of Sufficient Reason', in *Two Essays by Arthur Schopenhauer* (London: George Bell & Sons, 1889), pp. 42, 146.

2. It might be reasonably objected that what I have called the Thomist proof ought in fact to be called the *falsafa* proof or the Fārābīan proof, since it originated among Arabic thinkers. But with due apologies to Islamicists, I have chosen to call the proof Thomist, not only because Aquinas summarises them all, but primarily because Thomism is the only school that vigorously defends the arguments today.

It is gratifying to find that R. L. Sturch in his survey of the cosmological argument comes to virtually the same threefold typology as I do: the *Kalām* argument, the causal argument, and the contingency argument (R. L. Sturch, 'The Cosmological Argument' [Ph.D thesis, Oxford University, 1972]).

3. William L. Rowe, *The Cosmological Argument* (Princeton, N. J.: Princeton University Press, 1975), pp.3–4, 6–9.

4. Howard Krebs Congdon, 'The Principle of Sufficient Reason and the Cosmological Argument' (Ph.D dissertation, Purdue University, 1970), pp. 26, 59.

5. John Herman Randall, *Aristotle* (New York: Columbia University Press, 1960), p. 135.

6. Fazlur Rahman, 'Ibn Sīna', in *A History of Muslim Philosophy* ed. M. M. Sharif (Wiesbaden: Otto Harrassowitz, 1963), p. 482.

7. Etienne Gilson, *The Philosophy of St. Thomas Aquinas* [*Le thomisme*], trans. Edward Bullough (Cambridge: W. Heffer & Sons, 1924), p. 57; Etienne Gilson, *History of Christian Philosophy in the Middle Ages* (London: Sheed &

Ward, 1955), p. 370; Etienne Gilson, *The Christian Philosophy of St. Thomas Aquinas*, trans. L. K. Shook (London: Victor Gollancz, 1961), p. 64.

8. R. Garrigou-Lagrange, *God: His Existence and Nature*, 5th ed., 2 vols., trans. Bede Rose (London and St. Louis: B. Herder Book Co., 1934), 1: 181–91, 261–302.

9. Efrem Bettoni, *Duns Scotus: The Basic Principles of His Philosophy*, trans. and ed. Bernardine Bonansea (Washington, D.C.: Catholic University of America Press, 1961), p. 137.

10. G. H. R. Parkinson, *Logic and Reality in Leibniz's Metaphysics* (Oxford: Clarendon Press, 1965), p. 95.

11. For this view, see Bruce Reichenbach, *The Cosmological Argument: A Reassessment* (Springfield, Ill.: Charles C. Thomas, 1972), pp. 53–6.

12. Congdon, 'Principle', p. 46. This seems to be just sloppy writing on Congdon's part, for he later acknowledges that the principle of sufficient reason is not that of causality (ibid., p. 159).

13. E. L. Mascall, *Existence and Analogy* (London: Longmans, Green & Co., 1943), pp. 73–4; E. L. Mascall, *The Openness of Being* (London: Darton, Longman, & Todd, 1971), pp. 101–2, 117.

14. George A. Blair, 'Another Look at St. Thomas' "First Way"', *International Philosophical Quarterly* 16 (1976): 307.

15. Bettoni, *Scotus*, pp. 139–40.

16. Rowe, *Argument*, pp. 32–8, 48–50.

17. Joseph Owens, *The Doctrine of Being in the Aristotelian 'Metaphysics'*, 2nd ed. (Toronto, Canada: Pontifical Institute of Mediaeval Studies, 1963), pp. 172, 174.

18. Julius R. Weinberg, *A Short History of Medieval Philosophy* (Princeton, N. J.: Princeton University Press, 1964), p. 189.

19. Felix Alluntio, 'Demonstrability and Demonstration of the Existence of God', in *Studies in Philosophy and the History of Philosophy*, vol. 3: *John Duns Scotus,1265–1965*, ed. John K. Ryan and Bernardine M. Bonansea (Washington D.C.: Catholic University of America Press, 1965), p. 155.

20. They appear to take Leibniz's argument that an infinite temporal regress of events fails to explain why there is any world at all and apply this reasoning to an infinite essentially ordered series as well. But neither Leibniz nor Aquinas ever employed such an argument.

21. John Edwin Gurr, *The Principle of Sufficient Reason in Some Scholastic Systems, 1750–1900* (Milwaukee: Marquette University Press, 1959), pp. 15, 48–9.

22. Ibid., p. 6.

23. Dennis Bonnette, *Aquinas' Proofs for God's Existence* (The Hague: Martinus Nijhoff, 1972), p. 125.

24. Comments Rowe, '. . . if the Principle of Sufficient Reason were shown to be false, we could, then, fairly say that the Cosmological Argument had been refuted' (William L. Rowe, 'The Cosmological Argument and the Principle of sufficient Reason', *Man and World* 2 [1968]: 279).

25. Antony Flew, *God and Philosophy* (London: Hutchinson & Co., 1966), p. 83.

26. Schopenhauer, 'Fourfold Root', p. 17.

27. Noting that the principle of sufficient reason is primarily a logical principle, Jalabert comments,

> The proof from contingency has therefore in Leibniz a *logical generality* which the Thomist proof from efficient cause could not have. *It applies to everything relative, to everything which does not find in its own essence its very reason of existing or acting.* As for the principle of sufficient reason, which is the nerve of the proof, it applies itself even to God. We must realize the reasonableness of divine existence, as of everything. But here the determining reason is in the divine essence itself. *God exists by his essence.* In that we have a new opposition between Leibniz and Saint Thomas. God has no cause, does not need one, according to the Angelic Doctor. No being can be its own cause, for there cannot be a being which comes before its own existence. The principle of causality always goes back to an exterior principle. The concept of causality, drawn by Saint Thomas from experience, is in fact inapplicable to divinity. It is not the same for the concept of *reason.* To say of God that he is a *necessary Being* is to admit that he is in himself *his own reason* for existing. Therefore, the substitution of reason for cause authorizes a concept, *not negative any more, but positive, of aseity* (Jacques Jalabert, *Le Dieu de Leibniz* [Paris: Presses Universitaires de France, 1960], p. 110).

28. Schopenhauer himself clearly understood and illustrated the difference between a cause and a reason (Schopenhauer, 'Fourfold Root', p. 28), and he indicts his forebears for failing to do so (ibid., pp. 5–27). However, his conception of causation was that of a cause being temporally prior to its effect, and this chain of causes he believed to be necessarily infinite (ibid., pp. 38–9, 42–3). Hence, he maintained that when the cosmological argument denied the possibility of an infinite regress, it was surreptitiously shifting from talking about causes to talking about reasons in the sense of conditions for knowledge. There could not be an infinite regress of such reasons, for we must arrive at some self-evident first principles of knowledge. Thus, Schopenhauer believed the cosmological argument sought to arrive at a being which was self-caused (ibid., pp. 185–6.) Indeed, the notion of God as *causa sui* was prevalent in rationalistic circles at his time.

29. D. J. B. Hawkins, *The Essentials of Theism* (London and New York: Sheed & Ward, 1949), p. 41.

30. A. J. Wensinck, 'Les preuves de l'existence de Dieu dans la théologie musulmane', *Mededeelingen der Koninklijke Academie van Wetenschappen* 81 (1936): 47–8.

31. C. D. Broad, *Religion, Philosophy and Psychical Research* (London: Routledge & Kegan Paul, 1953), p. 186; Paul Edwards, 'The Cosmological Argument', in *The Cosmological Arguments*, ed. W. R. Burrill (Garden City, N.Y.: Doubleday & Co.; Anchor Books, 1967), pp. 101–23; Wallace I. Matson, *The Existence of God* (Ithaca, N.Y.: Cornell University Press, 1965), pp..76–7; John Hick, *Arguments for the Existence of God* (New York: Herder & Herder, 1971), pp. 50–3; John Hospers, *An Introduction to Philosophical Analysis*, 2nd ed. (London: Routledge & Kegan Paul, 1973), p. 443. *Contra*, see Rem B. Edwards, *Reason and Religion* (New York: Harcourt Brace Jovanovitch, 1972), p. 150; Donald R. Kehew, 'A Metaphysical Approach to the Existence of God',

Franciscan Studies 32 (1972): 113–14; John J. Shepherd, *Experience, Inference and God* (London: Macmillan Press, 1975), pp. 76–8.

32. Bertrand Russell and F. C. Copleston, 'The Existence of God', in *The Existence of God*, ed. with an Introduction by John Hick, Problems of Philosophy Series (New York: Macmillan Co., 1964), pp. 174, 176; Matson, *Existence*, pp. 82–3; Flew, *God*, p. 83; D. R. Duff-Forbes, 'Hick, Necessary Being, and the Cosmological Argument', *Canadian Journal of Philosophy I* (1972): 473–83; Hospers, *Introduction*, p. 442. *Contra*, see Hick, *Arguments*, pp. 48–50; John Hick, 'Comment', *Canadian Journal of Philosophy I* (1972): 485–7.

33. For a defence of logical necessity, see Rowe, *Argument*, pp. 202–21; Robert Merrihew Adams, 'Has it been Proved that all Real Existence is Contingent?', *American Philosophical Quarterly* 8 (1971): 284–91. On factual necessity, see R. L. Franklin, 'Necessary Being', *Australasian Journal of Philosophy* 35 (1957): 97–100; Terence M. Penelhum, 'Divine Necessity', in *Arguments*, ed. Burrill, pp. 158–60; John Hick, 'God as Necessary Being', *Journal of Philosophy* 57 (1960) 733–4; John H. Hick, 'Necessary Being', *Scottish Journal of Theology* 14 (1961): 353–69; Alvin Plantinga, 'Necessary Being', in *Arguments*, ed. Burrill, pp. 136–41; Bruce R. Reichenbach, 'Divine Necessity and the Cosmological Argument', *Monist* 54 (1970): 401–15. For an attempt to reduce factual necessity to logical necessity by means of reasoning remarkably similar to Scotus's ontological argument, see Adel Daher, 'God and Factual Necessity', *Religious Studies* 6 (1970): 28–30.

34. David Hume, *Hume's 'Dialogues Concerning Natural Religion'*, ed. with an Introduction by Norman Kemp Smith (Oxford: Clarendon Press, 1935), pp. 233–4; Matson, *Existence*, pp. 75–6. *Contra*, see Russell and Copleston, 'Existence', pp. 175–6; Stuart C. Hackett, *The Resurrection of Theism* (Chicago: Moody Press, 1957), pp. 196–7, 221–9; Richard Taylor, *Metaphysics*, Foundations of Philosophy Series (Englewood Cliffs, N.J.: Prentice-Hall, 1963), pp. 90–3; Ninian Smart, *Philosophers and Religious Truth* (London: SCM Press, 1964), pp. 101–7; Fernand Van Steenberghen, *Hidden God*, trans. T. Crowley (Louvain: Publications Universitaires de Louvain, 1966; St. Louis: B. Herder Book Co., 1966), pp. 174–5; Hick, *Arguments*, pp. 48–50; John Hick, 'Brand Blanshard's "Reason and Belief"', *Journal of Religion* 56 (1976): 403.

35. Bruce Reichenbach, *The Cosmological Argument: A Reassessment* (Springfield, Ill.: Charles C. Thomas, 1972), pp. 1–22; Leonard J. Eslick, 'The Real Distinction: Reply to Professor Reese', *Modern Schoolman* 38 (1961): 149–60; George P. Klubertanz and Maurice Halloway, *Being and God* (New York: Appleton-Century-Crofts, 1963). *Contra*, see Stephen L. Weber, 'Proofs for the Existence of God: A Meta-Investigation' (Ph.D. dissertation, University of Notre Dame, 1969), pp. 119–40. For an extensive bibliography on essentialism see Nicholas Rescher, *A Theory of Possibility* (Oxford: Basil Blackwell, 1975), pp. 223–47.

36. R. Garrigou-Lagrange, *God: His Existence and Nature*, 2 vols., 5th ed., trans. B. Rose (London and St. Louis: B. Herder Book Co., 1934), 1: 265; R. P. Phillips, *Modern Thomistic Philosophy*, 2 Vols. (London: Burns Oates & Washbourne, 1935), 2: 278. *Contra*, see Edwards, 'Argument', pp. 101–23; Patterson Brown, 'Infinite Causal Regression', in *Aquinas: A Collection of Critical Essays*, ed. Anthony Kenny (London: Macmillan, 1969), pp. 234–5;

Anthony Kenny, *The Five Ways: St. Thomas Aquinas' Proofs of God's Existence* (New York: Schocken Books, 1969), pp. 26–7.

37. For background on this problem, see Bernard Bolzano, *Paradoxes of the Infinite*, trans. Fr. Prihonsky with an Introduction by D. A. Steele (London: Routledge & Kegan Paul, 1950); Richard Dedekind, *Essays on the Theory of Numbers*, trans. W. W. Beman (New York: Dover Publications, 1963); Georg Cantor, *Contributions to the Founding of the Theory of Transfinite Numbers*, trans. with an Introduction by P. E. B. Jourdain (New York: Dover Publications, 1915); Abraham A. Fraenkel, *Abstract Set Theory*, 2nd rev. ed. (Amsterdam: North-Holland Publishing Co., 1961); Abraham A. Fraenkel, Yehoshua Bar-Hillel, and Azriel Levy, *Foundations of Set Theory*, 2nd rev. ed. (Amsterdam and London: North-Holland Publishing Co., 1973); Robert James Bunn, 'Infinite Sets and Numbers' (Ph.D. dissertation, University of British Columbia, 1975).

38. David Hilbert, 'On the Infinite', in *Philosophy of Mathematics*, ed. with an Introduction by P. Benacerraf and Hilary Putnam (Englewood Cliffs, N.J.: Prentice-Hall, 1964), p. 151.

39. Hackett, *Theism*, pp. 194–5, 294; G. J. Whitrow, *The Natural Philosophy of Time* (London and Edinburgh: Thomas Nelson & Sons, 1961; rev. ed. forthcoming), pp. 31–2; G. J. Whitrow, 'The Impossibility of an Infinite Past', *British Journal for the Philosophy of Science* 29 (1978) 39–45; Pamela M. Huby, 'Kant or Cantor? That the Universe, if Real, Must be Finite in Both Space and Time', *Philosophy* 46 (1971); 121–3; Pamela M. Huby, 'Cosmology and Infinity', *Philosophy* 48 (1973): 186. *Contra*, see Norman Kemp Smith, *A Commentary to Kant's 'Critique of Pure Reason'*, (London: Macmillan & Co., 1918), pp. 483–4; Bertrand Russell, *Our Knowledge of the External World*, 2nd ed. (New York: W. W. Norton & Co., 1929), pp. 170–1, 195; Bertrand Russell, *The Principles of Mathematics*, 2nd ed. (London: George Allen & Unwin, 1937), p. 459; G. E. Moore, *Some Main Problems of Philosophy*, Muirhead Library of Philosophy (London: George Allen & Unwin, 1953; New York: Macmillan, 1953), p. 180; C. D. Broad, 'Kant's Mathematical Antinomies', *Proceedings of the Aristotelian Society* 40 (1955): 3; R. G. Swinburne, *Space and Time* (London: Macmillan, 1968), pp. 298–9; W. H. Newton-Smith, 'Armchair Cosmology', *Philosophy* 47 (1972): 64–5; N. W. Boyce 'A Priori Knowledge and Cosmology', *Philosophy* 47 (1972): 67; P. J. Zwart, *About Time* (Amsterdam and Oxford: North-Holland Publishing Co., 1976), pp. 238, 242–3; Karl Popper, 'On the Possibility of an Infinite Past', *British Journal for the Philosophy of Science* 29 (1978): 47–8.

There is also a sizeable body of literature on the Zeno paradoxes that is relevant to this issue. See the Bibliography in Wesley C. Salmon, ed., *Zeno's Paradoxes* (Indianapolis and New York: Bobbs-Merrill Co., 1970).

Index